Productivity Measurement and Improvement

Productivity Measurement and Improvement

Organizational Case Studies

Robert D. Pritchard, *Editor*

Westport, Connecticut
London

Library of Congress Cataloging-in-Publication Data

Productivity measurement and improvement : organizational case studies
 / Robert D. Pritchard, editor.
        p.   cm.
    Includes bibliographical references and index.
    ISBN 0–275–93907–3
    1. Industrial productivity—Measurement—Case studies. 2. Labor
productivity—Measurement—Case studies. I. Pritchard, Robert D.
    HD56.25.P8228 1995
    658.5'15—dc20   94–32932

British Library Cataloguing in Publication Data is available.

Library of Congress Catalog Card Number: 94–32932
ISBN: 0–275–93907–3

First published in 1995

Praeger Publishers, 88 Post Road West, Westport, CT 06881
An imprint of Greenwood Publishing Group, Inc.

Printed in the United States of America

The paper used in this book complies with the
Permanent Paper Standard issued by the National
Information Standards Organization (Z39.48–1984).

10 9 8 7 6 5 4 3 2 1

To my children, Elissa and Matthew.
Know that I walk with you in love.

Contents

List of Contributors

Jen A. Algera, Hoogovens Steel Works and Eindhoven Technical University, Eindhoven, The Netherlands

Jörg Beckmann, University of Dortmund, Dortmund, Germany

Ad van Berkel, Eindhoven Technical University, Eindhoven, The Netherlands

Ilya Bonic, Organisation Consulting Resources Pty. Ltd., Sydney, Australia

Ingwer Borg, ZUMA, Mannheim, Germany, and Human Resources Consulting, Munich, Germany

Karlease Clark, Texas A&M University, College Station, Texas

Noga Gottesfeld, Texas A&M University, College Station, Texas

Amie Hedley, Personnel Decisions, Inc., Dallas Texas

Robert L. Hood, Rotoform, Chattanooga, Tennessee

Clyde Howell, Westinghouse Corporation, Savanna River, South Carolina

Annemarie M.C.M. van den Hurk, Eindhoven Technical University, Eindhoven, The Netherlands

Paul Janssen, Eindhoven Technical University, Eindhoven, The Netherlands

Steven D. Jones, Middle Tennessee State University, Murfreesboro, Tennessee

Uwe Kleinbeck, University of Dortmund, Dortmund, Germany

Ad Kleingeld, Eindhoven Technical University, Eindhoven, The Netherlands

Henriëtte Miedema, University of Amsterdam, Amsterdam, The Netherlands

Frederike van Oostveen, A.W.V. (General Employers' Association),
    Haarlem, The Netherlands
Lynn Ourth, University of Tennessee at Chattanooga, Chattanooga,
    Tennessee
Anthony Paquin, Texas A&M University, College Station, Texas
Robert D. Pritchard, Texas A&M University, College Station, Texas
Martina Przygodda, University of Dortmund, Dortmund, Germany
Patricia G. Roth, Clemson University, Clemson, South Carolina
Philip L. Roth, Clemson University, Clemson, South Carolina
John E. Sawyer, University of Delaware, Newark, Delaware
Klaus-Helmut Schmidt, Institut für Arbeitsphysiologie and Universität
    Dortmund, Abteilung Arbeitspsychologie, Dortmund, Germany
Thomas Staufenbiel, Philipps-Universität, Marburg, Germany
Jan Stolk, Vandra Corrugated Fiberboard, The Netherlands
Henk Thierry, University of Tilburg, Tilburg, The Netherlands
Harrie van Tuijl, Eindhoven Technical University, Eindhoven, The
    Netherlands
Margaret D. Watson, LaSalle University, Philadelphia, Pennsylvania

Illustrations

Acknowledgments

I express my heartfelt gratitude to all the authors in this volume for their willingness to work with me on this project and their considerable efforts to try out my ideas in their own research. Their faith has helped sustain me in those times when I wondered whether it was worth it all! I also thank those of my staff who helped with this book. Tony Paquin, Karlease Clark, Noga Gottesfeld, and Mark Stewart helped me summarize the chapters in preparation for the conclusions chapter, gave me excellent comments on drafts of my chapters, and helped in many other ways. Todd Wheeler, Paige Prickette, and Amiee Schwartz worked hard to put together the index. Finally, to my dear wife Sandy I say thank you for being there through it all, as always.

Productivity Measurement and Improvement

Introduction

Robert D. Pritchard

Improving organizational productivity is an issue that has been with us for some time and will continue to be important. All types of organizations need to be as productive as possible to best utilize their precious resources, to meet their customers needs, and to stay competitive with similar organizations. Productivity improvement is also important at a national level. As we continue to improve our national productivity, inflation is moderated, our standard of living improves, and jobs are created or retained.

There are two basic approaches to improving productivity within an organization. One can change technology or one can change how people work. The former is the realm of the engineer, the second is the realm of the behavioral scientist. Our approach is the latter. Although improving technology is, of course, important to long-range productivity growth, it is how people use this technology that makes it a worthwhile investment to the organization. Thus, our concern is how to structure work so that people can and will want to behave in a way that will maximize their productivity.

THE PRODUCTIVITY MEASUREMENT AND ENHANCEMENT SYSTEM

This book is about a specific approach to the measurement and improvement of organizational productivity: the Productivity Measurement and Enhancement System or ProMES. ProMES is a methodology for measuring productivity and then using the resulting measurement as feedback to personnel doing the work. Using this feedback, personnel are able to change the way they work so that they become more productive. This improvement in productivity is then documented by the ongoing measurement/feedback system. The measurement system is developed with substantial participation by those who will be measured. This helps insure validity of the system and acceptance by those being measured.

The most detailed description of ProMES is in an earlier book, *Measuring and Improving Organizational Productivity: A Practical Guide* (Pritchard, 1990), which describes the importance of productivity improvement, identifies important characteristics of productivity measurement systems, and describes the basics of ProMES and why it works. The rest of the book is devoted to a detailed discussion of how ProMES is implemented. There is also a German adaptation of the 1990 book available (Pritchard, Kleinbeck, & Schmidt, 1993).

This book you are reading is an extension of the earlier one. Since that earlier book, there have been many applications of ProMES in different types of organizations, with different types of jobs, using different technologies, and in different countries. In addition, there have been extensions, elaborations, and completely new applications of ProMES. The purpose of this book is to describe some of this work.

PRODUCTIVITY DEFINED

The term "productivity" means different things to different people. However, most definitions fall into one of three categories. The first is the economist/engineer definition, where productivity is an efficiency measure: the ratio of outputs over inputs, where both usually are expressed in dollar terms. An example of productivity (efficiency) under this definition would be the dollar value of refrigerators produced this month divided by the total costs to produce them. The second definition of productivity is a combination of efficiency (outputs/inputs) and effectiveness (outputs/goals). In this definition a company making refrigerators could measure productivity by a combination of the efficiency measure above plus an effectiveness measure, such as number of refrigerators divided by the objective or goal for the number to be produced that month. The third definition of productivity is the most broad and considers productivity as anything that makes the organization function better. In this definition, productivity would include efficiency and effectiveness, but also things like absenteeism, turnover, morale, innovation, etc.

Our purpose here is not to introduce a major discussion about the definition of productivity. There have been such discussions elsewhere (Ilgen & Klein, 1988; Pritchard, 1992; Tuttle, 1981; Sink & Smith, 1994). Some people have a fixed definition and feel any other definition is inappropriate. Others (myself included) realize that there are so many different definitions that insisting that only one is correct is not conducive to good communication. However, it is important to be clear on which definition one is using. The definition we use in this book is the second approach. We see productivity as a combination of effectiveness and efficiency. As I have stated elsewhere, productivity is how well a system uses its resources to achieve its goals (Pritchard, 1992). However, this approach can easily accommodate measures of quality, attendance, and any other type of measure that is seen as leading the organization to accomplish its goals.

A SHORT HISTORY OF ProMES

The original development of ProMES came from three very different forces that came together rather serendipitously. The first was the result of working with Jim Naylor and Dan Ilgen on a book (Naylor, Pritchard, & Ilgen, 1980) that has come to be known as NPI theory. This was a six-year effort (1974–79) to develop an integrated theory of work behavior — primarily individual behavior — that incorporated all the major constructs in the field into one unified theory. Thus, NPI incorporates individual differences, perception, motivation, roles, leadership, judgment, climate, etc. into one integrated conceptualization. It is a highly theoretical book that turned out to be the conceptual foundation of a very practical approach to productivity improvement, ProMES.

The second force was my own desire to find some form of intervention that would be feasible and effective at improving motivation and, thereby, performance in organizations. This applied interest was the compliment to the highly theoretical work done with the NPI book. I wanted something that was practical, that would actually be used, and that would have a real effect. I had settled on the area of performance feedback. The idea was that if you give people good feedback, their performance should improve. The literature agreed that such feedback was important but offered little information on how exactly to give such feedback. I started a research program funded by the Air Force Human Resources Laboratory (now called the Armstrong Laboratories) that looked at different ways of giving feedback and their effects on performance. This work was being done at about the same time as the work on the NPI book.

The initial work in this feedback research program was done in simulation settings, where subjects were hired for what they thought was a real job but which was actually an experiment (Pritchard & Montagno, 1978; Pritchard, Montagno, & Moore, 1978). In the late 1970s, I took what had been learned in the laboratory out into the field. I obtained the cooperation of a large Houston-based oil company to use some of their units to try different types of feedback and look at the effects on performance.

As one step in this process, we had to pick the jobs to use in the study. I needed jobs where people worked as individuals with no interdependence on others, where they only did one or two things, and where measures of output were readily available. These conditions were necessary so that my individual feedback approaches could be implemented. We looked for weeks to find such jobs. This was a huge organization with hundreds of jobs, but I could not find *one* that met these criteria!

I finally did find a couple of jobs, and we did the project (Pritchard, Bigby, Beiting, Coverdale, & Morgan, 1981), but I learned a powerful lesson. If I needed a job to implement my ideas about feedback that could be found only rarely in an actual organization maybe I was going about this in the wrong way. How could I find some practical, effective interventions that would actually make a difference if there were no such jobs with which to use them? It became clear that I needed a way of giving feedback in work settings that were much more complex: settings where each person did many things, different people did different things, and there were complex interdependencies among people within the unit and among units.

These first two streams of force (NPI and the feedback work) started to come together. It seemed to me that I could take the conceptual ideas in NPI theory and use them to develop a way of measuring performance and productivity in real organizations, with all their complexity. Some ideas started to form, and I began reading in the area of organizational productivity.

The final force that led to the development of ProMES came from the Air Force Human Resources Laboratory. They were interested in the idea of group feedback and goal setting. I believed that the approach I was developing, that is, to use NPI ideas as the basis of a productivity measurement and feedback system in complex settings, would fit into their ideas nicely. They agreed and in 1983 funded a project to try this new approach in the Air Force. This project was done from 1983 to 1987 and led to the development and first field evaluation of ProMES (Pritchard, Jones, Roth, Stuebing, & Ekeberg, 1988, 1989).

The project was very successful in that it was possible to develop ProMES, and, using the feedback, productivity improved substantially in all five units where it was tried. It became clear that ProMES had significant potential, and I followed up the first articles about it with the 1990 book describing ProMES in detail. I also had the good fortune to meet a number of researchers in different countries who were interested in ProMES and wanted to try it.

Since that time, ProMES has been tried in a number of other settings and by a number of different researchers. This book is a summary of what we have learned over the past ten years from these efforts. It describes a series of studies where ProMES has been used in a variety of different organizations. The cases in the book attempt to answer a series of questions.

Can ProMES be developed in different settings?

Does ProMES improve productivity?

What factors seem to be important for making ProMES successful?

How long does it take to do ProMES?

What improvements in the process of doing ProMES have been developed?

What are some of the other effects of ProMES?

For what other applications can ProMES be used?

What have we learned about why ProMES works?

What do we still need to know about productivity and ProMES?

PLAN OF THE BOOK

This book assumes a working knowledge of ProMES. If the reader does not have this background knowledge, a nontechnical summary of ProMES can be found in Pritchard, Weiss, Hedley-Goode, and Jensen (1990). Chapters 2 through 7 of the 1990 book give the most detailed description. Chapter 2 of this book, the first case study, presents a detailed description of how ProMES is developed in an organization, although it does not describe the background and logic of the system.

After this introductory chapter, the book is organized into three parts. Part I is a series of case studies using ProMES to measure and improve productivity in manufacturing settings. Part II is similar but devoted to ProMES in service settings. Part III is devoted to extensions and applications of the general ProMES methodology to different problems beyond strictly productivity measurement and improvement, such as evaluating training and doing performance appraisal. A conclusions chapter summarizes what we have learned about productivity and ProMES and attempts to answer the questions identified above.

The content of the cases covers many different jobs, organizations, and so forth. Across all 16 cases, ProMES was developed 45 different times. The settings for each case are summarized in Table 1–1. The first column of the table is the chapter number. The subsequent columns describe the type of industry where the case was conducted, the specific job where ProMES was used, whether the work and corresponding measurement and feedback were done on individuals or groups, the country where the project was conducted, and the type of project. Most of the projects were applications of ProMES to measure and improve productivity. The last four chapters shown in the table were done for other purposes. The last column notes whether productivity data are available for that case.

Those cases in the first set of rows on the table comprise Part I of the book. They are the projects done in manufacturing settings. The middle group of chapters are done in service settings and are Part II of the book. The last set of chapters in the table are the cases not done directly

Table 1-1 Summary of the Cases

Chapter	Industry	Job	Individual or Group	Country	Project type	Productivity Data Available
2, Part I	Electronics manufacturing	Testing & repair	Group	United States	Productivity improvement	No
3, Part I	Cardboard box manufacturing	Machine crews	Group	Netherlands	Productivity improvement	Yes
4, Part I	Electrical components manufacturing	Assembling	Group	Germany	Productivity improvement	Yes
5, Part I	Recreational equipment manufacturing	Assembling	Group	United States	Productivity improvement	Yes
6, Part I	Battery manufacturing	Assembly line	Group	United States	Productivity improvement	Yes
7, Part II	Computer repair	Repair technicians	Group	Australia	Productivity improvement	Yes
8, Part II	Photocopier repair	Service technicians	Individual and group	Netherlands	Productivity improvement	Yes
9, Part II	Photocopier repair	Service technicians	Group	United States	Productivity improvement	Yes
10, Part II	University	Faculty	Individual	United States	Productivity improvement	Yes
11, Part II	Bank	Clerical & service	Individual and group	Netherlands	Productivity improvement	No
12, Part II	Oil distribution	Clerical and sales	Individual and group	Netherlands	Productivity improvement	Yes
13, Part II	Commercial painting	Painters	Group	Germany	Productivity improvement	No
14, Part III	Steel manufacturing	Process control	Group	Netherlands	ProMES feasibility study	Not applicable
15, Part III	State mental health school	Caregiving staff	Individual	United States	Performance appraisal	Not applicable
16, Part III	Textile manufacturing	Various	Group	United States	Training evaluation	Yes
17, Part III	Electronic manufacturing	Management	Individual	Germany	Strategic objectives	Not applicable

for productivity improvement but to try a new application or develop a new ProMES-related idea.

These chapters contain an enormous amount of information about ProMES and productivity improvement. I hope you enjoy them as much as I have.

REFERENCES

Ilgen, D. R., & Klein, H. J. (1988). Individual motivation and performance: Cognitive influences on effort and choice. In J. P. Campbell & R. J. Campbell (Eds), *Productivity in organizations* (pp. 143–176). San Francisco: Jossey-Bass.

Naylor, J. C., Pritchard, R. D., & Ilgen, D. R. (1980). *A theory of behavior in organizations* (p. 299). New York: Academic Press.

Pritchard, R. D. (1992). Organizational productivity. In M. D. Dunnette & L. M. Hough, (Ed.), *Handbook of industrial/organizational psychology* (2d ed.) (vol. 3, pp. 443–471). Palo Alto, CA: Consulting Psychologists Press.

Pritchard, R. D. (1990). *Measuring and improving organizational productivity: A practical guide* (p. 248). New York: Praeger.

Pritchard, R. D., Bigby, D. G., Beiting, M., Coverdale, S., & Morgan, C. (1981). Enhancing productivity through feedback and goal setting. *Air Force Human Resources Laboratory Technical Report* (AFHRL-TR-81-7).

Pritchard, R. D., Jones, S. D., Roth, P. L., Stuebing, K. K., & Ekeberg, S. E. (1989). The evaluation of an integrated approach to measuring organizational productivity. *Personnel Psychology, 42,* 69–115.

Pritchard, R. D., Jones, S. D., Roth, P. L., Stuebing, K. K., & Ekeberg, S. E. (1988). The effects of feedback, goal setting, and incentives on organizational productivity. *Journal of Applied Psychology Monograph Series, 73,* 337–358.

Pritchard, R. D., Kleinbeck, U. E., & Schmidt, K. H. (1993). *Das Management-system PPM: Durch Mitarbeiterbeteiligung zu höherer Produktivität* [The PPM management system: Employee participation for improved productivity] (p. 255). Munich: Verlag C.H. Beck.

Pritchard, R. D., & Montagno, R. V. (1978). The effects of specific vs. non-specific, and absolute vs. comparative feedback on performance and satisfaction. *Air Force Human Resources Laboratory Technical Report* (AFHRL-TR-78-12).

Pritchard, R. D., Montagno, R. V., & Moore, J. R. (1978). Enhancing productivity through feedback and job design. *Air Force Human Resources Laboratory Technical Report* (AFHRL-TR-78-44).

Pritchard, R. D., Weiss, L. G., Hedley-Goode, A., & Jensen, L. A. (1990, Summer). Measuring organizational productivity with ProMES. *National Productivity Review, 9,* (Summer): 257–271.

Sink, D. S., & Smith, G. L., Jr. (1994). The influence of organizational linkages and measurement practices on productivity and management. In D. H. Harris, P. S. Goodman & D. S. Sink (Eds.), *Organizational linkages: Understanding the productivity paradox* (pp. 131–160). Washington, DC: National Academy Press.

Tuttle, T. C. (1981). *Productivity measurement methods: Classification, critique, and implications for the Air Force* (AFHRL-TR-81-9). Brooks AFB, TX: Manpower and Personnel Division, Air Force Human Resources Laboratory.

PART I

ProMES in
Manufacturing Settings

2

ProMES in an Electronic Assembly Plant

Philip L. Roth, Margaret D. Watson,
Patricia G. Roth, and Robert D. Pritchard

This chapter describes the development of ProMES in an organization involved in the production of electronic computer components. This setting was substantially different from previous ProMES sites. ProMES was originally developed in a military operation where the focus was on military readiness (i.e., effectiveness) and few productivity measures were available (Pritchard, Jones, Roth, Stuebing, & Ekeberg, 1988, 1989). The setting described in this chapter was a for-profit organization that focused on the efficiency of its operations and had a fairly sophisticated productivity measurement system in place.

Based on these organizational characteristics, the following research questions were asked: Can ProMES be successfully developed in a for-profit setting? What are the effects of adding ProMES to an organization that already has a relatively sophisticated productivity measurement system?

ORGANIZATIONAL SETTING AND PROJECT DESIGN

This section describes the larger organization, the unit in which ProMES was developed, and the project design.

Organization

The larger organization was a small (approximately 485 employees) production facility in the southwest United States that manufactured electronic components for the aerospace industry. This facility was a very dynamic and visible part of its parent corporation, a Fortune 500 U.S. company. It demonstrated a strong commitment to employees by providing support for social activities for employees, preventing layoffs, and encouraging supervisors to resolve performance problems rather than fire employees. In addition, trust and open communications among all levels of the organization were highly valued. In addition to this commitment to worker satisfaction, management was constantly searching for new ways to improve operations and increase productivity.

The organization had a productivity measurement system in place before ProMES was developed. Amount of production, quality of production, and attendance were measured for each work unit in the facility. This system was superior to those often found in industry and had been quite successful in improving organizational productivity. Productivity measures were also available from the industrial engineering department. (The engineering indicators were intricate production formulas used mainly by higher management.)

The organization also utilized a recognition system that was based on its productivity measurement system. The work group with the highest overall productivity was designated "Team of the Month" or "Team of the Quarter."

The organization's interest in ProMES was to further increase productivity and to more equitably distribute the monthly and quarterly productivity awards. ProMES appeared to be a viable solution to both of these problems: previous research indicated that ProMES could successfully improve productivity, and ProMES productivity scores could be used to compare work groups performing very different tasks.

Project Unit

The larger organization was divided into two divisions that made different types of electronic components. The unit in which ProMES was developed was from division A, which was made up of assembly and specialty groups. The project unit, which will be referred to as Team A, was a specialty unit.

Team A was a five-member unit (including the supervisor). It was selected as the first project unit for two reasons. First, they had a particularly well-educated and skilled supervisor who was actively looking for ways to improve his team's productivity. Second, because of problems with the flow of components (described more fully below), it was especially difficult to compare the productivity of Team A with that of the other groups for the recognition awards. In other words, this unit was well-situated to evaluate the organization's two main interests in ProMES.

The specific duties performed by Team A included inspecting electronic components for loose wires, unacceptable levels of dirt, and unclear markings and labels; correcting problems by cementing and soldering electronic pieces; applying protective coatings to components;

and taking the components to final inspection. If final inspection found any errors in the finished products, the unit also was responsible for correcting them.

These duties were very different from those performed in the assembly teams and created special problems for the measurement and evaluation of Team A's productivity. First, the fact that different tasks were performed by Team A made it difficult to compare the productivity of Team A with the other teams. Second, Team A was not in control of many aspects of their own production. The component assembly process began with the assembly teams, who controlled the pace of their own work. When they worked harder, their output went up. Team A, however, served as an in-line inspection and repair group and could work only on the components finished by the assembly teams. Consequently, Team A's output levels depended on the flow of components from the assembly units. Simply working hard was not enough to ensure high output. This problem was complicated by management, who set a monthly output quota for each team. Team A often was prevented from achieving their output goal because they did not receive enough components from the assembly units. When this happened, they were unable to meet their goal, no matter how hard they worked. This prevented them from receiving recognition for their performance and substantially reduced their morale. The Team A supervisor knew that their productivity would eventually suffer because of this unfair situation.

Although it is common for work groups to be apprehensive about defining and measuring their productivity, this was not true of Team A. Because their productivity had been measured for several years by a less-extensive system, they had already resolved their concerns about what measurement would mean. Consequently, their initial reaction to developing ProMES was positive. They were pleased to be singled out for special treatment, interested in trying something new, and hopeful that the ProMES approach might end the equity problems in determining the productivity awards.

Project Design

Researchers met with Team A once every two weeks to develop the ProMES system. This timetable suited Team A because it did not distract them from their normal work schedule. Meeting more often would have required that too much time be devoted to system development. It also suited the researchers because it provided preparation and discussion time between meetings.

Because one of the research questions concerned how ProMES would compare with the existing measurement system, it was important to gather baseline data. The data that had been generated by the existing measurement system were gathered for Team A for the previous year and for the six months of project development. This resulted in 18 months of baseline data. Feedback of the ProMES productivity data was to start the nineteenth month. Baseline data were also collected for three assembly work groups from the same division as Team A and one from the other division. These groups were to serve as controls.

DEVELOPMENT OF THE SYSTEM

The team assigned to design ProMES consisted of facilitators, all members of the Team A work group, and the Human Resources Manager. The chief facilitator (Philip Roth) was an industrial/ organizational psychologist who had been involved with implementing ProMES in other organizations. Four other facilitator trainees were involved in various aspects of the process. The facilitator and facilitator trainees were members of Robert Pritchard's research team and, thus, were not members of the project organization.

The Human Resources Manager was a special member of the design team. He had provided access to the organization, had expressed a great deal of interest in the ProMES process, and wanted to be involved in the development of the system. This request presented an unusual situation for the research group. Members of upper management generally were not included on the design team. However, it was believed that he could be of benefit to the group, providing additional information of which Team A incumbents were unaware. He was instructed, however, to limit his participation in the process. This was necessary to prevent the team incumbents from abdicating development of the system to management. This process was often difficult to manage and was an ongoing issue for the design team and the facilitators.

The Team A members of the design team included the supervisor and the four job incumbents from the Team A unit. The supervisor of Team A was a key member of this group. He had been with the larger organization for some time and had been promoted into a supervisory position from a technician position. He was committed to his team members and their success within the organization. His role during the ProMES development was a complicated one, having several separate functions: to help facilitate the participation of the incumbents and to provide information, pertinent to the process, that was unavailable to his employees. This required that he be a leader and a contributing member of the team but not dominate the team. In spite of how difficult this can be, this process was managed fairly well. Participation by all team members was heavily emphasized by the facilitators and the supervisor. Decisions were made by consensus, with the supervisor's opinion receiving little extra weight.

Designing the productivity measurement system was accomplished by the typical four steps: develop products, develop indicators, develop contingencies, and put the system together (Pritchard, 1990; Pritchard et al., 1989).

Before generating the products, the facilitators learned about the unit's work. They made two tours of the workplace, talked to supervisors and incumbents, and observed the unit performing its various tasks. Each tour took one to one and one-half hours.

Following each tour (and each project meeting), the facilitators met for approximately an hour to discuss their experiences, give each other feedback on how well they had facilitated the group process, assess the progress made, and plan future activities. Although it is believed that this debriefing process is always a good idea, it is especially critical for facilitator trainees. These meetings serve as performance feedback for them and increase their understanding of ProMES and how to manage group process issues.

The facilitators also reviewed the existing productivity measures. This step was very helpful to the facilitators' understanding of the work environment.

To understand how the various teams had performed on these measures in the past, the facilitators talked to supervisors and management about the measures and conducted statistical analyses (e.g., descriptive statistics, intercorrelations) on the baseline data. Descriptive statistics, such as means and standard deviations, helped facilitators understand typical levels of performance and how much variation could be expected and helped guide the choice of maximum and minimum values during development of the contingencies. Intercorrelations between indicators helped guide the choice of indicators in the system. (For example, indicators that were very highly correlated [$r = .90+$] might be measuring the same thing. Thus, only one such measure might be needed in a productivity measurement system.) In addition, facilitators needed to be aware of the intercorrelations among indicators during contingency development. Two indicators with a strong correlation might inadvertently overweight some aspect of work. For example, two important indicators that were positively related might cause the overall productivity score to increase or decrease greatly when only one aspect of work group productivity really had changed.

Product Development

The facilitators started product development with a 20-minute briefing describing the development of products and indicators. The briefing focused on a hypothetical example of an organization developing the products and indicators. The briefing did not focus on contingency development; instead, the facilitators briefed the participants about contingencies immediately before they were developed.

Following the orientation briefing, members of Team A were asked to develop a list of products. They were told products were "a set of activities the unit/organization is expected to perform." The team members began by enunciating very small parts of the unit's work, as small as the duties of individual members. Because these small tasks were what incumbents focused on during their daily activities, it was a logical place for them to start to explain what their organization did. In addition, the facilitators' attention to the small tasks during the tours and discussions held prior to the beginning of the project may have reinforced this tendency. However, the term "products" refers to the objectives of the group as a whole. Hence, the facilitators had to redirect the group to focus on unit goals.

The facilitators managed to focus product development on larger work activities by reminding the Team A personnel that there were typically three to eight products for most groups. They also instructed members to focus on activities for which the whole group was responsible, rather than one individual. Other cues that moved the focus to the proper level of analysis included asking the questions What are some of the big things the organization expects you to accomplish? and What are the groups of tasks you are expected to do? The change of focus toward products was accomplished fairly quickly, taking approximately 45 minutes. The original seven products for Team A are listed below.

1. Maintain a high level of production
2. Make highest quality components possible
3. Maintain high attendance
4. Charge hours to contracts accurately and completely (this product addresses two of management's concerns: that the maximum number of hours be devoted to work that can be billed to the customer and that employees work as efficiently as possible while doing billable work)
5. Follow proper housekeeping and maintenance procedures (this product addresses the need for the work area to be free of contaminants and for all chemicals to be stored and used correctly within their allotted shelf life)
6. Strive to cut production costs
7. Maintain team rapport

Product development took three meetings of one and one-half hours each. Team A personnel were very interested in the development of the productivity measurement system at this stage, although they had some difficulty agreeing on the final list of products. Each member had his/her own ideas about what the system should include. Consequently, the frustration that is often found in consensus activities was present. This could be seen in how each member responded to the disagreements regarding what the products should be. After making suggestions that were not accepted, some members tended to emotionally withdraw from the group. Other members were reluctant to engage in the discussion at all unless specifically asked for an opinion.

In order to deal with this tension, the facilitators took care to ask each person what their thoughts were and to verbally and nonverbally support all attempts at group participation. The design team also discussed the difficulty of accomplishing a consensus group decision and encouraged the group to continue working. They were reassured that the work would be worth it when the final list of products was agreed upon. Although these discussions did not totally eliminate the group tension, they did reduce it substantially. It became clear later in the project, however, that probably more could have been done to resolve this problem. Although the system development went satisfactorily, more complete participation would have been useful.

The facilitators had two concerns with the product list. First, they were worried that products six and seven — "strive to cut production costs" and "maintain team rapport" — would be difficult, if not impossible, to measure in a meaningful way. Unless a method could be found to measure each product objectively and accurately, the product would not be a valid contributor to the system. Consequently, during product development, the facilitators questioned the Team A members about these products and urged the team to consider whether they could be measured. Because individuals typically made suggestions for cutting production costs only once or twice every year or two, it was argued that cutting production costs occurred too rarely to have a substantial impact on the system. It was further argued that maintaining rapport would show up in other products, that is, rapport affects production, quality, and attendance. However, the Team A incumbents were not persuaded by these arguments. They continued to assert that these were important objectives of the unit and should, therefore, be included in the system. The facilitators, on the other hand, still believed that the two products did not belong in the system.

This was the first time in the development process that there was a serious disagreement between the Team A members and the facilitators. The facilitators were in conflict about allowing the system to be totally the product of the ideas of Team A and needing the system to be valid. The Team A members, on the other hand, did not understand why the facilitators were "interfering" with their system. The conflict was resolved when the facilitators decided to postpone any further argument. They believed that this would be resolved during indicator development. When the design team tried to find indicators to measure these products, they would either find creative methods that the facilitators had not considered for measuring these products or understand the inherent problems in each product and be willing to drop them from the system. Consequently, products six and seven were kept on the initial list of products.

The facilitators were also concerned that the product "maintain high level of production" was multidimensional in nature, that is, the product had several conceptually distinct subparts. In this case, maintaining high production entailed producing enough components overall as well as producing a specific number of high-priority components. Although ProMES is very capable of dealing with multidimensional products, these products require very careful analysis by the design team. For the system to be complete, every aspect of a multidimensional product must be included.

Indicator Development

The next step was to develop indicators. Members of Team A were told that an indicator was "a measure of how well the organization was generating the product."

Team A members were initially quite comfortable with the concept of measuring performance. The company's original productivity measurement system had been in place for several years, and Team A had seen how easily certain parts of their productivity could be measured. However, as they began discussing indicators for the more complex portions of their jobs, their reaction was, "You can't really measure that part of my job." Although this type of reaction might prove somewhat disconcerting to facilitators, it seems to be a very common reaction to indicator development. To help expedite the process, the facilitators used their own experiences and ideas to suggest various indicators. Although many of these suggestions were unacceptable to the group, they seemed to help the group begin the process of defining possible indicators. The group also was able to construct some indicators by answering the questions What would you point to to show your boss how well you are doing? and How would you convince your boss the team deserved a raise for its work? A couple of products were left without indicators, however, until the next meeting.

During the second meeting, facilitators cued members of Team A for these indicators by asking the questions Do you know how well you are generating a particular product? followed by How do you know? The response of Team A personnel showed that the team members did use some implicit means for measuring these products. After these ideas were verbalized, they led to indicators. In addition, Team A personnel seemed to focus on the development of indicators rather than the concern that their jobs could not be measured.

The difficulty of developing meaningful indicators helped to resolve one earlier concern. The last two products, "striving to cut production costs" and "maintaining team rapport," were cut from the productivity measurement system at this stage. Team A members could not find a satisfactory way to measure these products. "Striving to cut production costs" did not lend itself to the desired monthly measurement, because methods to promote significant savings were very isolated events. Personnel also accepted the idea that the effects of maintaining rapport would show up in other products.

However, one other early concern continued to be a problem throughout indicator development. This problem had to do with measurement of the first product, "maintain high level of production." This product had a number of conceptually distinct subparts. To capture all aspects of this product, three indicators were needed. The first indicator represented the number of components completed compared with the number of components received from the other units. This indicator was basically an efficiency measure. The second indicator represented the number of high-priority components completed compared with the number needed. This indicator was a measure of percent of goal met. The third indicator was to represent the number of total components completed compared with the total monthly production goal. This was also a percent of goal met indicator. All team members perceived this third indicator as a very important indicator. The monthly goal and the percent of goal met were important measures to upper management. This is the indicator, however, that would be influenced by Team A's lack of control over the number of components received from the production units. The problems with this indicator were further complicated by the fact that the monthly goal was subject to substantial variability, ranging from as low as 600 (a very easy goal to meet) to as high as 1,000 (an extremely difficult goal to meet). A decision was made to weight the percent of goal met by the difficulty of reaching the goal. Many attempts were made to develop a formula that would weight the goals correctly. However, this turned out to be a more intractable problem than was expected. Because of time pressures, this indicator was finally dropped from the system. The plant management, however, committed to continue work on this indicator, because they perceived it to be an extremely important part of a complete productivity measurement system.

Development of the nine indicators took four meetings of one and one-half hours each with the total design team and a one-hour meeting with the supervisor. Listed below are the resulting five products and their indicators.

1. Maintain a high level of production
    Indicator 1: number of components sent to inspect, divided by number received, multiplied by 100
    Indicator 2: number of high-priority components completed, divided by number of components needed, multiplied by 100
2. Make highest quality components possible
    Indicator 3: number of components passed final inspection, divided by the number of components sent, multiplied by 100

3. Maintain high attendance

    Indicator 4: total hours worked divided by total hours available, multiplied by 100 (total hours available equals 40 hours per week per employee, minus holidays and extended sick leave)

    Indicator 5: number of occurrences divided by number of team members (an occurrence is being late to work or being absent for less than half a day)

4. Charge hours accurately and completely

    The work in this organization is done under a government contract with a fairly complex payment system. There are two categories of work hours: budget hours (those used in accomplishing company business, such as meetings and training) and billable hours (those for which the customer will pay). There are three types of billable hours: standard (predetermined hours that reflect how long it should take to complete each type of component), rework (time spent in correcting mistakes on components), and engineering changes (time spent in making corrections requested by the customer). The following three indicators utilize these primary categories of hours.

    Indicator 6: number of hours charged to contracts (billable hours), divided by number of team members (NAH)

    Indicator 7: number of hours actually charged to contracts, divided by number of hours available to be charged, multiplied by 100 (hours available to be charged includes total work hours minus budget hours)

    Indicator 8: number of hours available to be charged to contracts, divided by the standard time allowed for that type of work (the denominator includes standard hours only and does not include hours due to rework or engineering change)

5. Follow proper housekeeping and maintenance procedures

    Indicator 9: number of violations found during a general audit (violations include unclean work area or improperly stored or labeled chemicals)

The members of Team A seemed less positive during indicator development than they were during product development. This seemed to be the result of several different factors. First, indicator development is the most difficult step in developing the ProMES system. It is very important that the indicators measure what they intend to measure. Therefore, what may seem to be a very minor change in an indicator can result in very different outcomes. Thus, finding the right indicator is a quite complex and difficult process. It requires team members to be much more precise than most people are accustomed to. Consequently, the facilitators asked lots of detailed, specific questions, such as, Do you think of this indicator as a percentage or as the actual number of components? Thus, it often appeared to the team members that the facilitators were "being picky." The facilitators must communicate to the team members why this process needs to be so exacting and detailed.

Second, during indicator development, it becomes very clear if there are problems with any of the products. For example, if the product is not a measurable one, finding an indicator will be impossible (such as the suggested product of "maintaining rapport"). Consequently, some of the problems that were discussed but not resolved during product development arose again during indicator development. At this stage, the problems must finally be settled. This can be frustrating for team members, because these problems were typically delayed until indicator development for the very reason that they were so difficult. Facilitators must be particularly careful at this stage to ask all team members for ideas to be sure they remain actively involved.

Because there had been several "contested" products (products six and seven, "strive to cut production costs" and "maintain team rapport"), these had to be addressed during indicator development. In fact, this turned out to be a very simple process. Because these were the last two products to be discussed in terms of indicators, the design team had developed a fairly high level of sophistication regarding indicators through the development of indicators for products one through five. Consequently, when products six and seven were reached, the Team A members voluntarily suggested dropping them from the system. This seemed to be a viable solution to the disagreements between facilitators and the other design team members. By allowing the products to remain in the system until indicator development, two things were accomplished. First, the job incumbents formed a solid sense of ownership of the system. Second, through the indicator development process, the job incumbents developed design skills that made it much easier for them to understand the arguments the facilitators were making.

During indicator development, several important questions were raised. First, what level of control should members of Team A have over each indicator? Theoretically, control should be high to ensure a strong relationship between behavior of unit personnel and scores on indicators (Naylor, Pritchard, & Ilgen, 1980). If personnel work hard, they should see productivity change as a result. Thus, the facilitators stressed that Team A should construct indicators to measure parts of the job they could control. However, Team A had been encouraged by management to be motivated not only to do their best in controllable areas but also to cooperate with other parts of the organization in order to increase the flow of work to them. Thus, the team was leaning toward indicators that were less controllable. For example, on the indicator "mix of high-priority components completed," the indicator could have been either percent of demand mix met (i.e., percent of goal) or number of high-priority components completed divided by number of high-priority components received multiplied by 100 (i.e., percent completed). The problem with the first indicator is that Team A had little direct control over the flow of components. They could, therefore, be penalized for failing to meet the goal even when they had not received enough components to meet the goal. Although the second indicator was controllable, it did not encourage Team A to interact with the assembly teams to increase the flow of components. Team A wanted to use percent of demand mix met as the indicator. The facilitators wanted Team A to use percent completed as the indicator. After extensive discussion of these issues, the design team decided to use the first indicator and to simply live with the problems caused by the uncontrollability. This issue became pertinent again during contingency development.

The second question raised during indicator development referred to the relationship between the team members' ability to understand an indicator and how motivated they would be by the indicator. Do team members need to understand exactly how an indicator is calculated to be motivated by it to improve productivity? This question arose when facilitators noted that several group members did not completely understand how some of the indicators were calculated. For example, some Team A personnel did not understand the specifics of indicator 8, "charging efficiency." This complicated indicator is the number of hours actually billed to the customer divided by the number of hours available to be billed (hours available to be billed included total work hours minus hours used in completing other company business, such as meetings and training sessions). The design team discussed the trade-offs between understanding the indicators and measuring all important parts of productivity accurately and completely, even if it means including harder-to-understand indicators. Because measuring all parts of productivity is so important (Pritchard, 1990), the design team concluded that the complicated measures were appropriate as long as personnel understood them well enough to know what behaviors positively and negatively affected each indicator.

Both of the above questions are partially related to the purpose of the productivity measurement system. Pritchard and colleagues (1989) list several different purposes for productivity measurement, including motivating personnel to increase productivity and acting as a management information system. In this case, the primary purpose was to motivate personnel to increase productivity. Hence, the design team must be concerned with the amount of control that workers have over the indicators and how well they understand them. However, if the system was to be used as a management information system, summarizing the contribution of the human/technical system of Team A to the organization, these two concerns may not be nearly as important (Pritchard, 1990).

Contingency Development

This stage of the project was begun by describing contingencies to the team and the process of their development utilizing the hypothetical example used earlier in the briefing about products and indicators. The contingency briefing lasted about 35 minutes and focused on the development of contingencies, including specification of maximums, minimums, and zero points and drawing the contingencies. Within this briefing, the team was told that a contingency is "the relationship between the amount of an indicator and the effectiveness of that amount." Specific examples of contingencies were included, and their interpretation was discussed.

Maximums and Minimums

The first step of contingency development began with determining the maximum and minimum values of each indicator. The facilitator explained that the maximum was "the best possible performance a group could expect on an indicator if they did everything correctly for a given time period." Similarly, the minimum was "the worst possible performance the group could imagine actually happening to them." For example, the indicator for the quality product was "percentage of components passing final inspection" (Indicator 3). The design team determined that the maximum was 100 percent and the minimum was 99 percent. This means that if Team A did everything under their control correctly, 100 percent of their components would pass inspection. Further, the worst quality they could imagine was that 99 percent of their components would pass inspection.

After determining the maximums and minimums for each indicator, they were ranked by the design team, starting with the maximums. Team A personnel were asked, Which one of these maximums would contribute the most to the effectiveness of the organization? and If you could only have one of the maximums, which would you choose? The maximum that contributed most to the organizational effectiveness received a rank of 1, the one that contributed the second most received a 2, and so forth. Rating the maximums followed the ranking process. Because "percentage of components completed" (Indicator 1) was ranked first, it received a rating of +100 effectiveness points. The other maximums were rated relative to these 100 points. For example, the maximum for "attendance" (Indicator 4) was seen as only one-third as important as "components completed" (Indicator 1), so it received a rating of +33 points. Shown below are the rankings and ratings for the indicator maximums.

Ranking	Rating	Indicator Maximum
1	100	Indicator 1: Production completed
		115 percent of components received completed
3	95	Indicator 2: Production of high-priority components
		100 percent of demand mix met
4	70	Indicator 3: Quality
		100 percent of components passing final inspection

Ranking	Rating	Indicator Maximum
5	33	Indicator 4: Attendance 100 percent of available hours worked
6	25	Indicator 5: Occurrences 0 occurrences per team member
2	97	Indicator 6: Hours charged per employee (NAH) 32 hours charged to contracts per team member per week
7	12	Indicator 7: Percent of available hours actually charged to contracts 85 percent of hours available to charge contracts actually charged
8	11	Indicator 8: Hours charged compared with standard hours number of hours charged to contracts divided by standard time for work done during those hours is 6
9	10	Indicator 9: Housekeeping 0 violations on general audit

A very similar process was used to rank and rate the minimums. The minimum that detracted most from overall effectiveness was given the ranking of 1, the minimum that detracted the second most was given a 2, and so forth. However, the minimum that received the highest rank did not automatically receive a value of −100 effectiveness points. Instead, Team A personnel were asked to rate its negative effect on productivity relative to the 100 effectiveness points of the most important maximum. They were asked, If producing 115 percent of the components you received is rated at +100 points, how low should producing only 85 percent of the components be rated? This allows the minimum to be greater than, less than, or equal to −100, depending on the organization's circumstances. Team A felt that producing only 85 percent of the components would harm the organization as much as producing 115 percent of the components they received would help the organization. Hence, they rated this minimum at −100.

It is interesting to note that the same indicator received the rank of 1 for both the maximum and the minimum. This is not a requirement of the system, and, often, one indicator receives the highest rank while another indicator receives the lowest rank. Listed below are the ranking and rating of the indicator minimums.

Ranking	Rating	Indicator Minimum
1	−100	Indicator 1: Production completed 85 percent of components received completed
6	−73	Indicator 2: Production of high-priority components 60 percent of demand mix met

Ranking	Rating	Indicator Minimum
4	−80	Indicator 3: Quality
		99 percent of components passing final inspection
2	−97	Indicator 4: Attendance
		88 percent of available hours worked
5	−75	Indicator 5: Occurrences
		6 occurrences per team member
3	−85	Indicator 6: Hours charged per employee (NAH)
		16 hours charged to contracts per team member per week
7	−25	Indicator 7: Percent of available hours actually charged to contracts
		60 percent of hours available to charge contracts actually charged
8	−20	Indicator 8: Hours charged compared with standard hours
		number of hours charged to contracts divided by standard time for work done during those hours is 10
9	−7	Indicator 9: Housekeeping
		15 violations on general audit

The final part of the ranking and rating process examined the resulting weightings of the different products. Because each of the five products had from one to three indicators, it was important to be sure that those products with more indicators did not contribute a disproportionate number of points to the overall productivity scores. For example, the "maintain a high level of production" product had two indicators, and the "make highest quality components possible" product had only one indicator. The issue was whether or not production deserved to be weighted substantially more than quality. To check the relative weightings, the effectiveness scores for the indicator maximums were summed for each product. These summed effectiveness points are shown below.

Product	Sum of Maximums
Maintain a high level of production	195
Make highest quality components possible	70
Maintain high attendance	58
Charge hours accurately and completely	120
Follow proper housekeeping and maintenance procedures	10

Each product's total possible points were then compared with every other product's total possible points. Team A personnel were given a chance to correct any inappropriate weightings. The same process was followed for minimum points. The summed effectiveness points for the minimums are shown below.

Product	Sum of Minimums
Maintain a high level of production	−173
Make highest quality components possible	−80
Maintain high attendance	−172
Charge hours accurately and completely	−130
Follow proper housekeeping and maintenance procedures	−7

No changes were made in the relative weights assigned to each product for either maximums or minimums. The facilitators found this somewhat surprising. They had expected that following all of the previous judgments needed to determine maximums and minimums, some final adjustments would need to be made. The lack of any adjustment may have reflected that accurate relative weighting was already accomplished by the ranking and rating process, relative weighting judgments were very difficult to make following many other judgments, or some combination of the above. The facilitators believed that the first explanation was most likely correct.

Determining the maximums and minimums as well as their rankings and ratings required two meetings of 1.5 hours each.

During this first step in developing the contingencies, the Team A personnel had trouble with four issues. First, they had trouble with the term "minimum." In their organization, this term connoted the lowest level of *acceptable* performance instead of the lowest *possible* level of performance. Hence, it caused some misunderstanding during the initial ranking and rating discussions. To alleviate this misunderstanding, the facilitators changed from the term "minimum" to the term "worst" and from "maximum" to "best." However, this chapter will continue using the terms "maximum" and "minimum" for continuity.

A second problem was that several members of Team A did not initially understand how the maximum rankings and ratings could differ from those for the minimums. They reasoned that if producing components is the most important maximum, it should be the most important minimum. Abstract explanations such as "because an indicator's maximum makes the largest contribution to effectiveness does not necessarily mean its minimum detracts the most from effectiveness" did not help. However, one facilitator suggested a hypothetical example that illustrated this point very clearly. The example used the indicator for attendance, with hypothetical values of 100 for the maximum, 95 for the zero point, and 90 for the minimum. Using these numbers, it was pointed out that attendance might be only fairly important when it was near 100 percent, but it might be extremely important when it was below 95 percent. This is because when attendance is near 100 percent, there are plenty of people to do the work; however, when attendance is low, there are not enough people to do the required work. Team A immediately understood the issue, and the problem was resolved.

Another problem was that Team A members had difficulty determining the minimum indicator values, because they had never performed at that low level. Data from past years of performance helped set the minimum values, but team members still seemed uncertain when they rated the minimums. Cues such as "When would the supervisor's boss descend on you and ask what is happening here?" seemed to help the group understand what the minimum values should be and how they should be rated.

A final problem was that Team A personnel could more easily rank and rate the three most important and three least important maximums, but they had difficulty ranking and rating the middle three maximums. It seemed as if the group knew what was most and least important but seldom thought about the indicators that fell in the middle. The same problem occurred for the minimums, that is, the most and least important minimums were relatively easy to establish, while the middle three minimums caused more difficulty.

Drawing the Contingencies

The second major step of contingency development was to construct the contingencies. To draw the contingencies, the facilitators used an overhead projector, a series of blank contingency slides, and an erasable marker. The blank contingency slides were transparencies with the indicator and effectiveness axes printed but with no effectiveness points shown.

To illustrate the process of contingency construction, the development of the first attendance indicator, "percent of hours worked" (Indicator 4), is described below. The first step was to determine the size of the intervals between the maximum and the minimum points. The maximum was 100 percent attendance and the minimum was 88 percent attendance. The design team chose to use eight intervals of 1.5 percent after an unsuccessful attempt to use more intervals. Initially, the facilitators tried to use as many intervals as possible (e.g., 16) to capture as much detail in the contingencies as possible. However, this overwhelmed Team A with too much detail that required too many fine judgments. The use of eight intervals allowed the design team adequate opportunity to deviate from a linear function if the need arose but did not overwhelm them with too many small judgments. Experience gained by the facilitators during this and other projects suggests that most personnel are comfortable dealing with five to ten intervals.

The facilitators completed the second step by placing the maximum and minimum values on the contingency as they had been rated earlier. These points formed the ends of the function relating percent of hours worked to the overall effectiveness of Team A, as illustrated in Figure 2–1.

The design team next identified the zero point. The facilitators told Team A personnel that the zero point was "the expected level of performance, the level that is neither good nor bad performance." Several cues helped elicit zero points, including What is the point that separates good and bad performance? and What is the level of performance that does not result in a pat on the back or a kick in the pants? After some discussion, the consensus was that the zero point was 97 percent attendance.

The final step in contingency development was to determine the points on the contingency from the zero point up to the maximum and from the zero point down to the minimum. The facilitators used two different strategies to draw the contingencies. First, they started at the zero point for percent hours worked (i.e., 97 percent) asking Team A personnel what the effectiveness value would be after jumping one interval (i.e., 97 percent + 1.5 percent = 98.5 percent). That is, if the effectiveness value at 97 percent is 0, what is the value at 98.5 percent? After this number was obtained, personnel were asked for the effectiveness value after the next interval jump, and so on. Although this strategy had been successful on a previous project, it did not work well in this case. Team members had a difficult time determining the effectiveness levels for each level of an indicator. They tended to simply divide the total number of indicator points by the number of intervals. This resulted in an artificial solution that forced the contingencies to be linear from the zero point to the maximum and from the zero point to the minimum.

Hence, the facilitators and the Team A supervisor developed an alternative method that focused on where the biggest increases or decreases in effectiveness occurred. For example, before drawing from the zero point to the maximum of the attendance contingency, personnel were asked, Is there a big increase in productivity at some point, and if so, where is it? The design team determined that there was a big jump and that it was between 97 and 98.5 percent. The facilitators then asked, For how much of the total 33 points between the zero point and maximum should this jump account? Team A personnel decided it was 30 of the 33 points. An analogous process was used when drawing from the zero point down to the minimum, using the question, Is there a place where there is a big loss in effectiveness, and if so, where is it?

It is critical that this approach be used very carefully. It is possible that using this method will force contingencies to be nonlinear. Forcing contingencies to be either linear or nonlinear when this does not reflect policy is a serious problem that needs to be prevented. Consequently, facilitators must be careful in phrasing these questions to ensure that the design team is satisfied that the shape of each contingency is accurate.

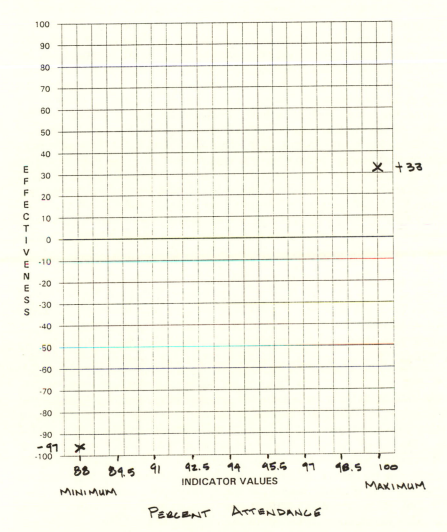

Figure 2–1   Form Used to Develop Contingencies

Although personnel from Team A seemed to have an easier time constructing the contingencies than developing the indicators, this step was also fairly difficult for the team. In fact, it was suggested by the team that a subset of team members would be in a better position to develop the contingencies, which could then be checked and verified by the entire team. Therefore, the process of drawing the nine contingencies required a small portion of one meeting of the whole design team, one meeting of one and one-half hours with a subset of the design team (selected by the entire design team), and one 30-minute meeting of the facilitators and the Team A supervisor. Examples of some of the contingencies, including the final version of the attendance contingency, are shown in Figure 2–2.

This process of using the subgroup seemed to work extremely well. The subset members were very interested in contingencies and grasped the process very quickly. In addition, they had the respect and confidence of the entire team, because they had been the informal leaders of the group throughout the development process. The entire team met later to approve the final list of contingencies.

It was at this stage that the team members came to a real understanding of how ProMES would work, what it would look like, and how it would help them. One member even reported that once he saw the "numbers on the charts," he could finally see what the system would look like and what it would mean to him personally. This was an exciting event for most of them and helped them see that the frustrations of the group process were finally going to pay off.

During the process of contingency development, there were three issues that required attention. First, when drawing the contingencies, facilitators must make unit personnel aware of the implications of their choices. Perhaps the most important one is the relationship among the effectiveness scores assigned to the various intervals of an indicator. For example, if the increase in effectiveness from 97 to 98.5 percent is 30 points but from 98.5 to 100 percent is only 3 points, the implication is that the former increase is ten times as important as the latter increase. The facilitators must ask group members if this is correct; if not, the contingencies should be modified. Checking the intervals is necessary to ensure that the contingencies are constructed accurately.

The second issue is that Team A personnel had more trouble drawing the contingencies below the zero point than above it. Because they had not performed at this low level recently, if at all, they had difficulty determining the appropriate effectiveness values. Facilitators should be ready for this phenomenon and try to encourage the best possible judgments from organizational personnel.

The third issue actually occurred throughout the process but was more pronounced during contingency development. This issue was a result of the different areas of expertise provided by the facilitators and the team members. It was clear that the Team A incumbents were the

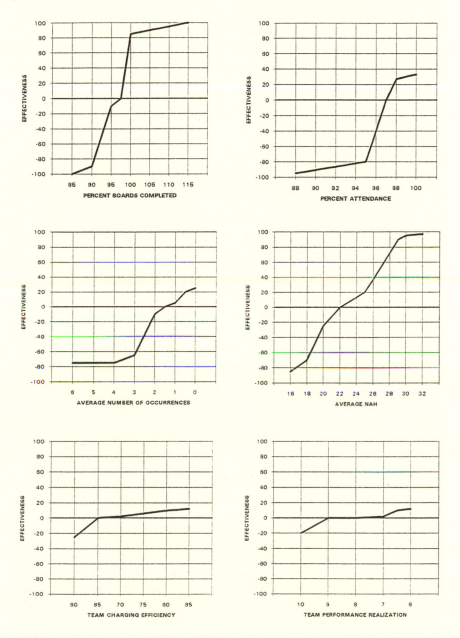

Figure 2–2   Example Contingencies

content experts on the design team; it was less clear, however, that the facilitators were the measurement experts. As measurement experts, they were charged with ensuring that the system was valid and had integrity. Because of these measurement issues, the facilitators often questioned and challenged the suggestions of the team members. This was necessary to ensure that the indicators captured what they were supposed to be measuring, that the maximums and minimums were neither too lenient nor too stringent, and that the total system was valid. Consequently, it could appear to the team members that the facilitators had some preconceived ideas about what the measurements should be and were simply waiting for the team member to "give the right answer." For example, facilitators questioned many of the initial suggestions for maximum and minimum values and encouraged the team to consider either a more extreme or less extreme number. Because the facilitators understood the implications of these judgments for the completed productivity measurement system, they were trying to ensure that the judgments were correct. It was easy to see, however, how the team members could be confused about the intent of these questions. Consequently, it is very important that this issue be identified and discussed openly with the team. After team members understand this process, they work more easily and effectively with the facilitators, and a more accurate system is developed.

Put the System Together

Putting the productivity measurement system together involved developing a formal feedback report, obtaining management approval, and training Team A personnel to use a computer program to generate the feedback report.

To obtain management approval, two levels of the organization above the Team A supervisor were briefed on the system by the facilitators, a subgroup of incumbents, and the Team A supervisor. The one-hour briefing reviewed the products, indicators, contingencies, and feedback report. Management requested no changes in the Team A productivity measurement system.

Both the process and the result of this meeting were somewhat out of the ordinary. Past development of ProMES has found a management briefing following development of products and indicators to be very helpful to gain management approval and involvement. However, the Team A supervisor informally briefed his superiors on several occasions before the formal management briefing. In addition, as was mentioned earlier, the Human Resources Manager of this plant was a member of the design team. Thus, management already knew a good deal about the measurement system. Other projects to develop ProMES have resulted in management briefings in which managers and incumbents negotiated some changes in the measurement system, particularly in the contingencies.

Although management did not suggest any changes in the system, they suggested a direction for future research. They indicated that contingencies might be more useful in certain situations if the vertical axis was in terms of dollars, or financial impact, rather than effectiveness points. They believed that the dollar metric would be a good guide for management decisions. Consequently, a future project might investigate whether a dollar metric could be used on the vertical axis, what the implications of this metric would be, and in what kinds of situations it should be used.

Feedback Reports

Two facilitators met with the supervisor of Team A to teach him how to use the computer program that generates the feedback reports. The initial meeting in which the program was introduced to him took 30 minutes. Later meetings were planned to completely train him. A sample of the feedback report is given in Table 2–1.

The basic information in the feedback report is the indicator and effectiveness data for the period. This includes the list of products and indicators and the level of each indicator for the period with its associated effectiveness value. Total effectiveness for each product is also shown, along with overall effectiveness. This information is on the feedback report in Table 2–1.

In addition to this basic information, the report also contained historical data. Data were included from the previous month along with data from the current period, and the amount of change between the two months was shown. This allows personnel to readily see improvements or decrements in productivity.

ProMES also offers a way to develop a clear set of priorities for improving productivity. The feedback report shows the amount of each indicator for that period and the associated effectiveness levels for those amounts. It is a simple matter to look at the contingency for each indicator and calculate the effectiveness gain that would occur if the unit went up one increment on each of the indicators during the next period. If, as is indicated in Table 2–1, the unit had a Percent Completed of 101 percent in June, for them to improve one interval on the contingency shown in Figure 2–2 would mean that they would increase by 6 percent, going from 101 to 107 percent. Examining the contingency, this would mean going from an effectiveness value of 86 to an effectiveness score of 92, for a gain of 6 effectiveness points. Thus, with a percent completed of 86 in June, if they improved to a score of 92 percent completed in July, their effectiveness gain would be 6 effectiveness points.

A gain of this type is calculated for each indicator. The indicator data for the current month are shown in the Indicator Data From column.

Table 2–1   Sample Feedback Report

Indicator and Effectiveness Data
Period: June

Products and Indicators	Indicator Data	Effectiveness Score
Production		
Percent completed	101	86
Percent mix (high priority)	96	80
Quality		
Percent quality	100	70
Attendance		
Percent attendance	97.5	10
Average occurrences	1.5	0
Charging of hours		
NAH	25	20
Charging efficiency	73	4
Realization factor	6.2	11
Housekeeping and maintenance audit violations	4	2

Effectiveness Totals

Product	Product Effectiveness	Overall Effectiveness
Production	166	283
Quality	70	
Attendance	10	
Charging	35	
Maintenance	2	

Effectiveness Change from Last Period to Current Period

Indicator	Last Period		Current Period		Change in Effectiveness
	Indicator Data	Effectiveness Score	Indicator Data	Effectiveness Score	
Percent completed	99	57	101	86	29
Percent mix (high priority)	98	91	96	80	-11
Percent quality	99.95	68	100	70	2
Percent attendance	97	0	97.5	10	10
Average occurrences	1	5	1.5	0	-5
NAH	27	55	25	20	-35
Charging efficiency	69	1	73	4	3
Realization	6	11	6.2	11	0
Audit violations	2	6	4	2	-4

Potenial Effectiveness Gains for Next Period

Indicator	Indicator Data		Change in Effectiveness
	From	To	
Percent completed	101	107	6
Percent mix (high priority)	96	104	15
Percent quality	100	100	0
Percent attendance	97.5	99.9	23
Average occurrences	1.5	0.3	22
NAH	25	28	53
Charging efficiency	73	78	5
Realization factor	6.2	5.4	0
Audit violations	4	1	6

The value of the indicator if it was increased by one interval is shown in the Indicator Data To column. The gain in effectiveness that would occur with that improvement is shown in the Change in Effectiveness column.

This information communicates exactly what should be changed to maximize productivity. In the example, it says that the best thing the unit can do is to increase their NAH. This would produce the largest improvement in overall effectiveness. Once this is done, or if increasing this factor is not possible, the priority data suggest that the next best thing they could do is to improve percent attendance and average occurrences. Improving percent quality and realization factor are the least important in increasing productivity, because no gain in effectiveness is possible.

Thus, the feedback report gives information on priorities that personnel can use to guide efforts to increase productivity. Although it is necessary for unit personnel to combine the priorities data with information on factors such as cost and difficulty of making each change, the priorities information should aid in decisions about resource allocation and where to focus in identifying barriers to productivity.

Feedback Meetings

After feedback reports were designed, the plan was to have regular meetings with supervisors and incumbents to review the feedback reports. Such a feedback meeting was to be held after each feedback report was done. This is a very important part of ProMES. The meetings should be conducted by the supervisor. During the meeting the feedback report would be reviewed and areas where productivity increased or decreased would be explored. The group would then focus on the reasons for improvement or decrement in each area.

RESULTS

At approximately the same time that productivity feedback was to begin, top management at the corporate headquarters in another state announced a major organizational change. A decision had been made by the parent company to test a different organizational design. Instead of several assembly work groups sending components to Team A for review, all groups in the organization would function as assembly groups and share the tasks and duties of Team A. This resulted in the breakup of Team A.

Because Team A no longer existed, implementing the feedback system was precluded. This prevented the research team from collecting the data needed to fully answer the second research question. The first research question asked if ProMES could be developed in a for-profit organization. The answer to this question is clearly yes. The design team successfully developed the system and was ready to institute feedback at the time of the organizational change. Unfortunately, only anecdotal information is available to answer the second research question. It asked what the effects of ProMES would be on productivity in a for-profit organization that already had a large number of productivity measures in use. Specific comments made by both the Team A supervisor and the Team A members indicate that ProMES was seen as a clear improvement over the existing productivity measurement system. The supervisor described ProMES as a "total system as opposed to a little tool." He knew that it would allow him to proactively intervene with his group, based on his knowledge of what was actually happening within the team. The team members also expressed the feeling that they would know where to focus their efforts and were disappointed that the system was not fully implemented. Thus, it seems that ProMES could have produced positive effects in the team's productivity if the full system had been implemented.

DISCUSSION

This section discusses lessons learned in the course of the project and conclusions.

Lessons from the Project

In spite of the organizational change that precluded feedback, the facilitators learned a number of important lessons about developing ProMES that could benefit future development efforts. These lessons fall into the categories of personnel concerns, product development, indicator development, and contingency development.

Personnel Concerns

The first lesson was that the correct composition of the design team is very important in efficiently designing a high-quality productivity measurement system. In this project, the design team included all Team A incumbents. The high proportion of incumbents to supervisors (i.e., four to one) encouraged incumbent participation but had the effect of diminishing the relative input from the Team A supervisor. Supervisory input is extremely important, because it provides a perspective that incumbents do not have. In particular, the supervisor is aware of management needs and how the work group fits into the larger organization. It is very important that these issues of supervisor versus incumbent participation be discussed by the research team. The pros and cons of group composition must be clearly delineated and the decision made as to which approach to take. Based on this experience, it is recommended that the design team include a few representative incumbents and the immediate supervisor from the unit in question such that the ratio of incumbents to supervisory personnel is lower than in this instance. This composition has a number of advantages: it allows the supervisor to have more input into the system, because fewer incumbents are involved; it allows workers to participate in ProMES development but does not burden uninterested workers; and it allows the unit to accomplish more of its regular work. If the facilitators are concerned about too little incumbent participation, the design team could periodically present their work to the entire work group for approval.

The second lesson gained from this project was the clarification of the facilitators' role. The facilitators are responsible for three distinct tasks: leading or moderating the meetings; recording product, indicator, and contingency information; and watching and directing group dynamics. Because one facilitator would have difficulty accomplishing all three tasks, having two facilitators is recommended. If two facilitators are available, one should lead the meeting and the other should record information. Because group dynamics are so important to the success of the design efforts, both facilitators should watch group dynamics.

The most important aspect of group dynamics during the development process is each group member's reaction to the frustrations and tensions associated with achieving consensus. As tensions arise, members may become withdrawn, dominant, argumentative, or even sullen. The facilitators need to draw out each member, insuring that everyone is included in the process and encouraged to share their perspective. Each idea deserves to be heard, regardless of whether or not it is accepted. Unless open interactions are maintained, there is the possibility that the resulting system will be less valid and/or less accepted.

A third lesson about personnel issues was that the facilitators need to be concerned about the conflicting priorities between project participants. As was mentioned earlier, entry to this organization was gained from the Human Resources Manager, who also sat on the design team. Therefore, although most of the work was done with Team A, management was involved as well. Although there was a difference between the views of management and employees that subtly influenced the entire design process, there were times when the managerial view was quite different from that of the workers. This was particularly true regarding the conflict between the need for employee control over productivity measures and the need to encourage cooperation among teams. Although the employees originally agreed with management that it was important to encourage cooperation among teams, they did not fully understand the impact of this decision until contingency development. Thus, during contingency development, the views of management and employees diverged. Consequently, during the discussions to resolve this problem, the facilitators felt somewhat caught in the middle and had to work diligently to manage the group process.

Product Development

Two major lessons emerged from the process of product development. First, the facilitators must keep the design team focused on products that represent the work of the whole group. The natural tendency of individuals is to talk about the part of the group's work they know best — their own job. The facilitators should remind the design team that products by definition are those activities the unit is expected to perform that contribute to the functioning of the entire organization.

Second, the fact that some products may be multidimensional must be kept in mind. In this instance, the term "multidimensional" refers to products with distinctly different parts. For example, the "maintain high production" product was concerned with both the total amount of production and the amount of production of a few high-priority components. Facilitators must help the group to recognize these multiple dimensions and ensure that all dimensions are measured.

Indicator Development

The process of indicator development highlighted three major issues facilitators should consider. First, it is important to use an iterative process to develop indicators. Multiple meetings allow design team members to create or propose an indicator during one meeting, review and evaluate it between meetings, and revise it at the next meeting. The iterative process is particularly essential when developing new indicators. The time between meetings also allows facilitators to consider which behaviors the measures motivate and allows unit personnel to consider how comfortable they are with various indicators. In this project, three different indicators were proposed during a meeting in which most members of the design team were enthusiastic about utilizing them. However, further consideration showed that each had major flaws and should not be included in ProMES in their original form. Two of these indicators with flaws were reworded and included in the system; one indicator was dropped completely from the system. This iterative process is also helpful when the design team is considering using existing measures. It gives them time to determine whether the indicators measure what they are purported to measure.

A second issue that the design team should consider is what level of understanding of the indicators workers need. This may depend on the purpose of the system. Generally, greater worker understanding is needed when ProMES is used as a motivational tool rather than as a management information system. Motivational systems can probably use existing complex measures if workers know how to change their behavior to change the indicator values. However, using new complex indicators may, at least initially, leave workers with less understanding of what behaviors they must change to change the indicators.

A third issue highlighted in indicator development is that the amount of control workers will have over the indicators has direct implications for how the group will rank and rate the indicators and draw the contingencies. For example, Team A chose to increase their motivation to cooperate with assembly groups by developing some indicators that relied on the combined efforts of all work groups. However, they achieved this motivation to cooperate at the expense of control. In spite of attempts made by the facilitators to explain the trade-offs between degree of control and ability to encourage cooperation, the implications of this choice did not become fully clear until contingencies were developed. Team A personnel discovered that cooperative indicators mean they are evaluated not only on how well they perform but also on how fast other teams give them components. During the ranking and rating of the indicators, Team A personnel were reluctant to rank even a very important indicator highly if it measured things they could not control. Similarly, when drawing contingencies, members of Team A were particularly concerned about the part of the contingency below the zero point; they did not want to receive negative effectiveness scores due to factors outside their control.

Consequently, it appears that it may be very difficult for team members to fully understand the trade-offs between control and encouraging cooperation until the productivity measurement system is nearly finished, or even in operation. To counteract this problem, facilitators should consider encouraging the team to include both controllable and uncontrollable indicators in the system. This strategy insures that the team members are encouraged to cooperate with their fellow employees at the same time that they are not unduly punished by uncontrollable indicators.

Contingency Development

Several things were learned during contingency development. First, it was found that the size of the intervals between the maximum and minimum indicator values should not be too small. If the intervals are too small, a large number of indicator values must be included on the horizontal axis. It was found that the number of increments on the horizontal axis of the contingency generally should be kept in the range of five to ten. This allows flexibility to construct a linear or nonlinear contingency but does not overwhelm design team members with too many small judgments. Asking members to make small judgments results in a large number of points on the contingencies. The effect of deciding on a large number of points is that individuals must process a great deal of complex information. It appears that it is unreasonable to expect individuals to process more than five to ten specific judgments.

A second lesson was that facilitators must be careful when dealing with minimum points. They should make sure that personnel view the minimum as the lowest possible level of performance, not the lowest acceptable level. In addition, facilitators should not be surprised if group members are more tentative in making judgments about minimum values. However, this is seldom an important problem, because most organizations do not function at such a low level of productivity and, hence, probably will not use this part of the contingency often.

Third, there was a concern about the relative weighting of products. The weighting was explicitly considered after the ranking and rating process, but there were no changes to the weights assigned to different products. It was unclear whether this was due to the precision already present in ProMES or the difficulty of making more complex decisions by Team A personnel. The facilitators felt the former reason was the case.

A fourth lesson was the success of the alternative method of drawing the contingencies. Asking Team A members if there was a big jump in productivity and where it might occur stimulated a great deal of thinking. After the thinking and discussion had started, drawing the contingencies came very naturally.

The final and most striking lesson was how easily members of Team A were able to construct contingencies. Most people could contribute ideas, see the implications of these thoughts, and discuss the shape of the contingency. This is, indeed, striking when one considers how complex a contingency is. It conveys the evaluation of the productivity of the maximum, minimum, expected, and all levels of performance in between with a level of precision seldom seen in the workplace.

Conclusions

In conclusion, researchers were successful in using the ProMES approach to develop a productivity measurement system in a for-profit organization engaged in team-based manufacturing. They were also able to learn more about the ProMES development process. Unfortunately, only anecdotal data could be collected to assess the expected impact of ProMES on the productivity of this organization.

REFERENCES

Connolly, T., Conlon, E. J., & Deutsch, S. J. (1980). Organizational effectiveness: A multiple constituency approach. *Academy of Management Review*, 5, 211–217.

Naylor, J. C., Pritchard, R. D., & Ilgen, D. R. (1980). *A theory of behavior in organizations* (p. 299). New York: Academic Press.

Pritchard, R. D. (1990). *Measuring and improving organizational productivity: A practical guide* (p. 248). New York: Praeger.

Pritchard, R. D., Jones, S. D., Roth, P. L., Stuebing, K. K., & Ekeberg, S. E. (1989). The evaluation of an integrated approach to measuring organizational productivity.

Personnel Psychology, 42, 69–115.

Pritchard, R. D., Jones, S. D., Roth, P. L., Stuebing, K. K., & Ekeberg, S. E. (1988). The effects of feedback, goal setting, and incentives on organizational productivity. *Journal of Applied Psychology Monograph Series, 73,* 337–358.

Schmidt, F. L., Hunter, J. E., McKenzie, R. C., & Muldrow, T. W. (1979). Impact of valid selection procedures on work-force productivity. *Journal of Applied Psychology, 64,* 609–626.

3

ProMES as Part of a New Management Strategy

Paul Janssen, Ad van Berkel, and Jan Stolk

THE SETTING: VANDRA CORRUGATED FIBREBOARD

Vandra Corrugated Fibreboard is a medium sized firm that produces corrugated packaging for a large variety of customers. It employs approximately 200 people, and 120 of them work in the production department, in two shifts. In a commercial sense, Vandra has prospered over the past decade. The number of people employed has almost doubled since 1983. Sales also have doubled, at least. Return on investment stayed at a level regarded as high in this field of operation. Despite its highly successful performance, Vandra changed its strategic business orientation in the late 1980s. Until then, Vandra operated in a way that is typical for this type of business. The company focused primarily on selling large numbers of packagings. Due to fierce competition among different manufacturers, profit margins on single packagings were fairly small, but by turning out large volumes, the company had been able to maintain good profits.

Now their view changed. Vandra decided that it would be much more profitable to focus on small orders, very short delivery times, and a flexible way of meeting customer demands, getting better prices in return. It is obvious that for such a change, a complete turnaround of the organization was necessary.

Until then, Vandra was a fairly traditional organization. Management decided that a new type of organization was necessary to accomplish their goal. Their ideal was a fairly flat organization, where responsibilities were handed down as much as possible to people on the shop floor and communication between management and the shop floor was direct and straightforward. With regard to quality, for example, management was opposed to the idea of a separate quality control department. Management, the production manager most of all, was convinced that quality control should be an integral part of everyone's job. In their view, a separate quality control department would weaken attention and motivation for quality on the shop floor, because it would be viewed as other people's responsibility.

With regard to the process of change, management favored a gradual process of change over a drastic, one time reorganization. The concept of a "learning organization" appealed to them very strongly. They were convinced that it would be much better to allow people to adapt gradually to the demands of the new situation and to learn how to cope with it. This way, changes in the organization and procedures could grow in a natural way.

Management was also very much aware that existing values, such as keeping costs low, concentrating foremost on production speed, and following routine procedures without questioning them, had to be replaced by new ones. Flexibility, reliability, and meeting customer demands became much more important. Most of all, people all over the organization had to become aware of the impending changes, and they would have to learn how to incorporate these new values in their own job behavior.

Right at the time when management was pondering how to prepare people on the shop floor for these changes, Vandra's production manager met the senior author of this chapter, who had just acquainted himself with the ideas of Pritchard on performance management and enhancement. After an initial feasibility study, the author proposed to do a pilot project with ProMES in one of the production groups. The production manager agreed on the condition that he could find a group that was willing to engage in such a project on a voluntary basis.

For Vandra, the goal of this pilot project was to find out whether ProMES is effective in altering the attitude and working behavior of people on the shop floor and, thus, leads to improvements in the performance of production groups, ultimately resulting in higher productivity and improved quality. Right from the start, Vandra made it clear to everybody involved that there would be no direct link between ProMES and (individual) performance appraisal or pay.

For the research team of Eindhoven University, the project posed an opportunity to find out whether a system like ProMES could be applied in a Dutch organization. Actually, it was the first attempt to implement the system in Europe, so basic questions like Will the system work here? How will people react to the system? and How will ProMES fit in with the existing organization and its culture? predominated the research.

THE EXPERIMENTAL GROUP

The group of workers willing to try the system operated a die cut machine that produces various kinds of corrugated board boxes. It consisted of four people: a senior operator, an assistant operator, and two fellow workers. Their machine, called the "Cuir," after its French manufacturer, consists of two printing units and a die cutting unit. Sheets of corrugated board, produced by another department, are fed into the machine at the front end. After passing through the printing unit, they are fed into the die cutting unit, where they are cut and molded. At the end of the line, the cut and printed sheets are stacked according to customer specification and transported to the shipping department.

In a technical sense, the process is not very complicated. It is a fairly straightforward production process. In order to operate it in a profitable way, however, sound knowledge of the machine, speed, and accuracy are important.

The setup of the machine, in particular, is critical, because it is directly related to both quality and quantity of production. Each time a new order is produced, the machine setup has to be altered. This means changing the rubber stamps and the ink in the printing units, installing a new cutting form, and adjusting it to the die cutting drum. The average number of new orders in one shift was eight. At the start of the pilot project, the average time needed for the setup of an order was 22 minutes. During setup, production is halted. This means that, on an eight-hour shift, almost three hours of production time were spent on setup activities. Therefore, it is clear that short setup times are very important for good performance. Speed of setup, however, is not the only important factor. A thorough setup of the machine is crucial to the quality of the boxes produced as well as to the speed with which the group can operate the machine during the production run.

The die cutter is operated in two shifts. The crew of only one shift was involved in the project. The crew from the other shift made it very clear right from the start that they did not want to participate in the project and that they would certainly not take part in the development of the system. Despite their initially fairly antagonistic attitude to the project, the presence of an almost identical group created an opportunity for comparison between the two as a means to establish the impact of ProMES. We will come back to this later.

DEVELOPMENT OF THE SYSTEM

The development of ProMES was largely done by way of interactive group discussion (Pritchard et al., 1989; Pritchard, 1990). The design team consisted of all four of the machine operators, their supervisor, an assistant production manager, and two facilitators, one of them the senior author of this chapter. Each week, one session of one and one-half to two hours took place, either right before the group started its shift or after they finished working. Operators received their normal hourly pay for the extra time that was spent on developing the system.

Initially, actual participation in the group discussions varied a great deal. The least educated and experienced operators especially had great trouble expressing their thoughts and ideas. At this stage the facilitators stressed the fact that ultimately the system should be "owned" by the group as a whole and, therefore, participation by all members of the group in the discussions and the decision making was of great importance. The facilitators often had to slow down the process and help clarify the reasoning of other members in order to keep the developmental process clear and make everybody understand the steps taken. All things considered, the development of ProMES constituted a slow but deliberate learning experience for all involved, including the supervisor, the assistant production manager, and the facilitators.

The frequent interactive group discussions and the difficulties the group had to overcome in order to develop a system everybody could agree with also had a clear team-building effect: people learned how to work together and solve problems as a team. The way in which the facilitators supported the process provided a role model for the supervisor and the group with respect to communication and problem solving.

The developmental process differed from the one Pritchard used in two respects. First, at the start of the formal ProMES meetings, the group listed various problems they encountered regularly in their daily work. These ranged from small technical problems to problems in coordinating their own efforts with those of other departments. Minor improvements were made with help from the production manager and the technical department. As this is something that occurs in most projects, but at a later point in time, it is not considered a major deviation from ProMES as Pritchard described it. We look upon these discussions as an integral part of the developmental effort. Actually, we are convinced that the initial problem analysis helped the group to share their knowledge and experience on the job and focus on the really important issues when they started to define products and indicators.

The second aspect in which the developmental process differed from Pritchard's was the extensive use of historical data in establishing contingencies. In order to balance effectiveness scores for different indicators, some financial calculations were made with regard to the economic value of indicator scores. The group used these data to corroborate the effectiveness scores they deducted themselves.

The development of ProMES for the experimental group took 22 meetings (approximately 40 hours), between April and October 1989. In November 1989, the system was operational. Although the number of meetings is fairly large, one has to take into account that for all participants involved, this was the first attempt at introducing ProMES. Later, with other groups, the number of meetings was reduced a great deal. On the average, development of ProMES took 20 to 25 hours of interactive group discussion.

THE PRODUCTIVITY MEASUREMENT SYSTEM

The productivity measurement system the design team finally came up with was largely in accordance with the criteria Pritchard (1990) listed. Of five products, the most important were quality, speed of production, and effective use of machine time, the last being a product that is very much influenced by speed of setup. These are fairly conventional measures for a production group of this type. It is interesting to note that some of the indicators chosen were fairly gross measures of the responsibilities of the group. Some of them contained considerable variance that was beyond the control of the group. Speed of production, for instance, was partly dependent on the type of order the group had to produce and partly on the size of the order; both factors were beyond the control of the group. Attempts to take these factors into account in defining indicators showed, however, that to do this would result in a measurement system that was too complex and too difficult for at least some of the operators in the group. In order to keep the system simple and easy to comprehend, the design team preferred measures that were less than perfect in terms of controllability but easy to understand. For the facilitators, this was a difficult decision. Had the organization been planning to use the ProMES data in performance appraisals or decisions about pay, the facilitators would have been very reluctant to agree with such a decision. Vandra, however, had stated officially that there would be no direct link to performance appraisal and pay. To the facilitators, the decision of the design team was compatible with the goals of the organization. Therefore, in the end, they agreed.

Developing a valid, meaningful, and cost effective indicator for the product "Quality" initially posed a problem. As we mentioned before, management was opposed to a separate quality control function, which could have provided the necessary data. In the absence of these data, the design team decided on two other indicators for "Quality": the first, and most important, was the number of customer complaints, the second was the number of "internal complaints," that is, the number of times faults are made that are detected in time inside the organization so that they do not reach customers.

With regard to measurement of "Customer complaints," a technical difficulty did arise. Complaints often did not reach the company until several months after the date of production. Therefore, complete feedback on the performance of the group on this indicator could be given only after a long interval. This is contrary to the demands of effective feedback (Kopelman, 1990). Feedback should be given within a couple of days after a production period ends, and it should be complete. All other indicator scores were available within a couple of days after the end of a period. The chosen solution was to leave the score for the indicator "Customer complaints" out of the report initially and give priority to the speed with which feedback is presented. Six months later, when, according to experience, all complaints could be expected to have reached the company, the effectiveness score for "Customer complaints" was reported to the group and added to the scores for all the other indicators for the month in which the order was produced. Thus, six months later, the feedback report is completed. (Although the score is added only after six months, the actual complaint is brought to the attention of the group immediately after it is reported to the organization and is analyzed and discussed by the group.)

Another point of interest is the type of feedback scores the group gets. After the indicators were defined and contingencies developed, it became clear that some effectiveness scores and the overall effectiveness score could vary substantially from one period to another. This was caused mainly by characteristics of the indicators chosen. For instance, fairly small differences on an indicator score like "Customer complaints" can cause large differences in effectiveness scores. Although we look upon this as true variance, reflecting true differences in performance, the facilitators were not sure how the group would react to this. They thought that large and sudden differences in overall effectiveness scores from one month to another could create the subjective impression that chance is a major factor. It could also induce the group to "explain" low scores in a way that is favorable to them.

One solution we considered was to reduce variances by lengthening the report period. A decision was needed whether to do this, thus, "diluting" the feedback, or to accept the large variances in monthly scores. In this case, the design team opted for a compromise: each month the overall score for that month is presented along with the progressive mean overall score for the last four months. The feedback report, thus, contains an overall effectiveness score for all indicators minus "Customer complaints" for the month that has just expired; an overall effectiveness score including "Customer complaints," lagging six months behind; and two progressive mean overall effectiveness scores, one for the imminent period and one for the period six months back.

Starting from November 1989, the group received a monthly feedback report. Each month this report is reviewed in a one-hour meeting in which the group itself, its supervisor, and the assistant production manager take part. Scores are reviewed, problems discussed, and solutions offered. Action and decisions are recorded by the group itself. Sometimes, if problems cannot be solved by the group itself, other departments or management is involved. Finally, management also uses these meetings to inform the group of their plans and ongoing affairs.

THE RESEARCH DESIGN USED

The research design used to evaluate the effects of this pilot project on productivity was basically a times series design. For practical reasons, the inclusion of a baseline period after development finished and before feedback was given was not possible. There was no way in which the researchers could withhold feedback from management and the group once the system was completed. However, at Vandra, like at every other modern organization, a tremendous amount of information is gathered routinely on numerous aspects of performance. Inspection of the information recorded showed that it was possible, for research purposes, to calculate historical baseline scores on the five most important indicators. Only on two minor indicators were no data available, and at their maximum, these accounted for no more than 15 percent of the maximum overall effectiveness score. Throughout this chapter, where overall effectiveness scores are calculated and reported, both these indicators are treated as if their effectiveness scores were zero.

To evaluate effects of ProMES on productivity, effectiveness scores before, during, and after development of the system were calculated and compared. Scores for a period of one year before development started were calculated on the basis of historical data from production records. During development, scores were registered (but not fed back to the group). After feedback started, scores were available for a period of a little more than two years. At the end of 1991, there occurred many changes in the work and the organization of the experimental group. A second, technically improved "Cuir" die cutter was installed, the order package produced at the "old" die cutter changed, and half of the operators were transferred to the new machine. Although the group still uses ProMES, it does not make any sense to compare effectiveness scores before and after this point in time.

RESULTS OF THE PILOT PROJECT

The top half of Figure 3–1 shows the mean overall effectiveness scores for the experimental group (as a percentage of the maximum score) during the baseline period (one year), the developmental phase (eight months), and the feedback period (more than two years after completion). It is clear that productivity scores for the Cuir group increased significantly during the developmental phase and after completion of the system. To evaluate the impact on productivity, we calculated the effect size of ProMES, using the procedure Guzzo, Jette, and Katzell developed for their meta-analysis of productivity

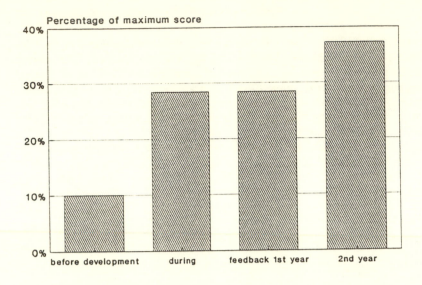

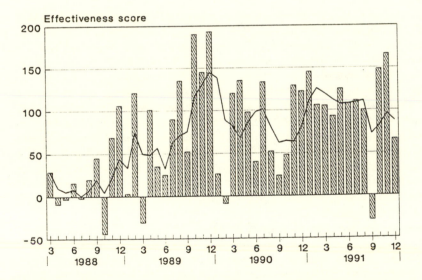

Figure 3–1   Mean Overall Effectiveness Scores for the Experimental Group

The top half of this figure depicts the mean overall effectiveness scores before, during, and after development of ProMES; in the bottom half, the monthly scores from March 1988 through December 1991 are presented.

interventions (1985). The effect size was calculated relative to the baseline period before development of the system started. The effect size for the developmental period was 0.92; for the feedback condition, it was 1.24. The effect size for feedback relative to development was 0.22. Compared with effect sizes Guzzo and colleagues (1985) reported for different studies using feedback to enhance productivity, ranging from 0.08 to 0.62, these results look very favorable.

It is interesting to note exactly when and how these improvements occurred. The bottom half of Figure 3–1 depicts the monthly overall effectiveness scores for the experimental group from March 1988 until December 1991. From March 1988 to the end of February 1989 represents the baseline period; in March and April 1989, the group engaged in their initial problem analysis; and from May to October, development of the system was underway. Finally, in November 1989, the group was presented their first feedback report.

As the bottom half of Figure 3–1 shows, effectiveness scores improved rather dramatically during the final part of the developmental phase. After feedback was installed, scores dropped a little, but, on the average, they remained at a level higher than during either the baseline period or the developmental phase. The question is what caused these effects.

Let us first turn to the increase in scores during the developmental phase. A slope like the one depicted in Figure 3–1 could be regarded as evidence for a Hawthorne effect, learning, or role clarification (Locke & Latham, 1990). Although there is some evidence for all these causes, there appear to be two other important factors in play.

First, as was discussed before, in this case, the development started with a short, fairly general analysis of problems the group encountered in their normal work. Suggestions from the design team resulted in some structural changes regarding work practices and the organization of the work. Although we see this as an integral part of a ProMES project, one could argue that some improvements in productivity, in particular, in the first months of the project, were partly caused by actions taken as a result of this specific effort, not so much by goal setting and feedback.

Second, in the latter stages of the developmental process, something interesting happened. In field research like the Vandra project, one has to be aware of the ingenuity of people to obtain data pertaining to their performance once their curiosity is heightened by a project like this. There really is no way to prevent this. One could even actually argue that it would be unwise and demotivating to try to do so. In this project, there is evidence that after it became clear to the group what products and indicators would figure in their reports, they tried, successfully, to obtain performance data pertaining to these products and indicators. In a way, feedback started to be available some months before it was intended.

Next, we focus on the decline in effectiveness scores two months after formal feedback started. The explanation actually is fairly simple. As happens in field research, sometimes there are unexpected incidents and decisions that go against the goals of a project. In this case, the senior operator, who was officially in charge of the machine, was transferred to another group, along with one of his fellow workers. This happened on January 1, 1991. His assistant, until then the second in command, was promoted to first operator, and two new operators joined the crew. Although they were thoroughly introduced to ProMES and the job at hand, obviously, the group needed some time to regain their former level of proficiency. Actually, when asked, the newly appointed first operator stated that he willingly slowed down production to adapt to the level of proficiency of the new members of his team and that he took time off to instruct and train them on the job. It is obvious that under these circumstances, effectiveness scores should drop to a lower level. It is significant, however, that their scores for that year stayed well above the level before ProMES was introduced. Overall, management was very pleased with the way in which the new Cuir group performed in spite of personnel changes.

From a research perspective, we infer that long-lasting, consistent improvements in productivity were made by the experimental group as a result of developing and introducing ProMES.

HOW DOES ProMES WORK?

Next we turn to the issue of how different indicators contributed to this overall improvement. Inspection of the change in mean effectiveness scores on the three main indicators from baseline to feedback shows that the effectiveness scores on "Quality" improved by 55 points, on "Effective use of machine time" by 20 points, and on "Speed of production" by just 10 points. These findings show that improvements were not a result of frenetic work behavior but of better awareness and attention to quality demands and a more effective organization of setup activities. The indicators that changed most were those that were dependent on making intelligent decisions, anticipation, and maintaining high work standards. When asked, workers made it clear that they did not feel they were working any harder than before but that they felt more knowledgeable, involved, and responsible for their work. All this confirms Pritchard's (1990) summarizing statement that ProMES brings people to "work smarter, not (necessarily) harder."

We can highlight the way in which operators learned from using ProMES with a typical example. One month, shortly after feedback started, the effectiveness score of the group dropped remarkably when compared with their scores in the previous month. On inspection, it appeared that the indicator "Effective use of machine time" had dropped sharply. Further exploration brought to light that the machine operator, who took pride in his job, had tried to overcome problems in setting up an especially difficult job all by himself. Instead of the approximately 18 minutes that it would have taken him normally, it had taken him almost four hours. In doing so, he had shown great persistence and a strong commitment to quality. His choice, however, was erroneous. As the feedback report showed, the indicator for production time had dropped sharply, and as a result, overall scores for that period were disappointing. In discussing this with the group and his supervisor, they came up with a better strategy to cope with future problems of this kind. Instead of going through all kinds of pain and trouble to do a good setup job, in the future, he should decide to put the order aside, start working on the next order, work out the problem with the difficult setup away from the production line, and put the job back on again after the problem was solved. ProMES stimulates such thinking about priorities by showing the impact of alternative decisions and strategies on overall effectiveness. It helps people to learn from mistakes and become more effective.

PRODUCTIVITY CHANGES IN THE ALTERNATE SHIFT

As mentioned before, the production at Vandra operates in two shifts. In addition to the experimental group, there is another group that operates the same machine in the other shift. Both groups are identical except for the fact that one group developed ProMES where the other refused to take part in the project. The second group initially showed a fairly negative attitude toward the experimental group. They refused to cooperate in attempts to change work practices. They even engaged in a fierce competition with the experimental group, trying to outperform them. The authors, therefore, decided initially that a control group design to evaluate the impact of ProMES on productivity was not feasible. However, as time went by, relations between the two groups improved and got back to normal. Therefore, a comparison of productivity data of both groups over a period of some years can give at least some evidence of the effects of ProMES. To compute effectiveness scores for the control group, we extracted indicator data for this group from company records and used the contingency functions developed by the experimental group to translate these into effectiveness scores. Figure 3–2 shows the "mean overall effectiveness scores" of both groups for the years 1988 to 1991. Remember that development of the system in the experimental group took place in 1989 and that the group started to receive feedback in November of that year.

In 1989 and 1990, both groups succeeded in improving their performance substantially. We partly ascribe this to the fact that the control group benefited from structural improvements that resulted from suggestions from the experimental group. However, improvements in productivity for the control group also partly were due to the fact that

Figure 3–2   Mean Overall Effectiveness Scores for the Experimental Group and the Control Group from 1988 to 1991

they did their very best to outperform the experimental group. Later on, in 1991, with relations between both groups back to normal, the experimental group maintained their high level of performance, whereas the control group slid back to substantially lower effectiveness scores.

It is interesting to note that the two groups increased productivity in different ways. The experimental group improved in performance on "Quality" and succeeded in bringing down setup times. The effectiveness score on "Customer complaints" improved steadily from 16 points in 1988 to 79 points in 1991. The control group raised their productivity in a more traditional way: they exceeded previous standards of "Production Speed" by far, thus, turning out large volumes of production. On the negative side, their performance on "Quality" did not improve at all. The average effectiveness score on "Quality" for the control group was 16 in 1988, 0 in 1989, 16 in 1990, and 8 in 1991.

When interpreting these results, one should keep in mind that for the organization as a whole, "Quality" was a major strategic issue. Therefore, considering that the experimental group had to cope with personnel changes while the control group did not, both the improvement and the makeup of the effectiveness scores for the experimental group look very favorable.

SUBJECTIVE REACTIONS TO ProMES

One of the key elements of ProMES is the sense of ownership it creates in people at the shop floor. Because of the small number of people involved, we decided to evaluate subjective reactions of the operator group, their supervisor, and management through interviews. When asked, the operators revealed that they looked upon the system very much as their own. They stated that they felt much more involved, both with their own work and with the organization as a whole. As a result, there were frequent suggestions for improvements. Also, in their view, their performance as a team and communications with their supervisor and management had improved significantly. Both the operators and management stated that knowledge and influence in the group of operators were more equally shared than before ProMES. More important, these changes last. When asked in 1993, almost three years after the development of ProMES was finished, the group of operators working at this machine still expressed the same feelings and opinions about ProMES. Throughout the years, the group and the operators transferred to other groups have acted as ambassadors for ProMES in other parts of the organization.

We also asked the people involved how they evaluated the developmental process. Those who were engaged in the process state that it was a fairly difficult task. To them, concepts and instruments used in ProMES were not easy to understand completely, partly because they are not used to abstract reasoning. Because the facilitators thought that the developmental process took rather long, they asked the group whether they would have preferred a faster and less time-consuming approach. This they denied unanimously. Their feeling was that a shortened or more compact approach would have provided less understanding and less working knowledge of the system. Both management and the supervisor shared their opinion.

AN ECONOMIC EVALUATION OF RESULTS

For organizations like Vandra, statistical significance or a large effect size, criteria often used in psychological research, is not enough to justify the amount of energy, time, and money required for a project like this. A project aimed at increasing productivity has to show sizable economic effects. Therefore, we evaluated the project also from this angle.

First, let us turn to the costs of the project. Roughly estimated, the development of ProMES for the experimental group took 40 hours. Because development took place after normal working hours, there was no loss of production time. Extra hours were paid at the normal rate; no overtime allowance was given. In operator wages, the costs were approximately $3,100. Although the supervisor and the assistant production manager participated in their normal working hours, it is fair to calculate their time also. Expressed as wages, this amounts to another $2,500. In this case, because of the nature of the pilot project, the facilitators did not charge the company. The net time investment for one skilled facilitator would normally amount to 60 hours, and in external consulting fees, this would mean an extra $5,000. Total investment would be somewhere around $10,600.

Next, we calculated the financial benefits from the pilot project. The method we used is called Activity Based Costing. First, we calculated the economic value of scores on each of the indicators. From there, it is easy to calculate the economic value of changes in indicator scores attributed to ProMES. Elaborating on this approach, we also calculated the value of a change of one unit on the effectiveness scale for each of the different indicators. Our results show that, by and large, an improvement of one unit on the effectiveness scale equals $90 in productivity gains per month. There are no huge differences in this respect among different indicators. We interpret this as an economic validation of contingency functions in the system. With regard to the economic value of productivity improvements brought about by ProMES, according to our calculations, the productivity improvement of just over 90 points in effectiveness scores, which was the mean improvement over 1989 to 1991, represents an economic value of $8,200 each month. Considering the relatively small investment that was needed, the results are fairly convincing.

However, some caution is necessary when interpreting these data. An Activity Based Costing approach enables only a fairly limited view of the real benefits, because it does not take into account profits (or losses) generated by the company as a whole. If, for instance, ProMES leads to increased productivity of the Cuir group and if the excess capacity that is generated that way is used to produce more orders or to put people on other tasks, then revenues of these activities could be considered profits resulting from ProMES. If, on the other hand, the excess capacity is not put to use, there is really no extra profit gained from the project. That is why a broader perspective is needed to evaluate the economic consequences of an intervention like ProMES.

A promising but rather complex solution to this problem is an evaluation based on a Cash Flow Model. We are planning to use such a model in future evaluations at Vandra and have been engaged in some preliminary research.

EXTENSION OF ProMES INTO THE ORGANIZATION

As a result of positive evaluations of ProMES at the Cuir, Vandra decided in 1990 to extend ProMES to other production groups and the shipping department. Sufficient data for evaluation are available for a total of eight groups, the Cuir group included. Figure 3–3 shows the mean cumulative overall effectiveness scores, expressed as percentage of the maximum score for these eight groups, before, during, and after development of ProMES. A period of one year before ProMES was introduced serves as a baseline period. Development extends over a period of four to six months, depending on the group. Data on the feedback condition cover a period of one year.

Overall, these scores follow the same pattern as the scores for the experimental group. Although improvements in productivity vary from one group to the other, the data show a clear increase, both during development and during feedback. The mean effect size for the change from the baseline to the feedback condition for these seven additional groups is 1.67. One group shows a small negative effect size of −0.30. For the other groups, the effect sizes are 0.80, 1.39, 2.04, 2.09, 2.58, and 3.11. The negative effect size is caused mainly by an industrial accident the group encountered recently and by high turnover in the original group just when feedback started. Although the scores for this group also show a clear positive trend in general, the weight of their score for safety is such that the overall effect size drops significantly.

In early 1993, by chance, a very unexpected and interesting possibility for research arose. At that time, Vandra installed a new management information system, developed by an external agent. As it happened, the new system did not function properly in the beginning. For a period of four months, no productivity data were available, so, temporarily, no feedback to the ProMES groups was possible.

Figure 3-3 Cumulative Overall Effectiveness Scores for Eight Groups Before, During, and After Development of ProMES as a Percentage of Maximum

Thereafter, normal feedback was resumed. Afterward, we were able to calculate effectiveness scores for the period that no feedback was possible from company records. Thus, we were able to monitor changes in productivity as a result of withholding feedback to the groups. In 1992, with feedback provided on a monthly basis, the mean cumulative overall effectiveness score for the ProMES groups was 620 points. During the breakdown of the system, this score dropped to a mean of −80 points. After feedback was resumed, the cumulative score over the next four months went up again to 428 points. It is important to note that no other major changes took place during this time, so, most of the changes can be attributed to lack of feedback.

From these data, we conclude that feedback played a major role in creating the productivity improvements we reported above. The effects of learning and increased role clarity, although evident, seem limited, because all groups did use ProMES for at least one year when feedback was intermittent and neither the level of proficiency of the operators nor the clarity of their role changed.

VIABILITY OF ProMES

In 1993, four years after the first experimental group started, ProMES is still expanding in the organization. At this time, ProMES is operational in 11 groups. In two more groups, development is almost done. With only two other groups remaining, almost all of the production groups use ProMES. In addition, development is planned in the model making department and, possibly, some groups in sales.

Meanwhile, the company is changing in the direction management has planned. Gradually, the work in the production department is getting more difficult and complex. The number of hierarchical layers in the organization is reduced. Interaction between different departments is much more dynamic and open than it was five years ago.

In a series of interviews the authors recently held, people all over the organization expressed their commitment to ProMES. Because of changing demands, existing ProMES systems will be up for a systematic review in a couple of months.

CONCLUSIONS AND FINAL REMARKS

From the results of this project, we conclude that ProMES can lead to substantial productivity improvements. It is obvious that the system can be applied in Europe as well as in the United States. In general, people react favorably to ProMES. It is also evident that ProMES, as it is used at Vandra, is a fairly complex organizational intervention. There seem to be a lot of causal factors in play, which, together, create a strong positive effect on productivity.

Learning seems to be an important factor early on in the process. There is also some evidence for a Hawthorne effect. Both factors, however, can explain only a small part of the improvements in productivity.

More important is the fact that by taking feedback reports as a starting point for analysis and problem solving activities, the ProMES groups are able to suggest substantial improvements with regard to working methods, the organization of their work, and the way they interact with other groups or departments. We attribute these effects to ProMES.

Feedback seems to be a major factor. As soon as feedback was available to the experimental group, productivity started to increase. The decline of effectiveness scores when feedback was omitted during the breakdown of the management information system and the quick recovery when feedback was reinstalled are rather strong signs that feedback as provided by ProMES causes productivity improvement in itself.

Apart from direct productivity improvements, but, for many organizations, at least equally important, is the effect ProMES can have on the attitude and the working behavior of the work force. Organizational communication and coordination also are improved. There is a better understanding of interdependencies among different groups in the organization. Operators are more aware of the way in which other groups affect their performance, and vice versa. When necessary, they communicate their preferences and their demands to other groups, either directly or through their supervisor. Thus, ProMES triggers improvements in intergroup relations and communication.

For management, regular ProMES meetings constitute an important communication channel, especially when the supervisor plays an active part in linking discussions to broader organizational issues. Especially when organizational change is needed, companies often encounter great difficulties in getting the message down to the shop floor and explaining how these changes affect the work of every day. In this project, ProMES has proved to be of great help in this respect.

A word of caution is also in place. According to our experience in this project, ProMES is not a technique that guarantees success in an easy way. It takes a lot of commitment and effort from people on the shop floor, supervisors, and management to get the system going. Once installed, constant effort is needed to keep the system alive. Organizations have to be willing to commit themselves to ProMES and integrate the system in their day-to-day business to get results.

REFERENCES

Guzzo, R. A., Jette, R. D., & Katzell, R. A. (1985). The effects of psychologically based intervention programs on worker productivity: A meta-analysis. *Personnel*

Psychology, 38, 275–291.

Kopelman, R. E. (1990). Objective feedback. In E. A. Locke (Ed.), Generalizing from laboratory to field settings. Lexington, MA: Heath.

Locke, E. A., & Latham, G. P. (1990). A theory of goal setting and task performance. Englewood Cliffs, NJ: Prentice Hall.

Pritchard, R. D. (1990). Measuring and improving organizational productivity: A practical guide (p. 248). New York: Praeger.

Pritchard, R. D., Jones, S. D., Roth, P. L., Stuebing, K. K., & Ekeberg, S. E. (1988). The effects of feedback, goal setting, and incentives on organizational productivity. Journal of Applied Psychology Monograph Series, 73, 337–358.

Pritchard, R. D., Jones, S. D., Roth, P. L., Stuebing, K. K., & Ekeberg, S. E. (1989). The evaluation of an integrated approach to measuring organizational productivity. Personnel Psychology, 42, 69–115.

4

Productivity Measurement and Enhancement in Advanced Manufacturing Systems

Martina Przygodda, Uwe Kleinbeck,
Klaus-Helmut Schmidt, and Jörg Beckmann

This chapter describes the effects of developing and implementing ProMES in a factory involved in the production of safety devices for electric control systems. The production section of the factory consisted of several interrelated manufacturing centers. Two of them formed the research setting of the present study. Both centers were characterized by a high degree of automation and allowed the flexible production of different products sized in varying lots. In comparison with conventional production units, advanced manufacturing systems like these generally are expected to offer better conditions for reacting rapidly to changes and diversification in market demands.

These technological facilities, however, are to be maximized only with crews who know thoroughly how their behavioral input is transformed into the final output of such systems. In practice, this knowledge is difficult to acquire because of the complexity and the multitude of intervening mechanical processes, which, in addition, are not all under the immediate control of the operators. Moreover, the commonly applied output measures for evaluating the system's functioning, such as number of pieces produced or time per piece, neither provide clear information about what the crews can influence nor show how this influence can actually be used to contribute effectively to the productivity of the whole sociotechnical system. Modern production systems put increasingly higher demands on the abilities and skills of people necessary to cope with organizational complexity.

As a behavior oriented measurement and feedback approach, ProMES would represent an appropriate instrument for assisting the operators in overcoming these difficulties. Therefore, the following research questions were asked: Can ProMES provide the information needed for operators to control advanced manufacturing systems more effectively? Will the ProMES information actually be used by the operators to improve the productivity of advanced manufacturing systems? To find answers to these questions, we started a research program in April 1991, the first phase of which ended in March 1993.

ORGANIZATIONAL SETTING AND PROJECT DESIGN

The organization for which ProMES was developed and implemented was engaged in the production of circuit breakers. The factory was medium sized and was located in the midwestern part of Germany; it produced electrical equipment such as contacts and relays for a large number of domestic and foreign customers. Because of the rapid technical changes in this kind of factory, management was confronted with difficulties in keeping the working crews informed about the functioning of the machines and the effects of their own working behavior on the whole system's performance. At the time the project started, top management was looking for new organizational principles to promote effectiveness of the crews, especially in using complex machines in advanced manufacturing departments.

Both groups selected for the field experiment worked in highly automated flexible production centers. One crew (N = 5) assembled circuit breakers in a flexible assembly center (FAC). The main tasks of these operators were the maintenance of the whole system, loading and unloading of parts, tool change and inspection, and supervisory control of the manufacturing process. The second experimental group (N = 3) produced a special part of the circuit breakers — the coils. The flexible coiling center (FCC) delivered the coils directly to the FAC and also to other departments. The tasks of the operators in this group were similar to those in the FAC. Both groups used materials from other departments of the factory, so, their work was in part dependent on the quality of parts for which they themselves were not responsible.

For evaluating the effects of implementing ProMES in both groups, a special experimental plan was used. One shift each of the FAC and the FCC served as experimental groups for which ProMES was implemented; the respective other shift of both centers was observed without training them to use ProMES. This was done to determine whether the expected effect of ProMES on productivity had been caused by ProMES and not by any other factor that could possibly have come into play. If it can be shown that there are changes in performance in the experimental group and no changes in the control groups, the probability increases that the observed effects are due to the ProMES implementation and not to other factors that come in by chance.

After having developed products, indicators, and contingencies, resulting effectiveness values were recorded for six months in the FAC and for five months in the FCC. This created a baseline that could be used for comparisons with effectiveness scores collected during the period when systematic feedback reports had been introduced for the experimental groups. In the FAC, feedback was given for six moths; in the FCC, for five months. (For more technical information on the experimental plan, see the Technical Appendix at the end of the chapter.)

The research team successfully convinced workers and the management to agree to these experimental procedures. As a third party, the works council agreed. Members of the works council play an important role in such field studies. As a group elected by the workers, their task is to engage themselves for the well-being of the workers. Without their support, it would have been impossible to conduct this study. In talking with all three parties together and with each of them alone, it could be made clear that ProMES would create information to improve productivity that was not yet available in existing productivity measures; until that time, productivity measures mainly indicated overall quality and quantity information not at all related to the behavior of the crews and their members. The research team stressed the fact that ProMES adds information about the relation between working behavior and system output. Furthermore, it elaborated the idea that ProMES functions as a tool to strengthen the skills for self-organization in working groups, which should help crew members to coordinate their efforts, especially in reacting to the demands of the advanced manufacturing systems in which they were working. As a special feature, ProMES offers a measurement system that focuses on the relations between group (or individual) behavior in relation to valuable outcomes as they are defined by organizational management. Especially in the discussion with the works council, it became important to make sure that ProMES would not increase work stress as a result of productivity improvements.

DEVELOPMENT AND IMPLEMENTATION OF ProMES

Identification of Products and Indicators

As expected because of earlier experiences (Pritchard, 1990; Pritchard, Kleinbeck, & Schmidt, 1993), products were developed easily using two meetings (lasting nearly two hours on the average) in both experimental groups. Table 4–1 shows that both groups developed two products, one related to the quality of work, the other pointing out effective production control. The indicators were done in five meetings; they turned out to be similar for the two experimental groups. The FAC group described one indicator for the first product, daily number of defective pieces needing rework. For the second product, the group identified two indicators, daily amount of time to identify and repair machine breakdowns and daily number of pieces passing inspection.

This last indicator points to an inspection task of the crew, which consisted of two parts. At first the circuit breakers pass an automatic inspection (ensuring appropriate electric functioning of the pieces) before crew members make a last visual check and verify manually whether the parts are in the correct position.

Members of the FCC group identified two indicators for the first product (quality of coils) and one for the second product (effective production control). The first indicator was daily number of rejected coils under the control of the group. Furthermore, the crew decided to describe one more quality indicator, daily number of rejected coils partly under the control of the group. The first indicator points to errors due to soldering and errors in labeling that the workers could avoid by using the right strategies and investing an appropriate amount of effort. The errors in the second indicator were not so easy to control, because they were partly influenced by the material used. These errors occurred mainly in the starting phase of the coiling process and were partly dependent on the quality of the wire. As a third indicator, the group developed the total amount of time to identify and repair machine breakdowns.

The listed indicators reflected the controllable parts of the working process and were developed in accordance with the definition of an indicator as it is defined in the ProMES system. In addition to these indicators, members of the experimental groups also described factors that were not under their control but could influence their productivity. These factors were, in most cases, under the control of other units delivering parts to the experimental groups. Knowing about the effects of factors having their origin outside the groups helped the crew

Table 4–1   Products and Indicators in the FAC and the FCC

FAC
Product 1. Quality of produced circuit breakers
    Indicator A.   Daily number of defective pieces needing rework
Product 2. Effective production control
    Indicator B.   Daily amount of time to identify and repair machine breakdowns
    Indicator C.   Daily number of pieces passing inspection

FCC
Product 1. Quality of coils
    Indicator A.   Daily number of rejected coils under the control of the group
    Indicator B.   Daily number of rejected coils partly under the control of the group
Product 2. Effective production control
    Indicator C.   Total amount of time to identify and repair machine breakdowns

---

members to see their own role clearer and kept them from taking responsibility in cases where they really did not have control.

Two of these factors will be discussed here. One factor specified rejects caused by false construction. These errors in the construction of parts increased the overall number of rejects within both groups. No one in the working group had any influence on the quality of the parts, because they were delivered from another unit of the plant. A possible solution to this problem would be an information system between the two units in order to increase the quality of the material. As a first consequence coming from the implementation of ProMES, management reacted upon these observations by recommending and establishing an official communication link between the production manager and the design engineer of the plant.

A second example of an uncontrollable factor was the time to repair machine breakdowns caused by computer controlling. Bugs in the computer program, which was developed in a special department, caused errors in the production process or a total machine breakdown. A short machine breakdown led to a temporary increase in work load because the team tried to compensate for the deficient output. If the machine breakdown took longer, there would have been no chance to compensate for the deficit, and the productivity would have decreased. The recording of this kind of breakdowns gave the organization information about the amount of production loss and strengthened the necessity to counteract these troubles. One possible solution for this problem could be seen in the increased availability of computer experts or in improving the training of the operators. Recording these factors in addition to the controllable indicators increased the transparency of responsibilities and reduced false attributions of outcomes.

During this first part of system development, a remarkable discussion started among the group members in the FAC. It focused on a problem typical for an organization with high demands on both quality and quantity. The supervisor responsible for effective production control strongly emphasized output criteria, while the one responsible for the quality of parts mainly focused on quality criteria. This kind of management behavior was supported by the traditional organizational structures found in this factory. Before the implementation of ProMES, organizational management had not been aware of this situation, which inevitably created role conflicts on the side of the working crew. Several times per month, they received instructions with respect to quantity and quality of their work from different supervisors without being ale to estimate priorities for themselves. After having developed products and indicators, this conflict potential became clear, so that management could change the organizational structure by opening channels for communication among those who were responsible for quality and quantity of production. ProMES stimulated organizational change, leading to a close cooperation on the management level. It helped to identify potentials for conflict, provided clarity of organizational roles, and served as a basis for an increase in productivity during the process of ProMES implementation.

The development of products and indicators in itself influenced important aspects of organizational performance. It made working roles clearer and showed those parts of the working process controllable by the workers and those where they did not have control. During such a developmental process, workers and supervisors learned to reduce false attributions of outcomes with the positive effect of not being blamed for failures for which they were not responsible. On the management level, the first steps of the ProMES implementation could help to identify unclear organizational conditions.

Development of Contingencies

The final set of contingencies for the FAC and the FCC is presented in Figure 4–1. For the product "effective production control" in the FAC, both contingencies show a relatively steep slope, which points to the importance of these indicators. For the daily amount of time to identify and repair machine breakdowns and the daily number of defective pieces needing rework, the negative effectiveness scores have a flat slope, showing that an increase in indicator values does not contribute in a linear way to a decrease in effectiveness. In the FCC, all contingencies are nonlinear. The steepest slope is found for the only indicator related to the product of effective production control: total amount of time to identify and repair machine breakdowns. For the product quality of coils, the two indicators, daily number of rejected coils under the control of the group and daily number of rejected coils partly under the control of the group, show flatter contingencies.

The process of developing the contingencies brought some difficulties, indicating that workers had to make decisions in an informational vacuum, leading to a high uncertainty of their judgments. After a first set of contingencies was developed in two sessions, baseline data were recorded. Comparing baseline data in the FAC group with the contingencies revealed an unexpected discrepancy between the actual mean performance of the group and information contained in the contingencies for one indicator. For the daily number of pieces passing inspection, the zero point of effectiveness (indicating what is expected, what is seen as neither especially good nor bad performance) was much higher than the mean actual performance of the group. The group had estimated 2,300 pieces per day, although their mean performance was 1,700 pieces.

Furthermore, the employees mentioned that they had no influence on the number of persons assigned to do the work. Because the output of the system depended on the manpower input, the group decided to

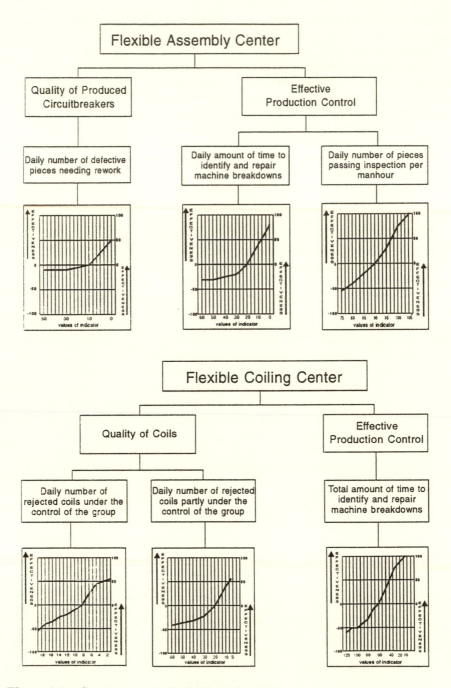

Figure 4–1 Contingencies in the FAC and the FCC

define as a final measure "the daily number of pieces produced per manhour."

At the same time, baseline data from the FCC group showed a discrepancy with respect to the contingencies of two indicators, the daily number of rejected coils under the control of the group and the daily number of rejected coils partly under the control of the group. For both indicators, the actual performance generally exceeded the expected value as defined by the zero point of effectiveness in the contingencies.

Discussions with the groups about these observations supported the assumptions of the research team that these discrepancies might have been caused by a lack of information in the groups. When asked for the first time during the implementation phase of ProMES to estimate the effect of their behavior on productivity outcomes, they could not do it. This failure clearly indicated that they were not able to see the relation between their own behavioral input and system outcome, which is not unusual in advanced manufacturing systems. Inspection of the baseline data stimulated the groups to discuss the contingencies again, leading to the already presented final set after two more sessions.

The uncertainty of the crews could be seen during these steps of the ProMES implementation procedure. This discovery then led to a correction in the definition of the contingencies, thereby, overcoming the deficit in information. The whole crew, including its leader, got more realistic with respect to what could be expected. Reactions of the management showed that they were surprised by these observations. They had not been aware of these problems and, therefore, had no idea how to handle them. Using ProMES helped them, too, to pay more attention to strategies for keeping their workers informed about the result of their activities.

Development of the Feedback Report

After having adjusted the measurement system, feedback reports were produced. The feedback reports showed the effectiveness scores of the last two weeks for each indicator and the overall effectiveness scores. Because the indicators were recorded daily, the effectiveness scores were also computed daily. As a consequence, the feedback report used the mean effectiveness score of daily effectiveness over the last two weeks. The feedback report also contained the effectiveness scores of the foregoing feedback period. Furthermore, it listed the values of important work factors not controllable by the workers, which were important to the group to identify obstacles in their work and for the supervisors and higher management to recognize general organizational problems.

Summary of the Developmental Process

Products were identified in both groups without major problems. Describing appropriate indicators and establishing contingencies proved to be more difficult. The development of contingencies, especially, suffered from a lack of information in the experimental crews, which lengthened the process and resulted in a redefinition of some of the indicators. However, with the help of ProMES, this problem was discovered and made more clear. After these lacks of clarity in the production process were identified, ProMES could be introduced and used to establish a valid measurement and feedback system. The recording of the factors not controllable by the workers helped to unburden the workers of unrealistic demands of performance and to supply the management with information necessary for optimizing the production process.

Both experimental groups started with the development of the measurement system in April 1991. The whole list of products, indicators, and contingencies was completed after nine sessions by the end of July 1991. For the FAC baseline, data were recorded from August 1991 to January 1992, and from February 1991 to July 1992, feedback reports were presented and discussed systematically every two weeks. Because of a longer absence period of one of the operators in the FCC, the baseline period had to be lengthened to May 1992. Feedback reports were given in intervals of two weeks until June 1992.

USING ProMES FOR BASELINE MEASUREMENT AND FEEDBACK REPORTS

After the measurement system was implemented, data were collected to establish a baseline for six months in the FAC and for five months in the FCC experimental and control groups. According to the experimental design, these data were compared with effectiveness data in a feedback phase following the baseline period. During this latter phase, feedback reports were presented every second week to the experimental groups. They were given to every crew member in the previously described form. A facilitator (from the research team) summarized the reports and supplied the group with additional graphic aids. During feedback sessions, the moderator tried to stimulate a discussion about the effectiveness scores and trigger ideas for the development of strategies to improve productivity. The feedback reports were given for six months in the FAC and for five months in the FCC experimental groups. The control groups, for which only indicator data were collected, were given no feedback.

RESULTS

After the ProMES system was implemented, the baseline data were recorded, and systematic feedback was introduced, the data could be analyzed to find answers to the two research questions — Does ProMES provide information necessary for improvements in productivity? and Will crew members use this information? According to the logic of the research design, an analysis of variance described by Shine (1973) was used that considers the single subject (group) character of the design (one group with many times of measurement). It appeared to be the appropriate analytical tool for a design with repeated measurements, especially when there are not more than 50 measurement points (which would be a recommendation for using time series analysis).

The expectations of the research team were, of course, to find an effect in the experimental groups after the ProMES implementation. If ProMES really works as a management instrument contributing to an increase in productivity, effectiveness in the experimental groups should be enhanced after systematic feedback is introduced on the basis of products, indicators, and contingencies, while the control groups should stay unaffected.

The FCC showed the expected effects: although effectiveness increased from baseline to feedback for the experimental group, it did not in the control group. This effect turned out to be statistically significant (detailed results of the analyses of variance are summarized in the Technical Appendix at the end of the chapter). Looking at the group means in the upper half of Figure 4-2 shows that the experimental group started with a relatively low effectiveness in the baseline compared with the control group. After systematic feedback was introduced in the experimental group, effectiveness was doubled. On the other hand, however, the control group stayed relatively stable. On the basis of these results, the effect of ProMES turned out to be clear and strong, indicating an increase in productivity.

Furthermore, the main intervention effect (not considering the group membership) also came out as significant, strengthening the evidence of a powerful ProMES application, if it is seen together with the former effect. The overall high effectiveness of the control group in comparison with the experimental group proved to be significant, too. This last effect made it clear that the control group worked on a higher effectiveness level compared with the experimental group for the whole time of data collection. This is an observation not unusual in field studies, indicating the selection practice of management. Organizational managers are interested to invest effort in supporting groups that need help. From this perspective, it is not surprising to find a rather low effectiveness of the experimental group (FAC) at the beginning of the study.

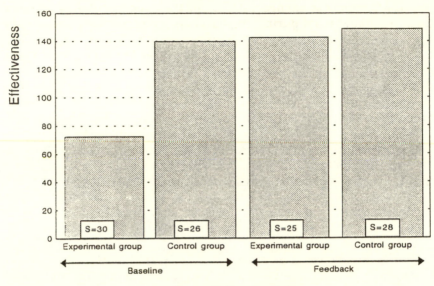

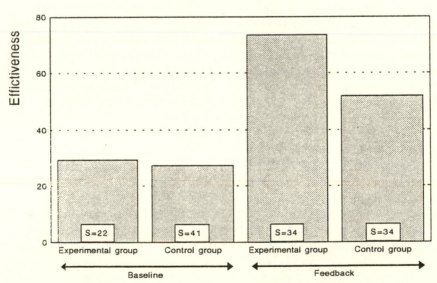

Figure 4–2 Effectiveness Scores in the FCC and FAC during the Baseline and Feedback Periods

The expected effect was also found for two of the three indicators, the number of rejected coils under the control of the group and the total amount of time to identify and repair machine breakdowns. In both cases, a similar change of means could be observed compared with the overall effectiveness changes. Although the experimental group was lower in effectiveness during the baseline compared with the control group, the differences were reduced after the introduction of feedback.

For the second indicator, total amount of time to identify and repair machine breakdowns, there was a strong significant effect of the intervention factor, showing that the intervention, as such, increased effectiveness to a significant degree. The group effect of this indicator was only weakly significant. For the first indicator, number of rejected coils under the control of the group, the intervention effect was not significant, but the group effect was weakly significant; this made it clear that the effectiveness of the control group on this indicator was slightly higher than in the experimental group. For the third indicator, daily number of rejected coils partly under the control of the group, there was only a significant group effect.

Figure 4–3 shows the overall effectiveness scores for experimental groups in the FCC (upper half) and the FAC (lower half). In both cases, the course of the scores over two-week periods shows a variable pattern with a clear-cut increase after the feedback sessions had been started.

These results provide rather clear evidence for the expected ProMES effects in the FCC (Figure 4–3, upper half). They were not so clear-cut for the FAC (Figure 4–3, bottom half). Only the intervention factor turned out to be significant, which, of course, seemed to indicate a ProMES effect with increasing effectiveness during the feedback phase. However, because this effect held not only for the experimental group but also for the control group, it was not possible to attribute the effects clearly to the ProMES specific intervention.

The picture was very similar for the indicator daily number of pieces passing inspection. Only the intervention effect was significant. For the indicator daily amount of time to identify and repair machine breakdowns, only the difference between the groups becomes significant, showing a higher effectiveness for the experimental group in both the baseline and the feedback periods. For the indicator daily number of defective pieces, no effect appeared significant.

DISCUSSION AND PRACTICAL CONCLUSIONS

ProMES could be successfully developed and used as a participative management tool in an advanced manufacturing system. There is evidence in the results of this study indicating such an answer to the first research question. ProMES can provide the information needed for operators to control highly automated production systems more effectively. Especially the results reported in relation to the

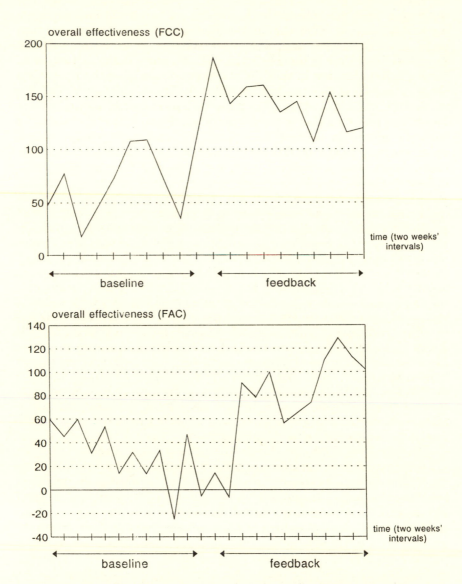

Figure 4–3 Overall Effectiveness Scores in Two Week Intervals for the Experimental Groups in the FCC and FAC

implementation phase of ProMES support these statements. When the indicators were developed, organizational conflict could be identified, because it became clear that two supervisors gave instructions that were not coordinated and, therefore, sometimes aroused conflicts. Because of this flaw in the organizational structure of the factory, crew members did not know in such cases whether to set priorities on quality criteria (as one of the supervisors wanted them to do) or on quantity factors (as was asked by the other supervisor). In addition, the identifying and recording of productivity factors not under the control of the crew helped to produce role clarity, which helped unburden crew members from responsibilities that were outside their roles. All this information was provided by using the ProMES system and was accepted by workers and management to improve the conditions of their work behavior.

Before ProMES had been introduced, members of the experimental groups did not make use of any productivity indicators and did not attempt use of the technical information system. This lack of use of an advanced manufacturing system could be successfully aided by using ProMES as a management system, recording indicator data on a regular basis, and feeding behavioral outcomes back systematically.

The second research question can now be answered on the basis of the reported results. ProMES effects turned out to be powerful, as can be seen in the significant results that were found for the FCC. In this center, the control group started with a higher effectiveness than the experimental group in the baseline period. It remained at that high level without significant change after the introduction of systematic feedback in the experimental group. The experimental group increased its effectiveness from a previously low score to a higher one after systematic feedback was introduced. These results offer the evidence for a successful increase in productivity through the implementation and application of ProMES.

In addition to this effect, the feedback itself proved to be effective in the FCC data, which can be interpreted as further proof for the power of ProMES. The effect seems to be so strong that it became significant, although there was no real change observed in the control group. The significant group effect indicates a higher effectiveness for the control group, which is interesting for the purpose of comparing both groups but has nothing to do with the interpretation of the positive ProMES effects. The overall effectiveness data of the FCC can be used as a convincing argument for the conclusion that ProMES not only changed important aspects of the organization but also clearly contributed to increased productivity.

Inspection of the indicator data support these conclusions for the FCC in general. For the indicator total amount of time to identify and repair engine breakdowns, the statistical analyses show very similar results compared with the overall effectiveness. The same pattern is also found for the daily number of rejected coils under the control of the group, but less clearly. The third indicator, daily number of rejected coils partly under the control of the group, is different. It is not at all in line with the overall expectations. Taking into consideration the definition of indicators as factors that can be controlled by the crew members, this result is not so surprising. Because this indicator does not allow full control by the workers, it does not show the expected productivity improvement.

The interpretation of the FAC data produces some difficulties. Although the data show changes in the right direction with an increase of effectiveness in the experimental group from the baseline to the feedback period, the difference between the experimental and the control groups was not so large. One explanation for this could be the simultaneous increase in effectiveness in the control group. It is not quite as strong as in the experimental group but enough to keep the differences nonsignificant. There is a main effect of the feedback, indicating either a ProMES effect for both groups or an effect of an external factor that has nothing to do with the experimental intervention. Unfortunately, there are no hard data to decide between these alternatives, but from informal discussion with members of the FAC, one possible explanation for the unexpected behavior of the control group emerged. As the second shift, the control group working at the assembly machine tried to observe the results in the experimental group (working during the shift before). Knowing about the improvements in the experimental group could have stimulated the members of the control group to increase their effectiveness.

Effectiveness data for the indicator daily number of pieces passing inspection show a pattern similar to that observed for the overall effectiveness, and this also holds for the indicator daily number of defective pieces needing rework, coming up with a similar pattern but without any significant result in the analysis of variance. For the indicator daily amount of time to identify and repair machine breakdowns, no relevant effects could be found except one for the group factor showing that the experimental group is higher in productivity than the control group over the whole measurement period.

Taking all the results together, the data seem to indicate that ProMES works. It contributes to an increase of productivity in working groups. Data also made clear (especially those in the FAC) how difficult it is to realize experimental plans in field experiments. Further conclusions from these data with respect to the uncertainty of the psychological processes behind these ProMES effects cannot be deduced, but some speculations might be helpful to get some ideas about these processes that could be useful for further experiments.

The observed increase of productivity was related to the feedback phase of the study, pointing strongly to the fact that feedback might be a powerful variable to explain the results. Feeding back the information of the measurement system is not only expected to facilitate role clarification and to promote the building of more effective work strategies but also should enhance the motivation of the workers. At first, the feedback information may help the group members see the results of their efforts. This should strengthen the connection between effort and productivity and, thereby, improve the effort-performance-expectancies, which, according to expectancy theory approaches, are considered as strong determinants of work motivation (Campbell & Pritchard, 1976; Vroom, 1964). Furthermore, by separating the effects of factors that group members can control from those not under their control, the members are made accountable for their productivity. This may strengthen the workers' feelings of responsibility and, at the same time, prevents them from attributing low productivity rates to external conditions like technical processes and management strategies. In addition, experiencing that they have control on the production process, the workers develop a sense of task competence or self-efficacy (Bandura, 1982; White, 1959), which is another powerful determinant of a high work motivation.

Moreover, the feedback information may stimulate the workers to set their own productivity goals. This process can be supported by a formal training in goal setting strategies that explains the effectiveness of goal setting and shows how goal setting is to be managed in a group of workers and supervisors. By this, they learn to set specific and challenging but attainable goals that meet the unanimous approval of all involved in the goal setting process (Locke & Latham, 1990). On the basis of this training, a formal goal-setting program can be introduced to shape the group activities in line with the organizational goals.

All these motivational effects presuppose that the group members accept the measurement and feedback system. This is a very important issue for the success of its implementation. However, high acceptance of the system can be expected, because the workers are heavily involved in all the different steps of developing and implementing it. They have control over the identification of products as well as establishing indicators and contingencies. It is also possible for them to modify the elements of the system to bring it in close correspondence with the situational requirements.

There was one special characteristic in the developmental phase of ProMES in this study that is worth mentioning. It has to do with the self-corrective potential of ProMES. During the baseline period, after the sets of products, indicators, and contingencies were developed, both experimental groups noticed that they had described at least one indicator that was not under their control and that they had developed contingencies that were quite unrealistic compared with their actual performance. ProMES provided information to enable the members of the experimental groups to overcome these gaps of knowledge. It generated the necessary information in the course of the implementation process, which then could be used to adapt the measurement system to the new situation.

Finally, ProMES proved to be a management information system. In the advanced manufacturing system of this study, ProMES furnished information about the range of possible performance of the workers and the influence of the groups to increase productivity. Furthermore, the developmental process clarified the source of obstacles in the production process that had their origin in the organizational structure. The recording of factors that are not under the control of a single unit promoted steps to an expansion of ProMES to the whole organization. The uncontrollable factors of a single unit often were controllable indicators of other units or the higher management. The identifying of these structural dependabilities supported processes that initiated a reformulation of responsibilities and improved the communication between the units of an organization. As a result, the bottom up process of ProMES could be complemented by a top down process that engages the supervisors and the higher management in an overall organizational ProMES. This expanded form of ProMES should improve communication processes and enhance the productivity of the whole organization.

During the whole process of ProMES implementation and evaluation, management learned step by step to use the system for improving their own managerial behavior. This could be observed when the research group was present in the organization. Whether ProMES will be used by the organization itself without the direct support of the research team in the sense of a system to strengthen self-regulation in semiautonomous working groups (e.g., in lean production) will depend very much on the organizational design. It could be hypothesized that ProMES will be most successful in flat organizations that make use of the organizational principle to delegate responsibility down the organizational hierarchy. To find evidence for such a hypothesis will be a future research task.

TECHNICAL APPENDIX

The experimental procedure used can be described as a three factorial design with one group factor (experimental versus control), one intervention factor (with baseline and feedback periods as two stages of the factor), and one trial factor that included the repeated measures for the experimental and the control groups (Shine, 1973).

Analysis of Variance Results

Factor	df	F	p
Analysis of Variance for the FCC			
Variable: Overall effectiveness			
Group (G)	1.5	84.20	<.01
Intervention (I)	1.5	84.25	<.01
G x I	1.5	54.78	<.01
Variable: Daily number of rejected coils under the control of the group			
Group (G)	1.5	6.25	>.05
Intervention (I)	1.5	3.20	>.05
G x I	1.5	5.35	>.05
Variable: Daily number of rejected coils partly under the control of the group			
Group (G)	1.5	20.38	<.01
Intervention (I)	1.5	4.00	>.05
G x I	1.5	0.37	>.05
Variable: Daily amount of time to identify and repair machine breakdowns			
Group (G)	1.5	4.17	>.01
Intervention (I)	1.5	33.61	<.01
G x I	1.5	31.10	<.01
Analysis of Variance for the FAC			
Variable: Overall effectiveness			
Group (G)	1.6	3.60	>.05
Intervention (I)	1.6	36.92	<.01
G x I	1.6	3.31	>.05
Variable: Daily number of defective pieces needing rework			
Group (G)	1.6	2.43	>.05
Intervention (I)	1.6	2.60	>.05
G x I	1.6	1.67	>.05
Variable: Daily amount of time to identify and repair machine breakdowns			
Group (G)	1.6	24.19	<.01
Intervention (I)	1.6	0.93	>.05
G x I	1.6	2.47	>.05
Variable: Daily number of pieces passing inspection per manhour			
Group (G)	1.6	0.52	>.05
Intervention (I)	1.6	15.13	>.01
G x I	1.6	0.30	>.05

ACKNOWLEDGMENTS

The research was supported by a grant from the Deutsche Forschungsgemeinschaft (KI 408/10-1). The cooperation and assistance of employees and managers in the firm where the research was conducted is gratefully acknowledged. We also thank Burkhard Daume for assistance in data collection and analysis.

REFERENCES

Bandura, A. (1982). Self-efficacy mechanism in human agency. *American Psychologist, 37*, 122–147.

Campbell, J. P., & Pritchard, R. D. (1976). Motivation theory in industrial and organizational psychology. In M. D. Dunnette (Ed.), *Handbook of industrial and organizational psychology*. Princeton: Van Nostrand.

Locke, E. A., & Latham, G. P. (1990). *A theory of goal setting and task performance*. Englewood Cliffs, NJ: Prentice Hall.

Pritchard, R. D. (1990). *Measuring and improving organizational productivity: A practical guide* (p. 248). New York: Praeger.

Pritchard, R. D., Kleinbeck, U. E., & Schmidt, K. H. (1993). *Das Management-system PPM: Durch Mitarbeiterbeteiligung zu höherer Produktivität* [The PPM management system: Employee participation for improved productivity]. Munich: Verlag C.H. Beck.

Schmidt, K. H., Przygodda, M., & Kleinbeck, U. (1995). Development of a productivity measurement and feedback system in a firm of commercial painters. In R. D. Pritchard, (Ed.), *Productivity measurement and improvement: Organizational case studies*. Westport, CT: Praeger.

Shine, L. C. (1973). A multi-way analysis of variance for single-subject designs. *Educational and Psychological Measurement, 33*, 633–636.

Vroom, V. H. (1964). *Work and motivation*. New York: Wiley.

White, R. W. (1959). Motivation reconsidered: The concept of competence. *Psychological Review, 66*, 297–333.

5

ProMES in a Small Manufacturing Department: Results of Feedback and User Reactions

Steven D. Jones

One of the tests of an intervention is that it can be implemented in a variety of settings. ProMES was developed and successfully tested in five work groups in a military setting (Pritchard, Jones, Roth, Stuebing, & Ekeberg, 1988, 1989). Although the results of that study were impressive, they would be more convincing if they could be replicated in the private sector. This chapter reports on such a study in a manufacturing department of a small, but successful, corporation.

The purpose of the study was to develop two ProMES systems in two different departments, then test the effects of feedback by giving feedback to only one department while using the other department as a comparison group. A secondary purpose was to assess user reactions to the measurement system using an interview format so that the domain of user reactions could be understood.

The survey was designed to explore two issues in developing ProMES. The first issue is How do the users react to the measurement system as developed by the design team? Because a measurement system put the users "under a magnifying glass," they may have reactions to the system that cannot be anticipated fully by the design team. The second issue is Depending on the reactions of the users, should the measurement system be revised? In other words, the initial measurement system may be viewed as a prototype that will be modified and improved based on user reactions.

The methodology used in this study differed slightly from the standard ProMES (Pritchard, 1990). The differences were primarily in use of a model to guide the measurement system and how the importance weights were assigned. Where these differences occurred, they will be discussed.

ORGANIZATIONAL SETTING

The measurement system was developed for a highly successful but small retail corporation (225 employees) in the outdoor sports industry located in the western United States. They are considered to be highly successful in their industry, and they have been used as a model for their customer service and product warranties. The corporation consisted of four departments: retail, buying, wholesale, and manufacturing. The retail department, the buying department, and the manufacturing department participated in the study. The results of the retail department are not reported here because the work cycle of that department was of a much longer duration than that of the other two departments. The major duties of the manufacturing department included purchasing raw materials, cutting raw materials, sewing, inspecting, packaging, and shipping outdoor software such as rain gear, sleeping bags, and tents for outdoor outfitters nationwide. Annual sales for manufacturing approached $1 million. They made a large variety of products in relatively small batches. They changed products frequently so that the manufacturing process was flexible and responsive. They also designed and developed new products. The buying department purchased products for the corporation's retail stores. The manufacturing department was a product supplier for the buying department.

Comprehensive measurement systems were developed for the manufacturing and buying departments. ProMES feedback was given to the manufacturing department, while the buying department served as a comparison group. Although these two departments have different functions, the purpose of the comparison group was to rule out changes in the manufacturing department due to organization-wide improvement efforts.

This project took place during 1991–92 while the recession was at its deepest level. During this time, retail sales declined, as did orders to manufacturers. Organizations , such as this one, operating on the west coast of the United States were particularly hard hit by this recession. Pressure placed on this organization by the recession forced management to look for every opportunity to cut costs. In the manufacturing department, this pressure translated into an initial emphasis on labor efficiency. The implications of this pressure will be seen in the discussion of the results of feedback.

MEASUREMENT SYSTEM MODEL

The reason for using a model is to avoid developing a measurement system that is inconsistent with the values of the organization. When a design team is developing a measurement system, their focus is on a detail level. This "micro" focus is necessary to develop a sound measurement system, but it may obscure the "big picture." To retain a focus on this big picture, we used a model that contained the organization's values, strategic plan, and customer needs. There are a number of theoretical models for organizations (Cameron & Whetten, 1983; Connolly, Conlon, & Deutsch, 1980; Goodman & Pennings, 1977). Each model has a better fit to certain types of organizations or departments. A manufacturing organization may be best fit by a goal model, while a service organization may be best fit by a multiple constituency model. We select a model or combination of models that is consistent with the kind of organization in which we are developing the ProMES.

In order to develop the measurement system, we took the following steps, based on a measurement model presented by Jones, Powell, and Roberts (1990). The model draws from the open systems model of Katz and Kahn (1966). Additional influences came from the centrality of the customer in Deming's (1986) approach to quality, measurement processes reported by the American Productivity and Quality Center (1986), and the goals and multiple constituency models of organizational effectiveness. The steps of the model (Figure 5–1) are sequential, as presented below.

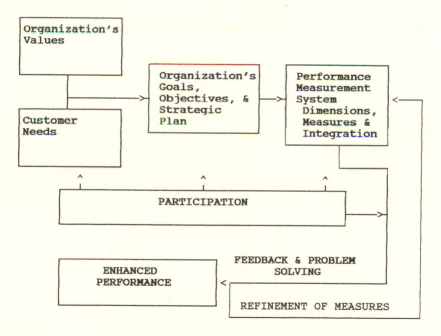

Figure 5-1   Organizational Performance Measurement Model

1. Through interviews with management, an understanding of the values of the organization and the departments was developed. This included the shared values on which this organization perceived that its

success was based. This understanding provided consistency between the dimensions to be measured, their relative importance, and the value system of the organization.

2. Interviews were conducted with customers to gain an understanding of customer needs for each department. Customers were both internal and external, for example, the wholesale and retail departments were customers of manufacturing.

3. Through interviews with management, an understanding of business strategy and specific organizational goals and objectives was developed. This understanding highlighted measures for inclusion in the measurement system.

4. Dimensions of performance of the departments were developed. These dimensions were identified by interviewing groups and individuals. Each dimension led to identification of one or more measures. These measures were combined into a composite index termed "overall effectiveness."

The model accommodates refinements to the measurement system, recognizing that the initial system may be a prototype requiring modifications. Refinements may be made to improve reliability, validity, and acceptability to users. Refinements also may be made to reflect a revised business strategy.

Example of the Measurement System — Manufacturing

As a result of proceeding through the first four blocks (values, customer needs, and strategy) of the model, it was determined that the manufacturing department had five major dimensions of performance. (We used the term "dimension," rather than the ProMES term "product," because this department manufactured "products," and they would have been confused if we had used the term "product" in a different way.) These five dimensions were quality, cost control, labor efficiency, sales, and product innovation. In a departure from the standard ProMES methodology, the dimensions were weighted for importance to avoid a dimension becoming weighted by the number of measures in it. The total of the importance weights was set at 100, which put the overall effectiveness score on a percent scale. Therefore, the highest possible overall effectiveness score was 100, and an effectiveness score of 80 was 80 percent of maximum possible.

The relative importance weights of the dimensions were determined through a brief survey of supervisors and employees. Responses were averaged, and management made a determination of the final weights based on those averages.

Eight measures were required to capture the five dimensions adequately. (The term "measure" was used instead of the ProMES term "indicator," because "measure" was more consistent with the organization's terminology.) Quality was measured by percent of lower quality items, that is, "seconds," and percent of returned goods. Cost control was measured by the difference between actual and planned budget. Labor efficiency was measured by actual units sewn divided by the engineering standard and the average number of days late to ship finished orders. Dollar value of goods sold measured the sales dimension. Product innovation was captured by two measures: number of ideas for new products submitted each month (calculated as a three month rolling average) and number of new product ideas put into production (three month rolling average). Of these eight measures, only the first and third measures had been used in this form by the organization; the other six measures were either modifications or entirely new measures.

Importance weights of the measures were ascribed a percentage of the dimension weight. If a dimension was captured by one measure, the importance weight was 100. However, if two measures were required, weights summing to 100 were divided between the measures, reflecting their relative importance within that dimension. The measurement system recognizes that the importance of a measure could change depending on whether the organization is performing well or poorly on that dimension. For instance, when performance in the innovation dimension is poor, the number of ideas submitted becomes more important than the number of ideas put into production. Thus, if the department is performing poorly in product innovation, ideas for new products are neither being suggested nor put into production. In this negative scenario, getting ideas suggested is more important; therefore, ideas submitted have a weight of 60 percent, whereas ideas into production have a weight of only 40 percent. Conversely, under a positive scenario, when the organization is doing well in terms of innovation, putting ideas into production becomes more important. Similarly, a rationale was required for each importance weight. Input on measures and importance weights came from employees and supervisors via survey, and these weights were reviewed by management.

Contingencies were developed using the standard ProMES method. Also, an overall effectiveness score was calculated for each month of the baseline time period.

Assessment of User Reactions and Refinement of the System

After the measurement system was developed, users were given one month of feedback with the system. Subsequently, they were interviewed concerning their reactions to the measurement system. Initial reactions were unanimously positive to global questions such as How satisfied are you with the measurement system? On a hunch that these were "Yea-saying" responses, a structured interview was developed. This interview was designed to detect problems with specific components of the measurement system, such as adequacy of the individual measures and understanding of the contingencies. Although the interview was designed primarily to detect deficiencies in the measurement system, questions were asked that provided an opportunity for positive responses. An introduction to the interview included a request that the interviewee be candid and not respond with what he or she thought the interviewer wanted to hear. The structured interview is reproduced in the Appendix.

Responses to the interview are presented in the results section. As will be seen, there were slightly more positive reactions than negative reactions. The bulk of the negative reactions focused on the reliability and validity of the measures. Because reliability and validity of the measurement system was crucial, all of these concerns were addressed, resulting in a reviewed system. Respondents, however, were not interviewed again following the revisions to the system.

In the revised system, the measures for quality were changed to dollar value of returned defective merchandise rather than the percent of returned goods. This modification weights the importance of a returned item by its value. The percent of seconds was dropped as a measure of quality because of problems in recording this data consistently and the extremely low number of seconds. A measure of raw materials usage was added to the dimension of cost control. This addition addressed key duties of the cutting department, whose contribution had not been measured in the original system. This new measure was the dollar value of raw materials purchased this month divided by next month's sales. If the department was purchasing too many or too few raw materials, it would show up in this measure. Contingencies were created for these new measures, historical data were collected on them, a corrected baseline was established, and feedback was continued. In addition to refining the measures, the measurement system was explained again to personnel at all levels for clarification.

Feedback to the Manufacturing Department

Feedback was given to the manufacturing department at the beginning of each month. This feedback was based on the measurement system and consisted of performance graphs of each of the measures, a graph of overall performance, and a feedback report. The feedback report consisted of the "raw data" for each measure and the corresponding effectiveness score. Feedback meetings for the manufacturing department were conducted by the researchers and attended by at least two managers and those employees who could be spared from their work. During the feedback meeting, the data were discussed, increases and declines were noted, and the reasons for them were explored. Problem solving was stimulated by asking why the managers and employees thought the performance measures were changing. A particular effort was made to ask what they were doing differently during months when individual measures and overall performance increased. They were asked to look at changes in overall performance as the effects of trade-offs, such as emphasizing labor efficiency over innovation.

Comparison Group

The buying department served as a comparison group for the manufacturing department. Using the measurement model, a measurement system was developed for the buying department, and the data were collected and combined into the overall effectiveness index. The data were collected over the same time period as for the manufacturing department, but feedback was not provided to the buying department. The buying department was used as a comparison group because it would be comparably affected by changes at the corporate level as well as by environmental changes, such as the recession.

RESULTS

Reactions to the Measurement System

To understand the user reactions, categories for the interview responses were developed. After the responses were reviewed, an initial set of categories was defined. Responses were independently placed by three judges into those categories, and unclear categories were redefined until a 75 percent agreement criterion was reached.

As a result of this process, five categories were obtained that met the agreement criterion. These were reliability and validity of the system, understanding unique features of the system, changes in behavior or in level of understanding the organizational policies as a result of measurement system development, overall reactions to the process of being measured, and overall reactions to the outcome, or end result, of being measured. Because of the nature of the interview questions, all but a very few of the responses tended to be either complementary or critical of the measurement system. Therefore, responses were categorized as either a predominantly positive or a predominantly negative reaction to the system within each of the five categories. For a few of the responses, the judges could not agree on whether the response was a positive or negative reaction. These neutral responses were omitted from the frequency counts.

The categories, frequency counts, and representative responses are given in Table 5–1. In looking across the five categories, there were slightly more positive than negative responses (52 positive, 42 negative). Thus, the reactions to the measurement system were somewhat positive in spite of the fact that the interview was designed to detect problems, rather than elicit positive comments. Also, these interview questions were asked prior to the refinements made to the measurement system. Those refinements addressed the concerns of the interviewees about the system, particularly the reliability and validity concerns. Project staff also repeated explanations of the system with

Table 5–1   Responses to Structured Interviews

Category	Frequency	Sample Response
Reliability and validity (positive)	19	"I can't think of much that is not covered."
Reliability and validity (negative)	25	"Direct labor needs to be involved more." "I'm not sure where the cutting department fits in."
Behavior and attitude changes (positive)	15	"I tend to think about the customer a little more since it is heavily weighted." "Thinking more about the overall picture."
Behavior and attitude changes (negative)	4	"Nothing's been changed."
Overall reactions to the system outcome (positive)	10	"It told us that communication was worse than we thought it was. For other measures, it confirmed what we felt but could not quantify."
Overall reactions to the system outcome (negative)	4	"It doesn't tell me enough about the bottom line." "It doesn't give any recommendations about what will improve the bottom line."
Overall reactions to the system process (positive)	2	"The apparent fact that this exercise was done interests me." "Spawns new ideas and opens eyes."
Overall reactions to the system process (negative)	9	"It touched the surface, but you can't get much deeper without spending lots of time."
Understanding unique features of the system (positive)	16	"What has been useful is the consolidation of data, put into charts, reflecting sales, the recession; it's all shown in the graphs."
Understanding unique features of the system (negative)	10	"It's been confusing because of the negatives and the positives, and putting everything into numbers."

manufacturing personnel and management to increase user understanding. Therefore, it may be assumed that the user's reactions to the system became even more positive following these changes and explanations.

Looking within categories, the system seemed to elicit a number of positive reactions in terms of behavior and attitude changes. For instance, more attention was given to customer related measures and the overall big picture. The system also elicited predominantly positive reactions to the overall outcome of the system and to its unique features.

The concerns about the reliability and validity of the measurement system shown in Table 5–1 were the most troubling. We made several changes in the measures to accommodate those changes, as mentioned earlier. It should be noted that most of the measures used in the system already existed in the manufacturing department. If the users did not have confidence in the data contained in their own preexisting measures, this would affect their perception of the ProMES. It was the author's opinion that there was a lack of confidence in their own data and that this perception affected the responses to the interview. Although this lack of confidence in the data is a problem, it is typically a long-term problem that the ProMES can impact only gradually.

The other area of concern from the interview responses was the overall reactions to the process of being measured. Some of the respondents felt that the ProMES did not get deep enough into the functioning of the department. This may be a reflection of the fact that ProMES is oriented to outcome measures that indicate the result of various processes. A desire for a deeper level of measurement may indicate a need for measurement of the processes themselves. Process oriented measures, however, are labor intensive. It was felt by the design team that adding process oriented measures would unduly burden the current system.

Effects of ProMES Feedback

To assess the effects of feedback, the overall effectiveness of the manufacturing department during the feedback period was compared with that during the baseline period. This change between baseline and feedback was then compared with change in the comparison department. Figure 5–2 shows the monthly overall effectiveness scores during the baseline and feedback periods for the manufacturing department. Two conclusions may be drawn from this graph. The first is that the average effectiveness score was higher during the feedback period than it was during baseline. The average score during baseline was –5.23, while the average during feedback was 10.43; this 15.66 point improvement represents a 14.9 percent improvement. This percent was calculated by dividing the actual improvement (15.66) by the maximum possible improvement of 105.23. For the comparison group, the average overall effectiveness score during the baseline period was 8.96, and it dropped to –8.60 for the time period when manufacturing was receiving feedback.

The other conclusion that can be drawn from the graph is that the overall effectiveness of the manufacturing department was declining during both the base line and feedback periods. This decline may be seen in Figure 5–2 by looking at the trend lines. This decline was most likely due to the recession, which affected all retail industries and particularly those on the west coast. The improvement may, therefore, be looked at as the difference between the downward slope of the baseline period and the slope of the feedback period, in other words, the difference between the department's performance with feedback and where it would have been without feedback. This difference is the distance between the two trend lines in the graph. This distance is 51.8 points, a percentage increase of 41 percent. The reader interested in the statistical analysis of this data may wish to see the technical publication of this study (Jones, Buerkle, Hall, Rupp, & Matt, 1993).

It is interesting to examine the contribution of each of the indicators to the improvement in overall effectiveness. The prime contributors were sales and the two measures for innovation. The other measures either declined or remained stable from baseline through feedback periods. Labor efficiency continued to decline slightly during the feedback period.

As mentioned earlier, this organization's business was hurt by the recession, and, as a result, a decision was made to focus on increasing labor efficiency in the manufacturing department. This efficiency effort occurred during the baseline period and may have contributed to the decline. After management received the ProMES feedback, they changed strategies to increase sales (which also meant increasing innovation so there would be new products to sell). Some portion of the improvement seen in Figure 5–2 for the feedback period was due to this change in strategy.

LESSONS LEARNED

The implementation of this feedback system and the interview responses taught the organization and project team four key lessons. First, ProMES can be effective in a manufacturing department of a successful corporation. Feedback improved their overall level of performance and helped them offset the downward trend caused by the recession. The comparison group showed no improvement, indicating that the improvement in the manufacturing department was not due to an overall improvement in the larger organization.

Second, we can learn a lot by asking for the user's candid reactions to the measurement system. The design team constructed what it

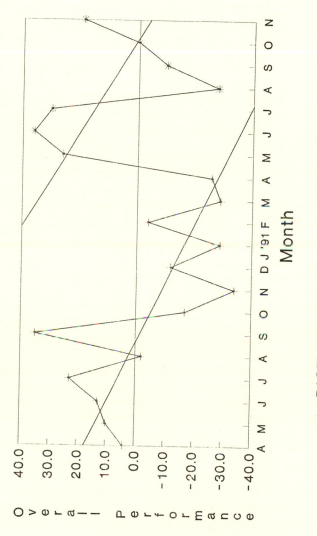

Feedback began: May 1991

Figure 5–2   Overall Manufacturing Performance

perceived as a finished system. However, results of the interviews demonstrated that, although the measurement system may be positively perceived in an overall sense by the users, the system may require a refinement phase based on user reactions before it is fully accepted. This may be because the users cannot completely react to the system until they have used it and then are asked probing questions to get their reactions to specific issues. The users cannot have the same level of understanding of the ProMES as those who have designed it.

After they begin to receive feedback based on the system, however, the full implications of the system become clearer to them. They then can have more specific reactions to the measures. Their reactions present an opportunity to improve the system and to get a greater commitment to it. Continuing this line of reasoning, we may view ProMES more as a continuous process with periodic refinements, so that the measurement system is dynamic rather than static.

The third lesson concerns the comprehensive nature of the measurement system. When organizations react to a problem, such as a recession, they often lose their view of the big picture and focus on only one strategy for improvement. If this is the wrong strategy, it may not become evident for some time. With ProMES, they continually see the big picture, and they can see the effects of an improvement strategy relatively quickly. The management of this corporation was absolutely convinced that improving labor efficiency was the correct strategy. When they saw that overall effectiveness was declining even though labor efficiency was improving, they reconsidered their strategy and changed to a strategy of increasing sales. This ability of ProMES to monitor the impacts of strategy changes on the big picture is one of its most valuable features for organizations.

The fourth lesson was learned from the processes that manufacturing changed to increase sales. It may seem paradoxical to the reader that the manufacturing department could increase sales during a recession. They did this by working more closely with their main customers, primarily the buying department. By providing more responsive delivery dates and new products, the manufacturing department was able to increase sales even during a recession. The lesson learned here is that a comprehensive feedback system promotes working smarter.

APPENDIX: STRUCTURED INTERVIEW QUESTIONS

Instructions: Recall the dimensions of performance of your department. (These were reviewed for them.) Recall that performance in these areas was measured by _____ (a list of the measures was given to the interviewee). These measures were combined into an overall effectiveness score that was plotted over time, giving an overall effectiveness graph.

1. How well do the dimensions cover the responsibilities of your department?
2. What areas are not adequately represented?
3. How accurate are each of the measures? (each measure addressed separately)
4. Which areas are not adequately measured?
5. What does the measurement system tell you that you did not already know?
6. What improvements would you make on the system?
7. What, if anything, are you doing differently as a result of the measurement system?
8. In what ways has it gotten you to think differently about your department?
9. Was what you got out of the measurement system worth the time you put into it?
10. What did you get out of the overall effectiveness graph?
11. What did you get out of the contingencies?
12. What did you not like about the system?

REFERENCES

American Productivity and Quality Center (1986). *White collar productivity improvement*. Houston: American Productivity and Quality Center.

Cameron, K. S., & Whetten, D. A. (Eds.) (1983). *Organizational effectiveness: A comparison of multiple models*. New York: Academic Press.

Connolly, T., Conlon, E. J., & Deutsch, S. J. (1980). Organizational effectiveness: A multiple-constituency approach. *Academy of Management Review, 5,* 211–217.

Deming, W. E. (1986). *Out of the crisis*. Cambridge, MA: Massachusetts Institute of Technology.

Goodman, P. S., & Pennings, J. M. (Eds.) (1977). *New perspectives on organizational effectiveness*. San Francisco: Jossey-Bass.

Jones, S. D., Buerkle, M., Hall, A., Rupp, L., & Matt, G. (1993). Work group performance measurement and feedback: An integrated comprehensive system for a manufacturing department. *Group and Organization Management, 18,* 269–291.

Jones, S. D., Powell, R., & Roberts, S. (1990). Comprehensive measurement to improve assembly line work group effectiveness. *National Productivity Review, 10,* 45–55.

Katz, D., & Kahn, R. L. (1966). *The social psychology of organizations* (2nd ed.). New York: John Wiley.

Pritchard, R. D. (1990). *Measuring and improving organizational productivity: A practical guide*. New York: Praeger.

Pritchard, R. D., Jones, S. D., Roth, P. L., Stuebing, K. K., & Ekeberg, S. E. (1988). The effects of feedback, goal setting, and incentives on organizational productivity. *Journal of Applied Psychology Monograph Series, 73,* 337–358.

Pritchard, R. D., Jones, S. D., Roth, P. L., Stuebing, K. K., & Ekeberg, S. E. (1989). The evaluation of an integrated approach to measuring organizational productivity. *Personnel Psychology, 42,* 69–115.

6

ProMES with Assembly Line Work Groups: It Is More than Just a Technology

Steven D. Jones

One of the staples for increasing productivity has been that of feedback to individuals, work groups, and organizations. It has not, however, been uniformly effective. For example, in a review of objective feedback applications in organizations, Balcazar, Hopkins, and Suarez (1986) found that feedback was ineffective in 15 percent of the studies and that 57 percent of the studies reported mixed results (significant improvements in some but not all of the dependent variables, or an improvement for some but not all subjects). Although other reviewers (e.g., Guzzo, Jette, & Katzell, 1985) have found more consistent improvements with feedback in the workplace, the variability of the results indicates there is still much to learn about applying feedback in organizations.

The purpose of this chapter is to describe the development of ProMES and the results during feedback for two manufacturing work groups. By examining both a successful and an unsuccessful application, issues are raised that may aid our understanding of ProMES not just as a technique but also as an improvement effort.

METHOD

Parent Organization and Local Facility

The work groups involved in the project (referred to here as group 1 and group 2) were part of a manufacturing facility in the southeastern United States that is, in turn, a part of a Fortune 500 corporation. The corporation holds the largest market share of its principle product relative to competition and is constantly striving to increase quality and efficiency. The parent corporation and the manufacturing facility both are dominated by engineers in the management and technical ranks. Management would be described best as having a benevolent autocratic style, with significant discretion given to plant and department managers to manage in their own style.

As with most large manufacturing firms, the manufacturing facility had numerous measurement systems that were the focus of management attention. Although different dimensions of productivity were addressed in those measurement systems, there was little, if any, integration of different dimensions (e.g., quality and quantity) of productivity to determine overall improvement.

Even though there was daily and, with some measures, hourly feedback, it was thought that ProMES could make a contribution because of its ability to integrate different measures into a single index and because it could provide a feedback system that would be meaningful to supervisors and workers.

Two ProMES projects took place with two different groups in the manufacturing facility. These two projects will be described separately, and implications from each will be discussed together toward the end of this chapter.

Group 1

Group 1 consisted of 14 employees, mostly male, working in a chemical processing assembly line. These employees averaged 9 years of experience in Group 1, ranging from 3 to 13. Their ages ranged from 26 to 43. All shifts were included in the study. Group 1 blends, compacts, and granulates powdered chemicals together. These blended chemicals are then used by other assembly lines of the plant to manufacture the final products. Group 1 was considered to be a relatively highly functioning group.

This group was participatively managed. Before the beginning of the development of the measurement system, the workers were accustomed to problem-solving meetings where they made specific suggestions for improvement, and management responded formally to these suggestions.

The project was conducted in two phases: development of the measurement system and feedback.

Phase 1: Development of the Measurement System

The development of the measurement system will be described primarily as it was developed for group 1. The development for group 2 was similar. Where there were differences, these will be pointed out. Also, where the methodology for the development of the measurement system differed from the standard ProMES methodology as described by Pritchard (1990), these differences will be explained.

To begin the measurement process, the author believed it was important to orient the measurement system to the organization's "big picture." Measurement in an organization has a tendency to be problem oriented, and, thus, the measures that evolve over time are those that control key problems. Partially for this reason, ProMES does not accept an organization's existing set of measures without question. Instead, it backs up a step and asks what the work products are and proceeds from that understanding to measures or indicators. This tactic results in a measurement system that is comprehensive, as opposed to problem oriented.

In the author's experience, efforts that attempt to improve organizations often fail for three key design reasons: they are in conflict with the organization's value system, they have an insufficient objective input, and they are static and, so, become quickly outmoded. Following this logic, three additions were made to the basic ProMES model. The first was to develop an understanding of the organization's culture and value system so that the measurement system and the feedback based on it were consistent with the values that were unique to this organization. The second addition was to understand the needs of the customers. This was done to increase the objectivity of the measurement system by balancing the tendency that members of the organization have to see only what they believe is important. The third addition was to include an understanding of the strategic plan and the organization's objectives so that the measurement was consistent with the direction the organization is going as well as what its current objectives are. From this basis of understanding, ProMES was developed.

In understanding the culture of the organization, we found through informal interviews that the following features determined the culture and values of group 1: pride of ownership, participative management style, a high skill level in their group, a high level of responsibility where minimum supervision was required, an emphasis on open communication with each other and the "customers" in the subsequent department in the production process, and highly demanding customers.

Through informal interviews with the customers of group 1, that is, the other departments downstream in the production process, we found the following customer needs: quantity of product to meet schedule, minimum downtime because of product quality problems, and a safe working environment.

Similarly, we found the objectives and strategic plan of group 1 to be as follows: maximize machine utilization of the next downstream department, make the optimal changes to cope with variation in incoming raw product, operate as safely as possible, produce enough product to meet plant production schedule, and continuously improve the product.

These three bases of understanding provided a perspective from which the ProMES could be developed so that it would be consistent with the important features of group 1 and the larger organization. In the following sections, it will be explained how using this model provided some different measures and different importance weights than would have otherwise been developed. Following the completion of the three bases of understanding, the measurement system was developed through the following six steps.

Step 1: Develop products. Through discussion with managers of group 1, four products were determined to be significant enough to be measured: quality, quantity, safety, and employee involvement. Although the first three products are givens for any manufacturing facility, the product of employee involvement was a direct reflection of the culture of group 1.

Step 2: Develop indicators. Through discussion with supervision and management of group 1, the following nine indicators were found to be necessary to comprehensively measure how well the four products were being "produced":

Quality
1. Machine utilization (actual number produced/number of units that could be produced minus units lost to mechanical downtime). This utilization referred to the machines in the customer's department (the next unit downstream in the production process). The higher the quality of the product produced by group 1, the faster the customer's machines could run, thus, the higher their utilization.
2. Percent of batches reblended (product batches that pass quality control inspections but have to be recycled through the blending process because they do not run well).
3. Percent batches doctored (batches that fail quality control inspections, thus, requiring additional ingredients).

Quantity
4. Percent of standard pounds of the product produced (based on engineering capacity standard).

Safety
5. Number of Occupational Safety and Health Administration (OSHA) recordable injuries/man-hours.
6. Number of safety violation reprimands/man-hours.
7. Air quality level.

Employee Involvement
8. Number of ideas suggested by employees in meetings/number of manufacturing problems x 100.
9. Number of ideas implemented/number of problems x 100.

To illustrate the importance of understanding customer needs in the measurement system, it was noted that the first indicator for quality, machine utilization, was a measure obtained from the next production unit downstream from group 1. This important indicator might have been overlooked had we not assessed customer needs before developing the measurement system.

The two indicators for employee involvement fit the culture of group 1. Employees participated in identifying production related problems and suggested potential solutions. Management determined feasibility of the solutions, and employees and management jointly implemented the approved solutions. A large number of high-quality suggestions were needed for the employee involvement effort to be viable, requiring an indicator for quantity (#8) and an indicator for quality (#9) of suggestions.

Indicators 1 through 7 were ones that the organization already formally measured, but the data were kept by different departments. Indicators 1 and 4 were kept by Manufacturing; 2 and 3 were kept by Quality Control; 5, 6, and 7 were kept by Human Resources. Indicators 8 and 9 were created for this project. That the data were kept by different departments does not imply that these indicators all were not seen by management; in fact, they were, but the indicators were treated separately.

Step 3: Develop contingencies. Contingencies development began by weighting the products and indicators of group 1 for relative importance. This development of the importance weights had some differences from that described by Pritchard and colleagues (1988, 1989). It was similar in that the importance weight for the maximum value of an indicator could be different from the importance weight for its minimum. The difference lies in how many indicators are compared at once to get the importance weights. In the traditional ProMES method, the maximum values of the indicators are weighted simultaneously across all products (and, separately, the minimum values are weighted simultaneously). For example, if there were ten indicators, the ten maximum values of those ten indicators would be ranked and rated for importance, resulting in ten importance weights. In the method presented here, the products are weighted first for importance; then, the indicators within a product were weighted in comparison with each other.

These four products of quality, quantity, safety, and employee involvement were not judged to be equally important. Each supervisor and the department manager independently assigned importance weights to the products. These weights and the reason for them were discussed, and consensus judgment produced the following weights: quality — 50 percent; quantity — 30 percent; safety — 10 percent; and employee involvement — 10 percent. Although products are not rated for importance in the traditional ProMES approach, product importance ratings were done here to avoid the problem of inadvertently assigning too much importance to a product just because it took more indicators to capture it than a product that required less indicators. By weighting the products, a limit was set on how important the set of indicators for each product could become. That limit was the product weight. Therefore, if there were three measures of quality, the total weight of the three indicators would be 30 percent.

As in the traditional ProMES methodology, the relative importance of each indicator can differ if it is at an effective or an ineffective level. Some indicators were more important on the downside than they were on the upside. For example, if group 1 was effective in involving employees, then indicators 8 and 9 were judged to be equally important. However, if the employee were not involved, indicator 8 became more important. A low ratio of ideas to problems would indicate to management that employees were losing interest and that the involvement process was in trouble. This would be a more significant indication of trouble in the area of employee involvement than a low ratio of implemented ideas. The indicator weights were established through consensus-seeking discussions with management. Rationales were required to justify the positive and negative weights, just as they were for the weights of indicators 8 and 9.

Generally speaking, these changes in importance followed the degree of management attention. For instance, machine utilization represented 75 percent of the importance of quality on the positive side, but on the negative side, it increased to 85 percent of quality. Low quality would adversely affect subsequent production lines, thus, attracting negative attention from management. The relative importance ratings are presented in Table 6–1. The first column lists the products, and the second column provides the importance weights for each product. The third column gives the indicators for their associated products. The fourth column gives the importance weight of each indicator on the positive side, that is, when the group was effective in that product area. The fifth column gives the product weight on the negative side, that is, when the group was ineffective in that product area. For instance, when group 1 was producing a high-quality product, machine utilization was 75 percent of the product quality, but when quality was a problem, machine utilization was 85 percent of the product quality. The negative sign in front of the 85 indicates that the group was ineffective, or below expectations, in the product area of quality. Shown in the last two columns of the table are the final indicator weights. These were obtained by multiplying the product weight times the negative and positive indicator weights. We can get the final indicator weights for machine utilization as follows: on the positive side, 50 x 75 converted to percent equals 37.5 percent, and on the negative side, 50 x –85 equals –42.5 percent. Now we have indicator weights that sum to +100 and –100 and can be treated like percents.

The managers of group 1 came up with this approach to weighting the indicators. They reported that it offered three advantages. The indicator weights were more understandable to them because they

Table 6–1   Products, Indicators, and Weights for Group 1

Product	Weight	Indicator	Percent of Product +	Percent of Product −	Weight +	Weight −
Quality	50	Machine utilization	75	−85	37.5	−42.5
		Batches reblended	20	−5	10.0	−2.5
		Batches doctored	5	−10	2.5	−5.0
Quantity	30	Percent standard produced	100	−100	30.0	−30.0
Safety	10	OSHA recordables	60	−80	6.0	−8.0
		Reprimands	20	−10	2.0	−1.0
		Air quality level	20	−10	2.0	−1.0
Involvement	10	Number ideas/number problems	50	−70	5.0	−7.0
		Number ideas implemented/ number problems	50	−30	5.0	−3.0
Total					100.0	−100.0

were in percent formats with totals of 100. Also, it gave the overall effectiveness score more meaning (an overall effectiveness score of 64 was 65 percent of the maximum possible). They also reasoned that if other groups developed ProMES, they would have more easily comparable scores, because they would all have the same maximum possible effectiveness score of 100.

Figure 6–1 presents the contingency for the indicator of machine utilization. Several features of Figure 6–1 highlight how the contingencies were constructed. The horizontal axis for the indicator of machine utilization ranges from a low of 60 percent to a high of 95 percent, that is, the machines in the "customer's" department could run as low as 60 percent to as high as 95 percent of their capacity as determined by engineering standards. Recall that the higher the quality of the product sent to this "customer" by group 1, the more efficiently the machines could run and, thus, the higher the utilization. The 60 percent and 95 percent values were best and worst case scenarios, which were determined from historical data. The vertical axis ranges from +37.5 to −42.5 overall effectiveness. These two values were taken from the relative importance of the indicators as shown in the last two columns of Table 6–1.

Next, the "zero point" was established; it is 77 percent in the example. Machine utilization of 77 percent was seen as neither good nor bad performance; it was the level that was minimally acceptable to management. The goal of the department was 85 percent, because at this point they can begin to build inventory and perform preventive

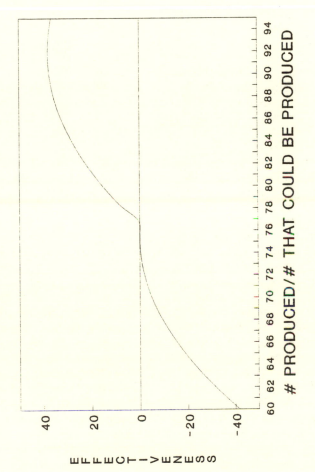

Figure 6–1   Machine Utilization Contingency for Group 1

maintenance. Note that as the machine utilization approaches the goal of 85 percent, this is the steepest section of the contingency, signifying that improvement in this range will generate the greatest gain in overall effectiveness. At the higher levels of machine utilization, the function presents a curve of diminishing returns, that is, higher levels of production improve overall effectiveness (because it adds to inventory) but less so as inventory limits are approached. At the very upper end, around 92 percent, effectiveness actually begins to drop. Because the product has a limited storage life, excess inventory above a certain amount actually begins to be ineffective. It was determined that a machine utilization rate of 92 to 94 percent begins to produce inventory that can create storage life problems.

On the downside, the curve is a negative accelerating function. Subsequent lines can still run if production was in the 74 to 77 percent range. Below 74 percent, overtime becomes necessary, and at even lower levels, subsequent lines begin to be shut down. Thus, effectiveness drops off rapidly.

A contingency graph for each indicator was constructed by following the steps outline above. Rationales were requested for the shape of the curve, the zero point, and any inflection points. The contingency graphs were drawn by hand, discussed, and confirmed by group consensus of managers and supervisors.

The process of contingency development went very smoothly. Managers and supervisors seemed to have no difficulty understanding and using the concept of the contingencies. In fact, a supervisor and a manager, who were both engineers, readily took to the contingency development procedure and were able to offer modifications to ProMES that seemed to be improvements. The first improvement was the weighting of the indicators as described above in percent format with a total of 100 percent. Two other improvements, both of which are described below, were contributions of these two engineers in group 1.

Step 4: Develop computer program for feedback reports. A spreadsheet program was developed for the measurement system with the intention of using it to produce feedback reports and graphs. This spreadsheet program was written in Lotus 1-2-3 by the two engineers. The purpose of the spreadsheet program was to make data storage, calculation, and graphing of the effectiveness scores as easy as possible. The program was written around formulas that described the contingency curves. The engineers graphed each contingency in the spreadsheet. This required a set of X and Y coordinates where X was the raw score for the indicator and Y was the effectiveness score as determined by the contingency graphs. Following this, they computed a regression equation (a function of Lotus 1-2-3). For a contingency that was curvilinear, a logarithmic term was employed. This regression equation then became the equation in the spreadsheet that described the contingency. Each of the nine contingencies had a single regression equation. These nine equations were put into separate cells in the spreadsheet program so that the cell that had the raw score was linked to the cell that contained the equation describing the contingency. When the raw scores were entered into the program, effectiveness scores were computed and summed to get overall effectiveness. The final result of the spreadsheet program was to produce a feedback report for group 1.

The feedback report used the same format as other ProMES projects. The report contained columns for the name of the indicators, the raw indicator data, the effectiveness scores, and the percent of maximum effectiveness. Group 1 placed an emphasis on the percent of maximum, because from that data, it could readily be seen which indicators had the most room for improvement and how much room for improvement there was.

A second page of the feedback report gave the changes in effectiveness from the last period to a current period for each indicator and for the overall total. In addition, each indicator was graphed in terms of raw indicator values over time; also, overall effectiveness was graphed over time.

Step 5: Collect baseline data. After the measurement system and the spreadsheet programs were completed, baseline data were recorded. These data were taken on all of the indicators for group 1 during the time period when the measurement system was being developed and prior to the beginning of feedback. In addition, many data were available prior to the development of the measurement system from the organization's records, because the majority of the indicators were measures that already existed. Inclusion of this archival data allowed the extension of the baseline over a longer period of time.

In order to have complete data for all indicators during this extended baseline, the problem of missing data for new indicators that did not exist prior to the development of the measurement system had to be resolved. It was decided to substitute means for the months where data were missing by taking the average of the months that did exist. This only affected indicators 8 and 9.

The data for each indicator were entered into the spreadsheet program, which calculated the overall effectiveness score and a feedback report for each time period. Graphs were then made for each indicator and overall effectiveness over the baseline period.

Step 6: Determine priorities for improvement. In order to determine which areas had the greatest potential for improvement, a "what if" analysis was done, using the spreadsheet program. Management reasoned that a 10 percent improvement in each indicator was feasible. From the eight month baseline, the average of each indicator was input into the program and the effectiveness values (from the contingencies) were recorded. Next, a hypothetical 10 percent increase for each indicator was input into the spreadsheet program, and the changes in effectiveness were calculated. Machine utilization averaged 80.2 percent during baseline, resulting in an effectiveness score of 18.2. If it increased by 10 percent, it would be at 88.23 percent, or an effectiveness score of 36.0. Subtracting 18.2 from 36.0 gave a potential effectiveness gain of 17.8. All other indicators yielded much lower potential improvement gains; therefore, machine utilization was targeted for improvement.

This potential effectiveness gain calculation is very similar to that presented by Pritchard and colleagues (1988, 1989). The only difference is that it is calculated in terms of a percent gain of the indicator rather than a unit increase as presented by Pritchard and colleagues (1989). Again, changing to a percentage methodology appeared to be more readily understandable to managers and supervisors. Also, using a percentage approach avoided the need to have the same number of increments for every indicator on the horizontal axis of the contingencies.

It seemed relatively easy for managers to make a judgment that a 10 percent increase was feasible for each indicator. How accurate this judgment was remains unknown; however, it did appear to have an intrinsic appeal, because the managers readily took to the notion of calculating potential gains through use of the contingencies. In fact, the two engineers initiated this calculation on their own after the idea had been briefly explained to them.

From this data it became clear that the greatest gain would come from improving machine utilization. (Recall that machine utilization was an indicator of how efficiently the "customer's" machines ran and was directly impacted by the quality of the product produced by group 1.) From this analysis, it was decided to attack this indicator first while maintaining the other indicators at their baseline levels. It was reasoned by management that this strategy would provide the workers a specific target and a higher chance of early success than if they had tried to improve all the indicators at once. This decision was made just prior to the formal beginning of feedback to all employees.

Phase 2: Feedback

Phase 2 consisted of giving feedback to the members of group 1 based on the ProMES measurement system established in Phase 1. Preceding the first feedback session, a meeting was held with the workers to explain the meaning of the graphs, the measurement system, and the purpose of the project. The feedback was not separated by shift; results were averaged across all shifts. This was done to streamline the feedback computations and to encourage cooperation rather than competition between shifts, which was felt would be counterproductive.

Feedback began, and the overall goals and objectives of the project were explained to group 1 employees by management. Up to this time, the employees had not been involved in ProMES; only the supervisors and department manager were involved in the development of the measurement system. The two engineers who were previously mentioned had the largest roles in the development of the measurement system. Although the other supervisors and employees appeared to understand the system enough to use the feedback reports, they also appeared to have less investment than the engineers.

The baseline data, the indicator (machine utilization) that management determined had the greatest potential for improvement, the method of intervention (feedback), and the means of improvement measurement were discussed with group 1 employees.

With the initial introduction of feedback, weekly meetings were held to monitor the progress of the indicator targeted for improvement as well as the other indicators and overall effectiveness. The targeted indicator received the most attention. Weekly feedback was used in the beginning of the project because management felt that frequent feedback was necessary to get the project off to a quick start. Each group was used to meeting once a week at the change of shift, and it was relatively easy to introduce feedback into these meetings. The supervisors conducted the feedback meetings, which were attended by all employees. Ideas and suggestions for solutions were solicited in these meetings. All group 1 employees were encouraged to participate openly and freely in idea suggestion for problem solutions. After the first two months, it was felt that the project start-up had been accomplished. Thereafter, feedback meetings were held monthly, although the employees continued to make and process suggestions for improvement on a weekly basis just for the targeted indicator.

Results of Feedback: Group 1

Figure 6–2 presents the graph for the targeted indicator for group 1, machine utilization over nine moths of the baseline period and five months of feedback, and the graph for overall effectiveness during that same time period. Notice that the graph for machine utilization has a sharp upward trend from month 4 to month 6, which was due to an improvement in the chemical formulation of the product. Feedback began at the beginning of month 10, and the data were taken at the end of the month. Machine utilization during feedback was 11 percent higher than it was during the eight months prior to feedback. If we ignore the period before month 3, when the chemical formula was changed, the feedback period represents a 4 percent improvement in machine utilization.

Because one measure was targeted for improvement, the question became What happened to the other eight indicators during this time period — did they suffer while machine utilization improved? This question is addressed by the graph of overall effectiveness, because it combines all nine indicators. The graph of overall effectiveness, which is also shown in Figure 6–2, demonstrates the trend of all indicators combined.

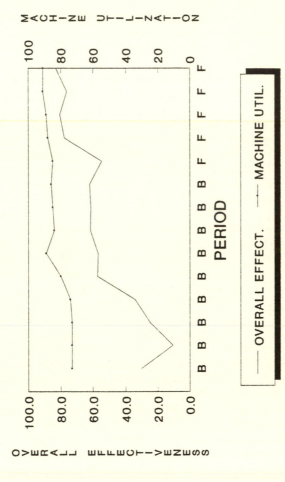

B = BASELINE   F = FEEDBACK

Figure 6-2   Overall Effectiveness and Machine Utilization for Group 1

As can be seen from the graph, overall effectiveness increased during the feedback period, so that the gains in machine utilization were not offset by declines in other indicators. In fact, the improvement comparing the entire baseline period with feedback was 68 percent (change of 29.9/baseline average of 44.36). If we ignore the period before month 5 of the baseline (to remove the impact of an improvement in the chemical formulation of the product that occurred during that time), there was a 24 percent gain in overall effectiveness (change of 14.64/ baseline average of 59.86). Thus, the other indicators actually improved while machine utilization improved. This illustrates the point that without a means to integrate the indicators into a single index, it would have been difficult to assess the overall impact of the improvement effort.

Currently, group 1 is no longer using ProMES. One of the key supervisors (one of the two engineers) was promoted to another department. This was the person who knew the system the best, wrote the spreadsheet program, and performed the effectiveness calculations. A new supervisor has been trained in using the system but has not yet implemented it. It should be noted that this new supervisor manager came from a different department and would be expected to take several months learning the technology used in group 1's department.

Although this project appears to be an early success, as indicated by the improvements in Figure 6–2, the discontinuation of the project following turnover of a "project champion" raises issues that are addressed in the discussion section.

Group 2

Participants in group 2 were members of an assembly line that produces products on a line that is labor intensive and not highly machine paced. Included in the group were both the first and second shift workers, supervisors, and maintenance mechanics, totaling 42 employees. The mean years of experience of the workers in group 2 was 3.6, with the range being 3 months to 13 years. Most of these workers were women, ranging in age from 28 to 62 years. Like group 1, group 2 was considered to be a relatively highly functioning group within the larger organization.

The work of this group was highly repetitious, the principal diversions being job rotation every two hours and the social interaction of the workers. The management style was benevolent authoritarian; the workers had little or no experience with suggesting ideas for improvement during their tenure with this group.

Phase 1: Development of the Measurement System

The products and indicators were developed for group 2 through meetings with the department manager, the supervisors, and the assembly line workers. Typically, the meetings with workers were one-on-one, because they had to be taken off the assembly line, which could not be shut down, and they could not be paid overtime for meeting to develop the measurement system. Meetings with managers and supervisors were also typically one-on-one because of their work schedules. The four products and seven indicators for group 2 are presented below:

Quality
  1. Percent of quality control inspections passed.
  2. Number of finished units returned by customers for quality problems under the control of group 2.
  3. Dollar value of units scrapped.
  4. Number of units put "on hold," that is, not packaged for shipment to customers, by quality control inspectors.

Quantity
  5. Utilization — the percent of the production standard met.

Safety
  6. Number of OSHA recordable injuries.

Teamwork
  7. Mean score on the teamwork survey. To measure teamwork, a survey was developed that could be completed by the personnel manager on the basis of weekly discussions with the group 2 personnel. The survey comprised 17 items using a Likert scale format that was designed to measure three areas: supervisor facilitation, between-shift cooperation, and morale.

After the products and indicators were developed, they were weighted for importance just as they were in group 1, beginning by weighting the products for importance. The only difference from group 1 was that the effectiveness scores were not put into percent format; thus, the effectiveness score could sum to more than 100. Contingencies were drawn using the traditional ProMES approach, and a computer program was written to produce the feedback reports and graphs.

Phase 2: Feedback

An introductory meeting was conducted by the department manager, who presented the feedback graphs to the workers and entertained any questions they had regarding the graphs or the feedback process. In this first feedback meeting, group 2 workers were shown graphs for each of the seven indicators and overall effectiveness for the 22 week baseline period. This first feedback meeting occurred in a meeting room separate from the production area and on company time. Extensive discussions occurred in this meeting, which lasted approximately 90 minutes. Subsequent feedback meetings took place in the production area in front of the project bulletin board and lasted 10 to 15 minutes.

Discussions were minimal in these meetings because of the noise level from the nearby assembly lines.

The weekly feedback was given to workers through conspicuous (14 by 14 inch) graphs posted on a bulletin board so that all workers could easily view the group's results. There were graphs of each indicator and one for overall effectiveness, all of which were updated weekly. The weekly feedback meetings were held in front of the bulletin board. Members of both shifts were present, because the meeting was held on Friday at the time of shift change. The previous week's results were presented by management, and suggestions for improvements were solicited from the group members.

After eight weeks, the ProMES feedback was discontinued, because the supervisors were dissatisfied with the results. This dissatisfaction was due primarily to the fact that productivity did not improve during the eight weeks of feedback. Although there seemed to be many other reasons (presented below), if productivity had improved, it is the author's opinion that group 2 would have continued using the ProMES feedback even though they may have had other reservations about the system. Data were collected for 18 weeks on all of the indicators following the termination of feedback. This additional collection of data after the termination of feedback allowed a more sophisticated test of the effects of feedback.

Results of Feedback

As mentioned earlier, there was a change in the level of worker experience in group 2 during the feedback period. This change in worker experience is overlaid on the graph of overall effectiveness and presented in Figure 6–3. Along the horizontal axis of the graph are the time period, which are either under the baseline (i.e., no feedback) or the ProMES feedback condition. Because productivity measurement was done weekly, each of these points represents a given week either before, during, or after ProMES feedback. Both worker experience and overall effectiveness of group 2 are represented on the vertical axis. Because worker experience was measured as percent of the workers with three or more weeks of experience, it has a maximum of 100, and there is little change except when new workers entered group 2 during the feedback period. Overall effectiveness, represented by the solid line, shows considerable variation on the graph, starting with a slightly negative score and rising to a score of approximately 180 during the eighth week of the baseline period.

Visual inspection of this figure reveals two key features: there appeared to be no increase in the level of overall effectiveness during the feedback period, and the decrease in worker experience apparently had a negative impact on overall effectiveness.

Because worker experience was thought to influence effectiveness, it was necessary to remove this influence so that the effects of ProMES

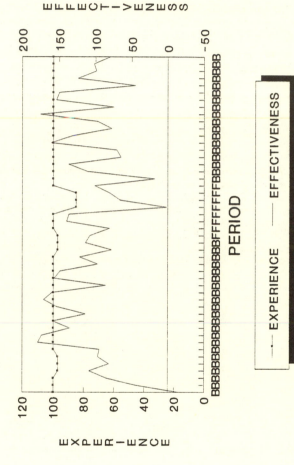

B = BASELINE   F = FEEDBACK

Figure 6-3   Worker Experience and Overall Effectiveness for Group 2

feedback on overall effectiveness could be more clearly determined. To remove the impact of worker experience, it was used as a control variable in a statistical analysis (multiple regression). The results of the analysis revealed that the introduction of feedback did not have a significant effect upon overall effectiveness when the effect of worker experience was statistically removed. Likewise, feedback did not have an effect on any of the seven indicators.

Qualitative Analysis

Because there were no significant improvements during feedback in group 2, all workers and supervisors were interviewed about their impressions of the feedback system. Their responses were classified in five categories based on inspection of the entire set of responses by the author. The number of responses that fit into each category indicated the relative importance of that category as a reason for the lack of results.

Resistance to change was the most common theme in the interview responses. There were 26 responses that fit into this category. Three sample responses were, "I didn't go to the meetings because I figured nobody would listen anyway." "People don't care if they do any more or not; you could put a graph over every machine and people wouldn't do anymore." and "They believe that if they talk in a meeting, they will be thought of as a troublemaker."

The second most common response when asked about the lack of results concerned intershift conflict. The measurement system combined the performance data for both the first and second shifts. There were 20 responses that fit this category. Two example responses were, "We don't work together between shifts because day shift doesn't leave us any components." and "If the feedback was separated for the two shifts, you could tell more about it."

The third most common response concerned the meeting logistics. The feedback meetings were held at the change of shifts in an area adjacent to the production line. There were 12 responses for this category. Two sample responses were, "There was not interest in it because it was at the wrong time [quitting time], and our minds were on walking out." and "I couldn't hear too well what was being said — too noisy on the floor."

The next most common response was that the feedback system was not adequately explained. There were ten responses in this category, such as, "It [the feedback system] was not presented well." and "We thought that they [management] were trying to find something to make the work harder."

The least frequent type of response concerned the incremental information provided by the feedback system. There were four of these responses. Sample responses were, "We already knew everything it was telling us." "The girls on the line know when they do good and bad work;

it didn't add anything new. When you've been on the line for 13 years, you know how you are doing."

DISCUSSION

ProMES measurement systems were developed and implemented as feedback systems in two highly functioning manufacturing work groups in a plant that had a substantial measurement system prior to the introduction of ProMES. The results indicated an improvement during the ProMES feedback period for group 1 but not for group 2.

There are six major differences between the conditions of this study and those of the original ProMES study reported by Pritchard and colleagues (1988). First, groups 1 and 2 were both performing at a much higher level during baseline than were the military work groups in the original ProMES study; therefore, there was less opportunity for the dramatic initial improvements due to feedback shown in the original ProMES study.

Second, in both groups 1 and 2, the measurement system was developed more quickly than in the Pritchard and colleagues (1988) study (four months as opposed to one year). These figures are calendar time in both cases; actual meeting time (in the organization) for groups 1 and 2 was two to three hours every two weeks. Although this shorter development time did not appear to impact group 1, it may have not allowed sufficient time for understanding by supervisors and workers in group 2. Reason number three (feedback system not adequately explained) from the qualitative analysis of group 2 bears on this limitation. It appears from this study that supervisors and workers may require fairly long "incubation time" and thorough explanations, particularly in cases where the institution of a feedback system represents a change in the information the group is getting and a change in what is expected of them to adequately use this new information.

Related to the second difference, for group 1, the measurement system was developed with supervisors and managers and then explained to the workers. Obviously, this shortened development of the system. The positive results for group 1 indicate that worker participation in development of the measurement system may not be necessary in all cases. Group 2 was extensively involved in development of the measurement system; virtually every worker was pulled off the assembly line (a costly procedure) for individual meetings to determine products and indicators. A lesson learned was that in spite of this much involvement, the interviews indicated a lack of understanding of the system.

A third difference concerns the tasks of the work groups. Group 2, in particular, performed tasks that were highly repetitive, at the rate of 10 to 15 repetitions per minute. Under these conditions, workers in group

2 developed methods of mentally disengaging from the tasks. In the military units of the original ProMES study and in group 1, the majority of the tasks were repeated only a few times per day, and it seems less likely that workers had developed disengagement strategies. The sample responses for interview response category 1 (resistance to change) seem to point to a resistance to involvement in the feedback meetings that could be expected in repetitious jobs and particularly where participation is not a part of the culture of the organization. Group 1, on the other hand, was accustomed to giving input on how the work could be improved.

Fourth, group 2 already had in place feedback every two hours for quantity of work. Several of the other indicators were readily apparent to the workers on a daily basis; therefore, the feedback system provided little additional information, as demonstrated by category 5 (feedback provided no additional information) in the interview responses of group 2. In contrast, in the original ProMES study, the feedback system provided much additional information to the military groups, who typically received feedback only when they had made a mistake.

Fifth, the logistics of the feedback meetings for group 2 were a problem. In both the original ProMES study and in group 1, meetings were held in a place and at a time that signified that something special and important was happening. Meetings in these cases were held in rooms or offices where it was quiet enough to encourage thoughtful discussion and participation by workers. In contrast, group 2 met on the production floor a short distance from the assembly lines, which were quite loud. In fact, the noise limited most conversation to one or two sentences; this setting was not conducive to either discussion or involvement.

Thus, there were a number of differences between group 1 and group 2 that help to explain the lack of results in group 2. Most of these differences are also differences between group 2 and the military groups where the initial successful ProMES results were reported. The differences between these groups and how ProMES was instituted provide some insights into how ProMES projects should be managed.

Looking back at the interview responses for group 2, the second through the fifth reasons for the lack of positive results in group 2 are project management issues. For example, where there is substantial intershift conflict, the management of a ProMES project requires special considerations. One of the key issues in this case was whether to combine the results of both shifts or to separate them. To separate the results would have required a feedback system for each shift, effectively doubling the work to maintain the system, and it would have encouraged competition between the two shifts. Because much of the work required cooperation between the shifts, it was decided to combine their results into one feedback system. However, intershift conflict became the second most important reason for the lack of results. In retrospect, it would have been better to address the conflict between the two shifts before making the decision to combine or separate the feedback system. Management became more aware of the intershift conflict during the ProMES development and feedback. As a result, the department manager responsible for group 2 requested an intergroup team-building session for the two shifts, but we decided this was outside the realm of the ProMES design team.

Explanation of the feedback is a project management issue that also requires careful consideration. In the case of group 2, the feedback was explained by the department manager to all workers; however, it seemed that the workers did not understand, and they did not ask questions. Similarly, meeting logistics and the amount of additional information in the feedback system can be thought of as project management issues.

An additional project management issue concerns turnover of key personnel in the organization. Typically, a ProMES project requires a "project champion" internal to the organization who will take a large share of the responsibility for making the project work. When the project is successful, this person often gets the credit. There is a problem when the "project champion" leaves the organization or changes positions. His or her replacement will not have the intimate knowledge of ProMES nor will they be able to get credit for its continued success, because it was someone else's project. The loss of project continuity because of turnover of the project champion, as occurred in group 1, then becomes a critical project management issue. In this regard, ProMES requires careful project management and extensive project support to facilitate its implementation.

The results of the interviews with group 2 workers indicated that the most frequently stated reasons for the lack of positive results addressed the larger context within which the feedback system was used. This larger context consisted of the social system of the workers and supervisors and the prevailing management style. For instance, group 2 was not participatively managed. In addition, like many assembly line groups, group 2 had a longstanding conflict between the day and night shifts.

With feedback systems, improvements in productivity and effectiveness typically come from improved strategies: working smarter rather than working harder. These strategy improvements require both cooperation and some degree of employee involvement to be successful.

Participation and employee involvement run contrary to many management practices, and they also run contrary to assembly line work, where workers learn to turn off their minds beyond what it takes to perform repetitive tasks. When an intervention attempts to elicit involvement in such a situation, resistance is generated that undermines the effectiveness of the intervention itself. Understanding and resolving such conflicts and resistance may need to be done prior to and throughout the introduction of the intervention to avoid falling into the "technique trap," that is, implementing a technique without a supporting change in the culture of the organization (Belcher, 1987).

In a study similar to the one reported here, Nadler, Mirvis, and Cortlandt (1976) developed a feedback system for bank employees that combined both objective feedback of group performance and attitude survey feedback. In bank branches where the system was used extensively, the authors found improvements in both attitudes and performance, but there were no improvements in branches where the system was not used extensively. Extensive use was defined as occurring when a branch encouraged employees to participate in using the feedback and where joint problem solving and goal setting took place. The choice of how extensively to use the feedback lay with the branch managers. Of the branches, 50 percent chose not to use the system extensively, and consequently, they showed no improvement. One of the managers who chose not to use the system extensively was quoted as follows: "All of a sudden it seemed to kind of take the management of the branch a little bit out of our hands. We spent a lot of time answering employee questions as to why we were doing things, and we never really had to do that before" (p. 74).

This statement is the management equivalent of this worker's response from group 2: They [workers] believe that if they talk in a meeting, they will be perceived as a "troublemaker." Indeed, the introduction of a feedback system may be perceived as "trouble" for both management and workers in groups where participation has not been established as part of the culture.

Regarding the other culture issue, intershift conflict is common in manufacturing firms. Potential productivity and effectiveness improvements may depend on improved cooperation between shifts. A quote from one of the workers interviewed underscores this issue: "We don't care to cooperate with day shift — we've bent over backwards — they [day shift] don't leave us as many lids [assemblies] as we leave for them. They should cooperate — the work would go better if there was cooperation between the shifts." A productivity feedback system by itself may do more to accent an existing conflict than to facilitate cooperation. Workers and supervisors seldom have the specialized skills required to solve such problems, which may require an organization development effort such as intergroup team building.

Although feedback systems are not typically considered organization development (a planned organizational change in the culture of the organization), the introduction of a feedback system poses many of the same implementation issues as do organization development efforts. This is because the processes that are necessary for the feedback to result in increased effectiveness, such as increased employee involvement and improved cooperation, are the same processes that are specialty areas of organization development. The failures or mixed results of feedback studies, such as those of group 2 and those described by Balcazar, Hopkins, and Suarez (1986), may well have more to do with organizational change considerations than with the feedback system per se.

In conclusion, a ProMES intervention can be successful, as it was with group 1 and in the military units described in the original ProMES study by Pritchard and colleagues (1988, 1989). The results of group 1 give a preliminary indication that ProMES can facilitate improvements even in a private sector organization that is already performing well. ProMES embodies many features that can allow it to be highly successful, such as its design as a feedback system, the overall effectiveness score, and the possibility of doing "what-if" analysis to set priorities.

There is an important additional consideration of ProMES, however; it is a large-scale intervention that may either mesh well with the fabric of the organization or be resisted by it. Such resistance can prevent the system from getting off the ground, and it may require external support to keep the system operational. A thorough understanding of such resistance forces and conflicts between the implicit values of ProMES and the organization's culture may be a critical component of the knowledge base for design and implementation of ProMES projects.

REFERENCES

Balcazar, F., Hopkins, B. L., & Suarez, Y. (1986). A critical, objective review of performance feedback. *Journal of Organizational Behavior Management, 7,* 65–89.

Belcher, J. G. (1987). *Productivity plus.* Houston: Gulf.

Guzzo, R. A., Jette, R. D., & Katzell, R. A. (1985). The effects of psychologically based intervention programs on worker productivity: A meta-analysis. *Personnel Psychology, 38,* 275–291.

Nadler, D. A., Mirvis, P., & Cortlandt, C. (1976). The ongoing feedback system. *Organizational Dynamics, 4,* 63–80.

Pritchard, R. D. (1990). *Measuring and improving organizational productivity: A practical guide* (p. 248). New York: Praeger.

Pritchard, R. D., Jones, S. D., Roth, P. L., Stuebing, K. K., & Ekeberg, S. E. (1989). The evaluation of an integrated approach to measuring organizational productivity. *Personnel Psychology, 42,* 69–115.

Pritchard, R. D., Jones, S. D., Roth, P. L., Stuebing, K. K., & Ekeberg, S. E. (1988). The effects of feedback, goal setting, and incentives on organizational productivity. *Journal of Applied Psychology Monograph Series, 73,* 337–358.

PART II

ProMES in Service Settings

7

ProMES and Computer Service Technicians: An Australian Application

Ilya Bonic

Although the development, implementation, and evaluation of ProMES by Pritchard, Jones, Roth, Stuebing, and Ekeberg (1988, 1989) was strikingly successful, a number of issues remained unresolved. This chapter describes further ProMES research aimed at examining two of these unresolved issues.

The first issue considered related to the generalizability of the ProMES system. Pritchard and his colleagues examined ProMES in the U.S. military context. The present research examined the extent to which the ProMES system could be successfully developed and implemented in the Australian business environment; specifically, would ProMES work with Australian computer service technicians?

The second issue related to the contingencies that serve as the algorithms that allow the conversion of raw measures of performance into the standard effectiveness unit of measure that forms the basis of the ProMES system. Pritchard and colleagues (1988, 1989) and Pritchard (1990) place a good deal of emphasis on the generation of full nonlinear contingencies. They imply that full nonlinear contingencies more accurately reflect the significance of performance changes in the work environment and, thus, more accurately measure changes in effectiveness than do simpler contingencies; however, the generation of full nonlinear contingencies is likely to be more complicated and, thus, a more time-consuming and costly process than is the generation of abbreviated contingencies. The present research was designed to examine the extent to which a full nonlinear contingency-based ProMES system provides an organization with any meaningful gain over and above an abbreviated contingency-based ProMES system in terms of either the ease of ProMES development and implementation or the magnitude of productivity enhancement.

METHOD

Organization

The present study was conducted in a branch of a service division of a multinational computer systems organization. ProMES was developed within two of the branch's service groups.

Service groups are responsible for the maintenance and repair of computer systems that are contracted to the organization by its customers. Service groups consist of a number of field technicians, a field coordinator, and a group supervisor. When customers experience technical difficulty with their computer systems, a service call is lodged with the service group via the organization's information system. The field coordinator allocates the call to a service technician, who then proceeds to attend the call and deal with any identified faults. Technicians work individually, but technicians within a single work group service the same customers.

The two groups that formed the basis of the present study were comparable in terms of both their function and structure. Group 1 consisted of nine service technicians (including the field coordinator) and one group supervisor. Group 2 consisted of 16 field technicians (including the field coordinator) and 1 group supervisor.

ProMES Development and Implementation Procedure

The process of ProMES development and implementation was carried out over a five to six week period in five major steps.

Workflow Analysis

Before ProMES was developed, a workflow analysis of the service branch was performed. The purpose of the analysis was to provide the researcher with a detailed insight into the objectives, their indicators, and functioning of the two work groups that formed the basis of the study.

ProMES Development Questionnaire

The information derived from the workflow analysis allowed a ProMES development questionnaire to be constructed and distributed to each technician within the two service groups. The questionnaire served two purposes: first, it made work group members aware that a productivity system was being developed, and second, the questionnaire provided technicians with an early opportunity to help shape the productivity measurement system with minimal disruption to their work activities.

Technicians were required to complete three sections of the questionnaire. The first section required the identification of products. The second section required the identification of product indicators. Finally, a rank ordering of indicators was required. A worked example was provided to assist technicians in completing the questionnaire. The worked example was constructed on the basis of the information derived from the workflow analysis.

ProMES Development Meeting

The results of the questionnaire were collated and presented to management for examination. This provided management with information that allowed them to assess the degree to which the work groups' perceptions of their primary function matched the organization's understanding of the groups' principal work objectives. In brief, it represented the first stage of clarifying and communicating work group objectives.

Following the progress review, a separate ProMES development meeting was held for each of the work groups. The meeting was attended by a representative number of technicians (five from group 1 and seven from group 2) without their supervisor.

At the development meeting, the ProMES system was described and discussed in detail. Technicians were presented with the product, indicator, and rank ordering results of the questionnaire. The products and indicators identified with the questionnaire were the same as those identified during the workflow analysis. Furthermore, because both service groups performed the same functions, only in a different environment, the same products and indicators were identified for both groups. In all, three products and six indicators were identified:

1. Quantity of repair
    Indicator 1: percent call demand met
2. Quality of repair
    Indicator 2: successful call rate, that is, the percentage of successful calls
    Indicator 3: call back rate, that is, the percentage of calls returned within three days of initial successful repair
3. Timeliness
    Indicator 4: average down time
    Indicator 5: average repair time
    Indicator 6: average response time

The meaning of the products, indicators, and the significance of the rank ordering in the context of the ProMES system were discussed. During this process, some modification of the rank ordering of priorities occurred. The contingency generation process of ProMES development, as outlined by Pritchard and colleagues (1988, 1989), was next undertaken.

There were four steps involved in generating the indicator contingencies. First, an importance weight was assigned to each indicator. Second, the maximum and minimum realistic levels of performance for each indicator were identified. Third, the expected level of performance for each indicator was defined and assigned an effectiveness value of zero. Finally, the contingency curve was completed by placing the defined maximum, minimum, and expected levels of performance for each indicator together with their corresponding effectiveness values on a contingency template and extrapolating a straight line between these three points.

At this stage of the ProMES development process, contingency development departed from the procedure recommended by Pritchard and colleagues (1988, 1989). The contingencies generated by technicians in the present study were essentially linear, with a single inflection point at the zero effectiveness level. In contrast, Pritchard and his colleagues suggest that the generation of full nonlinear contingencies is preferable to the generation of abbreviated contingencies because full nonlinear contingencies should more closely reflect the relationship between the level of indicator performance and the effectiveness of that amount. The implication is that of the two contingency formats, full nonlinear contingencies should represent the more accurate indicators of performance.

Figure 7–1 shows that abbreviated contingencies are essentially simplified versions of full nonlinear contingencies. Although both contingency formats have a major inflection point at the zero level of effectiveness, the abbreviated contingency illustrates a linear relationship between raw performance and effectiveness from the zero level to the extremes.

According to Pritchard and his colleagues, full nonlinear contingencies are generated by taking individual indicator points between the defined maximum, minimum, and expected levels of performance and assigning each an effectiveness value. In the present context, this process was rejected for two reasons: first, because the design team experienced difficulty in reaching consensus on the effectiveness values of indicator amounts between the maximum, minimum, and expected levels, and second, because the present study was aimed at comparing abbreviated and full nonlinear contingencies. For the purpose of this comparison, abbreviated contingencies were generated in group 1, while full nonlinear contingencies were generated in group 2. The full nonlinear contingencies in group 2 were generated by the group supervisor in a later step of the ProMES development process.

Group 1: Sample abbreviated contingency

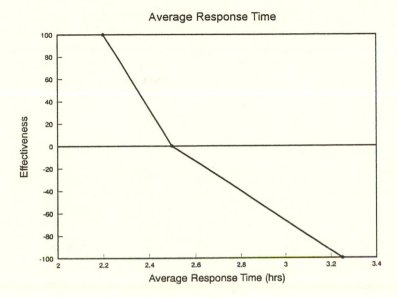

Group 2: Sample full nonlinear contingency

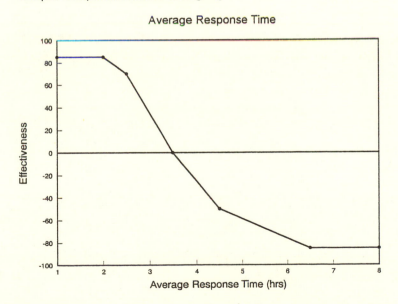

Figure 7–1   Sample Abbreviated and Full Nonlinear Contingencies

Management Review

Results of the ProMES development meeting were presented to management and group supervisors for review. For both groups, modification was considered necessary.

Group 1 contingency modification. In group 1, the maximum, minimum, and expected levels of group performance were modified by the group supervisor in consultation with higher management to levels considered by the organization as more realistic given the context of the group's operation. During the management review process, the group supervisor, together with higher management, proceeded to construct contingencies for each indicator in the same manner as outlined above.

Two of the outcomes of the management review process were particularly salient. First, not all contingencies required modification. Call back rate and average repair time remained unchanged. Of the remaining contingencies, the expected levels of performance (and, to a lesser extent, the maximums and minimums) defined by the design team required considerable adjustment. Specifically, expected average down time was adjusted from eight hours (design team) to five hours, successful call rate from 80 percent (design team) to 85 percent, and average response time from 5 hours (design team) to 3.5 hours.

The second outcome of the management review was a management decision to eliminate the quantity indicator of percent call demand met. The logic underlying this decision was twofold: first, the group consistently met close to 100 percent of call demand, and second, failure to meet close to 100 percent of call demand would result in a dramatic increase in the average down time indicator. Given the relationship between average down time and percent call demand met, it was decided that the information provided by the quantity indicator was redundant.

Group 2 contingency modification. In group 2, the expected levels of group performance for two of the indicators were also modified by the group supervisor in consultation with higher management. Expected average down time was modified from 5 hours (design team) to 6.5 hours, and expected average response time was adjusted from 3.5 hours (design team) to 4.5 hours. The remaining indicators remained unchanged. As with the management review process in group 1, higher management and the group supervisor proceeded to construct contingencies for each indicator. Unlike the abbreviated contingencies in group 1, the group 2 supervisor and higher management generated full nonlinear contingencies in the manner recommended by Pritchard and colleagues (1988, 1989). This approach was adopted because the design team itself experienced difficulty when this process was attempted. It is quite probable that this difficulty may have been overcome had the supervisor been a member of the design team itself. The supervisor's role in development and its implications are considered in more detail in the discussion.

In the later stages of the study, the performance of group 2 had improved to such an extent that further revision of the maximum, minimum, and expected values of indicators, together with their contingencies, was required. For example, expected average down time was adjusted from 6.5 hours to 5.5 hours; expected successful call rate was adjusted from 87 percent to 89 percent; and expected average response time was adjusted from 4.5 hours to 3.5 hours.

The process of a second revision of contingencies was somewhat a reversal of the development procedure. First, management and the group supervisor met and defined the new maximum, minimum, and expected levels of group performance. Second, the group supervisor met with the field technicians, discussed the outcome of the management review, and proceeded to construct the new contingencies with the group members.

ProMES Implementation

Following the management review and group supervisor revision of the contingencies, a ProMES implementation meeting was held with the field technicians. This meeting was attended by the entire group, including the field coordinator and group supervisor. At the implementation meeting, the revised contingencies were presented and discussion focused on the reasoning underlying management's revision of the expected levels of performance.

Feedback. After the revised contingencies had been presented to group members and their significance was understood, 19 weeks of prior performance data were presented to the group in both raw form and effectiveness value form using a trend graph.

Subsequent discussion of the data trends was led by the group supervisor, and areas requiring attention were identified. Following this discussion, group members were informed that at the beginning of every week they would receive a feedback report that illustrated group performance for the previous week. As with the feedback reports developed by Pritchard and colleagues (1988, 1989), field technicians were provided with feedback in both its raw performance data from and its corresponding effectiveness value form.

Following the implementation of the feedback system, a feedback meeting was held at approximately monthly intervals and attended by all group members. Group performance data for the previous month were presented at each feedback meeting, and discussion focused on identifying trends in group performance, identifying areas that required attention, and developing strategies aimed at improving performance.

Goal setting. Goal setting was implemented in group 2 after five weeks of performance feedback. Performance objectives for goal setting were defined at the feedback meetings. Difficult but realistic goals were set by the group under the guidance of the supervisor.

As with earlier feedback, a goal attainment feedback report was provided at the beginning of each week. It should be noted that this form of feedback allowed goal setting to be implemented without the need to adjust the expected levels of performance in the ProMES contingencies.

Goal setting was maintained in group 2 for the remaining seven weeks of the study. Three weeks following the commencement of the goal-setting intervention, the expected levels of performance defined in the ProMES contingencies for group 2 were adjusted. These adjustments were necessary because at this point of the study, the organization's expectations of the group's performance were identified to have changed following the transfer of two field technicians and one customer from group 1 to group 2. For reasons of customer service expectations, the organization did not consider its own performance expectations of group 1 to have changed.

Goals in group 2 were adjusted at a group feedback meeting by group members in conjunction with the group supervisor. Given that group members were aware that additional resources had been devoted to the group, the goal adjustment process was accepted as both necessary and allowing the opportunity for clarifying performance expectations.

Importantly, goal setting was not implemented in group 1. In group 1, large improvements in performance had been observed during the feedback phase of the ProMES trial. A management review of the progress of group 1 after six weeks of ProMES feedback revealed that the group was attaining close to the level of performance expected by the organization. Specifically, in the context of the group's work environment, these levels of performance were meeting the expectations of the group's customers. In brief, group 1 was performing at an acceptable level, and management agreed that this provided the opportunity for an experimental manipulation. Goal setting was added to the group 2 ProMES feedback system but not to the group 1 system. The purpose of this manipulation was to determine the degree to which a goal-setting intervention may (or may not) add to the productivity enhancement potential of ProMES.

Project Time Line

The ProMES development process for the two groups was undertaken concurrently in four major steps. The workflow analysis involved approximately 40 hours of work over a two week period. The questionnaire development, data collection, and analysis phase was completed in eight work hours over a further two weeks. Products and indicators were finalized in two meetings of two hours over a two week period. Contingencies were developed in two meetings of one hour over a two week period. The management review of the results of the design teams was undertaken in one meeting of two hours. Approximately two hours was devoted to explaining to the work group the finalized system and presenting initial feedback at the implementation meeting.

RESULTS

The ProMES study was conducted over a 31 week period.

In group 1, 13 weeks of baseline data were gathered from the organization's information system prior to ProMES development. The ProMES development process extended over a six week period. The feedback intervention was implemented following ProMES development, and group 1 received feedback for a total of 12 weeks.

In group 2, 14 weeks of baseline data were gathered prior to ProMES development. The ProMES development process extended over a five week period. The feedback intervention was implemented following ProMES development and maintained for five weeks. A goal-setting intervention was then added to the feedback. In sum, group 2 received feedback for a total of five weeks and feedback plus goal setting for six weeks.

The results presented below use three types of data. First, effectiveness as a percentage of maximum effectiveness is listed and serves as a weighted index of group productivity. This measure was derived using the procedure outlined by Pritchard and colleagues (1988, 1989). The sum of the maximum effectiveness scores for each indicator served as the denominator. The numerator was derived by summing the actual effectiveness scores for weekly performance. For example, in group 2, the sum of the maximums was an effectiveness score of 395. If the actual effectiveness in one week was 100, the effectiveness as a percentage of maximum measure would be equivalent to 100/395, that is, 25 percent. Where the sum of the effectiveness scores was negative, it was divided by the sum of the minimums and the resultant value was given a negative sign. Second, changes in the effectiveness data for individual indicators are also provided. Finally, to put the changes in effectiveness into a more practical perspective, mean changes in raw indicator data for individual indicators are also listed.

Group 1

The upper half of Table 7–1 lists the group 1 changes in average effectiveness as a percentage of maximum effectiveness, individual indicator effectiveness, and raw performance changes across the baseline, development, and feedback periods of the study. To illustrate what is critical in the tale, consider the average down time indicator in isolation. The baseline raw data show that the average down time in the 15 weeks prior to ProMES development was 5.33 hours. The feedback column shows the average down time in the 12 weeks following ProMES implementation was 4.83 hours. The corresponding effectiveness value changed from −48 to −13, implying that performance on the average down time indicator had improved from a level well below performance expectations to a level of performance much closer to these expectations. Similar trends are observed on the remaining indicators. Table 7–1 shows that improvements in the performance of group 1 across all indicators were observed through the development and feedback phases of the study.

Note that because the effectiveness as a percentage of maximum effectiveness measure provides a weighted index of productivity across each important aspect of work group functioning, this measure provides a good summary of the pattern of change in group performance over the course of the study. Inspection of Table 7–1 reveals that effectiveness as a percentage of maximum effectiveness changed from an initial average of −44 prior to the development of ProMES to −5 during the ProMES development phase and to an average of +4 during feedback. In brief, by the end of the present study, group productivity had improved from a level well below that expected of the group prior to ProMES to a level more closely approximating the organization's expectations.

Group 2

The lower half of Table 7–1 lists the group 2 changes in average effectiveness as a percentage of maximum effectiveness, individual indicator effectiveness, and raw performance changes across the baseline, development, feedback, and goal-setting periods of the study. Improvements in the performance of group 2 across all indicators, except call back rate, were observed following the implementation of the feedback and goal-setting interventions.

Although the raw changes in performance in group 2 appear much larger in magnitude than those observed in group 1, the actual changes in performance as measured by the effectiveness as a percentage of maximum effectiveness measure are very similar in magnitude to the changes observed in group 1. This result is consistent with the fact that there was greater room for improvement in group 2 than group 1. In brief, productivity improved from levels well below that expected at the beginning of the study (effectiveness = −36) to levels approximating that expected of the group toward the end of the study (effectiveness = +1).

Combined Results: Group 1 and Group 2

Figure 7–2 illustrates the trend in overall effectiveness averaged across group 1 and group 2 for the pre-ProMES development, development, and post-ProMES development and implementation periods of the study. Given that groups 1 and 2 are part of the same service unit,

Table 7–1 Group 1 and Group 2 Indicators Means by Treatment in Both Raw Data and Effectiveness Value Form

Group 1: Indicator Means by Treatment

Indicator	Baseline		Development		Feedback	
	Raw	*Effectiveness*	*Raw*	*Effectiveness*	*Raw*	*Effectiveness*
Effectiveness as a percent of maximum	n/a	-44	n/a	-5	n/a	+4
Down time	5.33 hr	-48	4.49 hr	+6	4.83 hr	-13
Successful call rate	78.0%	-64	82.0%	-21	83.0%	-10
Response time	2.85 hr	-21	2.51 hr	+11	2.39 hr	+41
Call back rate	16.6%	-26	12.3%	-19	12.3%	-1
Repair time	1.48 hr	-33	1.27 hr	0	1.30 hr	-3

Group 2: Indicator Means by Treatment

Indicator	Baseline		Development		Feedback		Goal Setting	
	Raw	*Effectiveness*	*Raw*	*Effectiveness*	*Raw*	*Effectiveness*	*Raw*	*Effectiveness*
Effectiveness as a percent of maximum	n/a	-36	n/a	-32	n/a	-2	n/a	+1
Down time	12.13 hr	-52	11.58 hr	-49	6.92 hr	-11	6.55 hrs	-2
Successful call rate	82.0%	-21	83.0%	-10	88.0%	2	87.0%	-1
Response time	5.09 hr	-54	4.70 hr	-28	3.19 hr	23	2.93 hrs	+40
Call back rate	4.7%	-12	6.3%	-27	6.9%	-18	6.4%	-28
Repair time	1.19 hr	-6	1.29 hr	-16	1.19 hr	-6	1.20 hrs	-6

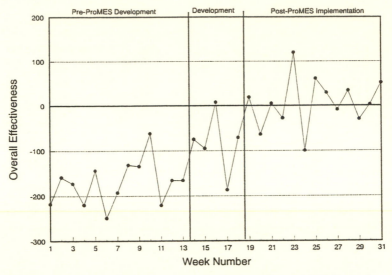

Figure 7-2   Overall Effectiveness Averaged across Group 1 and Group 2

these averaged results provide management with meaningful information relating to trends in the unit's productivity. Because of the initial
large negative effectiveness values illustrated in Figure 7–2, it is
immediately obvious that the service unit's performance prior to
ProMES development was at a level well below the organization's
expectations. Clearly, unit performance improved markedly over the
course of the study to reach a much more acceptable level. The
magnitude of this improvement becomes more salient when monthly
performance data are inspected in their raw form. Such data are
displayed in Figure 7–3.

Figure 7–3 illustrates monthly trend data averaged across groups 1
and 2 for measures the organization placed most emphasis on prior to
the development of the ProMES system. The measures contained in
Figure 7–3 include average down time, average puzzle time, and
average response time. Puzzle time represents time unaccounted for
(lost time) per service call and is highly correlated with the successful
call rate. Note that although the organization has traditionally tracked
puzzle time, the measure was not included as a ProMES indicator,
because successful call rate was considered as a more tangible and
relevant area for the groups to direct their attention. Given the
organization's historical tracking of puzzle time, however, management
considered it appropriate to examine puzzle time in evaluating the
success of the ProMES system.

Inspection of Figure 7–3 reveals a very stable baseline for each
measure followed by a marked trend toward improvement subsequent

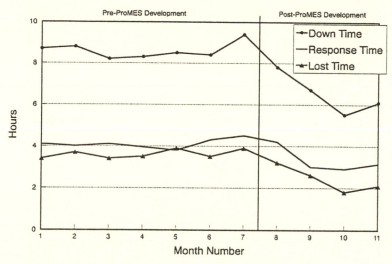

Figure 7-3 Group 1 and Group 2 Pre- and Post-ProMES Average Performance by Month

to the development and introduction of ProMES. Down time fell from a baseline average of approximately nine hours to six hours by the end of the study, an improvement of around 30 percent. Puzzle time fell from approximately 3.5 hours pre-ProMES to 2 hours post-ProMES, an improvement of approximately 40 percent. Finally, average response time fell from an average of four hours pre-ProMES to three hours post-ProMES, a performance improvement of 25 percent. Clearly, large performance improvement was observed across all measures following the development and implementation of ProMES.

Problems of Causal Attribution

There can be little argument that improvements in the productivity of both group 1 and group 2 were observed over the course of the present study. However, the extent to which these improvements can be attributed to the development and implementation of ProMES itself must be questioned by identifying and examining other variables that may provide plausible alternative accounts of the present findings.

The issue of causality was examined in some detail in the original study (Bonic, 1992). Importantly, this examination of alternative accounts for the pattern of productivity improvement observed led to the conclusion that the most plausible account was one that attributed causality to ProMES development and the ProMES-based feedback and goal-setting interventions. Briefly, the pattern of productivity improvement could not be explained by fluctuations in work load, resources, or any general organizational trend toward improvement performance. In fact, none of several comparable service units showed concurrent improvements in productivity.

DISCUSSION

The purpose of this research was twofold: first, to examine the extent to which ProMES successfully could be developed and implemented in the Australian business context with computer service technicians, and second, to examine issues arising from the development of a full nonlinear versus an abbreviated contingency-based ProMES system.

ProMES and Computer Service Technicians

Pritchard and his colleagues first developed, implemented, and evaluated ProMES in the U.S. military context. In the current study, ProMES was developed and implemented successfully in the Australian division of a multinational computer systems organization with little adaptation to the procedures advocated in the original ProMES study.

In both group 1 and group 2, significant improvements in productivity were observed. Although certainly impressive, the magnitude of productivity enhancement obtained in the present study was somewhat smaller than that obtained by Pritchard and colleagues (1988). It should be noted, however, that the Pritchard and colleagues study was carried over a 23 month period. The present study was completed after seven months. Furthermore, the present research was carried out in an organization that already possessed a sophisticated information system; Pritchard and colleagues make no mention of their organization possessing a similar system.

Importantly, the present research demonstrated that ProMES has the potential to facilitate meaningful increases in the productivity of an organization that already possessed an information system. This suggests that the information system was neither being used to its full potential nor providing workers with the information required to improve their performance. As well as providing management with diagnostic information and clarifying the roles and priorities of work groups, it is quite likely that ProMES (particularly through the ProMES-based feedback and goal-setting interventions) facilitated better and more appropriate use of the organization's information system.

To summarize, the evidence reviewed in the results suggested that the observed productivity increases would not be attributed to changes in work load, the investment of additional resources, or any general organizational trend toward improvement. The most plausible account for the pattern of productivity improvement observed is one that attributes causality to ProMES and the ProMES-based feedback and goal-setting interventions. As evidence by the present productivity gains in a computer services organization that already possessed an information system, the ProMES approach to productivity measurement and enhancement may be adapted quite easily for successful application in organizations in different contexts and with different structures.

Full Nonlinear versus Abbreviated Contingencies

The second issue examined concerned the ProMES contingencies. Could any meaningful difference in either the ease of ProMES development and implementation or the magnitude of productivity enhancement be attributed to a full nonlinear contingency-based ProMES system over and above an abbreviated contingency-based system? Through a qualitative examination of the pattern of results and consideration of anecdotal evidence, some relevant conclusions were drawn.

First, because large productivity improvements were observed in both groups, there appears little reason to suspect that a full nonlinear contingency-based ProMES system is likely to provide the organization with greater enhancement of productivity than is an abbreviated contingency-based system. Second, because the process of developing abbreviated contingencies is simpler and less time-consuming than is the process of developing full nonlinear contingencies, an abbreviated contingency-based system may have a cost advantage over a full nonlinear contingency-based system.

Significantly, although Pritchard and colleagues (1988, 1989) argue that a full nonlinear contingency-based system has the advantage of providing a more accurate measure of effectiveness, it may also be open to greater distortion than an abbreviated contingency-based system. Specifically, if ProMES is to be expanded to measure the productivity of many, or even all, groups within an organization, some consistency of contingency generation is required if the resultant effectiveness values are to be comparable among groups. A full nonlinear contingency generation procedure allows groups to alter the slope of curves to maximize positive effectiveness for performance improvements and minimize negative effectiveness for performance declines. Although the contingency generation procedure advocated by Pritchard and his colleagues is designed to counter such unsystematic distortion through the process of management review, a problem of consistency is likely to arise if different management groups (e.g., management from different branches of the organization) review contingencies from different work groups. In contrast, the abbreviated contingency generation process is less likely to produce such contingency distortions within, because only maximum, minimum, and expected levels of performance are identified and a connecting line is extrapolated between these points to determine contingency slope.

In summary, the present study suggests that the use of abbreviated contingencies will not significantly hinder the ProMES development process or limit the potential for productivity enhancement.

Other Issues

As well as providing data that allowed closer examination of the above research questions, the present study also drew attention to other ProMES related issues. Closer examination of these issues is likely to expand our knowledge of ProMES and increase its efficacy as both a productivity measurement system and as a productivity enhancement intervention.

ProMES Development and Productivity Enhancement

One such issue relates to the mechanism underlying the productivity improvement observed during the ProMES development phase in group 1, where effectiveness as a percentage of maximum effectiveness increased to –5 from a baseline of –44. This increase in productivity was observed prior to the implementation of the feedback intervention. Close examination of the development process reveals that, for three reasons, the observed productivity improvement was not entirely unexpected. First, the ProMES development process draws attention to the need for increased productivity. Second, the ProMES development process provides management with the opportunity to clarify the work group's performance expectations by providing the group with an opportunity to examine the outcome of the magnitude, direction, and persistence of its current efforts. Third, in the present study, the organization's information system was available to the group supervisor to assist in examining group performance during the ProMES development phase; this condition may have been contaminated by feedback. Accordingly, it is quite expected that improvements in performance would result from a development process that facilitates such an examination of performance.

Curiously, although improvements in productivity during the development phase were not unexpected, there was no reason to expect that group 1 would show improved productivity during the development phase while group 2 (baseline effectiveness as a percentage of maximum = –36; development effectiveness as a percentage of maximum = –32) would not. Anecdotal evidence offers a plausible explanation for this result and raises the issue of goal commitment in moderating the success of ProMES.

The Role of Commitment

Group 1 and group 2 were led by different group supervisors. Where the group 1 supervisor quickly realized the potential of ProMES and was eager to embrace the system, the group 2 supervisor was much less interested. In effect, the group 1 supervisor displayed greater commitment. Given that field technicians received no performance related feedback during ProMES development, it is likely that any improvements in group performance during this phase of the study would be largely a function of the supervisor using the information system to more closely examine the magnitude, direction, and persistence of the work group's efforts and, consequently, better motivating and directing the work group. Although such a process was likely to have occurred in group 1, it is unlikely to have been duplicated in group 2 because of an apparent lack of supervisor commitment during this phase of the study. By implication, a lack of supervisor commitment should have moderated the performance of group 2 during the intervention phases of the study. However, the results show no such moderation. In accounting for this inconsistency, it is necessary to examine more closely the commitment variable.

Most research examining the relationship between commitment and performance is found in the goal-setting literature. The consensus is that commitment is a moderating variable (Locke, Latham, & Erez, 1988); without goal commitment, goal setting is unlikely to be a successful intervention. Drawing further on the goal-setting literature, the two most salient methods of gaining employee commitment to a goal are through employee participation in goal setting and through goal assignment from a person(s) in authority. Both of these methods of attaining commitment to ProMES were available during the development process; a third method was available during the intervention phases.

Commitment to the ProMES system during development was attained through an interaction between participation on behalf of work group members and strong direction on behalf of management. After the interventions were introduced to the group, the feedback itself served to commit both the group supervisor and work group members to ProMES and the goal of productivity improvement. The ability of feedback to generate commitment was largely a function of the method in which it was provided. Management, the group supervisor, and field technicians received weekly feedback reports. Feedback reports provided an objective history of work group performance. Because these same feedback reports were made available to management, neither the group supervisor nor the field technicians could ignore their concrete performance history. In effect, feedback generated commitment to ProMES by making the work groups accountable for their performance.

Deviation from the Standard ProMES Procedure

There were a number of areas in which the present study differed from the typical ProMES application, and these deserve discussion.

Development differences. As noted earlier, unlike the typical ProMES development procedure, the work group supervisor was not a member of the design team. The rationale for this deviation was largely in response to organizational culture. Specifically, management in the organization did not have a history of being participative in style. It was agreed by management prior to ProMES development that the design teams would develop the system in the absence of the group supervisor and management. From management's perspective, it was hoped that this approach would elicit the group's expectancies without the possibility of being significantly influenced/hindered by the presence of the supervisor.

Although the design team did develop the system, it is noted that a number of modifications were made later during the management review. The implication is that without the supervisor, the design team did not have sufficient knowledge of the work group, its objectives, and its role in the broader organizational context to generate contingencies that more closely approximated management's views. In hindsight, it is likely that the inclusion of the supervisor as part of the design team would have significantly improved the contingency generation process.

Consistent with the above development approach and consistent with organizational culture, management review and modification were undertaken without the presence of the design team. Following management review, the modifications were then put before the design team and the changes and reasoning behind the changes were discussed. The design team's reaction to the modifications was interesting: the changes were accepted, and it appeared unlikely that commitment to the system was in any way diminished. Three reasons likely contributed to this reaction. First, the modifications made were realistic, and the expected levels of performance defined were attainable. Second, the reasoning behind the modifications was sound, that is, the changes in expected levels of performance were explained in the context of the broader organization, including reference and discussion relating to the group's historical levels of performance, customer expectations (as defined by contract), and the amount of resources devoted to the group. In brief, the discussion significantly clarified the group's role and the organization's expectation of the group. Finally, the management review and modification approach was consistent with the organization's more directive culture.

A conclusion drawn from this experience with ProMES is that the development procedure should not be rigid but, rather, flexible enough to be adapted to match the organization's culture. It should be remembered that although work group participation is likely to increase understanding, acceptance, and commitment to ProMES, the system also needs to gain management acceptance and commitment.

The expected level of performance. Pritchard (1990) defines a zero or expected level of effectiveness as performance that is neither good nor bad, where one would neither be praised for nor complimented about. In the present study, a more literal definition of expected was adopted. Specifically, in the present study, attaining the expected level of performance was considered to be good performance. To keep consistency between the two groups in defining expected levels of performance, variables considered included the group's historical level of performance, work group customer expectation, organizational policy, and the amount of resources devoted to the group. The resultant expected levels of performance were difficult but attainable.

The reasoning underlying the present interpretation of the expected level of performance was considered a logical extension of the purpose of the system's implementation. From the organization's perspective, ProMES was implemented with the aim of enhancing productivity. ProMES does have parallels with goal-setting theory and its approach to productivity enhancement. From goal-setting theory, we know that clearly specified, difficult but attainable goals lead to the greatest performance enhancement. We also know that goal acceptance and goal commitment are important moderating variables in the goal difficulty— performance outcome relationship. ProMES generates acceptance and commitment to an expected level of performance. It was hypothesized that gaining commitment to an expected level of performance that was defined as good rather than defined simply as acceptable (neither good nor bad) would more likely result in significant enhancements in productivity. As the result of the present study showed, significant improvements in productivity were obtained using this more difficult definition of the expected level of performance.

Feedback. In the original ProMES evaluation (Pritchard et al., 1988), work groups received performance feedback at a monthly feedback meeting. In the present study, performance feedback was given to the work group on a more regular basis. Each week, the work group members received a group performance feedback report. Once a month, work group members were brought together to discuss performance trends and to develop performance improvement strategies. This approach was adopted for two reasons. First, from a performance improvement perspective, the feedback literature consistently shows that the closer performance feedback is to the event, the more relevant and useful is that feedback. In the present organization, it was both appropriate and possible to give work groups weekly feedback. Second, monthly feedback meetings were the most practical and acceptable to both the work group and management. Weekly feedback meetings were not considered simply because they would have too often interrupted the work group's functioning.

Maintenance of ProMES

A final issue deserving some discussion relates to the degree to which the ProMES system was maintained following the departure of the researcher. In the present study, the researcher gathered, processed, and returned performance related information to the work group, supervisors, and management. Upon the researcher's departure, the technical manager (one level of management above the group supervisors) assumed this role. Within a few weeks of the researcher's departure, the organization underwent an extreme restructuring and downsizing. It was at this stage that the ProMES system ceased to operate.

The failure of ProMES to be maintained beyond a few weeks following the researcher's departure highlights the importance of management commitment to the system's survival. Given the dramatic changes that occurred following the researcher's departure, it is clear that, in the context, ProMES was not a management priority and, subsequently, the support required to maintain the system was not provided.

On a more encouraging note, some five months after the researcher's departure, the field coordinator from group 2 was promoted to the position of group supervisor, and on his initiative, ProMES was reintroduced.

Twelve months after the initial study, the organization's management expanded the application of the system. ProMES is currently functioning in eight service groups across six Australian states. For group feedback purposes, indicator performance data are collected, processed, and distributed by the quality manager at the head office. Feedback is now provided on a monthly basis, it incorporates a monthly goal-setting component, and it has proved particularly useful as a tool for identifying problem areas and, subsequently, acting as a catalyst for problem solving aimed at enhancing group productivity.

In summary, the procedure adopted in developing and implementing ProMES in the present study differed in many respects from the typical ProMES approach. Some particularly important observations were made. First, it is likely that including the work group supervisor as part of the design team would be of significant benefit in developing the system. Second, it is important to keep the ProMES development approach consistent with the organization's culture or norm; ProMES must be accepted not only by work group members but also by supervisors and management. Finally, as evidenced by the decline and gradual reintroduction of ProMES following the researcher's departure, management commitment to ProMES is critical to its maintenance.

CONCLUSION

ProMES-based feedback and goal-setting interventions were implemented in the context of an Australian computer services organization with the aim of modifying work group behavior and enhancing work group productivity. The results of the intervention were certainly impressive. Dramatic increases in productivity levels were attained in both of the groups in which ProMES was developed and implemented. Importantly, the evidence reviewed suggested that the productivity increases observed could not be attributed to changes in work load, the investment of additional resources, or any general organizational trend toward improvement. The most plausible account for the pattern of productivity improvement observed was one that attributed causality to ProMES and the feedback and goal-setting interventions employed.

REFERENCES

Bonic, I. D. (1992). *ProMES: The use of group-based feedback and goal setting interventions in enhancing productivity*. Unpublished master's thesis, University of New South Wales, Sydney, Australia.

Locke, E. A., Latham, G. P., & Erez, M. (1988). The determinants of goal commitment. *Academy of Management Review, 13*, 23–39.

Pritchard, R. D. (1990). *Measuring and improving organizational productivity: A practical guide* (p. 248). New York: Praeger.

Pritchard, R. D., Jones, S. D., Roth, P. L., Stuebing, K. K., & Ekeberg, S. E. (1989). The evaluation of an integrated approach to measuring organizational productivity. *Personnel Psychology, 42*, 69–115.

Pritchard, R. D., Jones, S. D., Roth, P. L., Stuebing, K. K., & Ekeberg, S. E. (1988). The effects of feedback, goal setting, and incentives on organizational productivity. *Journal of Applied Psychology Monograph Series, 73*, 337–358.

8

Individual and Group Productivity Enhancement in a Service Setting

Ad Kleingeld and Harrie van Tuijl

This chapter focuses on the development and implementation of ProMES for about 300 technicians servicing photocopiers at client offices throughout the Netherlands. The case illustrates some of the complexities of real-life work situations ProMES can handle. Three points will be dealt with in particular. First, because service technicians in this case were in some respects dependent on their colleagues but in other respects not, the system developed was partly based on individual performance data and partly on data gathered at the group level. Second, the differences among the photocopiers serviced by the department could be dealt with adequately only by a rather complex ProMES system: separate sets of contingencies had to be developed for each type of photocopier. Third, the relationship between ProMES and performance appraisal and reward issues had to be dealt with. The main reason was that, in this case, ProMES feedback reports contained precise information on the performance of individuals. Supervisors got copies of the feedback reports, that is, they knew exactly how well each technician was doing his or her job. This knowledge could not be ignored in the annual performance appraisal assessments. In addition, performance appraisal scores influenced the amount of bonus received by technicians at the end of the year. So, the issue of how to deal with ProMES scores in the context of performance appraisal and rewards had to be settled. At several places, we will refer to these three points.

We will successively describe some context information: the company, the immediate motivation for installing ProMES; the procedure followed in developing ProMES; the system and its implementation; the preliminary results; and, finally, some adaptations of the system instigated by those preliminary results.

SOME CONTEXT

ProMES was developed at the field service department of a company selling and servicing office equipment (faxes, laser printers, and photocopiers) in the Netherlands. The service department was chosen because of the management's intention to make service the company's competitive edge. Probably for the same reason, the management wanted to install a payment by results system in the service department, as they already had done in the company's sales department. ProMES could provide the performance data necessary for such a system. A final consideration was the technicians' recurring request for feedback. A large amount of performance data were gathered already by the company, but very few of these data were fed back to the technicians. Because the vast majority of service resources were spent on repairing and maintaining photocopiers, it was decided to leave faxes and laser printers out of the ProMES to be developed.

The service department was organized geographically. There were 11 geographical regions at the start of the project, and there are 14 now. Each was serviced by a group of approximately 20 technicians headed by a supervisor. The technician's job consisted of repairing machine malfunctions and doing preventive maintenance. The maintenance was done at the same time as the repairs, in that there was no prearranged schedule for preventive maintenance. The regular course of action ran more or less as follows: The client makes a phone call to the company, indicating that the photocopier is out of order. A first attempt is made to solve the problem by giving the client some instructions on the phone. If this does not succeed, the planning department instructs a technician to go to the client, repair the machine, and do the preventive maintenance suitable at that time, given the maintenance history of the machine. The technician drives to the client's location, repairs the machine, follows the prescriptions with regard to preventive maintenance, fills in a card containing information on the machine's repair history, and leaves for the next client. Before he does so, he makes a phone call to the home office, informing his dispatcher about the time he took to travel to the customer, the time needed to repair and maintain the photocopier, the spare parts he used, and the number of copies on the counter. He also orders additional spare parts as he runs out of stock. (The supplies asked for are delivered at the technician's home address by a special service.) The dispatcher tells him his next job, and off he goes. It is important to know that his next job can be at any client in his region: the planning department allocates technicians to jobs in such a way that agreements with clients regarding service within a certain time limit are fulfilled. For that reason, there are no fixed connections between technicians and clients: any technician can be allotted a particular repair, provided that he has the requisite knowledge. It is the planning department's responsibility to use the available technicians efficiently and, at the same time, to fulfill the company's obligations to the client.

The following are the most salient aspects of the technician's job: The job is a rather individual one. The technician works on his own, meets his colleagues only at monthly meetings, and meets his supervisor, at most, one or two times per month during a repair visit for a client. He is primarily dependent on his own knowledge and skill, but he can ask for help from a product support department when unable to solve a technical repair problem on his own. To a certain degree, he is dependent on others, too: he has a hard time repairing and maintaining a machine serviced on a prior occasion by a colleague who did a bad job. In such a case, he has to invest a lot of time and spare parts to make good the damage caused by his colleague. The way a photocopier is handled by a client is important, too, because it influences the occurrence of malfunctions. The timeliness with which the warehouse fulfills his requests for spare parts influences the technician's stock of parts he carries in his car and, in turn, the percentage of repairs that cannot be finished adequately because of lack of spare parts. In such cases, a return visit is necessary.

Some of the company's characteristics are quite relevant for understanding what happened during the process of development and implementation. First, there was a lack of communication both horizontally and vertically, caused by the nature of the service work to be done. Technicians had very few opportunities to communicate with one another and with their management: their supervisor and the levels above the supervisor. Because of this lack of communication, all kinds of prejudices arose and continued to exist. Second, the company's culture could be characterized as top down: decisions were made at headquarters, and technicians should do as they were told. In addition, there were large differences in culture between the sales and the service department and between headquarters and the field: sales and headquarters could be characterized as a white-collar culture, field service as a blue-collar culture. Also, feelings of inequity existed in the field service regions because sales representatives and managers could earn significant incentives, whereas service technicians could not.

PROCEDURE

The company had decided to develop ProMES for the service technicians of the field service department for the previously mentioned reasons. In addition, it was decided to first develop and implement the system in two regions and to install the system developed by the two trial regions later in the remaining regions, provided that the implementation in the two trial regions had been successful. The two regions were selected on several grounds. One was an urban region — Utrecht — the other a rural one — East. One was cooperative, the other one critical with regard to a system like ProMES. Next, it was decided to develop ProMES in each of the two regions separately, in monthly meetings during paid overtime hours, with design teams consisting of all the technicians of the region (about 20 people, all male), the region's supervisor, and two facilitators (this chapter's authors). This choice necessitated several interregion meetings in which consensus between the two regions had to be reached before elements of the system could be discussed with the management. The decision to work with all the technicians in the design team was made because of the highly isolated nature of the technician's job. Communication among job incumbents during working time simply was impossible. This decision resulted in extremely large design teams. To structure the discussions in these teams, several methods (to be discussed in more detail later) were used in addition to the normal interactive group discussion, such as nominal group technique and discussion in subgroups (at monthly meetings) and delphi method (to stimulate between-meeting information exchange). ProMES was first introduced to the supervisors of all regions, and their consent was obtained. Next, the two trial regions were informed. The reactions of the critical region were such that the management was urged to give a written guarantee that the system to be developed would not be used for performance appraisal or reward purposes until all parties concerned (i.e., both management and technicians) agreed that it would be a good thing to do so. After this guarantee was given, the development process was executed according to plan.

In each region, it took 13 meetings of about 2.5 to 3 hours each to develop the system. Because there were no meetings during holiday periods, the whole development process took 1.5 years, from June 1989 until September 1990. During this period, two students spent each, one after the other, eight months full time on the project to fulfill their master's thesis obligations. Their job was to prepare the meetings, to act as cofacilitators, to adapt the company's computerized information system to produce ProMES reports, and to do all the paperwork involved (e.g., reports, the delphi material).

The following products and indicators were developed.

1. Quality — to repair and maintain photocopiers as effectively as possible
    Indicator 1.1: mean copies between calls — the average number of copies made between a technician's repair visits and the first malfunctions after those visits
    Indicator 1.2: percentage repeat calls — the percentage of repair visits made by a technician within five working days of the original repair (because of inadequate repair)
    Indicator 1.3: compliance with preventive maintenance prescriptions — percentage of preventive maintenance procedures correctly followed

2. Cost — to repair and maintain photocopiers as efficiently as possible
   Indicator 2.1: parts cost per call — the average amount of money spent on replacement parts
   Indicator 2.2: labor time per call — the average amount of time used for repairing and maintaining photocopiers
   Indicator 2.3: percentage return calls due to car stock — the percentage of visits caused by a lack of spare parts in the technician's car stock
3. Administration — to keep records of repair and maintenance activities as accurately as possible
   Indicator 3.1: accuracy of history card — percentage of required information filled in correctly
   Indicator 3.2: completeness of claims — percentage of potential claims (parts replaced within their warranty period) submitted
4. Attendance — to spend the available time on work related activities
   Indicator 4.1: percentage of capacity used — the percentage of labor contract hours actually spent on the job
5. Ambassadorship — to behave as correctly as possible on the job
   Indicator 5.1: correctness of behavior — the percentage of important social behaviors demonstrated on the job.

Products and indicators were generated by the design teams according to the procedures described above. During the discussions, several products and indicators were rejected. For example, the proposed product "paper sales" (technicians were supposed to turn the client's attention to the fact that the company was selling paper, too) was rejected, because technicians considered this an activity that had nothing to do with their core responsibilities (repairing and maintaining photocopiers) on which they should spend their time and effort. When this issue was discussed with the management, the decision to exclude that product from the system was confirmed. The discussions with the management of the field service department were intense and valuable; this was partially because for many technicians, this was the first real contact with the managers.

Management expressed their appreciation for the work done by the design teams. Several important issues were settled in direct interaction. For example, management insisted on technicians wearing official company work clothes, but the work clothes were not delivered on time, so that technicians often had to do their job dressed unofficially. A similar problem had to do with the delivery of spare parts. Management asked for low percentages "return calls for car stock," but the warehouse made many mistakes in supplying the technicians. It was not possible to resolve all these issues, but they were brought to the attention of management and taken seriously by them. The controllability criterion that products and indicators should fulfill was discussed here. Responsibility was accepted by the technicians only in cases where solutions could be given or promised for the near future. One general solution offered was to use running averages over larger periods as measures in addition to scores per month. By taking averages, the influence of chance factors resulting in accidentally high or low scores is minimized, thereby, giving a more accurate picture of a stable "true" score.

It should be mentioned that the discussion with the management also resulted in the addition of an indicator. Indicator 1.3, "compliance with preventive maintenance procedures," was not in the list generated by the design teams. In discussing the products and indicators proposed to management, management felt that improving performance on the proposed indicators could be beneficial to the company in the short run but disadvantageous in the long term, because preventive maintenance could be neglected easily in favor of labor time and parts cost per call. The net short-term effect would be high scores on these indicators and acceptable scores on "mean copies between calls" and on "percentage repeat calls," both short-term quality indicators. A probable long-term effect would be a decrease in the general condition of the photocopiers, eventually resulting in high machine malfunctions. To prevent this, a new indicator was developed that measured preventive maintenance quality. The indicator consisted of a large checklist covering the main elements of the preventive maintenance procedures for each type of photocopier at several points in the machine's history. It was agreed that supervisors would check the preventive maintenance done by technicians by sampling. Because of the impracticality of taking large samples, it was decided that this indicator would result in a score for the region, not for individual technicians. The same decision was made with regard to "accuracy of history card" and "correctness of behavior," both indicators measured by means of a checklist filled in by the supervisor on a sample of technicians' visits.

Apart from the impracticality of gathering individual performance data on the checklist indicators continuously or by taking large samples, there was another reason to deal with these indicators at regional level. As mentioned above, technicians were, to a large degree, dependent on the quality of repair and maintenance done by their colleagues. If every technician does proper preventive maintenance and correctly records repairs done, parts replaced, and so forth, colleagues who have to do the next call are in a comparable starting position, that is, individual scores on indicators such as "labor time," "parts cost," "mean copies between calls," and "percentage repeat calls" are valid indicators for individual performance only if all technicians correctly execute the preventive maintenance and administration part of their job. So, group commitment with regard to decisions on these indicators is needed.

The four indicators "compliance with preventive maintenance procedures," "accuracy of history card," "correctness of behavior," and "percentage of capacity used" were indicators newly developed by the design team. The company already gathered information on the other indicators, but, as we shall see, there were doubts on the validity and meaningfulness of that information. The main reason for the latter point was that data concerning different types of photocopiers, that is, high volume, middle volume, and low volume machines, were not comparable. Even though this was known, the company simply added the scores across these types of copiers, resulting in feedback that was not meaningful. As will be shown, the contingency technique offered by ProMES can solve this problem: seemingly incomparable scores on identical indicators can be added in the same way as scores on different indicators.

OPERATIONALIZING THE INDICATORS

The operationalization of the indicators turned out to be a very time-consuming and complex activity. Between development meetings, the facilitators worked on the indicators with the help of product support specialists, supervisors, and a programmer. The results were reviewed by the design team during development meetings.

Level of Measurement

An objective of this ProMES system was to measure the productivity of service technicians both as individuals and as a group. The indicators under the control of individual technicians should be measured individually. For three indicators, however, it turned out to be too costly and time-consuming to do so. For that reason, it was decided to measure individual performance by sampling and to use the sampled scores as scores for the whole group.

Type Dependency

It was found that five indicators were "type dependent," that is, technical characteristics of each type of copier determined to a large extent the possible performance levels on these indicators. For example, historical data showed that on model X a mean copies between calls of 15,000 is an excellent result, whereas on model Y it is just average, and on model Z it is very bad. This has far-reaching consequences for the development of contingencies, because for these five indicators, a separate set of contingencies had to be developed for each of the 26 types of copiers included in the system.

Some indicators turned out to be similar to measures already in use in the service department. However, most existing measures were not suited for measuring productivity on an individual level, did not take into account differences between types of copiers, or included elements the technicians could not control. The existence of these measures meant that much of the data needed for the ProMES indicators were already being reported by the service technicians on a daily basis (e.g., how long did the visit take, which spare parts were used). Hence, the operationalization focused on defining the indicators and combining the data. All definitions refer to a measurement period of one month, which was customary in the service department.

There were ten indicators in all, three of which are measured type independently at the group level (compliance with preventive maintenance prescriptions, accuracy of history card, and correct behavior). The other seven indicators were measured individually. Five of these were type dependent (mean copies between calls, percentage repeat calls, labor time per call, parts cost per call, and percentage return calls due to car stock). The remaining two indicators, completeness of claims and percentage of capacity used, were type independent.

Difficulties in Operationalizing the Indicators

For a few indicators, the operationalization process was rather straightforward. Most indicators, however, posed serious difficulties, three of which will be discussed.

The first problem is related to the existence of return calls, visit(s) following the initial visit that are necessary to complete repairs and maintenance. These occur because the technician lacks spare parts or the time or knowledge to complete the initial call. In about 10 percent of the cases, the return call is handled by another technician, which complicates the allocation of labor time and spare parts usage to the individual technicians involved. Keeping in mind the objective of measuring individual productivity, it was decided to exclude calls involving more than one technician from the set of calls used to calculate parts cost per call and labor time per call. In that way, the results of individual technicians are not influenced by their colleagues.

The second complicating factor is a time-lag that sometimes exists before indicator values can be calculated. An example is mean copies between calls. In order to get this measure, the counters are compared for two consecutive calls on a machine, the difference being the number of copies made between the two calls. This is attributed to the technician involved in the first of the two calls. Averaged across calls, the mean copies between calls is calculated per type of copier. So, it is not possible to calculate the number of copies between calls until the next call has occurred. This makes it difficult to calculate the mean copies between calls for a technician at the end of a month, because it is very likely that not all of his repairs in that month have resulted in a new call. In fact, before the end of the month, only the less successful repairs will have resulted in new calls, the mean copies between calls of which would not be an accurate measure of the technician's performance. For this reason, the design team decided to attribute mean copies between calls results to the month in which they can be calculated. This is the only way to arrive at complete information, although part of the mean copies between calls results originated from months prior to the feedback period.

Third, it was found that there were no existing measures available for the indicators "compliance with maintenance," "accuracy of history card," and "correct behavior." Although some technicians were skeptical about introducing subjectivity into the system, the consensus eventually was that the region supervisor would be the person most capable of measuring to what extent the technicians met the demands posed by these indicators. He could do that on two occasions: during a visit, by watching the technician at work, or after a visit, by looking at the results of the work done by a technician the previous day. Yet, on practical grounds, it would be impossible to get an accurate monthly measure of all 20 technicians' individual performance. This is unfortunate, because two of these indicators reflect the interdependence between the technicians and could be used to insure the validity of performance data on the individual indicators. For example, a technician could obtain a high effectiveness score on labor time per call by carrying out only part of the maintenance procedure. This must be avoided, because it negatively influences the long-term quality of the machine. It was decided to measure the above indicators by sampling, resulting in group level indicator values that are allocated to the region as a whole and to all individual technicians. This, again, emphasizes the fact that the interdependencies among technicians are mainly reflected in the indicators "compliance with maintenance procedure" and "accuracy of history card" and that there is a joint responsibility to perform well on these indicators.

Most of the work on these checklists was done by the facilitators. Critical incident interviews were conducted with supervisors, field service management, and product support specialists. These resulted in two checklists per indicator, to be used during a visit and after a visit, respectively, and a procedure for applying these checklists.

Evaluation of This Phase

The operationalization process was characterized by a general lack of involvement of the design team. Most major decisions were made during the development meetings, but the facilitators, rather than the technicians, did most of the thinking and deciding. Although this was the only procedure possible, there was a risk of causing limited insight into the system, low perceived validity, and, as a consequence, low commitment on the part of technicians and supervisors.

There, indeed, was a temporary lack of insight into the system: during the last development meeting and the first feedback meetings, the facilitators were called upon to explain how certain indicators were operationalized. Most doubts about the validity of the indicators were taken away when the facilitators explained why certain choices were made. An important limitation in this respect is the fact that most indicators are not 100 percent controllable by individual technicians. The indicators were operationalized to exclude as many as possible uncontrollable factors from the indicators without diminishing the relevance of the indicator. The technicians agreed with most choices that were made. Some minor changes were suggested and incorporated into the system.

All in all, the indicators were operationalized satisfactorily. However, problems did occur in gathering data in accordance with these operationalizations. These are discussed with the feedback meetings.

CONTINGENCIES

The design of this stage differed in some respects from the usual approach (Pritchard, 1990). First, the first two stages in the development of the contingencies ("identifying maximums, minimums, and zero points" and "establishing maximum and minimum effectiveness scores") were switched. Second, scaling techniques were used extensively in the initial stages of establishing maximum and minimum effectiveness scores. Third, historical data were used to establish minimums, maximums, and zero points for the type dependent indicators. These differences will be discussed.

Establishing Maximum and Minimum Effectiveness Scores

Paired Comparisons

To get a first impression of the relative importance of the indicators, the technique of paired comparisons (Edwards, 1957) was used. In applying this technique, the individual technicians were asked the following questions for each pair of indicators: "Suppose you perform at the expected level (not good/not bad) on all indicators; on which of these two indicators would you want to perform maximally to maximize the value of your performance for the organization?" The results of these paired comparisons were converted into a ratio scale for maximum effectiveness scores by giving the maximum with the highest importance an effectiveness score of +100 and deciding on the effectiveness score of the least important maximum (close to but above zero). The latter effectiveness score was determined by asking how effective a maximum value on this indicator would be compared with the effectiveness of +100 for the most important maximum. The effectiveness scores in between are determined by the results of the paired comparisons. The minimum effectiveness scores were determined in an analogous way, the effectiveness score of the minimum with the highest importance being determined by the design team.

Ranking

A ranking technique was used in both regions, in addition to the paired comparisons. Each individual technician was asked the following question: "Suppose you perform at the expected level on all indicators. What is the first indicator on which you would want to perform excellently to maximize the value of your performance for the organization? What is the second one? Third one? etc." An analogous question was asked for the minimum effectiveness scores. By averaging the rankings across technicians, a ranking of maximum and minimum effectiveness scores was calculated.

Discussion

The initial effectiveness scores determined by paired comparisons and ranking were the starting point for group discussion on the exact positioning of minimum and maximum effectiveness scores. Two additional criteria were used in this discussion: First, the relative importance of the products should be correctly reflected by the indicators. This criterion was used because not all indicators are completely independent. For example, there is a dependence between mean copies between calls and percent repeat calls: if a technician succeeds in lowering his percent repeat calls, then his mean copies between calls will probably be higher. Consequently, the product being measured (in this case, quality) might be overweighed in the measurement system.

The importance of each indicator was determined by taking the range from minimum to maximum effectiveness score. This is a better way of establishing the relative importance of indicators than comparing the maximum scores, provided the minimum effectiveness scores also are determined with relative certainty. In addition, problems with determining the importance of indicators having a maximum effectiveness score of zero or with indicators having asymmetrical effectiveness scores (e.g., −65, +40) are avoided using this approach.

Second, maximum effectiveness on quality should compensate for minimum effectiveness on cost, and vice versa. The design team felt that there was a trade-off between the two products quality and cost. This trade-off should be reflected in the maximum and minimum effectiveness scores of the indicators belonging to those products. Therefore, a technician with maximum (minimum) effectiveness on quality and minimum (maximum) effectiveness on cost should have a total effectiveness score of about zero, indicating his performance is about average.

Identifying Maximums, Minimums, and Zero Points

During the development of the indicators, it became clear that the design team would not be able to identify maximums, minimums, and zero points for most of the type dependent indicators. Therefore, it was decided to generate historical data to help identify these points. The following decisions were made in generating the data:

The data should be collected per type of copier.

A minimum monthly number of 5 calls per technician per type of copier was used to avoid atypical results. For example, a technician performing a single call on type X might have either 0 percent or 100 percent repeat calls. Neither indicator value would be very informative.

The data should cover a one year period to make sure any seasonal trends are incorporated into the contingencies.

For all type of copiers, a frequency distribution of indicator values was generated for all five type dependent indicators.

In a discussion between management and the design teams, management stated that, in their opinion, the service technicians had performed according to expectations during the period concerned. Therefore, they suggested that the average national indicator values on all types of copiers be considered the expected level of performance (not good/not bad). The design teams agreed with this point of view. The facilitators suggested that the range of results in the frequency distribution might be used to determine minimum and maximum indicator values. Management and the design team agreed, indicating that this would be the only practical way to determine these values.

It has to be noted that it would probably be incorrect to base contingencies on historical data without having management and the design team ask themselves whether the resulting maximums, zero points, and minimums, which are of a descriptive nature, can be used normatively. In the worst case, this might result in contingencies formalizing ineffective policies. In this organization, the service department used procedures and working methods that were quite sophisticated when compared with many companies in the industry, so, there was no risk of reinforcing ineffective policy.

For the 26 types of copiers, minimum, maximum, and zero points were established for the five type dependent indicators, using historical data. For the remaining 50 types (constituting less than 10 percent of all calls), no accurate values could be established because of the very small amount of historical data. These types were excluded from the system.

The maximum, minimum, and zero points of the five type independent indicators were determined through discussion, as is usually done in a ProMES development.

Possible Consequences of Switching Stages

The first two stages in the development of the contingencies (identifying maximums, minimums, and zero points and establishing maximum and minimum effectiveness values) were switched to bridge the time needed to collect the historical data to be used to establish minimums, zero points, and maximums for the type dependent indicators. Two possible pitfalls were identified.

First, this sequence does not take into account indicators that have a maximum effectiveness score of zero (i.e., equal to the expected level). In this case, a few indicators might have had such contingencies, for example, compliance with maintenance procedure. Yet, when the technicians' attention was called to this, they held the view that they should have the opportunity to "score some points" on each indicator, that is, that every maximum should have a positive effectiveness score.

Second, this procedure also neglects possible differences among types of copiers concerning the relative importance of indicators, requiring different strategies. For example, type X may be a relatively labor-intensive type, where labor time is a very important cost indicator, whereas type Y may be a relatively parts-intensive type, where parts cost per call is a very important cost indicator. These differences would not be reflected in the system, because the maximum and minimum effectiveness scores of the indicators are the same for all types of copiers. Although these differences among types exist, it was decided by facilitators and management not to take them into account, because it was felt that the resulting complexities could not be handled.

Drawing the Complete Contingencies

The objective of this stage is completing the contingencies by filling in the remainder of the points. The total number of contingencies was 135, consisting of 130 type dependent contingencies (5 indicators for 26 types of copier) and 5 type independent contingencies.

In determining the precise form of the contingencies for the type dependent indicators, a well-known type was used as an example. Using transparencies, the facilitators started by simply drawing straight lines between minimum and zero point and between zero point and maximum. This caused an inflection point at the zero point for all indicators, which, according to the design team, would not correctly reflect the change in effectiveness going from an indicator value just below the zero point to one just above. This change in effectiveness should, in their opinion, be about linear. Keeping in mind that most technicians generally have indicator values around the zero point, it was decided to draw contingencies that were relatively steep around the zero point and relatively flat near the minimum and maximum. The exact location of the resulting inflection points was determined using the frequency distribution of historical indicator values. The design team decided that 10 percent of the observations should be above the upper inflection point and that 10 percent of the observations should be below the lower inflection point.

After the design team had developed the completed contingencies for this type of copier, the facilitators were authorized to develop the contingencies for the remaining 25 types of copier, applying the rules mentioned above. Figure 8–1 shows two type dependent contingencies (mean copies between calls and percent repeat calls) for two types of copiers (type 4100 and type 7150). Note that the shape of the contingencies is roughly the same for the two types. However, the type of copier determines to a large extent which indicator values correspond to minimum, zero, and maximum effectiveness.

The type independent contingencies were determined through discussion.

FEEDBACK REPORTS

Background

Generally, in designing feedback systems, interdependency between group members has to be taken into account. The ProMES system for these technicians is aimed at employees who work individually but are dependent on their colleagues. According to Matsui, Kakuyama, and Onglatco (1987), in a case of high interdependence among group members, effectiveness of task feedback is maximized when it provides information on individual and group performance. Just providing group feedback will not cause those individuals who are below target to improve their performance if the group is on target. Also, possibilities for social loafing are created. Just providing individual feedback will not cause individuals who are on target to improve their performance when group performance is below target. Mitchell and Silver (1990) argue that setting individual goals in an interdependent task results in lower performance than setting group goals, group goals plus individual goals, or no goals at all because of dysfunctional effects of competitive feelings, strategies, and behavior resulting from individual goals.

Keeping in mind the interdependence among technicians, it is clear that there should be not only an individual feedback report but also a group feedback report. From a practical point of view, a group feedback report is indispensable as a common frame of reference and a means to stimulate mutual help to improve the effectiveness of individual technicians and, thereby, the effectiveness of a group as a whole.

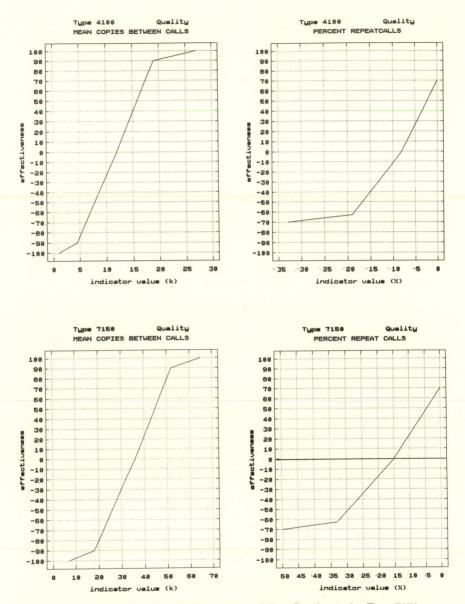

Figure 8–1   Two Contingencies Type 4100 and Two Contingencies Type 7150

Process

As a basis for discussion in the design team, the facilitators prepared a first draft of an individual and a group feedback report, based on their ideas on what would be useful feedback and how it might be presented. Three questions were posed by the facilitators, dealing with the feedback report, feedback meetings, and the extent to which the reports should be private or public.

1. "What information on your own performance and on the performance of others would you like to have?"

   After some discussion, there was agreement that every technician should have detailed information on his own performance. In addition, every technician should have information on group performance.

2. "How would you like to use the reports during the feedback meetings?"

   Initially, there was difference of opinion in the design team on how to use the feedback reports. Some technicians argued that every technician should judge for himself how to use the feedback reports. Only when the individual effectiveness score compares unfavorably with the region effectiveness score should a technician try to improve. Other technicians argued that communication and exchange of information among technicians would be essential to improve the effectiveness of individual technicians and, thereby, the region effectiveness, especially for the type dependent indicators. The knowledge and experience of technicians who perform well on these indicators should be shared with technicians who experience problems on these indicators. After ample discussion, the former technicians were convinced by the latter. In this discussion, the facilitators stressed that a feedback meeting should be a fact-finding exercise, not a search for excuses or a method for attaching blame. This might have put some technicians at ease who still appeared to have some fears concerning objectives and use of the feedback meetings. Finally, the design team reached agreement on the following general procedure during the feedback meetings:

   a. Type independent indicators: discussion in full session, conducted by the supervisor. The supervisor should, among other things, present his findings pertaining to the region indicator checklists.

   b. Type dependent indicators: discussion in small "type" groups (about five technicians). The groups should be discussing one or two types of copier on which all members receive feedback. Information per type of copier, especially information on individual differences, would be necessary in order to have fruitful discussions on causes of performance differences among technicians.

   c. Plenary announcement of the decisions and strategies arrived at in the "type" groups and written confirmation of decisions and points for attention in the next month(s).

3. "Who should get (parts of) the feedback reports?"

   There was agreement in the design team that the region supervisor should have access to all individual information. The general opinion was that the supervisor is responsible for the functioning of the technicians in his region. Consequently, he should be able to approach technicians individually in all matters regarding the functioning of individual technicians. The service management should receive region feedback reports, because they are responsible for the effectiveness of the regions as a whole.

A revised draft of the feedback reports, approved by the design team, was presented to management. Management agreed with most of the design team's suggestions on how to use the feedback reports. However, management objected to including detailed information per type of copier in the reports, because this would take too much time to program and maintain. As a consequence, some improvising would become necessary in order to get information per type of copier to be used in discussion in small "type groups."

Results: Feedback Reports

Resulting from this final stage in the development of ProMES are a three page individual feedback report and a two page region feedback report.

Moving Averages

During the operationalization of the indicators, it became clear that there would be large fluctuations in individual monthly indicator values (especially for percent repeat calls and percent return calls due to lack of car stock). The design team felt that feedback covering a larger period would be necessary to detect whether an indicator is really improving. A six month period was considered long enough to get a more stable measure. Using a moving average of six months also increases the reliability of the values of the indicators measured by the supervisor when it was doubtful whether the monthly sample would be large enough.

Percentage of Maximum Effectiveness

To be able to compare productivity of technicians, the monthly over-all effectiveness score is expressed as a percentage of maximum possible effectiveness. This index is a measure of how well the technician is doing relative to how well he could be doing. This measure, in addition to the total effectiveness score, had become necessary because the possibility existed that data on some indicators were not available in a certain month. For example, a technician may not have had the opportunity to claim spare parts; in this case, the indicator "percent claims" does not apply to him, and, therefore, neither an indicator value nor an effectiveness score can be obtained.

Individual Feedback Report

The first page of the report showed how the total effectiveness score was composed of the effectiveness scores of products and indicators for the past month and for the past half year.

The type dependent indicators were described on the second page of the report. The monthly indicator values for the type dependent indicators are calculated as follows: The total effectiveness score for an indicator was the weighted average of the effectiveness scores calculated for the different types of copiers. The weight was the number of calls the technician performs on each type, indicating the relative importance of each type of copier in that particular month. Only indicator values based on five or more calls on a type of copier are included. Suppose a technician performed 25 calls on type X with an effectiveness score of +20 on percent repeat, and 50 calls on type Y with an effectiveness score of −10 on percent repeat. In this case, the overall effectiveness score on percent repeat would be 0.

As explained, some of the results of mean copies between calls originated in previous months but were attributed to the month in which they can be calculated. Therefore, the calls used as weights in calculating the effectiveness score on mean copies between calls were not the same ones as the ones used as weights for the other type dependent indicators.

The moving average effectiveness scores were not directly linked to the moving average indicator values, because the contingencies were based on monthly indicator values. It would be incorrect to use these contingencies to calculate the effectiveness scores of indicator values averaged across a six month period, which have a smaller variance.

The composition of the effectiveness scores on the type independent indicators was shown on the third page of the feedback report.

The region feedback report was an aggregate of the feedback reports of all individual technicians in the region. All technicians contributed equally to the region report. The region effectiveness score on each indicator was the average of the individual effectiveness scores on that indicator (except, of course, for the group level indicators). The structure of the region report was identical to pages one and three of the individual report.

Programming of Feedback Reports

The technical implementation of the system was performed by a programmer from the data processing department, based on detailed specifications drawn up by the facilitators. This included programming of feedback reports and input and output facilities and took about six weeks. The facilitators entered the contingencies into the system. The result of the technical implementation is a program that generates (per month, per region) a set of individual feedback reports and a region feedback report.

FEEDBACK MEETINGS

Pilot Meetings

At the start of the implementation, the idea was to incorporate the feedback meetings into the monthly region meetings that were conducted by the supervisor. However, it was decided to hold the first feedback meetings separately, because they would take considerable time (about 2.5 hours). They were conducted in part by the facilitators, in part by the supervisor. The first five feedback meetings will be discussed.

Each month, data on the individual indicators and group indicators were collected, and feedback reports were generated for all technicians in both regions. The feedback meetings took place between the fourth and ninth workday of each month, to insure timeliness of the feedback. It was decided to distribute the feedback reports during the feedback meetings. After each feedback meeting, a memo was sent to all participants, confirming decisions and points for attention.

Procedure during Feedback Meetings

Region Level Indicators

The supervisor's observations during the past month pertaining to "compliance with maintenance procedure," "history card," and "ambassadorship" were discussed with the entire group. The supervisor explained how the effectiveness score on each indicator came about — using the contingencies — and compared it with effectiveness scores of previous months. He illustrated his evaluation with (anonymous) examples of positive and negative incidents he witnessed in the past month, some of which were shown on transparencies. Because of the routine nature of most elements of which the indicators consist, discussion was usually limited to directing attention to one or more areas that might be improved and getting group commitment on improving them.

Type Independent Individual Indicators

In the initial discussions on the indicators "percent capacity used" and "percent claims (value)," it became evident that there were major problems with the accuracy of the data.

In the case of "percent capacity used," the facilitators tried to solve the problem by introducing the system to the planners in the central planning department who are responsible for entering data on the technicians' activities into the information system. As a result, the planners decided to check on missing data at the end of each month. Meanwhile, a number of technicians kept a written log on all time spent in order to check on the ProMES data. This resulted in accurate data by the fifth feedback meeting. However, even after such efforts, this indicator still remains very susceptible to errors, which can be very detrimental at the individual level.

"Percent claims (value)" turned out to be a hopeless case, primarily due to the complexities of the claiming procedure used by the department handling the financial aspects of claiming, which prevented accurate feedback to individual technicians. In all, these problems took a lot of time during feedback meetings and left little time for discussing the type dependent indicators, which are considered the most important part of the system.

Type Dependent Individual Indicators

Individual interpretation of reports. During the third feedback meeting, the technicians were asked to individually interpret their own feedback reports using the contingencies and a description of the calculations involved. A number of questions were asked: Which aspects of the feedback report are not clear yet? What does the feedback report tell you about your strengths and weaknesses and about the strategies you follow? Are you satisfied with your effectiveness score? If not, what strategies could you try out to improve your effectiveness?

According to expectations, the lack of participation of the technicians in the operationalization of the indicators and the complexity of this part of the report led to a number of questions that could be answered by the facilitators, either immediately or after checking with the programmer.

There was, however, one exception: "percent return calls due to lack of parts in car stock." The objective of this indicator — measuring to what extent a technician avoids return calls by maintaining a sufficient level of car stock — could not be achieved. Technicians are allowed to order car stock parts together with non–car stock parts. It cannot be determined whether the car stock part was ordered to finish the call or as a normal resupply of the car stock, preventing accurate measurement of a technician's supply control.

Visual representation of effectiveness scores. Although most technicians agreed that the feedback reports were useful tools to monitor and improve performance, the reports were considered complex and difficult to interpret, especially for the type dependent indicators. For that reason, visual representation of effectiveness scores was added to the feedback reports. This consisted of line graphs representing individual and region effectiveness score over time for the type dependent indicators. Using these graphs, the technicians could see at a single glance where they stand, and whether they have succeeded in improving both in absolute terms (compared with zero point) and in relative terms (compared with the region as a whole). Unfortunately, it was not possible to have the computer system generate the graphs. Therefore, the technicians had to fill in these graphs themselves. Although some technicians found this to be useful, others had serious reservations about this "clerical" exercise. Although these graphs were very simple, a lot of technicians for the first time got an idea about which (often implicit) strategies they had been using. For example, some technicians appeared to have a "high quality–high cost" strategy, whereas others appeared to have a "low quality–low cost" strategy. Because quality and cost were about equally important in the system, both strategies could be, in principle, equally effective. By comparing their graphs with colleagues who have approximately the same models, strengths and weaknesses of individual technicians become apparent.

Discussion in small groups. The objective of small group discussion was learning about causes of performance differences among technicians by discussing individual performance data of those who work on the same types of copier. The focus should be on how to learn from each other and how to work more effectively and efficiently by using better strategies. Only during the fifth feedback meeting was this type of discussion attempted, and this was only partially successful. Some technicians did not like to talk about their individual performance. Yet, this had become necessary because of the lack of information per type of copier: technicians had to exchange a lot of information to get to know the extent of individual differences. Because of the limited experience with these discussions, no definite conclusions can be drawn.

In summary, the first five feedback meetings were partially successful. The part of the meetings that focused on the group indicators progressed satisfactorily. Yet, the recurring discussions on the validity of some of the indicators and lack of insight into the feedback reports hindered effective discussions on how to improve productivity on the individual indicators. Effects of the feedback meetings on productivity will be discussed later.

GENERAL INFORMATION

In this section, data are presented on time spent and costs involved in developing and implementing the system in East and Utrecht.

It took 16 months to develop the complete ProMES system, from June 1989 until September 1990. In both regions, there were 13 development meetings, including two review and approval meetings with management and one meeting to reach consensus between the regions. Developing the indicators turned out to be the most time-consuming activity, taking 2.5 and 3.5 meetings in East and Utrecht, respectively. The development of contingencies took three meetings in East and two meetings in Utrecht; these numbers would have been much higher if the scaling techniques had not been used. As is usually the case, developing products did not take a lot of time (1 meeting in East and 1.5 meetings in Utrecht). There were review and approval meetings with both regions about the products and indicators and about the contingencies. Before the second review and approval meeting, there was one meeting in both regions to achieve consensus on the system and one interregion meeting to prepare for the second review and approval meeting with management. In the last development meeting, the design team developed the feedback report and discussed ways of handling the feedback meeting. In both regions, 33 hours were spent on the development meetings.

Some costs involved in the development meetings were costs in connection with meetings (meeting rooms/aids/dinner) — approximately $16,000 — and payment of technicians and supervisors — approximately $13,000. The first feedback meetings were conducted in November 1990. Costs in connection with payment of technicians and rooms, aids, and dinner were about $1,000 per feedback meeting.

RESULTS

Design

Effects of the system are evaluated using a time series design with two experimental units (East and Utrecht) and nine control units (the nine other regions). In both experimental regions, there was only one month of baseline data (October 1990). In the experimental regions the system was implemented by means of monthly feedback meetings, during which there was feedback, but no specific goal setting. In the nine control regions, data on all indicators were collected, but no information was fed back. The supervisors of these control regions were familiar with the ProMES system. Their task was collecting the data on the group level indicators in order to get complete control group data. They received explicit instructions not to feed back any more information on these indicators than they had done in the past.

Evaluation of Effects

The period under consideration is October 1990 until May 1991. Feedback meetings in East and Utrecht took place from October until March. The meetings in April and May were used to evaluate the system. This will be discussed later, as well as results from June 1991 to June 1992.

Group Level Indicators

The group level data is shown in Figure 8–2, using a three month moving average. In the experimental regions (East and Utrecht), the total effectiveness score on the group level indicators improved remarkably after the first feedback meeting (from −33 to 25). In the following months, the effectiveness score dropped a little and stabilized around 15. Overall, the mean effectiveness of the experimental groups during the feedback period was 14, and the overall mean for the control groups was −16.

The effectiveness of East and Utrecht during feedback is significantly higher than the effectiveness of the control regions. The small increase in the control regions may have been caused by the fact that collecting data on the group indicators supplied the supervisors with useful information.

It should be noted that the feedback of information on group level indicators has had an immediate positive effect on productivity in Utrecht and a smaller and delayed effect in East. This was to be expected, because Utrecht's supervisor listed points for attention in a tell and sell way, which is considered effective, whereas the supervisor from East seemed less able to communicate the results clearly, especially during the first few feedback meetings.

Individual Level Indicators

*Type dependent indicators.** The experimental regions show a slight increase in productivity (about 10 points) compared with the control regions during the first six months of feedback (Figure 8–3, in which a three month moving average is used). During the first six months of feedback, the mean effectiveness of the experimental groups was 14 and the overall mean for the control groups was 17. The absence of large effects might be explained in part by the fact that relatively little attention had been paid to these indicators during the feedback meetings. Intensive group discussion, which was considered necessary to arrive at better strategies to improve productivity, hardly took place.

Type independent indicators. Because of difficulties in obtaining valid data on percent capacity used and percent claims, data are not available on these measures. However, there is some qualitative evidence of some improvement in East and Utrecht. According to the planning department, after feedback started, technicians from East and Utrecht were concerned about attaining 100 percent use of capacity: they would contact their dispatcher for an extra call if they felt they might not be able to "make their hours." Also, during the feedback meetings, it became clear that the technicians had been paying special attention to claims in order to check the validity of data that is fed back.

---

*Excluding percent return calls, because of difficulties in obtaining valid measures. Evaluation of effects includes those individual indicators that were considered valid at the start of the feedback period: mean copies between calls, percent repeat calls, parts cost per call, and labor time per call.

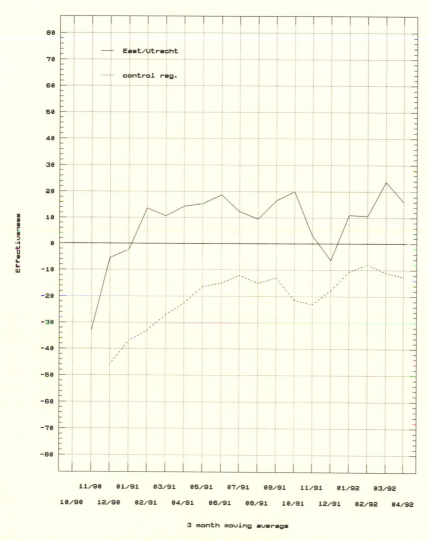

Maintenance Proc./History Card/Behavior

Figure 8–2   Effects of ProMES: Group Indicators

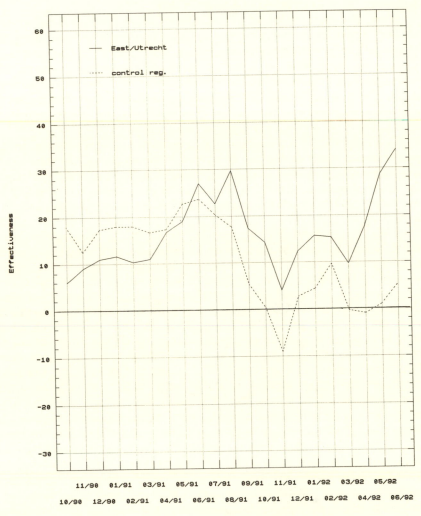

Figure 8-3   Effects of ProMES: Individual Indicators

DISCUSSION

Although there were improvements made in group level effectiveness, both management and facilitators were disappointed about the overall effects of the feedback provided by the ProMES on the performance of the technicians who had developed the system. The following steps were taken to deal with this.

First, the basic issue of potential performance improvement was settled: technicians were of the opinion that, notwithstanding the effects of performance-improving measures taken at earlier times by the management, there still was room for additional improvement. The management, when asked informally, was of the same opinion. Although they could not give indications as to the degree of potential performance increase, they could give anecdotal evidence indicating that at least some efficiency improvement had to be possible.

As a next step, a list of possible causes for the absence of substantial performance improvement on the individual indicators was made with the help of supervisors and technicians. The facilitators added some factors to the list on the basis of theoretical considerations. The factors were discussed in each design team and rated according to perceived importance.

After that, the design teams together with the facilitators developed the following list of solutions, which corresponded to the main perceived causes of the problem. First, a clear management statement on ProMES was asked for. Technicians felt somewhat left alone, working for a very long period on developing ProMES without getting regular signals from the management that this was still appreciated and in conformance with management policies and intentions. "Is this still serious, or do they have other interests and priorities right now? If so, why should we bother?" Second, technicians asked for the removal of invalid indicators from the feedback reports. Lots of discussion time during feedback meetings was being spent on validity issues. Many times, technicians, with or without the help of the facilitators, successfully demonstrated that data in the feedback reports were incorrect. This resulted in feelings of distrust that did not stimulate performance improvement initiatives. Besides, not much time was left in the meetings for discussing such initiatives. Third, feedback reports were considered too complex. Technicians got overall ProMES effectiveness scores on each indicator and per indicator, for each type of photocopier separately, both indicator scores and ProMES effectiveness scores. To be able to discern trends, graphic presentation of this information was necessary, but it was not available. Therefore, it was proposed to present information on the valid indicators both graphically and in tabular form. The fourth solution also concerned the feedback report. In the past, performance on the indicators measured by sampling at the level of the region were included in the individual feedback reports of each technician, thereby, suggesting that the scores represented the individual performance of the technician during the period concerned. Technicians refused to be held personally responsible for the performance of their colleagues and asked for removal of these indicators from their individual reports. The solution proposed was to present a feedback report containing the overall region's scores on all valid indicators (including those measured only by sampling) to the whole group and individual feedback reports containing only information on the valid individual indicators to each individual technician. These latter reports could be discussed in bilateral meetings of an individual technician with his supervisor, where as the region report could be discussed in a feedback meeting of all the technicians of the region with their supervisor. A fifth cause played a role but did not come explicitly to the surface until the management reacted to the first four solutions proposed by the design teams. It had to do with the issue of "What is in it for us, if we succeed in improving our performance?" In fact, opinions on this point were mixed, ranging from "You are already paid for doing a good job, so why should you get more for eventually really doing a good job?" to "If we improve, the company earns a lot more money, why shouldn't we get our share; besides, it stimulates us to have the possibility of a reward."

The proposed solutions were brought to the attention of the management, and management agreed to arrange a meeting at which they would make a statement and react to the concrete suggestions of the design teams. The management statement at these meetings came as a surprise. In short, they took the position that, although ProMES had not brought the improvements expected, it was still very worthwhile to have it and use it for performance appraisal purposes. This statement caused a lot of confusion, given the guarantee at the start of the project to not do such a thing unless all parties concerned would agree. In a long discussion, several of the ingredients presented before were combined into a plan acceptable to all. To begin with, although the technicians were outraged at first, they soon understood that the management proposal fitted in very nicely with their fifth problem, the absence of a link between performance improvement and reward. It was agreed that their annual bonus would be linked to their performance as measured by ProMES. This would be done by making ProMES an integral part of the performance appraisal system, by means of which the amount of annual bonus is determined. The exact procedure would be worked out and presented to the technicians for approval. A precondition was that only valid information would be used, so, the discussion continued on the other solutions proposed by the technicians. In fact, all suggestions made were accepted by the management. In short, agreement was reached on the content of the individual feedback reports: only the indicators agreed to be valid were included. These were "mean copies between calls," "percentage repeat calls," "parts cost per call," and "labor time per call." Thus, only the two more important products, quality and cost, are included in the individual reports. The region report will contain information on the overall score of the region on those four individual indicators and, in addition, the scores on "compliance with preventive maintenance," "accuracy of history card," and "correctness of behavior," the three indicators measured by sampling by the supervisor. The request for graphic information presentation was granted, too. Finally, it was decided to have regular meetings with the management in the future to evaluate the progress on the ProMES project and to discuss mutual affairs.

It is interesting to compare these events with the data. Figure 8–3 shows the performance of the two experimental regions and that of the control regions on the four individual indicators during the period in which feedback was provided (November 1990–April 1991), the period during which the discussions on lack of improvement took place (May–June 1991), and the period after the agreement with management was reached (July 1991–June 1992). It can be seen from the graph that whereas in the first period the experimental regions are below the controls, their performance is superior in the period after the final agreement with management was reached. In the 12 month period following this final agreement, the overall mean effectiveness of the experimental groups was 20 and the overall mean for the control groups was 3.

Thus, after removal of the main causes of dissatisfaction with the system, at least some improvement occurred on the individual indicators. In addition, the performance increase on the group indicators was maintained. A third positive result was the high opinion the management had for the measurement part of the ProMES system: they were convinced that the complexities of the job of the service technicians were accounted for extremely well by the system and that, after the revisions described before, the system was valid. They were particularly enthusiastic about the way a previously unsolvable problem — the incomparability of performances of technicians on different types of photocopiers — was taken care of by introducing a separate set of contingencies for each type of copier. Not only the management but also all parties concerned were of the opinion that the measurement system offered by ProMES was a sound one and far better than anything used in the past. This was the main reason for management and technicians to agree to use the technicians' individual ProMES scores as input for the performance appraisal system and as a basis for determining the amount of annual bonuses.

Although many positive results have occurred in this case, we are still left with the question of why there is far less performance improvement than expected. So, which are the factors inhibiting success? In discussing potential inhibiting factors, we would like to use the control loop model as a metaphor. The essential elements of a control loop are norms or goals, and feedback. ProMES can be considered a procedure to develop and implement accepted control loops. According to such a line of reasoning, ProMES can be effective only to the degree that the feedback provided by the system that is developed and the goals implied by the system are accepted by those who are supposed to control their own performance by means of the system. Discrepancies between accepted goals and accepted feedback would result in attempts to reduce these discrepancies by investing effort in strategies leading to high performance.

The above mentioned model helps us to explain why the effects in this case were small compared with what has been found in other cases. In other words, it helps us to organize what we have learned in this case. For several reasons, feedback acceptance might have been low. As discussed above, the feedback reports were rather complex. The provided indicator data for each of the types of photocopiers serviced by a technician and combined these data through the contingencies that belonged to each type into overall effectiveness scores for each indicator and each type of copier. In addition to that, six month moving averages were provided. Some information was given as raw indicator data, others in the form of effectiveness scores. For most indicators, information referred to the prior month. The mean copies between calls indicator, however, referred to an undefined period in the past. For these reasons, most technicians had difficulty understanding the system, notwithstanding the fact that they had assisted in developing it themselves. It will, no doubt, be difficult to accept and use feedback that one does not understand completely. Acceptance will also have been lowered by recurring discussions on the validity of some indicators.

For accepted discrepancies between feedback and goals to occur, in addition to accepted feedback, accepted goals are a prerequisite. It is doubtful whether there were accepted goals in this case. The main reason for this stems from the way in which the contingencies were developed. In estimating maximums, zero points, and minimums, the performance data from all (about 300) of the company's technicians working all over the Netherlands were used. By implication, many technicians belonged in the lower half of this distribution and many in the upper half. The former group will receive mostly negative effectiveness scores, the latter group, positive ones. For this reason, a lot of technicians will have difficulty in accepting the maximums, zero points, and minimums as relevant for themselves as individuals. As a consequence, they will have difficulty in defining relevant performance ranges for themselves. In other words, instead of helping them to establish specific, difficult but attainable goals, the contingencies might very well confuse technicians about the goals to be strived for.

Accepted discrepancies between feedback and goals should result in the decision to invest effort in a strategy that leads to a maximum performance increase in the future. In this case, however, to decide for such a strategy is a complicated affair, because the contingencies of all the types of copiers the technician is servicing have to be taken into account. In fact, there are several options. The technician could choose to improve his or her performance on the type on which improvement on all the indicators would result in the largest increase of his or her overall effectiveness score. Of course, he or she could decide to use some combination of the two options mentioned. Because of the large number of variables involved, it is very difficult to determine the best strategy to follow (it is even hard to determine a good or acceptable one). In fact, the feedback report should help the technician by providing predictions on how his or her overall effectiveness score would behave if one or the other strategy would be followed. However, the feedback report does not contain that facility yet, because we lack a good optimization model.

In conclusion, notwithstanding some significant problems during the development and implementation of the system, positive effects on productivity could be established, both on the group indicators and on the individual ones. Larger increases in productivity might be expected to occur as soon as the assumed problem of indeterminate individual goals will have been solved.

The main factor responsible for these results, in our view, is the participative approach advocated by ProMES and scrupulously followed in this case. Both the identification of the major problems and the discovery of solutions to those problems resulted from that approach. Solutions that appeared to be decisive were those that made the system acceptable to the technicians. Of prime importance in this respect was the measurement system's perceived validity, caused both by the way data from different types of copiers were combined into meaningful scores and by the management's concession to remove apparently invalid indicators from the system. Another important factor was the link that was installed between performance and reward at the request of the technicians. The technicians experienced a lot of recognition from the management by getting their problems accepted as real ones and by being taken seriously in the process of finding solutions. Taken together, this resulted in a system trusted by those who have to work with it.

REFERENCES

Edwards, A. L. (1957). *Techniques of attitude scale construction*. New York: Appleton-Century-Crofts.

Matsui, T., Kakuyama, T., & Onglatco, M. (1987). Effects of goals and feedback on performance in groups. *Journal of Applied Psychology, 72*, 407–415.

Mitchell, T. R., & Silver, W. S. (1990). Individual and group goals when workers are interdependent: Effects on task strategies and performance. *Journal of Applied Psychology, 75*, 185–193.

Pritchard, R. D. (1990). *Measuring and improving organizational productivity: A practical guide* (p. 248). New York: Praeger.

9

ProMES in a Service Setting

Clyde Howell, Steven D. Jones, and Robert L. Hood

This chapter presents the implementation of ProMES in a customer service organization. The main purpose of the chapter is to describe the development of the measurement system and the results during feedback and goal setting. An additional purpose is to describe the interplay between ProMES and other ongoing attempts to improve the overall effectiveness of the organization. In doing this, there were several issues that had to be addressed: how to measure intangible products such as customer service, the relationship between ProMES and other ongoing efforts to enhance motivation, and the nature of the facilitator/employee/management relationship.

Also to be discussed in this case study are changes in attitudes that were apparent in the employees as the project progressed. These attitudes deal with the processes necessary for ProMES to be an effective productivity enhancement system; particular attention was paid to the goal-setting processes. These attitudes include acceptance of the ProMES feedback, acceptance and commitment to the goals set by the team, the expectations of the employees that they could achieve the goals they had set, and perceptions by the employees regarding their role in the achievement of company goals.

This project was conducted in the local office of a Fortune 500 business and office machine company. The company has embodied the entrepreneurial spirit in its operations, which are diverse and international in scope. It not only deals with photocopiers and facsimile machines but also is involved in corporate financing, office communications equipment, and business supplies. It is profit oriented, with every action being designed to cut costs and increase revenues.

The local office was composed of two distinct parts: the sales section, which canvasses prospective clients and sells the company's products and services, and the service section, which is charged with installing, repairing, and servicing the equipment already sold to customers. This latter part, the service section, was the organization in which the project took place.

The service section was composed of 12 customer service representatives (CSRs), including one female. These CSRs ranged in age from 27 to 51 years, with educational backgrounds ranging from high school to junior college or technical school. Experience in this capacity ranged from 6 months to 27 years.

Each CSR worked independently unless she or he needed help in responding to a specific problem or a particular type of machine. Each was responsible for the management of his or her territory to the degree of performing scheduled services and inspections. Unscheduled services and repair work was assigned from a central office by way of an automated message system as well as through the efforts of the service manager (in the event one CSR was overloaded or was unable to meet prescribed response times because of a particularly stubborn problem).

The company practiced a degree of employee involvement in developing new ways to increase revenues and offered incentives to encourage employee participation. These incentives included profit-sharing plans, stock purchase plans, college fund programs, and an extensive employee benefit plan. Employees offered their suggestions at any time, but there were special occasions specifically designed to solicit employee input. These included a "brown bag" lunch, which brought top company executives together with employees. During these lunches, issues of concern to employees were discussed, and employee suggestions for dealing with company problems were solicited. Additionally, there was a bimonthly meeting of the Council of Personnel Relations, at which employees were encouraged to air their concerns.

The parent company utilized a management by objectives program to enhance performance. Corporate level management set objectives for the company based on financial reports, customer satisfaction surveys, and employee input. These objectives were passed along to the next lower level of the organization, where goals and objectives were set and again passed along to the next lower level. At the lowest levels of the organizational structure, these goals and objectives took the form of individual performance targets in terms of dollars or percentages.

PROJECT DESIGN

The design team for developing the ProMES system consisted, initially, of seven members, primarily graduate students, and included the local service manager. The inclusion of the service manager helped to facilitate management support at the local level and to remove the threat from the process at later stages. This size of a design team was good for involving all CSRs during the initial one-on-one interviews to develop the measurement system. One-on-one interviews were necessary because of the work demands of the CSRs.

At the start of the feedback implementation, the project team was reduced to four members. This was sufficient to cover the number of CSRs during the later one-on-one interviews. There were no substitute team members taken in, and this helped continue the relationships formed during the crucial first months. At the start of the implementation of the goal-setting phase, the project team had decreased further to two members. By going on with the smaller number, the design team was able to solidify the existing relationships and gain increased openness and cooperation from the CSRs.

Operating Philosophy of the Design Team

Throughout the project, the operating philosophy of the design team was to achieve its purposes without interfering with or limiting the work performance of the CSRs. Because of the decentralized nature of the job, the CSRs were continually out in their customer's organizations. Also, there were no funds available within the organization to pay the CSRs overtime to sit in meetings with the design team. Therefore, team members prepared well in advance of their meetings with the CSRs and kept questions to the minimum necessary to develop the ProMES.

One of the design team's objectives was to develop a complete set of products and indicators as quickly as possible while still insuring that the total domain of the job had been covered. This objective was facilitated because this organization regularly tracked performance statistics.

We fed the information gained from our interviews as well as the ProMES system back to the CSRs as quickly as possible. We were careful not to create a gap in our credibility that might later fester into a problem that would ruin the ProMES system. These efforts included explanations at each step of the process of what we were trying to accomplish and how we derived the data we were using. We also sought management approval as we proceeded with each step in the process.

Another point of the operating philosophy of the design team throughout the project was to compare this organization's performance with its own baseline rather than with other offices within the parent company. Information was available as to how the service team was doing compared with other offices in the region, but we tried to deemphasize this information because of other factors that made such comparisons less valid indicators of effectiveness. These factors included the size and composition of the other service teams (in terms of experience and levels of ability) and composition of the work load (one

CSR working on only one type of machine as opposed to one CSR working on several different types of machines, as was the case in this office). By focusing on comparing the service team's performance with its own baseline, we strove to improve the effectiveness of the team within its unique situation.

Another aspect of the design team's operating philosophy was to check CSR attitudes toward the ProMES at several points. We surveyed each CSR at the beginning of system development and again once the system had been implemented. This was to detect resistance to the system at as early a date as possible. We also developed and administered a standardized survey that was administered at the beginning of the goal-setting phase and again four months later. The purpose of this survey was to allow anonymous expression of attitude changes as we got into this more sensitive stage of the project. In addition to the survey, open expression of attitudes was encouraged during goal-setting sessions.

A final point of the team's philosophy was to maintain a flexible approach to attaining the objectives of the project. For example, a new indicator was added at the start of the feedback phase. This indicator had not been apparent during the initial steps to either the design team or the CSRs. As the project progressed, however, this indicator became apparent, and the decision was made by the CSRs that it should be added. This required a total recalculation of the ProMES contingency values and a revamping of the baseline. Although this was a tremendous amount of work, it was necessary. First, it insured that the total domain of the job had been covered. Without this, the ProMES system would have been invalid. Second, by doing the work and presenting the results to the CSRs, we showed that we were committed to improving the productivity of the service team and not to a rigid process of some arbitrary measurement system.

Project Design — The ProMES System

This project was designed to follow the published sequence of development of the ProMES system (Pritchard, Jones, Roth, Stuebing, & Ekeberg, 1988, 1989; Pritchard, 1990), implementation of feedback based on ProMES, and the initiation of goal setting in order to increase the effectiveness of the service team. Some variations on the basic ProMES theme were employed on this project; those variations will be discussed.

We began by identifying those measures that the CSRs used as indicators that they were doing a good job. This was done beginning with individual verbal surveys given to each CSRs. The results of these surveys were compiled, and a pattern of performance indicators began to emerge. This information was fed back to both the service manager and the CSRs, and the main products of the service section as well as indicators of these products quickly emerged. The three products were customer service, revenues, and what was termed "required activities."

Customer service and revenues are self-explanatory. Required activities is not so clear. This latter product consisted of those activities, primarily internally administered inspections, that are required by law in order for the company to remain in business. After some discussion and the elimination of those activities over which the CSRs had no control, a single activity remained, this being the inspection of a certain type of office machines. Because these machines generated revenue that is the property of the U.S. government, inspections to insure their proper operation and to detect tampering were required by law.

The products were explored over a series of two meetings with the CSRs that took place two weeks apart. Potential indicators of each product were identified and then verified by management. We deleted those over which the CSRs and the manager had no influence.

Customer service required five indicators. The first indicator, response time, was the average response time (in hours) to respond to a customer call. The second indicator, response time targets met, was the percent of calls answered within prescribed time limits for each equipment type. The third, call backs, was the percent of equipment operating beyond the prescribed service interval. The fourth, calls incomplete due to parts, was the percent of total service calls left incomplete due to required parts being on order. The fifth, mean time to repair, was the percent of service calls completed within the prescribed repair time for the equipment being serviced.

The product revenues was captured by two measures. The first, billed labor, was the dollar amount of labor performed other than for existing maintenance agreements. The second, maintenance agreements sold, was the number of maintenance agreements sold/renewed by CSR during service calls.

The product required activities was captured by one measure, machine inspections. It was defined as the number of machine inspections, required by law, completed each month and expressed as a percentage of the performance target completed.

The next step was to rank the products as to which was most important to overall effectiveness. In the standard ProMES approach (Pritchard, 1990), only the indicators are weighted for importance. In this case, each product had a different number of indicators, and it was thought that a product (such as customer service) might become unduly important because of the sheer number of indicators needed to adequately measure that product. The product weights were easily made by the CSRs. These weights were expressed in terms of percentages with the highest ranked product (customer service) being weighted at 100 percent. The other products were weighted relative to this standard — revenue, 45 percent, and meter inspections, 22 percent.

Next, the individual indicators were ranked and weighted as to their relative importance on both the positive and negative sides of effectiveness. We did this without regard to the product area in which each indicator was found as is done in the standard ProMES methodology. This allowed a single indicator to have a more profound impact on organizational effectiveness than another single indicator, even though the less significant indicator may come from the product area deemed most important to overall effectiveness. For example, customer service is the mainstay of a service industry organization. Without satisfied customers who remain loyal to the vending company, there is no business and, hence, no revenue to sustain the company. However, the sale of maintenance agreements, which falls under the less significant product of revenues, has a greater single impact than does the mean time to repair product machines. A customer who purchases a maintenance agreement has made a commitment to the vending company and is, therefore, less likely to change vendors quickly.

To prevent a measurement system that did not correspond to the relative importance of products established earlier, we checked the relative importance of the indicators to insure that they totaled to the percentage assigned to the respective product area. This means that all customer service indicators totaled to 100 points, revenue indicators totaled to 45, and meter inspections equaled 22. This allowed a single indicator to show up as having a more significant impact than another single indicator without obscuring the relative importance of the product areas.

After the indicator positive and negative weights had been set, we developed the contingencies for each indicator, using the standard ProMES methodology.

After the contingency graphs had been drawn, they were evaluated by both management and the CSRs. Some contingencies were adjusted by adding points in the positive or negative range that indicated points of diminishing return or diminishing damage. It is important to note here that few of the contingency graphs were simple straight line relationships, even without the points of diminishing return or damage.

It is also important to note that in this organization, the zero points were set extremely high. We questioned the high values with both management and the CSRs. The answer given was that these were the minimum acceptable levels of performance set by the company within each indicator. Performance below these levels was simply unacceptable. Therefore, both management and employees set the zero points extremely high. The high zero points affected the overall effectiveness scores by making them quite low. The effects of this will be seen when the results are described.

The next step was to establish a baseline measurement against which to compare the results of the feedback and goal-setting efforts. Because the company routinely tracked the indicators selected, and has for some time, it was easy to draw upon company records to construct a baseline measurement from the past year. The past year's data were deemed acceptable because the service team had remained stable during that time except for the recent addition of one CSR. As with all steps in this process, the CSRs were consulted, and they accepted the past year as a suitable baseline. After this, we applied the ProMES contingencies to the baseline data and established baselines of each indicator and overall effectiveness.

The project began in January and had two meetings every month, lasting from 1 to 1.5 hours each, during which we explained the philosophy of the ProMES system, explored the various products and indicators with the CSRs, and presented the contingencies developed from these meetings for their approval. We also had approximately another two hours of one-on-one interviews with CSRs. By April, this totaled approximately eight to ten hours for each CSR for the development of the ProMES system. After the ProMES system had been developed, we moved directly into the feedback phase of the project.

Feedback Format

We designed the feedback, quite simply, around the ProMES effectiveness scores. However, there is more to effective feedback than simply putting the material in front of the intended audience. The feedback was designed to have the following characteristics:

Timely. The data for feedback was of the current month.

Relevant. Feedback pertained to the indicators over which the CSRs had control.

Provide complete information. The entire domain of the work was covered, and the indicators were integrated into an index of overall effectiveness.

Attention to the positive. The feedback did not dwell on those things that did not go as planned or expected. It acknowledged that things did not go as desired and then focused on how to change that.

Credible source. In order for feedback to be believed and to have an impact on the performance of the work group or an individual, it must be perceived as credible. Although an informal leader of a work group may have strong credibility within the group, the source most commonly perceived as the most credible is the work supervisor.

Allow consistent reaction to the feedback. Workers must be allowed to react to the feedback they receive in a manner that avoids knee-jerk reactions or "brush fires." Failure to allow this consistent reaction will eventually invalidate the feedback and result in a decline in performance.

The feedback system was designed with these characteristics as criteria. Feedback was generated via a ProMES feedback report, a graph for overall effectiveness, and a graph for each indicator. Feedback was delivered every month at the first regular meeting of the work group unless that meeting was later than the first week, in which case, the service manager arranged a special meeting for the purposes of providing the feedback. Feedback was presented whenever possible by the service manager with design team members providing clarification and explanation where required. After effectiveness scores had been fed back, discussion moved quickly to why performance had been good or poor and how it could be improved over the next month. Although the discussion did include specific indicators and products, the focus was kept at the level of overall effectiveness for each product and for the group's collective performance that month in an effort to prevent the "squeaky wheel syndrome," that is, where attention was given just to the lowest performing indicator.

Effectiveness data were charted during the feedback phase, which lasted from April through August. To asses the effectiveness of the feedback system, the CSRs were surveyed in June with an emphasis on their perceptions of the feedback system. Reactions were positive, and indications were that the CSRs were accepting the feedback at that point.

Relationship between ProMES on Ongoing Feedback Sources

As previously mentioned, the company already had ongoing efforts to improve effectiveness through increasing motivation. One of the foremost of these efforts was individual and group feedback of performance statistics to the CSRs and discussion of them during their meetings. These made heavy use of "stack rankings," which showed where each person and service team stood in relation to the other individuals and teams. The design team recognized that this could lead to either unhealthy competition or to resignation to the fate of always being on the bottom. In this work group, the latter was the case, and a great deal of rationalization took place regarding performance in relation to other individuals and teams. This lead to the emphasis on avoidance of being last and an atmosphere of "we're no worse than anyone else."

At first the service manager was reluctant to abandon this traditional approach to feedback and motivation. However, after a few months of using the ProMES feedback and interacting with his CSRs, he came to downplay the stack rankings and focus more on the ProMES approach.

Goal-Setting Phase

The feedback phase lasted five months, from April through August. Encouraged by partial success during the feedback phase, a decision was made to enter the goal-setting phase of the project in September. In this phase, the feedback continued, and goal setting was added.

This phase began with an explanation of what a goal-setting system was and how it worked. During this meeting, we emphasized those characteristics that have been found to be typical of effective goals. These included the following:

Relevant. Goals must deal with only those aspects of the job (indicators) that the work group can affect directly.

Positively phrased. Goals need to be phrased to emphasize positive aspects of performance and engender success. This allows follow-on goals to build on the successes of meeting previous goals.

Difficult but attainable. Goals should present the work group with a challenge that is within their capabilities. Starting with an easier goal and building to harder goals can be effective, but a goal that is too easily attained will not motivate the group to perform above previous levels, and a goal that is too difficult or is perceived as impossible will demotivate the group.

Specific. Perhaps the most important characteristic of an effective goal is the fact that it addresses specific behaviors and performance. A vague, generic "We'll do better" or "Do your best" will not work well. Goals need to address specific behaviors and performance.

The group must have a reasonable expectation that it can achieve the goal. If the group does not feel that it can reasonably attain the goal, the goal will have little effect on their performance. This is related to goals that are difficult but attainable except that this involves more the skills and abilities of the group members than the level of difficulty of the goals. The group must, somewhere within itself, possess the technical or other skills necessary to attain the goals. Further, the group must understand that it possesses these skills and abilities and that it can use them effectively to attain the goal(s).

Goals must elicit a sufficient degree of acceptance and commitment. To simply state a goal is not sufficient to insure that the goal will be met. The group members individually, as well as the group as a whole, must accept the goals as relevant, realistic, reasonable, and important to them. They must also commit personally to attaining the goals both individually and as a group.

With these characteristics in mind, participative goal-setting sessions began. The sessions were facilitated by a design team member with the intent of developing one of the CSRs to assume that position. The service manager excluded himself from the early sessions to prevent any perception of pressure from management to set particular goals. It was explained to the group that the service manager was available as an information resource during the goal-setting sessions. It was further explained that, as the process developed, the service manager would need to be included in the sessions.

As we moved into the process of actually setting goals, the facilitator reminded the CSRs of the characteristics of effective goals. There were initially some goals that were either too difficult or outside the abilities of the CSRs to influence. Each goal was evaluated by the group in terms of the following questions: Is the goal reasonable? Is it something we can affect? Is it specific enough to understand what we should do? Do we possess the skills necessary to attain this goal?

Additionally, there was some discussion of exactly how the group and each individual could go about attaining the goal. Goals were expressed in both group and individual performance targets for the next month. The final step was to project what effect goal attainment would have on the overall effectiveness of the group if everything else remained as it had been the previous month. This last point was especially important, because it appeared that the group had been "squeaky wheeling" their way through the past several months, possibly years, and raw performance data as well as effectiveness scores had fluctuated dramatically during that time.

Purposes of the ProMES System

The ProMES system in this situation came to have three main purposes. The first was an employee feedback system. The development of the system and the feedback report were designed to give the CSRs current, timely, and relevant feedback on the effectiveness of their performance.

The second purpose was to provide an index of overall effectiveness. Again, the system and feedback format was designed to provide the group and the service manager with feedback on the effectiveness of the service team's performance beyond the raw data generated by the company's statistics. The intention was that by providing the "big picture" of overall effectiveness, the organization would tend less toward an approach of focusing on the poor performance of a single indicator.

The project ended after one year because of modifications in the organizational structure that changed the way the service section operated. These changes were made by the corporate level of the organization and made the ProMES system that had been developed invalid.

PROJECT RESULTS

The results of this project were evaluated both subjectively and quantitatively. The subjective evaluation deals with the attitudes, opinions, and perspectives of the CSRs. The quantitative evaluation deals with the harder numbers of the ProMES system. We will look at these results in terms of the overall effectiveness of the service team as well as by each product area.

Quantitative Evaluation

Overall Effectiveness

The overall results of feedback and goal setting are presented in Figure 9–1. As seen in this graph, the overall effectiveness of the service team did not show a significant change when compared with baseline. Note that overall effectiveness is in the negative range during most of the months of the project, signifying that the organization was operating below expectations. This is a direct reflection of the zero points being set high, as previously mentioned.

Customer Service

Even though overall effectiveness did not improve during feedback and goal setting, it was felt that it would be instructive to look at the effects within each product area. The most important product, customer service, was a composite of five indicators. Examining this product alone revealed an improvement during ProMES feedback and goal setting. This can be readily seen in the graph of customer service effectiveness scores, which is the composite of the five indicators combined via their contingencies (Figure 9–2). This improvement that can be seen from visual inspection was verified by statistical analysis as significant. Not only did the mean score increase relative to baseline, but also the gap in maximum and minimum scores narrowed, indicating more consistent performance. Also note that customer service was consistently in the negative range during the months of baseline and that with feedback and goal setting, it was generally in the positive range.

Revenues

Performance in revenues also experienced a change during feedback and goal setting, although this change was not as dramatic as that which occurred in customer service. This change, however, was in the opposite direction from customer service (i.e., it got worse).

Meter Inspections

Meter inspections did not experience any significant effect during either feedback or goal setting. The effectiveness scores for the product of meter inspections did not change during feedback and goal setting in comparison with baseline.

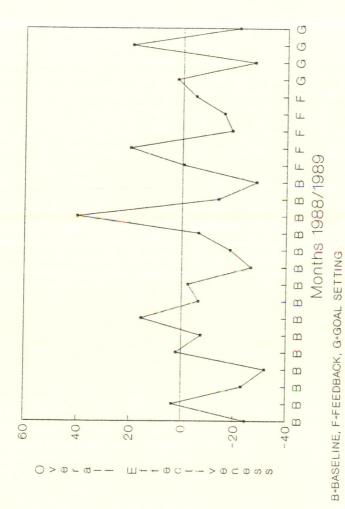

B=BASELINE, F=FEEDBACK, G=GOAL SETTING

Figure 9–1   Effects of Interventions on Overall Effectiveness

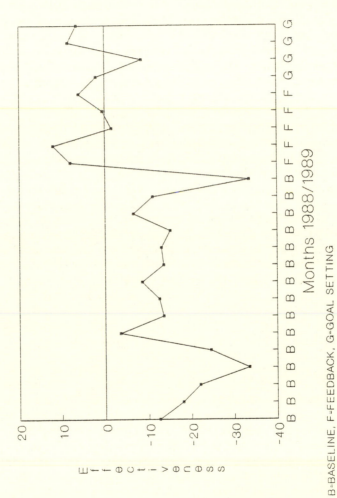

B=BASELINE, F=FEEDBACK, G=GOAL SETTING

Figure 9–2   Effects of Interventions on the Total Effectiveness Scores for Customer Service

Subjective Evaluations

CSR attitudes were surveyed one-on-one on two separate occasions during the early stages of the project. These interviews consisted of open-ended questions that gave much latitude in responding. The results of the first and second interviews were put through a simple content analysis, and it was found that, over the course of the development of the ProMES system, the CSRs had come to understand and accept the system as accurate and fair. Their initial skepticism had been replaced by confidence in the system's accurate reflection of their monthly performance. The results also confirmed that, overall, the relative rankings and weights of the products and indicators were still valid, even though there was one area in which there appeared to be some dissension. As a result of the interviews, it became apparent that there was a major difference between CSRs and management regarding the relative importance of the products of customer service and revenues. This dissension turned out to be very important and will be discussed at length in the following section.

DISCUSSION

At first glance the project would appear to be neither a success nor a failure. There was no apparent impact of ProMES feedback and goal setting on overall effectiveness. However, the ProMES system we developed in this organization was complex enough that a simple examination of the overall effectiveness index is not sufficient to determine the success or failure of the system. Instead, we must examine the effectiveness index for each product as well as look at the situational and cultural factors that impacted this project.

Product Areas

The simple statement of the effects of ProMES on the different product areas is that there was a positive effect in customer service, a negative effect in revenues, and no effect in machine inspections. However, even this simple statement is somewhat misleading.

Machine inspections are required by law to be conducted every six months. The organizational standard is to have them all done in five months. The standard by which this indicator was evaluated was the percentage of inspections completed relative to the target percentage for that month. In other words, if a CSR has a total of 100 machines to inspect, 20 percent (20) must be inspected during the first month of the reporting period. If the CSR inspects 20, she or he has done what is required and scores 0 in effectiveness. If only 18 are inspected, she or he scores −5 in effectiveness. Likewise, if 22 are inspected, she or he scores +5 in effectiveness. If more than 20 are inspected each month, the last month will have a target of less than 20, because these are the only ones remaining. There can be little fluctuation in performance on this indicator or the company will be decertified and overall business will suffer greatly. This indicator would tend to be stable regardless of a ProMES feedback and goal-setting system. However, it was decided to include this indicator in the ProMES because a lack of attention to it could have had serious consequences.

Concerning the product area of revenues, it was apparent from the beginning that the CSRs were not totally behind the idea that they should be generating revenue for the company. Their view was that they should be repairing machines and keeping customers satisfied and happy.

Recall that customer service had an importance weight of 100, while revenues had an importance weight of 45. Thus, the consensus was that customer service was roughly twice as important as revenues. However, we believe that the CSRs had much less commitment to revenues than this two-to-one ratio would suggest.

Recall from Figure 9–1 that overall effectiveness was in the negative range the majority of the time. This meant that the overall message to the CSRs was that as a group, they were below the minimally acceptable level of performance. We believe that this negative message about their performance combined with their weak commitment to revenues created a situation in which they were motivated to improve something, and that something that to which they had a commitment — customer service.

In retrospect, a fuller appreciation of this issue would have resulted in somewhat different importance weights in the ProMES, specifically, that customer service would have a greater importance weight on the negative side (when the organization was operating below expectations) than it did on the positive side.

Recall the importance weights reported earlier; note that call backs and billed labor have the same positive values of 23. This means that when things are going well in both the areas of customer service and revenues, the two indicators are equally important. However, call backs has a greater negative weight (−23) than billed labor (−22), which indicates that poor performance on call backs would do more damage than poor performance on billed labor. Both the CSRs and the service manager agreed that good customer service was the foundation for the company's continued operation. Thus, if things were not going well (negative effectiveness), call backs should get more focus. Certainly, this one-point difference is slight; in fact, the behavior of the CSRs indicates that, for them, customer service should probably have been weighted much more heavily on the negative side.

From the interviews and from the actions of the CSRs, we learned that their priority was almost exclusively with customer service and that their primary job was repairing machines. Their idea was that when things were not going well, the organization (service section) should concentrate on only those things that keep the company afloat (i.e., customer service and satisfaction). Doing this would guarantee survival.

Management had a different attitude, which was that by concentrating on only the essential elements for survival, the company would cease to grow and actually begin to stagnate. Thus, management placed a higher priority on generating revenues, which would allow continued growth and expansion into new market areas. Customer service was important, but after a good level had been attained, the emphasis should be placed on those activities that generated revenues for the company. This is clearly a more aggressive, "growth" attitude. Feedback from management dealt with all three product areas. As performance in revenues dropped off, feedback relating to this product increased.

Therefore, it appears that there were different policies operating at different levels of the organization. This is quite common. Often, contingency development can clarify and resolve these different policies. It did not in this case, and management continued to promote revenues while the CSRs put their efforts into improving customer service.

The feedback given to the CSRs apparently served to reinforce their view of what was important in their jobs. They focused on the customer service ratings rather than the revenue ratings. Obviously, this was a problem for management, and it was a topic of informal discussion at almost every meeting.

In an effort to understand why there was such resistance to revenues on the part of the CSRs, we found that the local sales office was charged with producing new clients and selling the company's products and services. Sales resulted in a commission for the salesperson and included commissions on maintenance agreements sold during the initial sale. CSRs generated sales leads with existing customers for follow-up by the sales force. Additionally, the CSRs were required to sell maintenance agreements to existing customers who either had no agreement or had an existing agreement that was about to expire. This sounds like a grand team effort for generating revenues except for one factor: the sales force received commissions for their success, the CSRs did not. This message was naturally interpreted by the CSRs that sales were really not that important for them. Additionally, the previous service manager had told the CSRs to concentrate on repair and leave the selling to the sales force. This doubly reinforced the CSRs' view that they should not be required to generate revenues.

In addition, the CSRs had come to identify with their customers to the extent that they tended to look after their client's interests. From this posture, billing labor and selling maintenance agreements were viewed as efforts by the company to "exploit" the customers.

Although these differences in viewpoint were known during the project, the strength of these differences was not apparent until the goal-setting phase. During the goal-setting phase, however, differences in points of view became more readily apparent when management applied pressure to increase revenues. In dealing with these differences there needed to be some sort of meaningful dialogue between the CSRs and management that addressed the issue of the different rewards for revenues.

This issue of resolving differences in values is normally considered outside the normal realm of a ProMES project, but it had an impact on the results. Clearly, revenues were sacrificed by the CSRs as a group in favor of customer service. The revenue index continued to fluctuate wildly in a general downward trend while the customer service index rose dramatically and stabilized. Discussion in CSR meetings tended to explore how effectiveness on the customer service indicators could be improved and tended to focus on justifying why revenues should not be part of the job. We found that a few CSRs continued to try to do well on revenues, while others simply abandoned the area altogether. However, before this issue could be addressed to this detail, the project was terminated by organizational changes directed from the corporate level.

Resolution of this difference between management and CSR views of the job domain would have required extensive discussions between CSRs and management. The ProMES system would have had to be reevaluated in terms of this new understanding. This was outside the charter of this project and was, also, not possible because of termination of the project.

Within the product of customer service, however, the ProMES system served its purpose in providing feedback to CSRs concerning to what extent their performance was good or bad and stimulated discussions as to how it could be improved. This resulted in more commitment to improving performance within this product, and the effectiveness index for this product rose and stabilized (Figure 9–2). Commitment to the goals set for customer service produced changes in performance over time, and indications were that this index would have continued to rise over time.

Dealing with the Issues

Another part of this issue was the potential threat to the CSRs from having someone enter the organization and take a long, inside look at how things were done. We were constantly tested by the CSRs to see if we were reporting everything directly to management. Great care was taken to answer management questions in general terms and to direct management's more specific inquiries to the CSRs. Nothing was reported directly to management without the consent of the CSRs. It was also very helpful to have a CSR working as a liaison between management and the CSRs in addition to the work done by the facilitator.

Such a relationship was essential to gaining the trust of the CSRs. Although they were up-front with everyone involved and did not hesitate to air their views to management at the local level, the very real threat of a conspiracy between management and the facilitator to accumulate information to be used in eliminating unruly employees was present. The appearance of this was carefully and constantly avoided.

Lessons Learned

Many familiar lessons were reinforced during this project. The first of these is the fact that support from management is vital to the success of any effort such as this. We were careful to gain the support of the local manager. However, the support of the managers above this level was not as solid. Management more than one level above this local office was aware of our efforts, but we did not have access to this level of management during the project. As a result, needed changes in the organizational system that would have removed the mixed signals regarding revenues were not possible. Additionally, there was pressure to improve performance on single indicators that were below the average level for the region. These indicators were not extremely important to the overall effectiveness of the work organization, and pressure to improve them resulted in decreases on other, more important indicators. Frequent access to these upper levels of management could have reduced or eliminated this distracting pressure. Therefore, the first lesson reinforced is that access to and the support of management at all levels is essential to a successful project. The involvement of the local or first-line manager in developing and executing a project such as ProMES is essential. To simply enter the organization, develop the system, hand it to the manager, and expect it to go as intended or even have a mild degree of success is an unrealistic expectation. By involving the local manager at the very first, we were able to eliminate the threat that is inherent in productivity projects such as this.

A major problem that we encountered was the existence of alternate forms of feedback that sent messages contrary to the ProMES feedback. ProMES is group level feedback that evaluates the group relative to expectations. There was a tradition of ongoing feedback that viewed performance in terms of who was doing the best and who was doing worse, not who was meeting standards. Rather than encouraging improvement, this alternate feedback seemed to engender an avoidance of being the worst.

The obvious lesson here is that alternate forms of feedback must be monitored and screened in order to prevent conflicting messages. If upper management sends these messages to the local manager, she or he should digest the information and, if required, pass it along in a form that is more compatible with the ProMES feedback. This could take the form of a suggestion of setting a higher goal for the work group or explanation of upper management's desires rather than simply declaring that "We are not doing as well as XYZ office." Such competition is destructive rather than constructive.

It is absolutely vital that the organization take ownership of the ProMES system. The role of the consultant is to help the organization develop the system and understand how it should work. At some point, though, the organization has to take over the administration of the system, or it will ultimately fail. This transfer needs to happen as quickly as possible but slowly enough that the participants have a good understanding of what needs to be done. The best way to achieve this transfer is to include an organizational representative from the beginning in the development and administration of the system. As the process goes along, this representative should be trained in facilitating the goal-setting sessions as well as in how to convey results to management and represent the work group's interests. This is vital if the ProMES system is to survive beyond the initial project.

What appeared to be a rather minor technical issue — the setting of the zero points during the development of the measurement system — became a significant motivational issue during feedback and goal setting. The setting of high zero points generally forced the overall effectiveness scores into a negative range (see Figure 9–1). Thus, the message to the organization was that they were operating below the minimally acceptable level for 11 months of the 15 month baseline period. Again, by looking at Figure 9–2, we can see that the response of the CSRs was to improve customer service. Unfortunately, they neglected revenues at the same time, and, thus, overall effectiveness did not improve.

In retrospect, the implications for high zero points was not sufficiently understood by the design team. On future ProMES projects, we recommend calculating the baseline effectiveness scores and checking them with management. This could be done without beginning feedback prematurely by asking management if they thought the organization was operating below, at, or above expectations during each month (or other time period) of the baseline. This judgment could then be checked against the effectiveness scores to see if the zero points are correct.

CONCLUSIONS

Although overall effectiveness did not improve during ProMES feedback and goal setting, the most important product area to the employees (customer service) did improve; therefore, from their point of view, it was a success.

From the design team's point of view, success was limited, ultimately by the different policies regarding the relative importance of products and the climate that produced those changes. Had the project continued, the next step would have been to address the problems that we found, and that have been discussed here, with upper management. By expanding the scope of this project, we would have gone beyond the ProMES system and begun to address changing the organizational culture, at least at the local level.

This project also illustrated that ProMES is more than a simple productivity measurement system. It can and does serve many other purposes for the organization within which it is used. These purposes include, but are not necessarily limited to, employee feedback on job or role and performance, management information system, and the facilitation of effective design and implementation of feedback and goal-setting systems at all levels for improving overall productivity and effectiveness.

REFERENCES

Pritchard, R. D. (1990). *Measuring and improving organizational productivity: A practical guide* (p. 248). New York: Praeger.

Pritchard, R. D., Jones, S. D., Roth, P. L., Stuebing, K. K., & Ekeberg, S. E. (1989). The evaluation of an integrated approach to measuring organizational productivity. *Personnel Psychology, 42,* 69–115.

Pritchard, R. D., Jones, S. D., Roth, P. L., Stuebing, K. K., & Ekeberg, S. E. (1988). The effects of feedback, goal setting, and incentives on organizational productivity. *Journal of Applied Psychology Monograph Series, 73,* 337–358.

10

Using ProMES to Evaluate University Teaching Effectiveness

Margaret D. Watson, Amie Hedley, Karlease Clark,
Anthony Paquin, Noga Gottesfeld, and
Robert D. Pritchard

This chapter describes the development of a ProMES system used to evaluate the teaching effectiveness of professors at a major U.S. university. This project was under the direction of Robert D. Pritchard, and it had several unique characteristics. First, ProMES was used to measure individual rather than group performance. The feedback was based on individuals, and improvements in performance were the responsibility of individual instructors rather than the group. Second, this setting was typical of institutions of higher education, where upper management exerts little control over members' performance. The management provided basic guidelines for performance but allowed a great deal of autonomy in how the organization's tasks were accomplished. Each faculty member had the right to conduct research on almost any topic, choose textbooks, select course content, and design tests that conformed to his or her own standards. Most of these decisions were not reviewed by others.

In addition, this setting, like all academic settings, was characterized by the concept of tenure. Tenure is typically granted to individual faculty who have performed at an acceptable level for a period of six or seven years and guarantees lifetime employment. Once tenure has been granted, the organization has even less control over the performance of faculty members (except in very rare situations such as unethical conduct or harassment of a student). Therefore, for tenured faculty, the evaluation of teaching performance can be mandated, but the data can be used in only limited ways. It can be used to determine the level of merit pay raises and to determine who should be promoted from the level of associate to full professor. For nontenured faculty, however, the measurement of performance can be mandated and the results used in making a variety of personnel decisions. These conditions resulted in a very unique application of ProMES.

Another unique characteristic of the project is that decisions were based on a thorough review of the teaching evaluation literature. This review indicated that there were a number of methods that could be used to measure classroom teaching. Among those were student learning, self-ratings, ratings by consultants, peer ratings, and student ratings.

The first three of these methods are used infrequently, for a variety of reasons. Student learning is not used commonly, because it is difficult to measure, but it has been found to be quite reliable and valid (Cashin, 1988; Kulik & McKeachie, 1975; Overall & Marsh, 1980). Self-ratings are rarely used to evaluate teaching, because of limited reliability and validity (Centra, 1973; Marsh & Overall, 1979); their primary use has been as a tool for motivating instructors to improve their teaching skills (Centra, 1980). Finally, consultant ratings, which appear to be valid and reliable, are rarely used, because of their cost (Centra, 1980; Marsh, 1987).

The other two measures of teaching effectiveness, student ratings and peer ratings, are commonly used to evaluate teaching. Peer ratings appear to be both reliable and valid when done without classroom observation (Blackburn & Clark, 1975) but have limited reliability and validity when they are based on observation (Braskamp, Brandenburg, & Ory, 1984). Student ratings have shown good test-retest reliability (Costin, 1968; Overall & Marsh, 1980), good internal consistency reliability (Marsh, 1987), and good interrater reliability (Cashin, 1988). Student ratings also appear to be valid measures of teaching performance because they are significantly related to other criteria of effective teaching, such as peer review of teaching, student learning, and consultant ratings (Centra, 1973; Kulik & McKeachie, 1975; Marsh, 1984, 1987; Marsh & Overall, 1979).

Because of the high levels of reliability and validity for both student and peer ratings of teaching, the system described in this chapter included both types of ratings. This chapter, however, will describe only the student rating system, because the peer review portion of the system is still being developed.

PROJECT EXPERIMENTAL DESIGN

The specific objectives of this research project were to answer the following questions: Can ProMES be used as a method for evaluating teaching in an institution of higher education? Will the resulting system be valid? Will the system help instructors improve their performance over time?

Organizational Setting and Project Design

The setting for this project was a college of veterinary medicine (CVM) at a large university located in the southwestern United States. The college was composed of five academic departments: anatomy and public health (45 faculty members), small animal medicine and surgery (39 faculty members), large animal medicine and surgery (46 faculty members), pathobiology (44 faculty members), and physiology and pharmacology (24 faculty members).

The mission of the CVM was to provide education at three levels: undergraduate and graduate training in biomedical sciences and professional training to students pursuing a doctor of veterinary medicine (DVM) degree. In addition, the CVM had an active commitment to medical research and patient care.

In general, the atmosphere at the CVM was congenial and hard working. Many of the faculty had worked together for a number of years and, thus, had established good working relationships with each other. The dean of the college, however, was fairly new to this setting. He was appointed only one year before this project began and, thus, was still in the process of building relationships with the other administrators and faculty when this project started.

The project was instigated by faculty members who saw the need for better methods of evaluating teaching and sought the support of the dean. The dean supported the project because he wanted a method for measuring teaching that would allow the faculty to improve teaching, as well as a method that would allow him to reward excellent teaching. Throughout the project, the dean supported the project verbally, financially, and through written communications. In addition, he was an integral part of all meetings held to explain the purpose and design of the system. Thus, there was little doubt that he supported the project.

Project Units

At the request of the dean, all five CVM departments were included in the research design. Three of these departments were basic science departments who provided instruction to undergraduate, graduate, and professional (DVM) students. The other two departments were clinical departments. These departments provided instruction only to professional students. They also were responsible, however, for providing patient care services to animals referred to the college by either local or state veterinarians.

Of the approximately 200 CVM faculty members, nearly 50 percent were tenured full professors. In addition, many had been on the faculty at this college for over 15 years. Thus, the faulty was quite senior and had limited professional experience in other educational settings.

Concerns about the Project

Although the five departments performed tasks that were quite similar to academic departments in other colleges and universities (e.g., provide teaching to graduate and undergraduate students, perform committee work, conduct research), the professional (DVM) curriculum also made them quite different. Many of the courses in this curriculum were taught by a team of faculty members rather than a single individual. This meant that the faculty placed a high priority on working well together as colleagues.

This issue also presented special problems in measuring their teaching effectiveness. Because many of the courses were taught by multiple instructors (usually three to seven individuals), students were required to evaluate a number of faculty members, some of whom had completed their teaching assignments several months prior to the collection of the evaluation data.

Many of the faculty were quite concerned about this issue. For the measurement system to be valid, students would have to remember the teaching behaviors of each individual faculty member. In addition, students would have to complete a large number of evaluation forms in each course. This could result in the loss of valuable class time in a curriculum that already included more information than there was time to present. This concern was serious enough to make some faculty question the value of student ratings.

There were also other concerns about developing an evaluation system. Some faculty felt that students were not the appropriate source for evaluation data; these individuals typically believed that only peers could provide valid and helpful information regarding teaching effectiveness. Other faculty members were opposed to the idea of evaluation in general. Although many of these critics were persuaded that the evaluation project could be quite helpful to them, some resistance continued throughout the project.

In addition to the concerns about evaluation and about using students to provide the data for the system, some faculty were uncertain about how the data generated by the system would be used by both departmental and college-wide administrators. They were concerned that the data would be used to deny tenure and merit pay increases rather than to reward good performance.

Although these were serious concerns on the part of a number of faculty, the majority of the faculty strongly supported the idea of teaching evaluations and were supportive of the idea of using student ratings of teaching as part of the project.

Project Design

The project used the standard ProMES approach in that the measurement system was developed by a design team, indicator data were collected, and feedback was given to faculty.

Development Process

In this setting, it was expected that the products and indicators would be consistent across the five departments. Therefore, a committee of faculty members served as the initial design committee to develop products and indicators for all five departments. This committee was the CVM Teaching Excellence Committee, a standing committee composed of representatives from each of the five departments. The TEC was charged with making improvements in teaching in the CVM. Experienced ProMES facilitators also attended meetings and helped the committee through the process.

The design committee met for approximately 1.5 hours, once a week. They identified products and developed indicators. These steps (along with development of contingencies and feedback reports) have been described in detail in the second chapter of this book, as well as in Pritchard (1990). Therefore, this section will describe briefly the process used to develop this system.

Product Development

An instructor has a set of activities or objectives that he or she is expected to accomplish in the classroom, which ProMES would call products. Because performance is a function of how well these products are being generated, the first step in the development of the teaching measurement system was to identify them.

After the design committee became familiar with the project and the steps involved, they developed the products by answering the question, What are the important things an instructor must do to be an effective classroom teacher? The committee discussed each of the suggested products until a consensus was reached. This insured that the completed list was comprehensive and accurate.

Developing products was fairly easy for the design committee and took only three meetings to complete. There was a sense that these products covered the important components of classroom teaching that could be observed by students. In general, the process of developing products was quite smooth and congenial.

Indicator Development

After the products were determined, the next step was to develop indicators of the products. An indicator is a measure of how well the instructor is generating the product in question. Because this project was based on student ratings of teaching, the indicators were items on a student rating questionnaire. Therefore, indicators were determined by asking the design committee to identify the behaviors a teacher would use in the classroom to accomplish each of the products and the questions to be asked of students to determine if the behaviors were being performed.

In order to facilitate the process of developing indicators as well as to build on the teaching evaluation literature, research team members obtained copies of existing student rating questionnaires. They reviewed the questionnaires and developed lists of items that could be used to measure each of the seven products. These lists were presented to the TEC, who reviewed them and selected items. Several of these items were included as indicators without changes, and some were included with minor wording changes.

Developing indicators was somewhat more difficult than developing products and required seven meetings of 1.5 hours each. During these meetings, there was some disagreement concerning the specific wording of some indicators, as well as whether certain behaviors were important enough to be included in the system. The committee members knew they needed to include all the important aspects of classroom teaching that students could observe but also knew that the questionnaire needed to be fairly short. It was felt that anything longer than 20 items would be redundant and too long for students to complete. In spite of these disagreements, consensus was finally achieved on 17 indicators, shown below the seven products.

1. Presented appropriate material in an organized fashion
   Indicator 1: The instructor was well organized.
   Indicator 2: The amount of material presented or assigned by the instructor was appropriate.
2. Demonstrated subject mastery
   Indicator 3: The instructor appeared to have a thorough knowledge of the subject.
   Indicator 4: Information and references provided by this instructor were relevant.
3. Communicated effectively
   Indicator 5: The instructor spoke clearly and was easily understood.
   Indicator 6: The instructor emphasized major points.
   Indicator 7: Concepts were presented in a manner that aided my understanding.
4. Promoted critical thinking and problem solving
   Indicator 8: The instructor's examination questions required me to do more than recall factual information.
   Indicator 9: The instructor helped me integrate facts, develop conclusions, and arrive at solutions.
   Indicator 10: The instructor raised challenging questions or problems for consideration.

5. Motivated students to learn
   Indicator 11: The instructor created and maintained an atmosphere that facilitated learning.
   Indicator 12: The instructor stimulated my interest in the subject.
6. Exhibited a positive attitude toward students
   Indicator 13: The instructor was courteous and easy to approach
   Indicator 14: The instructor was willing to help students outside of class.
7. Evaluated students fairly
   Indicator 15: This instructor's examination questions covered the important concepts presented in the course.
   Indicator 16: The examination questions from this instructor were reasonable in difficulty.
   Indicator 17: The examination questions from this instructor were graded fairly.

After the design committee completed the list of indicators, the system needed to be evaluated by students and faculty and approved by the college administration. A sample of students was asked to describe the meaning they ascribed to each item and if the items were understandable and clear. In addition, they were asked if the items could be answered easily and accurately and if they would be able to rate the teaching effectiveness of instructors, including those from team-taught courses. The students provided positive feedback about the instrument, although they recommended changes in the wording of a few indicators. The data from this review were presented to the TEC, who made some revisions to the items.

Next, the entire CVM faculty was given the opportunity to review and comment on the products and indicators. To obtain this input, a questionnaire was prepared that showed the products and indicators and asked for an overall judgment of their accuracy, completeness, and clarity. In addition, comments were requested on each of the items. Results indicated that most respondents (between 73 and 88 percent) felt that all important aspects of classroom teaching were covered by the instrument, that the questions were clear and understandable, that feedback from the items would aid the teacher in improving classroom teaching, and that feedback would be useful to administrators. These data suggested that the products and indicators were perceived as complete and accurate. Based on the responses to this questionnaire, the design committee finalized the products and indicators.

The final step in getting products and indicators accepted was to get formal approval from college administration, that is, the dean, his staff, and the department heads. This review was conducted in a joint meeting involving college administration, the five department heads, and the design team, including the research staff. The revised list of products and indicators was presented and, after a discussion, was approved unanimously with only one minor modification. As a result, it became college policy to evaluate teaching using this system.

Contingency Development

Contingencies are functions that describe the relationship between how well the instructor is rated on an item and how much contribution that level of the rating makes to overall teaching effectiveness. In other words, a contingency describes the relationship between the amount of the indicator and the effectiveness of that amount.

The contingencies developed at the CVM follow the same basic format as contingencies developed in other ProMES projects. The horizontal axis of a contingency is composed of indicator scores that range from the worst possible to the best possible level. In this setting, the horizontal axis is the mean rating on one of the items from the student rating questionnaire. Because a five-point rating scale was used (1 to 5), the worst possible rating an instructor could get was a mean of 1.0; the best possible rating was a mean of 5.0.

The vertical axis of the contingency represents effectiveness. The vertical axis usually ranges from −100 (minimum effectiveness) through 0 (the expected level) to +100 (maximum effectiveness). When this scale is used, the expected level is at zero, negative numbers indicate areas where performance is below expectations, and positive numbers represent performance that is above expectations. The departmental administrators, however, did not want to use negative numbers to describe effectiveness because they believed that receiving a negative number would be detrimental to faculty morale. Consequently, the vertical axis in this system used scores ranging from 0 (minimum effectiveness) through 100 (the expected level) to 200 (maximum effectiveness).

Contrary to the first two steps, the TEC determined that the contingencies would not be universal across departments. This was because the contingencies would capture how effective a specific amount of a teaching behavior as, that is, teaching policy. They expected that policies would differ across the departments. For example, an instructor teaching in anatomy might rely more heavily on lecture and the presentation of facts, whereas an instructor who teaches a more process-oriented subject such as a small animal multidisciplinary course might require the students to integrate disparate information and solve problems. This meant that the importance of these indicators (and, therefore, the slopes of the contingencies) would be quite different for courses in these two departments. Because of these expected policy differences, contingency design committees were convened in each of the five departments.

First, departmental contingency committee members determined the type of class for which they would develop the contingency set. It was expected that different types of classes offered by each department might require different sets of contingencies. This situation is analogous to the need for different contingencies among departments. In much the same way that we expected different teaching behaviors to have different effectiveness values among departments, we also expected different teaching behaviors to have different effectiveness values for different types of classes. For example, it might be very important that the instructor be extremely organized when presenting information to undergraduates, because undergraduates do not have a strong conceptual background for the topics presented. Graduate students, on the other hand, are expected to have a strong conceptual background in many of the topics presented; consequently, it might be less important that the instructor be extremely well organized. Therefore, the indicators were expected to have different levels of importance and, thus, different contingencies. Consequently, it was possible that the individual departments would choose to have two or more contingency sets (e.g., one for large lecture CVM classes, one for small graduate seminars).

To make this decision, each contingency committee considered the courses offered by their department, including undergraduate, graduate, and professional levels. Most departments contingency committees decided to begin the process by developing contingencies for the large lecture, DVM professional classes, which comprised the majority of their teaching loads. After this choice was made, the committee generated the contingencies , using the same basic steps that have been described in previous chapters.

After the first contingency set was complete, the design committees determined if the other types of classes taught by the department required different contingencies. Two departments felt that policies were different for different levels of class. One developed an additional set for laboratories in the professional curriculum, and the second developed additional sets for undergraduate classes and for graduate seminars. The contingency development process was repeated to develop each set.

The discussions about contingencies in all five departments were extremely lively, because teaching policy had never been explicitly discussed before. Consequently, every committee member had his or her own idea about teaching policy. In addition, because faculty are extremely independent, some discussions went on for quite a long time before consensus was achieved. Three departments were able to reach consensus within six to ten hours. Two departments, however, spent a total of approximately 20 hours discussing their first contingency sets. For the departments that developed a second or third set of contingencies, the total development process was slightly longer. Both departments that developed additional sets took their original contingency set and adapted it to conform to their expectations for the different classes. In those departments, two to five hours were needed to develop each additional set.

There were several major concerns expressed by the contingency committees. The most consistent concern dealt with the responsibility for determining teaching policy. Although the committees felt quite strongly that it should be the responsibility of the faculty rather than the administrators to determine policy, they were still somewhat uncomfortable making these judgments.

In addition, some of the contingency committees were concerned about how the students would use the rating scale. In other words, they were concerned that the students would interpret the scale differently and would give unnecessarily low ratings. Other contingency committees, however, had a great deal of trust in how the students would use the scales.

After the contingency set (or sets) was complete within each department, they were reviewed by the other members of the department and by the department head. Minor revisions were suggested in most departments and were made by the departmental contingency committees. Next, all sets from all departments were reviewed by a representative of college administration (the associate dean for academic affairs). This review process was similar to the review of products and indicators and provided an opportunity for the administration to insure that the teaching policy had been captured accurately. All contingency sets were approved without modification.

Feedback Reports

The final step in the development of ProMES was to design the feedback system and produce feedback reports. To facilitate this process, the standard report format (including indicator scores, effectiveness scores, average overall effectiveness scores, percent of maximum scores, overall percent of maximum scores, and priority data for improving effectiveness) was shared with the TEC, who agreed that this report format would be acceptable. Consequently, the reports used a format similar to those used in previous ProMES projects.

The reports also included summary data for the instructor, the department head, and the dean. The individual instructor's summary report included data for all classes taught that semester by that instructor. The department head's summary report included the data for all of the instructors in that particular department, and the dean's report included data for the entire college.

The effectiveness scores in this project must be interpreted slightly differently than scores in other projects described in this book. In this project, a score of 100 (rather than 0) means that the individual is meeting expectations, that is, performing at a level that is neither particularly good or bad. As the score moves above 100, she or he is exceeding expectations. The higher the score, the more expectations are being exceeded. When the score falls below 100, she or he is below expectations.

A feedback report was generated for each course taught by an instructor each semester. An example of one of the reports can be found in Table 10–1. This example only includes the first two products and the associated indicators; an actual report included all 7 products and 17 indicators and was three pages long.

Table 10–1   Example Feedback Report

BASIC FEEDBACK INFORMATION
Teaching Effectiveness Report for: M. Smith, Anatomy 391
Basic Effectiveness Data for: Spring 1992

Products and Indicators	Indicator Data	Effectiveness Score	Percent of Maximum
Appropriate material organization			
Instructor well organized	3.21	122	70
Material was appropriate	4.23	121	91
Evaluated student fairly			
Examination questions reasonably difficult	3.21	101	84
Examination questions graded fairly	2.83	83	65

Average overall effectiveness score = 107
Percent of maximum = 78

FEEDBACK REPORT PRIORITY INFORMATION
Teaching Effectiveness Report for: M. Smith, Anatomy 391
Potential Effectiveness Gains for Next Period

Products and Indicators	From Individual Data	To Individual Data	Effectiveness Gain
Appropriate material organization			
Instructor well organized	3.21	3.46	25
Material was appropriate	4.23	4.48	2
Evaluated student fairly			
Examination questions reasonably difficult	3.21	3.46	1
Examination questions graded fairly	2.83	3.08	13

SUMMARY FEEDBACK REPORT
Teaching Effectiveness Report for: M. Smith
Summary Data for: Spring 1992

Name	Department	Class	Average Effectiveness	Percent of
Smith, M.	VTAN	VTAN391	107	78
Smith, M.	VTAN	VTAN913	125	89

Average overall effectiveness score = 116
Percent of maximum = 84

RESULTS

In this section, we will discuss briefly the specific methods used to address each research question and the results obtained through those methods.

Research Question 1: Can the System Be Developed in This Environment?

Evidence to answer this question came from addressing several different issues. We first determined whether the system was developed as expected. We found that the design committees were able to complete the tasks assigned to them (i.e., develop products, indicators, and contingencies; present the system to the faculty and administrators; and obtain approval for the system) with reasonable ease and in a reasonable amount of time. Second, the design committees were able to achieve consensus regarding the system design. All TEC members and 95 percent of the contingency committee members reported that a true consensus was reached within their committee. Finally, the system components conformed to expectations. The products and indicators were consistent with what the teaching literature suggested, and the contingencies expressed differing levels of importance and were almost all nonlinear.

The second issue was whether the approval process was completed and viewed as acceptable by the various design committees. The products, indicators, and contingencies were formally approved by the departments, department heads, and administration, suggesting that the process was successful. In addition, the design committees reported that the review and revision process was completed smoothly and that their work was viewed positively.

The final measure of whether the system could be done in this environment was whether the system was continued after its development. The system has been used for two years since its development. In addition, the dean, associate deans, and department heads declared during the second year that the student rating system was to be used throughout the college for administrative reviews of teaching as well as for developmental feedback (prior to this decision, the system had only been used as developmental feedback). This statement of policy indicated the clear support that administrators felt toward the system and was further evidence that the system would continue to be used.

Research Question 2: Was the Resulting System a Valid Measure of Teaching Effectiveness?

The validity question is a difficult one to answer. As can be seen from a review of the teaching evaluation literature (Braskamp, et al., 1984; Centra, 1973, 1975; Kulik & McKeachie, 1975; Marsh & Overall, 1979), there is no single accepted criterion measure of teaching effectiveness that can be used to validate evaluation systems. Thus, there is no simple measure of system validity. However, partial assessments of validity can be determined through the use of two approaches, construct validity and absence of bias.

Construct Validity

In one form of validity, construct validity (Cascio, 1987, Guion, 1965), multiple aspects of validity are explored and the sum of the evidence is used to assess validity. The first aspect evaluated was whether the development process was valid. We answered this question by assessing the number and importance of changes made in the products, indicators, or contingencies after the system had been in use for some time. After the system was used for four semesters, no changes were made in products, indicators, or contingencies. The absence of any important changes suggests that the system was seen as complete and accurate, that is, valid, by the faculty and administrators at the CVM.

The second aspect of construct validity that was assessed was the psychometric characteristics of the instrument. The internal consistency reliability of the instrument for the total sample was .95, which is extremely high. Interjudge measures of reliability were also calculated using interclass correlations (Marsh, 1987). This analysis was broken down by class size, because the number of raters influences the size of this reliability estimate. The estimates for each class size ranged from a low of .62 (for classes with fewer than 10 students) to a high of .93 (for classes with more than 100 students) and averaged .86. Although the estimate for classes of less than 10 students was low, all other estimates were within accepted boundaries (i.e., above .80). suggesting that when there were enough raters, the interjudge reliabilities were quite good.

The final aspect of construct validity was how well the system predicted other measures of teaching effectiveness. Even though there is no single criterion of effectiveness, there are variables that can serve as partial criteria. The literature suggests that one such external measure is peer ratings.

To gather these peer ratings, department heads and faculty from the design committees were asked to identify the individuals who they believed were highly effective classroom teachers, of average effectiveness, and of low effectiveness. Faculty selected by at least three evaluators for a single level of effectiveness (e.g., high effectiveness) and not selected by any other evaluator for another level of effectiveness were determined. The percent of maximum scores for these three sets of instructors were then obtained. The percent of maximum score for the most effective group was 90.33, for the average group 75.28, and for the least effective group 61.83. Analyses indicated that the percent of maximum scores for the three groups were statistically different from each other. This indicates that the system was able to differentiate between above average, average, and below average instructors.

Sources of Bias and Validity

Bias in student ratings occurs when students rate the instructor based on some factor other than the quality of the teaching (Marsh,

1984, 1987). Thus, the presence of any major source of bias would indicate reduced system validity.

One type of bias would occur if large numbers of students rated an instructor at very low levels regardless of the quality of teaching. This would occur if students rated the instructor poorly due to the unpopularity of the course, the unpopularity of the instructor, or some other irrelevant factor. This possible source of bias was a concern of the faculty at the CVM, because they believed that students might give poor ratings to instructors who taught certain unpopular classes, thus, spuriously reducing their ratings.

This potential source of bias was evaluated through the examination of mean student ratings. The argument was that if a student was biasing his or her ratings, one source of evidence of this would be for the student to give very low ratings on *all* the items. It is unlikely that even a poor instructor is very bad at everything. We determined the number of students who had given such generalized negative ratings to an instructor. A generalized negative rating was defined as one where the mean rating was below 1.5 (where the rating scale ranged from 1 to 5). A mean below 1.5 would indicate that the student had given either the lowest or one of the lowest ratings to the instructor on all indicators.

The data indicate that across semesters and across the 266 classes, in 258 classes, none of the students gave generalized negative ratings; in only 7 classes did as many as 2 percent of the students give generalized negative ratings; and in only 1 class did as many as 4 percent of the students give such ratings. Therefore, it was clear that students were only rarely giving generalized negative ratings to instructors and that this was not a meaningful source of bias.

Research Question 3: Did the Resulting System Produce Increases in Performance over Time?

Because one of the primary purposes for developing the system was to provide feedback to faculty so that they might improve their teaching performance, it was important to determine if the system produced these results. Changes in teaching performance over time were used to answer this question.

There was no formal baseline in this setting because no quantitative measures of teaching effectiveness had been used before. Thus, the first feedback reports generated by the system were considered as the baseline because the teaching done that semester was done without the benefit of feedback from the system. These scores were then compared with the scores of successive semesters. If mean scores improved over time, that would be evidence of the system having a positive effect on teaching effectiveness.

To determine if scores improved over time, we gathered the teaching effectiveness scores for all individuals who had been evaluated more than once. Comparison of the data over time indicated that there was an improvement over time. The mean percent of maximum for the baseline period was 82.6 percent. This average improved to 87.3 for the second semester and was 86.1 for the third semester. Thus, there was an improvement after instructors received feedback from ProMES. This improvement was statistically significant.

However, many CVM faculty members had fairly high initial ratings. Thus, it was not likely that there was much room for these individuals to improve their scores. The individuals who were originally rated at lower levels could benefit more from the feedback provided by the system and, therefore, could make more substantial improvements in their scores. Thus, the subjects were divided into two groups, depending on whether their first (baseline) percent of maximum score was in the top 50 percent or the bottom 50 percent.

The means for these two groups (Figure 10–1) indicate that the means remained constant for the individuals whose initial scores were above the median, while the means continued to increase over time for the individuals whose initial scores were below the median. This meant that there were no significant changes in performance over time for those individuals who initially had high evaluation scores. Those who initially had low scores, however, did have large improvements in performance over time. In fact, the group initially in the bottom half of teaching effectiveness improved almost to the level of those initially in the top half.

CONCLUSIONS

Results of the study have, in general, affirmed the questions associated with the project. The system is currently being used by the college, several sources of information have confirmed the validity of the system, and instructors evaluated with the system have improved their performance.

However, although overall acceptance of the system is good, some of the faculty have continued to have concerns regarding the system. First, some of the faculty have voiced continued resistance to being evaluated by students. Many of these concerns should be reduced when the peer evaluation component of the teaching evaluation system is added to the student evaluation portion.

Another concern shared by some of the faculty pertained to how administrators would use the data yielded from the system. To address this concern, the administration did not use the data for evaluative purposes for the first four semesters. The idea was that this time would allow the faculty to become more comfortable with the system. However, a number of faculty continued to be concerned that the data would be

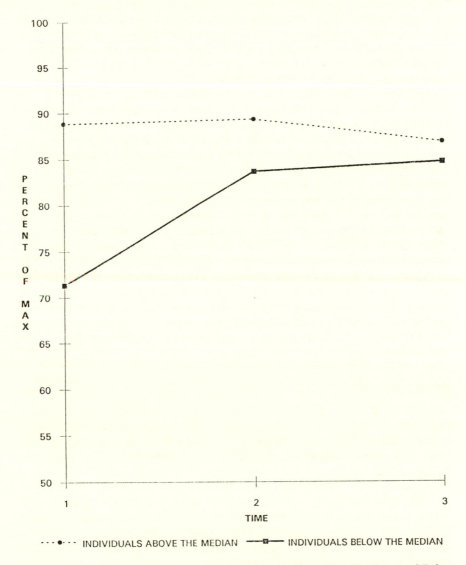

Figure 10–1 Teaching Effectiveness over Time for Those Initially Above and Below the Median

more likely to be used for punitive purposes than to determine rewards. Because the manner in which the system will be used is, in large part, beyond the control of the researchers, there was no simple solution to this problem. As such the researchers informed the administration of the faculty's concern and hoped that in the future the administration would be guided by sound managerial principles in the use of the data.

A third concern that persisted after the system had been put in place was a concern about the validity of the contingencies, held by a small but vocal minority of the faculty. These faculty worried that they did not have confidence in their own judgments of what was important for good teaching. The researchers pointed out to them that the faculty were the only ones who could determine this policy. However, a small minority was still not certain of their judgments.

Several other issues make this project somewhat unique. An academic setting is quite different from most of the other organizations used in the cases in this book. It is much more unstructured, with individual faculty having much more power over their work than in typical organizations. In addition, they tend to be much more independent. In addition, the assessment of teaching effectiveness is much less well defined than productivity in more typical organizations. Finally, all the indicators were subjective in this project. However, in spite of these differences, ProMES was successfully implemented and had a positive effect on teaching effectiveness.

There was also a set of issues associated with the fact that there were multiple departments doing essentially the same work. This is not unlike a setting where there are multiple departments in different geographic locations doing essentially the same tasks. The results of this project suggest that it is possible to streamline ProMES development by having representatives from different departments work together to develop products and indicators and then have contingencies done by each department separately. This allows each department to participate in the process, because they do contingencies, but reduces the total time to do ProMES considerably, because the development of indicators is the most time-consuming part of the process. However, it would be important, we feel, to include representatives from each department in the design team doing products and indicators and to give each of the departments an opportunity to review the products and indicators before they are finalized.

Another issue we were concerned about is the different departments using different standards. In this setting the work is very similar, but because each department does its own contingencies, differences in expected levels and other parts of the contingencies could produce different effectiveness scores for the same student evaluations. To assess this, we examined the contingencies after they were developed. Although there were some small differences, the overall result was that the contingencies were quite similar in the scores they produced. This suggests that different standards are not necessarily a problem. If there is evidence of different standards, one strategy is to use percent of maximum as the measure on which to focus when comparing different departments. Percent of maximum represents how close the person or group is to *their own* maximum. Thus, differences in standards are reduced or eliminated.

In conclusion, despite some concerns, the faculty and administration in general have accepted and become comfortable with the system. This, combined with the other results, demonstrates that ProMES can, in fact, be used to develop a valid measurement and feedback system in an institution of higher learning and, as such, used as a tool to improve teaching performance.

REFERENCES

Blackburn, R. T., & Clark, M. J. (1975). As assessment of faculty performance: Some correlations between administrators, colleagues, students, and self-ratings. *Sociology of Education, 48*, 242–256.

Braskamp, L. A., Brandenburg, D. C., & Ory, J. C. (1984). *Evaluating teaching effectiveness: A practical guide.* Beverly Hills, CA: Sage.

Cashin, W. E. (1988). *Student ratings of teaching: A summary of research.* IDEA Paper No. 20, September. Manhattan: Kansas State University, Center for Faculty Evaluation and Development.

Cascio, W. F. (1987). *Applied psychology in personnel management* (3rd ed.). Englewood Cliffs, NJ: Prentice-Hall.

Centra, J. A. (1980). *Determining faculty effectiveness.* San Francisco: Jossey-Bass.

Centra, J. A. (1979). *Determining faculty effectiveness: Assessing teaching, research, and service for personnel decisions and improvements.* San Francisco: Jossey-Bass.

Centra, J. A. (1975). Colleagues as raters of classroom instruction. *Journal of Higher Education, 46*, 327–337.

Centra, J. A. (1973). Self ratings of college teachers: A comparison with student ratings. *Journal of Educational Measurement, 10*, 287–295.

Costin, F. (1968). A graduate course in the teaching of psychology: Description and evaluation. *Journal of Teacher Education, 19*, 425–432.

Guion, R. M. (1965). *Personnel testing.* New York: McGraw-Hill.

Kulik, J. A., & McKeachie, W. J. (1975). The evaluation of teachers in higher education. In F. N. Kerlinger (Ed.), *Review of research in education*, Vol. 3 (pp. 210–240). Itasca, IL: F. E. Peacock.

Marsh, H. W. (1987). Students' evaluations of university teaching: Research findings, methodological issues, and directions for future research. *International Journal of Educational Research, 11*, 253–388.

Marsh, H. W. (1984). Students' evaluations of university teaching: Dimensionality, reliability, validity, potential biases, and utility. *Journal of Educational Psychology, 76*, 707–754.

Marsh, H. W., & Overall, J. U. (1979). *Validity of students' evaluation of teaching: A comparison with instructor self evaluations by teaching assistants, undergraduate faculty and graduate faculty.* Paper presented at the annual Meeting of the American Education Research Association, San Francisco.

Overall, J. U., & Marsh, H. W. (1980). Students' evaluations of instruction: A longitudinal study of their stability. *Journal of Educational Psychology, 72,* 321–325.

Pritchard, R. D. (1990). *Measuring and improving organizational productivity: A practical guide* (p. 248). New York: Praeger.

11

ProMES in a Bank

Henriëtte Miedema and Henk Thierry

This chapter describes the development of ProMES in a large Dutch bank. The bank's personnel and organization department was interested in ProMES in order to use it as an appraisal tool. The appraisal system in use did not work satisfactorily, according to both supervisors and subordinates (Miedema, Santbergen, Thierry, & Meyer, 1989). The traits that were used (like reliability and initiative) especially caused problems. Supervisors had trouble defining these criteria and assessing performance accordingly. Subordinates favored other assessment criteria such as effort or actual performance. The personnel and organization staff people expected that a system like ProMES could solve these problems because of its focus on actual performance, while the participative approach would further the acceptance of data by subordinates. ProMES was also favored as an instrument to allow the design of a more adequate payment by results system.

Because there is no precedent of an application of ProMES in a bank, we wanted to find out whether ProMES would cause any particular problem when developed for a bank facility. First, it was assumed from the beginning that all units of this facility would be involved, totaling approximately 45 employees. Eleven groups were identified, as well as two individual jobs. The criterion for the composition of the groups is interdependency. If employees are dependent on one another to do their work — or, put in ProMES terms, share the same products and indicators — they are considered to be a coherent group. Second, we were interested in applying ProMES to individual jobs, because there currently are few examples available relevant to individual job holders. Third, it is an intriguing point whether ProMES data can be used in the context of payment by results. Because ProMES tries to identify what is critical to group or organizational performance and how this can be affected by employees, ProMES seems to encompass major criteria for an effective performance related payment strategy.

ORGANIZATIONAL SETTING

In this section, the organization of the bank at large will be described as well as the particular facility in which ProMES is developed. Then, the design of the development process will be sketched. We refrain from giving details relevant to each of the groups concerned. Insted, we will highlight the results of one division — commercial clients — focusing upon the three groups that compose this division. Also, the development of ProMES for an individual job — in this case, the travel agent — will be described. Throughout, we will make some points of more general interest.

The facility in which ProMES was developed is one of approximately 800 cooperative facilities that are affiliated with the bank's head-quarters. Strictly speaking, it is not right to talk in terms of facilities: formally, each "cooperating" bank is autonomous. Consequently, headquarters may only suggest policy measures, not dictate them. In practice, however, the facilities act as if major policy directions are coming from the bank's headquarters. Thus, we use terms like "facility" and "headquarters" in the remainder of this chapter.

The bank at large is characterized by rather dynamic policy making. Also, because of Europe 1992, implying that internal boundaries among countries of the European Community have been eliminated, the bank is engaged in cooperative agreements with large banks in other European Community countries. Not all of these changes affect most facilities. However, a rather important development that does is that there is a change of opinion on whether or not the bank ought to have a facility in villages and small towns. Until recently, the bank's policy held that it should be represented in each small community. This has changed, not only because of relatively very high overhead costs (necessitating mergers among various small facilities) but also probably because of the vast increase in telebanking.

Headquarters' personnel and organization department asked the facility to volunteer for ProMES. The facility is located in the upper southern part of the country, servicing primarily various larger and smaller rural communities. Headquarters thought the facility to be fairly representative of all facilities concerned; it would, thus, provide for a good test of the feasibility of ProMES for the bank at large. Also, the facility had provided, on earlier occasions, an openness for innovations and opportunities for improvement, both economically and in terms of organizational behavior. It had faced a rather placid environment in the preceding years. The structure of the internal organization and its staff had been rather stable. Recently, however, a merge took place with a small facility in a neighboring village. The facility did not have a system of productivity measurement, nor were there particular directives for performance criteria. This implied that employees were very dependent upon their supervisors' performance assessment. Also, feedback was provided only once a year by the supervisor. Neither management nor employees were satisfied with this situation. They welcomed the idea of a more frequent and a more objective measurement of their activities.

The facility had three divisional groups: commercial clients, personal clients, and clerical support. The first two divisions, respectively, served commercial and personal clients on financing and investment matters. The main duties of the third division, clerical support, were to support the other two divisions and to carry out the necessary activities for periodically reporting the financial position of the bank to other parties involved. Additionally, there is a travel agency (one person) in the main office, belonging to the personal clients division. In the Netherlands, it is customary for branch offices to have a travel agency as a special service for personal clients. Furthermore, because of the current emphasis on personal investments, an advisor for personal investments had been recruited recently. Because its content was not yet clear, this advisor's job was not involved in the development of ProMES.

The facility manager was responsible for all three divisions. He had to account for the activities and results to the board members of his facility and to the bank's headquarters. He was assisted by his private secretary. Her activities were related only to him as a manager and not to the other divisions.

ProMES DEVELOPMENT

In the following sections, the development of ProMES will be described in main lines for the participating divisions and in particular for the commercial clients division as well as the travel agent job. Members of the ProMES team belong to the research group on compensation of the Department of Work and Organization Psychology of the University of Amsterdam (supervised by Henk Thierry). Henriëtte Miedema managed the ProMES team, supported by one junior staff member and two senior students. All employees, with the exception of the investment advisor and the "odd-job man," participated in the development of ProMES. Each group consisted of the supervisor and the job incumbents from the units concerned. Supervisors were key members in a group.

Researchers met with the groups once a week in order to develop the system This frequency was thought to prevent the participants from getting bored with the system. Furthermore, it would increase the commitment of employees, because it shows the importance management attributes to it in terms of time. Another advantage is that participants are able to keep good track of the development. It is easy to recall the last meeting if it is only a week ago, but when there are two weeks between the meetings, it becomes harder to do so. It was something of a problem to get everyone to attend the weekly meetings. They had to attend to the ProMES meetings during work hours, but at least one person had to stay at his or her desk to answer the phone or to receive clients. Nevertheless, with some shifting, it worked out quite well. At each meeting, one of the group members was assigned to report to those who could not attend the meeting. We agreed to try to develop the system in 10 meetings for each group concerned. Each meeting took about 1.5 hours. Longer meetings were not very effective, as we learned.

The process started in one division; after a number of meetings, a second division was brought in. A period of six months was available to develop ProMES in all groups. A baseline period of three months then would be taken to find out whether the system worked well. An attempt was made to gather baseline data from the period before the development of ProMES. Unfortunately, this was possible only for a few indicators.

Feedback reports would be provided on a monthly basis for the commercial clients and clerical support divisions and on a quarterly basis for the personal clients division. Although it is preferable to give feedback on a monthly basis (Chhokar & Wallin, 1984), financial reports as to personal clients are available only on a quarterly basis.

The supervisor of the commercial clients division was a progressive, enthusiastic person who was very cooperative in developing ProMES. The atmosphere in this unit was supportive, and the employees were not afraid to give their opinion, even on delicate matters. The supervisor stimulated his employees to talk about their work and to give their opinion on the various steps in the ProMES development. When information was not available to the other team members, he provided this or ordered it to be prepared. In spite of being skeptical about the feasibility of developing ProMES in his unit, he was very cooperative and helpful through all of the meetings. Although participation by all members was emphasized by the team, it was not always possible to get everybody to communicate or to become actively involved. Decisions were made on a consensus basis, with the supervisor's opinion receiving extra weight in some cases.

The development in the second group, clerical support, went according to plan. There was no need to split this group. Its members worked together, being responsible for the same products and trying to accomplish the same goals. The supervisor of this group had a strong facilitating role. He never dominated the group and encouraged all members of the group to participate.

The third group, personal clients, was split in three parts because of geography. The division supervises two branches situated in different villages, which will be referred to as "Branch 1" and "Branch 2." One of these branch offices had merged with the bank six months previously. Employees of this branch felt uncertain about what would happen to the branch and their own position. It was not clear at that moment whether the current work group would stay together in the near future. This was reflected in their behavior toward the system; apparently, they felt they were being watched and controlled. Therefore, the understanding with their new supervisor seemed uneasy. Although it was possible to identify products and to decide what indicators should be used in this group, it was not possible at that time to develop contingencies. Contrary to the other unit, they were not used to setting standards necessary to develop the indicators. Furthermore, they were afraid to do so. Thus, it was decided to develop contingencies on the basis of data gathered during the next six months. The development of ProMES in the other branch, which belonged to the facility for many years, went much better. The supervisor was not always present at these meetings, but problems did not occur. Employees took their work very seriously and set high standards for themselves. Because the branch groups performed fairly similar activities, the process went faster than in the other groups.

The development of the productivity measurement system was done in four steps: identifying products, analyzing indicators, designing contingencies, and putting the system together (Pritchard, Jones, Roth, Stuebing, & Ekeberg, 1989; Pritchard, 1990). Before the meetings were started with the groups, a short introduction on ProMES was given in which the steps in developing the system were explained. It was emphasized that ProMES could be useful as an information system. We explained that ProMES was still experimental. It was outlined that a relationship between performance and payment would not be considered during this phase. Only if the system worked satisfactorily for all parties concerned would the relation with pay be a point on the agenda. This is an important issue to emphasize, because pay is a delicate matter and employees felt uneasy about the purpose of ProMES.

There are various ways in which outside researchers or consultants may gain knowledge about the jobs and the work process of the groups with which they work. The team's initial idea was to get acquainted with the unit's work during the development of ProMES. It was thought that the ongoing process would be facilitated if the team members had just a global idea of the activities. This strategy also emphasized that employees themselves were responsible for developing the system. They were the experts, and our role primarily was to facilitate the process by helping them communicate and by explaining to them the several steps that were taken to develop ProMES. Previous to the meetings, policy plans, balance sheets, and turnover and absenteeism figures were analyzed by the research team. This was done not only to get a better picture of the facility's resources and effectiveness but also because it is part of our larger study to assess the discriminant and convergent validity of ProMES. Based on prior data from a questionnaire (BASAM) on the quality of work life (Biessen, 1992) and an additional questionnaire (BELON) on payment issues designed by Miedema and Thierry, we knew that the flow of information and communication were far from optimal in this bank. Employees did not keep one another properly informed on standards and important developments in their work.

In order to create an accessible file regarding both content and process issues in the development of ProMES, a format was designed where each meeting was recorded. It was a way of keeping good notes of what was happening in a meeting, to keep track of the process (like checking whether decisions were made according to former steps), and to see whether all important issues were covered in the end.

In each meeting, two team members always were present, one to manage the meeting and the other to make notes and provide support. Furthermore, little cards were used on which team members noted products and indicators. The participants had to fill in the job's components that belonged to these products and indicators between the meetings. It was thought that by listing job components, employees might get a fuller understanding of important features of their jobs and more in general of the products. Furthermore, by letting them do some work on their own, time was saved and it helped in keeping participants actively involved in the process.

Commercial Clients Division

The commercial clients division totals nine employees, including the supervisor. At an earlier meeting, the team had noticed that employees were puzzled by new concepts like products, indicators, and contingencies. Therefore, instead of introducing the various concepts jointly, each concept was explained at the time the group had to work with it. Members of the group were asked to tell about their activities. They began by enunciating very small parts of their daily work and their duties as individual members. Questions that worked well to encourage and help them to think at the unit level were What will happen if this unit would be eliminated? and What will be the impact for the organization? It turned out that many different activities were ongoing in what originally seemed to be one coherent group.

Thus, after two meetings with the entire group, it appeared that four groups could be identified with separate tasks, duties, and goals. The reason for belonging to one division was that they had a common consumer market: firms and companies. It was agreed with the entire group to further develop ProMES for each part of this division separately. The supervisor would be present at each meeting.

The first subgroup, financial advice, will be discussed in detail. ProMES development for the other three groups will be described globally. Only issues that are unique for these groups and that did not occur in the first subgroup will be discussed.

Financial Advice Subgroup

Product development. The first group in which ProMES was developed, financial advice, was composed of three members. They were highly qualified and worked relatively independent of each other. The supervisor played a dual role in this group, being a job incumbent as well. Discussions were very lively; the group members were skeptical about the system and quite critical in their comments. In their opinion, the development of ProMES would be possible only for industrial processes, because service related activities were not quantifiable. Furthermore, they argued that their results were, for the large part, determined by factors they could not control. They had, for instance, a limited package of services to sell, and prices and procedures for settlement were fairly fixed. Facilitators made it clear that the matter of control or influence is a very important issue. It was agreed that these factors would somehow be taken into account.

After these discussions, the process of developing the products went smoothly. The participants understood fairly quickly what was meant by products and had no problems in identifying them. The initial products for financial advice were effectiveness of advice, dealing with clients, credit control, active acquisition, and quality of clerical reporting.

Participants were given homework between the meetings. They were asked to think about the products they had proposed and to describe the activities that were involved in carrying out these products. An example of such a description for "effectiveness of advice" is being sensitive to customers' needs, preparing the right financing procedure, giving information about financial alternatives, selling services, preparing for future developments, and making requests for the credit commission. Important activities concerning this product relate to the need to be sensitive and to be able to prepare the right procedures but also to be aware of future developments in order to be successful.

Indicator development. In identifying indicators, it helped to have a proper description of the products that was done earlier through the little cards. When an indicator was selected, a check was made afterward to make sure all important activities were covered by the indicators.

In this stage, the group became aware of the possible implications of ProMES. As mentioned earlier, the group members were self-reliant and were not controlled by their supervisor. ProMES was perceived by them as an instrument to exert more control upon them than they wanted. However, in spite of this, the willingness of the group to cooperate was good. They seemed to consider ProMES as a kind of interesting brainteaser.

Some problems in developing the indicators were caused by the fact that in this setting it took a long time for effects or performance results to surface. Some useful indicators could not be analyzed because relevant data were not supplied by the clerical support group.

Compensators. Another problem was that this group, as well as all others, was afraid that the amount or supply of work would not be taken into account in ProMES. In some cases, fluctuations in the amount of work, partly due to seasonal influences, can be sizable. A great amount of work was not only a point per se but also made it more likely that errors would occur. Thus, it was important to define something like an average work load.

Trying to combine more than two variables into one indicator was not a good solution. It would make contingencies rather complex and difficult to understand. The problem is that a third variable (like amount of work) that does not have fixed values would have to be incorporated. This variable would affect the indicator and its effectiveness only when it reaches a certain specified level.

The problem was solved by introducing a so-called compensator whenever the amount or supply of work had to be taken into account for a specific indicator. Unlike an indicator, a compensator cannot be influenced by the group. Another aspect of a compensator is that it is tied to a specific indicator. Because a compensator cannot be affected, there is no ineffective area. The curve runs from zero to a positive maximum that affects the maximum of the indicator to which it belongs. If the amount of work is below average, a compensator will not apply.

An example of a compensator is shown in Figure 11–1. The upper half of the figure is the regular contingency, the lower half, the compensator for that indicator. The indicator "amount of additions on credit requests" is combined with a compensator "number of processed credit requests." Whenever the number of credit requests exceeds five, the compensator is used in combination with the indicator to determine the effectiveness score. If, for instance, the amount of additions on the indicator credit requests is one, the corresponding effectiveness score is 40. If the number on the compensator credit requests processed is 11, the effectiveness score is 20. In this example, the combined effectiveness score of indicator and compensator will be 60.

The final list of products, indicators, and compensators is:

1. Effectiveness of advising
    Indicator 1: number of additions (substantial/technical) on credit requests
    Compensator 1: number of processed credit requests
2. Keeping up with clients
    Indicator 2: number of clients handled/total amount of clients

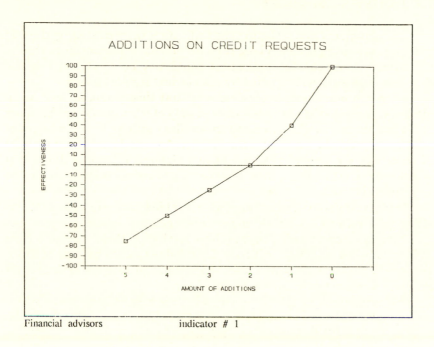

Financial advisors   indicator # 1

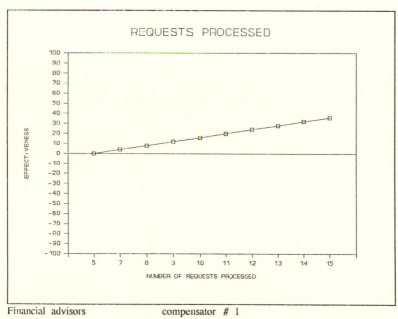

Financial advisors   compensator # 1

Figure 11-1   **Example: Contingency with Compensator**

3. Credit control
   Indicator 3: number of nonpersuasive arguments for credit entries on running accounts
   Indicator 4: number of non-completed dossiers
4. "Active" acquisition
   Indicator 5: number of calls and visits made on clients
5. Quality of reporting
   Indicator 6: number of unfinished documents

Although the volume of work appeared to be a very important point of discussion, it resulted in the addition of only one compensator for the first indicator, amount of additions on credit requests. In the end, six indicators were identified for this group. There was only one product, credit control, that needed two indicators.

Development of contingencies. The group was able to understand the meaning of this step very well. They had no problems with an example (Pritchard et al., 1989), although that was a totally different line of work.

Discussions were very lively; because they had good insight into the system, they discovered very soon that it might be sensible to set low standards for establishing the means for the indicators. This became a complicated issue because the supervisor was a job incumbent, too, and also could benefit from low standards. The ProMES team members intervened by telling them that they would fool themselves in this way; it would surface when proposals on standards had to be approved by the facility manager. After some meetings, participants seem to feel more comfortable with the purpose of the system; they viewed ProMES more positively and were not trying to beat the system in a negative way. Their general view held that ProMES may be useful in giving them more insight and perhaps even improve their activities.

Maximum and minimum scores. The first step in this stage of development was to determine the maximum and minimum values of each indicator. It was explained that the maximum was "the best possible performance of the group in any given period of time." The method of "critical incidents" was tried but did not work well. The group was not eager to talk about failures, nor could they identify extremely good results. It seemed threatening to them; they were involved personally. Some incidents were mentioned after a while, but they were not very helpful. A better approach was to depersonalize the issue: for example, if someone else would be working in your place and performed extremely bad, what would go wrong, or what would be the impact? Furthermore, several workers actually had been replaced temporarily, during vacation or sick leave. This made discussions easier, because they could talk about real events and incidents. It made them aware of critical factors in their work. Another strategy also worked well in this setting. One of the members suggested potential indicators while another member or the supervisor had the role of opponent, and vice versa. This worked quite well; there was a lively discussion.

After determining the minimum and maximum indicator scores, the indicators were ranked, based on their relative importance. Subsequently, the effectiveness scores for each indicator were established. There were two indicators that had equal weight in the maximum values. The group was very outspoken on this matter. The same was true for various minimum values. One of the indicators, amount of unfinished documents, received a low positive weight (40) but got the largest weight in the negative area (−90). Some activities just have to be performed and are not very important; however, if they are not carried out properly, there is a serious problem!

The final step in contingency development was to draw the contingency curve from the zero point up to the maximum and down to the minimum. First, the intervals for all indicators are determined. Then, the effectiveness score for each interval is established. It was a time-consuming job but not particularly difficult for the group, although it needed a lot of explanation. It should also be mentioned that the opinion of the manager was decisive in most discussions. This was particularly true when curves were nonlinear, which was true for four contingencies.

Insurance Subgroup

The insurance subgroup was a small subgroup, consisting of three members and a supervisor. They sold insurance policies to business clients. The group was also involved in mediating between clients and insurance companies and in the handling of damages. Because of its small size, it was not difficult for the participants to focus on the objectives of the group as a whole.

Communication between one of the group members and the supervisor was far from optimal. That employee felt threatened by ProMES. He thought that once he had set the standards, he would be forced to meet them, even if this was not possible for him. Finally, the supervisor and he agreed that it was not right to discuss this conflict during the meetings but could be solved better by the two of them. This obviously worked, because after some sessions, he softened his defensive attitude and became very actively involved and creative in developing the system.

There was a problem with one of the indicators, size of commission, which was very subject to seasonal influences and could be influenced only in small part by employees themselves. The group agreed, however, that this was one of the most important indicators. It caused one of the members to be hesitant in setting mean, minimum, and maximum scores. He felt that if the expected mean was set too high, he would not be able to reach it each month. According to his opinion, this particular facility was doing a lot better in selling products than comparable facilities, and it was not fair to compare his future results to his past results. Instead, his efforts should be compared with those of the other facilities. The supervisor did not agree with him and reminded him of their joint agreement they had made in the beginning of the year on the estimated size of commission. This was laid down formally in the policy-plan for insurance. This formal estimation was based on historical figures from the facility itself, not on figures from comparable facilities. This was one of the signs showing that ProMES formalizes agreements and policy issues.

Two members of the group continued to work on this indicator. Eventually, after the meetings were over, they suggested two excellent alternatives. Size of commission was, as mentioned, subject to seasonal influences and could be influenced only partly by the participants. They came up with a better option: advancing mean of commission. The size of commission in a particular month will be compared with the size of commission in the same month of the preceding year. If the commission in a particular month is subject to seasonal (and not to workers') influence, this will also be so in the same month of another year. By comparing these two months, the contribution of the employees can be estimated.

Commercial Support Subgroup

Six members were employed in this group as well as the supervisor. Their main activities were clerical in nature. An important feature of their jobs is accuracy. It was not possible to involve each group member in the developmental process. A few members apparently were not interested in ProMES. Team members tried to get them to talk about their job and asked them for their personal opinion on several matters, but it did not work. They were "merely present."

The supervisor played a very important role in this subgroup. Members were not used to thinking and talking about the relative importance of their activities; so, it was hard to rank these activities and come up with figures. The supervisor was very stimulating but, obviously, also very dominant in developing ProMES.

There were no problems in analyzing products for this group, but when ranking indicators, two members of the group who had been cooperative so far became quite recalcitrant. They felt that their activities were being evaluated as of secondary importance. In this opinion, the most important indicators were ranked lowest. By discussing this matter, it turned out that, although they formally worked in this group, they worked independently from the other members of the group. Thus, it was argued to distinguish another subgroup.

The new subgroup was called "desk activities." Further development of ProMES went well in this two-member group. They felt more comfortable as a separate group and were very cooperative now. The process went fast because there were only two products at which to look.

The measurement of one of the indicators was to be on an annual basis, because data were not available on a monthly or even quarterly basis. All other indicators were to be measured monthly.

ProMES for an Individual Job

ProMES was also developed for two individual jobs: the secretary and the travel agent. This section refers to the travel agent belonging to the personal clients division. At one of the first meetings with the personal clients group, it appeared that there were no connections between this job and the other jobs in the group; so, it was agreed to consider this job separately.

We used a slightly different approach here. Development of ProMES was done by just one of the team members. This was done to avoid the travel agent feeling uncomfortable being on her own and with two people; moreover, one facilitator was sufficient to do the work. The supervisor was asked not to be present at all meetings, only when important decisions were made, like the approval of the final list of products and indicators. This was also done to let her speak more freely; moreover, it reduced the supervisor's investment of time.

Developing Products

The process of identifying products did not take much time. A list of products and descriptions was designed in three meetings of approximately one hour. The following products were identified: effectiveness of advice, accuracy of clerical activities, stock control, and effectiveness of publishing.

The first and most important product, effectiveness of advice, can be influenced only to a certain degree, because the employee is restricted by time limits. Giving good advice is time-consuming, but she has to assist at the desk at "personal clients" from time to time when their work load is high. In her opinion, this was in conflict with her own work at the travel agency.

Developing Indicators

It was very easy for her to come up with indicators. She had no doubts, whatsoever, on the following list:

1. Effectiveness of advice
   Indicator 1: size of commission
   Indicator 2: number of trips sold
   Compensator 2: number of hours spent
2. Accuracy of clerical activities
   Indicator 1: number of errors in entries

The point that the travel agent was restricted by time limits to do her work properly, as mentioned before, was taken into account by adding a compensator "number of hours spent." Products such as stock control and effectiveness of publishing finally were omitted. The first one hardly could be controlled by the employee herself. The stock consists of travel brochures, which are provided by several tour operators. It was her responsibility to order them in time, but it depended on the tour operators whether they were delivered in time. An important aspect of her job was to advertise and publish in the local newspaper on special offers or newly offered trips. This product, called "effectiveness of publishing," was omitted, however, because this was already included in "size of commission" and "number of trips." If she did a good job in advertising and publishing, she would sell more trips, and the size of commission would be higher. Some correlation between number of trips sold and size of commission was to be expected, but it was very important to the employee to take both into account. It took just as much effort to sell an expensive trip as a cheap one, but the size of the commission was connected to the price of the trip. Thus, if only the size of commission was taken into account, this would provide an incomplete picture. From the point of view of the organization, voiced by the supervisor, size of commission, however, was the indicator that mattered, and that was related to the primary goal — survival. If selling cheap trips meant more losses (in terms of hours spent) than profits (in terms of commission), this would be the end of the travel agency.

It was a dilemma between the effort a person spent and the effectiveness in organizational terms in generating products. If the correlation between both indicators would be high, "number of trips sold" probably would be skipped.

Developing Contingencies

Problems did not occur in this stage of development. She understood its meaning and was capable of developing the contingencies by herself with the help of one of the team members. The supervisor was not present when contingencies were developed. Without any discussion, however, he agreed with the results. In fact, he was very satisfied with the minimums, maximums, and zero points she had set for the indicators.

Putting the System Together

The first step in putting the system together was to get management approval. In this case, only the facility manager had to approve the final results. He was informed during the entire development process and was eager to see the results. In his opinion, the final lists of products and indicators presented a good picture of the primary process of the divisions. He approved of the ranking and ratings of the indicator scores except for one indicator, belonging to "desk activities." The manager felt that the expected level should be set at a lower point. Team members addressed the supervisor and asked him whether an adjustment had to be made. He was quite outspoken on this indicator, however, and was reluctant to change his mind. Eventually, the facility manager gave his final approval.

Time Spent in Developing ProMES

Before starting the development of ProMES, we were asked by the supervisors to make time schedule for all groups involved, so everyone would know when meetings took place and how much time was to be spent by each one. Meetings lasted about 1.5 hours for the groups and about 1 hour for the individual jobholders. For commercial clients, it took about ten meetings for each subgroup to develop the system. For clerical support, there was more time involved, and it took 13 meetings to develop the system. For personal clients, each subgroup needed about 11 meetings to put the system together. For the two individual jobholders, eight meetings were needed for developing ProMES by the travel agent and nine meetings for the private secretary.

There are not many differences among groups in the time spent on ProMES. We were not always able to develop ProMES according to schedule — which was six months — because of work overload and problems with regard to the development of contingencies. On some occasions, data were not sufficient or available to design the contingencies. This affected the duration in some of the groups, which took about six months more than was scheduled.

FEEDBACK

Because points of interest and problems are very similar for all groups involved, feedback data will be discussed for all groups together. After the development of products, indicators, and contingencies, it was agreed to set a baseline of at least two periods (totaling half a year). After this period, outcomes would be analyzed to assess whether the system worked satisfactorily. Feedback reports would be explained as well as the way feedback was to be given after the baseline period.

At the time we finished developing the system, the work load was very high for all groups. Therefore, the groups were reluctant to put any more effort in the system. There was a general feeling of Why did we start all this? and the supervisors emphasized to the team that it was time to get the results as soon as possible. This feeling was partly due to the fact that relating ProMES to pay for performance became an issue of uncertainty. Headquarters did not take a stand on this, and the facility manger wanted to see ProMES work before he would decide on any payment relationship. Therefore, employees were left in doubt, and this had a very negative impact on the progress and acceptance of ProMES.

Another reason was the period between the start of ProMES and the moment data were about to appear. This took 16 months, and, thus, interest in ProMES was decreasing.

These problems surfaced within a rather short period. Moreover, there were still some indicators left to identify and some contingencies to be designed. Most important, however, were the doubts of both supervisors and subordinates concerning the applicability of the system.

Feedback data were expected to affect this feeling favorably. Special forms were made to facilitate data collection and to make sure the right data were collected. Analysis of data was done by the facilitators. In spite of this, data were either incomplete or incorrect. It was hard to get the groups to fill in the forms correctly and send them to the facilitators on time.

Supervisors were also reluctant at this time to decide on the contingencies that were still unfinished and to discuss alternatives for unsatisfying indicators. This caused a negative spiraling effect: because of incomplete data, it was not possible to make feedback reports in the baseline period. This had a very negative impact on the supervisors, who were convinced that it was important to come up with results as soon as possible. Because of all these problems, the baseline period took 11 months, much longer than was planned.

At this time, also, some important changes occurred in the bank office. Activities that were incorporated in ProMES were no longer relevant because of increasing automatization. Even the existence of an entire group, commercial support, became doubtful. Other changes were caused by new services that required new skills and a different orientation toward customers. For example, desk activities earlier consisted of a simple transfer of money or of checks from customer to employee or vice versa. Now it was expected that employees were actively involved in informing the customer on bank products and services. All this had its impact on ProMES. Some products or indicators did not apply any more, and norms and standards were no longer adequate. Eventually, of all 49 indicators and contingencies, 11 indicators and 16 contingencies had to be changed. Thus, technological and organizational changes that were not foreseen made major parts of ProMES data obsolete. It was expected, moreover, that many more changes would face the facility in the near future, also affecting quantity and quality of employment. Given the uncertainty about the ProMES performance pay link, it was decided not to install ProMES.

DISCUSSION

This section begins with the discussion of some general points concerning the process of development that may be worthwhile for future practitioners of ProMES. Furthermore, some specific issues concerning the development of products, indicators, and contingencies are discussed.

Conditions

We have learned from this project that certain conditions have to be met in order to implement ProMES successfully. A very crucial condition is the stability of an organization. At the time ProMES was developed and an attempt was made to implement the system, a large number of changes took place due to automatization, creation of new jobs, and growth. This had an incisive effect on products, indicators, and contingencies. They had to be changed repeatedly, and, therefore, it was not possible to make any useful feedback reports.

Another condition is management support. If management, for whatever reason, is not in favor of the system and does not support this, the implementation of ProMES will fail. The manager is a key figure both in the process of development and in giving feedback.

Preparation

It was found out the hard way (by trial and error) that it is vital to learn about the unit or group's work content previous to the starting of ProMES. Valuable time was wasted in the first meetings (product development) in order to familiarize the team members with the work of the groups.

Delegation

Although it may be attractive to get all members of a group to participate in all meetings, it does not seem to be a necessary condition to develop ProMES for small groups. Some of the groups consisted of a delegation of employees, and this operated rather well. In this case, it is important for the team members to monitor whether all other employees are kept informed.

Time Interval

An adequate time interval between the meetings is one week. Employees are still aware of what is going on. Moreover, the entire process (about ten meetings) is kept within everybody's view. However, when contingencies are developed, team members may need a two-week interval.

Homework

Much can be said in favor of giving group members some homework in the course of developing ProMES. First, it accelerates the process. More importantly, it increases commitment: through identifying products or considering contingencies, participants will consider ProMES more as their system. Participants are far less skeptical about the system if they can make suggestions.

Sensitivity

Team members need to be aware that some participants may feel threatened by ProMES: they view themselves as being watched and controlled. Others may even try to beat the system by trying to set the standards low. Also, the pressure of a superior may affect the openness of communication.

Norms and Standards

We were ale to compare two groups within the personal clients division having similar products and indicators. It appeared that the zero point of several comparable indicators was set differently: one group anchored this systematically different than the other. This implies a notion to be careful in generalizing scores from one group to another when both groups are doing the same kind of work. It also requires delicate decision making by the manager.

Definition of Products

The term "products" can be quite confusing: people may think of products as tangible, material things to hold or touch, as they consider these in very general terms, like "quality of service." For a better understanding, it helps to refer to "duties" or "responsibilities" for the unit in question. Thus, a product can be described as a number of parts of the jobs, or tasks. To help participants to identify indicators, they may use cards; on each card, the name of a product is listed, and participants make a description of the product in question.

Indicators/Contingencies

In order to keep ProMES as simple as possible, not more than two variables (the indicator and its effectiveness) should be implied into one contingency. If, for example, quantity or amount of work has to be used as a compensating factor for an indicator, this variable ought not to be inserted in the indicator in question but should be dealt with in a separate contingency. A compensator for the amount of work counts only when the amount of work is above average. When it is below average, employees can handle it properly within the normal schedule.

Properties of a compensator are no control over the amount of work, no scores in the ineffective area, and always related to a specific indicator.

CONCLUSIONS

With regard to the first issue mentioned in the introduction — the possibility of application of ProMES in a bank — researchers have been successful in using the ProMES approach for developing a productivity measurement system in a bank organization. There is, however, one exception: One group developed products, indicators, and some of the contingencies but could not put the system together. Initially, three separate groups were identified, based on the criterion of interdependency.

It turned out, however, that splitting these into 11 units was better, each with their own products, indicators, and contingencies. This means that ProMES becomes rather expensive and time-consuming for practical use in comparable organizations.

Concerning the second issue — application of ProMES to individual jobs — the team was successful in developing ProMES for an individual job. In groups, an average of ten meetings of 1.5 hours and, for individuals, five to six meetings of 1 hour, sufficed.

Regarding the third issue — tying pay to ProMES data — evidence is not available. Although, in theory, both individual and group applications to pay for performance appear to be feasible, this cannot be sustained by empirical results.

Although the research team indeed was successful in the development of ProMES, this does not apply to the implementation of ProMES. Changes were occurring so frequently that indicators and contingencies would need to be revised time and again. This is very time-consuming and restricts the use of ProMES data in practice considerably. Also, it was not clear whether headquarters, who started this experiment, was really interested and would consider ProMES as an instrument for bank offices in general. Moreover, it seemed that a group based pay system was not favored, while individual performance pay was.

This raises the question, Which are the right conditions for an organization to develop and implement ProMES successfully? Stability seems one of the most important conditions. In a dynamic situation, it does not seem to work so well. Indicators have to be changed regularly, and when new activities occur, it is not even possible to develop contingencies at first, because one has to gain insight in new activities for quite a while. This results in incomplete feedback reports. In such a situation, it will be hard to find support to keep the system going, because it does not offer much help.

Management support is another condition that is vital for a successful implementation. In our case, the gradual lack of support had a negative effect with regard to the motivation of employees to work with ProMES.

The third condition for a successful implementation has to do with the complexity of an organization. In our case, a relatively small organization (approximately 45 employees), 11 different groups, and two individual jobs had to be identified. This makes it very time-consuming to develop a system like ProMES.

These final conclusions may seem a bit negative, but that is partly due to use of ProMES in this specific case. We do hope it will alert future users of ProMES to develop and implement ProMES in supporting conditions.

REFERENCES

Biessen, P. (1992). *Oog voor de menselijke factor: Achtergrond, constructie en validering van de Basisvragenlijst Amsterdam* [Taking account of the human perspective: Background, construction and validation of the basic questionnaire Amsterdam]. Amsterdam: Swets & Zeitlinger.

Chhokar, J. S., & Wallin, J. A. (1984). A field study of the effect of feedback frequency on performance. *Journal of Applied Psychology, 69*, 524–530.

Miedema, H., Santbergen, B., Thierry, Hk., & Meyer, J. (1989). *Beloningsoderzoek bij de bankorganisatie* [Research on compensation at a bank] (Internal Report). University of Amsterdam: Work & Organizational Psychology.

Pritchard, R. D. (1990). *Measuring and improving organizational productivity: A practical guide* (p. 248). New York: Praeger.

Pritchard, R. D., Jones, S. D., Roth, P. L., Stuebing, K. K., & Ekeberg, S. E. (1989). The evaluation of an integrated approach to measuring organizational productivity. *Personnel Psychology, 42*, 69–115.

12

ProMES in a Small Oil Distribution Company

Henriëtte Miedema, Henk Thierry, and
Frederike van Oostveen

This chapter describes the development of ProMES in two units of a
small oil trading company: clerical support and sales. The company
wanted to use ProMES as a management tool in order to get a better
insight in the ongoing activities. Because there was no precedent of an
application of ProMES in small organizations that are relatively
unstructured, for example, without job grading, pay structure, or a
formal policy plan, the research team's first interest was to find out
whether ProMES would cause any particular problem. Second, the team
wanted to learn whether a slightly changed strategy — ProMES
development on a group level and ProMES application on an individual
level — would work.

ORGANIZATIONAL SETTING

In this section, the organization at large and the particular units
involved are described. Subsequently, the design of the development
process for each group will be sketched.

The organization in which ProMES was developed is one of the few
independent oil trading companies in the Netherlands with sales of
about 30 million gallons a year. Headquarters is situated in the eastern
part of the county. The company has two main activities: distribution of
oil products and management of gas stations. Customers are other
small oil companies, transportation firms, gas stations, and so on.

In the past ten years, the company has grown from sales of approximately $2 million to $3 million a year. Only one gas station was owned
when the current owner took over, there are 40 now. The number of
employees has grown from 4 to 25. This does not include those working

in the gas stations, because these employees work on a franchise basis. Due to the fast growth, more structuring of ongoing activities is needed, especially for sales and clerical support. Employees' activities are not adequately controlled, and their performance is not very well measured. Operations have changed considerably over the past three years, implying not only an increase in the quantity of work but also a need for automation of clerical support systems. Because of these changes, the director and the manager of clerical support welcome the idea of a system for measuring activities.

The company has five separate units. All units (except for clerical support) report directly to the director.

There are four main activities:

Clerical support for all operations. This is the only unit with an authorized manager who reports directly to the director.

Customer sales of fuels, propane/technical gas, and fire support systems.

Management of gas stations (this is part of the director's job).

Distribution of fuels and propane/technical gas. There are five truck drivers working in distribution.

Maintenance of gas stations and fire support systems, which is done by two technicians, respectively.

The last three operations, management of gas stations, distribution, and maintenance, will not be discussed, because these were not involved in ProMES development.

ProMES DEVELOPMENT

Members of the ProMES team belong to the research group on performance and compensation of the Department of Work and Organizational Psychology of the University of Amsterdam (supervised by Henk Thierry). Henriëtte Miedema managed the ProMES team, supported by one senior students. She was already familiar with the jobs and the work process in both groups, because she worked for the company in a staff position for several years.

Researchers met with the groups once a week; in the bank facility (Chapter 11) this frequency proved to be optimal. Meetings lasted usually about 1 to 1.5 hours but could be extended without any problem. A similar format as in the bank facility was designed (see Chapter 11) to keep notes. From the perspective of the work cycle, it seemed proper to collect feedback data on a quarterly basis. Reports and surveys that might be used as indicator measures were available only on a quarterly basis. Moreover, gathering data would be very time-consuming; therefore, the manager and the director preferred to do it on a quarterly basis.

The two units involved in this project were clerical support and sales. All employees of the two units participated in the development of ProMES. Clerical support consisted of the manager and three employees. Sales consisted of the director and two employees. The manager and the director were key members in the groups concerned.

Usually, ProMES is developed on a group level, but it can also be done on an individual level. What is critical is whether tasks of members of a group are interdependent. In clerical support, employees were, to some extent, mutually dependent. Consequently, ProMES was developed and measured at a group level. However, in sales, both employees performed exactly the same tasks in different areas of the country and were fully independent from one another. Thus, for sales, ProMES development occurred in a group setting with both sales personnel present, but contingencies were set for each salesperson individually and measures, likewise, were taken on each individual.

We used a stepwise procedure slightly different from the usual ProMES procedure. After the development of indicators, the relevant indicator data were gathered; the design of contingencies came afterward. This was done because employees were not used to evaluating their activities in a quantitative way. Therefore, they could not establish maximum, minimum, or mean scores. They had no idea how effective or ineffective their performance had been. Only the director and the manager had some global idea on the effectiveness of current performance levels.

By merely gathering data for a certain period, it was felt that employees would learn to grasp the essence of relating indicators to effectiveness scores. We expected this would allow them to draw the contingencies. Indicator data were gathered during four quarters for both groups.

Before starting the meetings with the groups, a short introduction on ProMES was given in which the steps in developing the system were explained. It was emphasized that ProMES could be useful as an information system for all parties involved. Also, it was explained that ProMES was still in an experimental phase and that a relationship between performance and pay was to be considered only if the system worked satisfactorily for all parties concerned.

Clerical Support

This unit totaled four people: three employees and the manager. The manager had a dual role — he also worked as an employee. We started by asking the unit members to talk about their daily work. This showed that each member had quite different activities and separate responsibilities. They were, to some extent, dependent on one another, for example, the employee who was responsible for controlling debts needed correct invoices in time from her colleague doing the invoice work.

It was decided to develop ProMES at a group level for two reasons. First, a member had to take over tasks from his or her colleagues in the case of absenteeism or work overload. Second, it helped group members to learn to think in terms of unit goals and unit policies rather than in terms of individual tasks.

The group identified the following sets of major activities: general accounts, accounts of gas stations, control of debts, and making invoices. General accounts was a job done by the manager himself. He was responsible for all incoming and outgoing payments and for making the monthly balance sheets in time. One of the employees was responsible for the accounts of the gas stations. He had to check whether operators of gas stations payed their debts on time. Another employee had to check if invoices were paid on time. The last main activity was to make invoices for products or services sold. This list of different activities showed the complexity of a relatively small unit. Each activity probably had its own products and indicators, although there were, perhaps, some links between activities from different sets.

It proved to be difficult for employees to bridge the gap between their own job and the objectives of the unit. We had observed this in other cases as well. Particular to this unit, however, was the wide variety of activities in which each individual employee was engaged. A question like What would happen if this unit would be eliminated? or What would be the impact for the organization? did not work. They were only able to think of this for their own set of tasks. These sets of tasks or activities became our starting point.

Product Development

After the description of the main activities, it was much easier for employees to identify products. They liked to talk about their jobs and to hear others talk about theirs. Discussions showed that the work efficiency might not be optimal. Answers to What is important in your job? or What is the impact on others? were difficult to give right away. For instance, the employee responsible for the accounts of gas stations and for checking the level of debts was asked, "Do you take any preventing action to check the debts?" He proved to be quite startled and had never thought about any such actions or of any control he could have in this matter. Tasks were just carried out, no more.

Each participant got some homework to do. They were asked to think about products and to try to describe activities concerned. This resulted in a list of products for each activity.

1. General accounts
   a. Processing of bank accounts
   b. Monthly balance sheets

   c. Control of computer systems
2. Accounts of gas stations
   d. Checking and processing daily reports
   e. Calculation of commission of gas stations
3. Control of debts
   f. Checking debtors' payments
4. Making invoices
   g. Processing invoices
   h. Solving invoice problems

Each activity appeared to have one or more products. This resulted in quite a large number for such a small unit. Because the primary objective in this study was to design a performance information system, they were kept intact and were not reduced to more abstract headings. This way, all group members were able to recognize their work.

Developing Indicators

The participants were quite skeptical initially. They considered the measurement of their performance to be very hard, if not impossible, to do. However, they were quite willing to cooperate. Because each employee had his own set of products, group discussions were not very fruitful. We first tried to keep the group together, because we noticed as products were developed, the group got a better sense of what the unit as a whole stood for. They learned their own contribution to the unit's goals. Thus, by keeping the group together in identifying indicators, it seemed to help to facilitate this process. However, it did not work. Only the person whose job was concerned was actively involved in the discussions; the others did not feel it was up to them to identify indicators for tasks they did not carry out, or they were simply not interested in discussing these matters. Besides, business was growing fast at that time, and they had trouble in getting the work done, so, it was hard to get the group together for 1.5 hours every week. After two meetings, it was decided that indicators would be set with each employee individually (the manager being present).

After the meetings with each individual employee were finished and the indicators were completed, a group meeting was held in which all products and indicators were explained. In this meeting, members of the group were encouraged to think about the relative importance of jobs, the consequences of bad or good performance, and the work relations among the members.

In the final list, there were 2 to 4 indicators for each activity, totaling 12 indicators.

Gathering and Recording Data

As mentioned previously, the objective was to set the contingencies after indicator data had been gathered for a period of six months. If available, data relating to the six months preceding the start of ProMES would also be taken into account. Special forms were made to record data adequately. Yet, data concerning the first two months were incomplete and incorrectly recorded, indicating some background problems with the data collection.

First, a problem occurred regarding customers complaints. Usually, a complaint concerned some (assumed) substandard behavior of a particular employee. A second employee was charged with making notes of these complaints. This made him or her feel uncomfortable, being in a position to have to "punish" the other employee. The issue was discussed with the group, and it was agreed that the manager was in a better position to make these notes instead of one of the employees. It was preferred to have a more objective indicator, but, unfortunately, there were no alternatives.

Second, part of the unit's tasks were being computerized at the time measures were taken. It was hard to interpret data and to set standards, because performance had not stabilized yet, and employees were still in a learning stage. Furthermore, there were few historical data that were useful with regard to past performance.

Third, it turned out that employees misunderstood the nature of indicators. They had selected indicators that were beyond their own control. Through assembling indicator data, they discovered their misperception; consequently, some indicators had to be revised. These problems were discussed with the manager and the director; results were much better for the following periods.

Developing Contingencies

Contingencies were then designed for the indicators that applied to each employee and the manager. Indicators first were ranked. This resulted in four indicators with a maximum effectiveness score of +100. These were indicators that belonged to different activities and that were carried out by different employees. They were seen as of equal importance. Two indicators had a maximum effectiveness score of 0, implying that zero activity is considered the normal state of affairs.

During the process, contingencies were set rather easily. Only minimum effectiveness scores were somewhat hard to establish. A helpful question appeared to be If you run out of time and everything goes wrong, what would you do first? Lines connecting zero, maximum, and minimum scores appeared to be exclusively linear in function. In particular, the director, having a clear understanding of what was requested in this phase, considered curvilinear functions as not applying.

Sales

This unit had no authorized manager; both employees reported directly to the director. From the beginning, one of the employees was frightened by a system like ProMES. He had a very defensive attitude during the discussions. When talking about their work, he stressed that because of market influences, his impact on job outcomes was only marginal. He was obviously afraid that once his performance was measured, this would have a negative impact on his performance appraisal made by the director. The other employee welcomed the idea of a more structured and systematic measurement of his performance; he thought he could benefit from such a system.

Developing Products

The process of developing products went easily and fast. Despite the defensive attitude of the one employee, there were no problems in defining the products. Both employees agreed on their final list of products: acquisition — retail and industry; acquisition — new gas stations; acquisition — new clients for gas stations; after sales; and clerical activities.

Acquisition was their main product but could be divided into different categories that received different weights according to their relative importance. Most important was acquisition in retail and industry, which had to be done throughout the year. Second in importance was acquisition of new gas stations, which was done only when other business was slow. Last in importance for acquisition was to get new clients for gas stations. Although the main task was acquisition, they also were responsible for keeping existing clients satisfied (called "after sales" here). There were also some clerical activities to be done — making reports of visits and registration of new clients.

Indicator Development

Both employees understood what was required fairly quickly. They had a good perspective on the use of the final ProMES data. This created more anxiety in the employee who was frightened. Again, his colleague had a more optimistic view.

Through developing products and indicators, it appeared that each employee had his own way of doing the job. This allowed the director to explain what was expected of each of them and to set priorities. For instance, the company made more money if "larger" clients were attracted. Yet, one employee felt more comfortable with "smaller" clients (making it necessary to acquire a larger number to get the same return). It was agreed that new clients' sales would be measured in order to evaluate the effectiveness of different sales strategies. Opinions on paperwork allowed the director and the employees to assess advantages and disadvantages of filing forms each time they visited a client.

In the final list, eight indicators were developed for all products.

Gathering and Recording Data

The objective was to set the contingencies after indicator data had been gathered for four quarters. This implied that the system could not be used for a period of one year. This was quite a long period, but the impression was that the group was not able to develop contingencies on the basis of less than four points of measurement. There were no accurate data available on the period previous to the development of ProMES.

Unfortunately, after collecting data for one quarter for this group, one of the employees became seriously ill, and this lasted for almost a year. Data collection was stopped at this time, because data could be gathered for only one person.

When the employee had recovered and returned to work, his job changed drastically. Insted of the activities he used to perform, he had to control and support the operators of the gas stations. This change in activities was related to a new company strategy. The company focus had moved from getting new clients and new gas stations to making the current ones more effective. At this time, it was not clear whether he was going to perform his old job ever again or whether someone else would take over his job. It was decided to wait to gather data until the company policy was more clear on this point.

Putting the System Together

Because the manager and the director had been present in the sessions developing ProMES, approval of the final results was done very quickly. With the team members, the director looked at the final results and did not make any adjustments.

ProMES development for the sales group went quickly. It took ten meetings to develop the system. There were only two employees involved, so, it was not hard to reach consensus for every step. The clerical group needed more time; the system was developed in 16 meetings here. Yet, considering the extensive list of indicators and the individual sessions, this was a reasonable amount of time.

FEEDBACK

Feedback will be discussed for the clerical support unit only, because it was not clear yet whether ProMES would have to be revised for the sales group. Feedback data were collected for four quarters to set the baseline. After this period, results would be studied to assess whether the system worked satisfactorily. In a previous study, we had noticed that participants had trouble understanding and interpreting the final results by means of the feedback reports. Detailed information on effectiveness scores mentioned in the reports did not seem to be understood. Only the information that effectiveness scores were positive or negative was appealing to them. Therefore, a graphical representation of the results was used to make it more understandable to them. As can be seen in Figure 12–1, in just one graph, it was clear how the group performed in a given period. Because all effectiveness scores were to be seen in this representation, the group easily could see on what indicators they performed well and on what indicators they did not perform well. By pointing out of the maximum and minimum scores, the impact of the score they obtained on each indicator became clear, too.

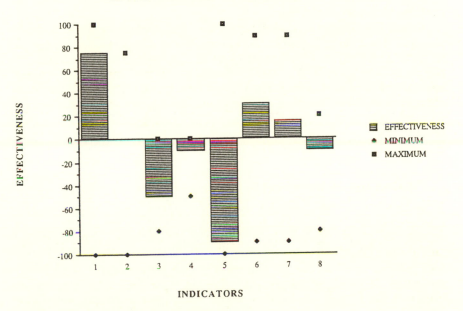

Figure 12–1   Example of Feedback Report

At the time we finished the phase of development, two members of the unit had been replaced by others. A session was held to inform them about ProMES. Results from past quarters were used to explain the system. One of these new employees grasped the meaning and consequences of the system very quickly, but the other one had difficulties in understanding. Hopes were that once she had to collect her own data and would see the results, she would get a better understanding.

The replacement of one of the employees had a considerable impact on ProMES results. After a learning period of about half a year, this employee was performing so much better than the one that left the company that it was necessary to adjust maximums, minimums, and zero points.

The manager was responsible for gathering data on time. Because work overload was very high for him, he never managed to do this on time. After data were collected for four quarters, the baseline results were fed back to the whole group (Figure 12–2). This graphical representation of the feedback results worked very well. It seemed to be better understood than the actual report. In just one sheet, all results were summarized clearly.

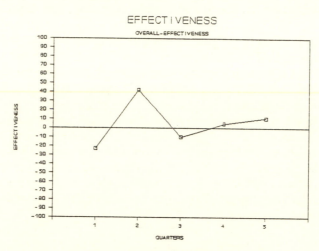

Figure 12–2   Overall Effectiveness Data for Five Quarters

When these results were shown, the general attitude of the group was very defensive. The overall effectiveness score, around the zero point, was not satisfying in their eyes. They were very concerned with results that were in the negative area and tried to explain these by work overload or by the need to learn a new task.

It was stressed by the team members that the overall effectiveness score was not bad but, instead, was neutral and quite normal for a start. The manager told them not to look for excuses but to try to find ways to improve negative results.

As can be seen in Figure 12–2, the group was able to improve their performance in the next quarter (quarter 5). The baseline was set for three quarters (quarters 1 to 3). Effectiveness scores fluctuated considerably during this period. In the last baseline quarter (quarter 3), some of the minimum, maximum, and zero points of the indicators were revised. Results stabilized more or less during the last three quarters. In quarter 5, there was a slight improvement (from 5 to 10) of effectiveness.

DISCUSSION

The following are some general points of interest.

Layout of Feedback Reports

Although it may seem trivial, it is very important to pay attention to the layout of feedback reports. We noticed on several occasions that a good presentation is crucial for understanding and accepting the results.

It seemed difficult for participants to understand the information given in the original feedback report. The effectiveness scores that were mentioned did not seem to have very much significance for the group. Only the fact that they were positive or negative was an indication of good or bad performance.

We have tried several formats and graphical representations and have asked the opinion of participants. The one that was the most appealing is shown in Figure 12–1. Group performance is visualized in just one simple representation. In this representation, all effectiveness scores are shown together. By the maximum and minimum scores of each indicator being pointed out, the impact of the effectiveness score that is obtained becomes clear.

Development for Complex Units

A unit like clerical support may not seem to be complex at first sight, but through development of the system, it turned out that several main activities went on. We recommend to identify these activities before identifying products. For each activity, a set of products can be identified.

The step of setting the minimum and maximum scores for the indicators is facilitated this way. By stating that each activity is equally important, one need only to rank the indicators belonging to a specific activity.

If one chooses the standard ProMES procedure, an exhaustive list of indicators will be identified, which makes ti very hard, if not impossible, to compare them with one another, not only because of the large number but also because it is not possible to prioritize activities: they are of equal importance.

Timing of Feedback

It is crucial for the success of the system that feedback is given as soon as the period of measurement is over. A delay may cause a loss of attention, because past results may not be of any interest. It may even have a demotivating effect to the extent that corrections cannot be effectuated during the current measurement period.

New Employees

Because the system is participatively designed, special attention should be paid to newcomers. They have not been involved in the process and do not see it as their own system. They are not as anxious to see the results as the ones who did participate. They seem to be less committed to the system than the ones who developed the system.

CONCLUSIONS

Before addressing the questions raised in the introduction, the company's current situation must be understood to make it clear why certain changes with regard to ProMES had occurred. The company's strategy had changed considerably during the two years of developing and implementing ProMES. This was partly because of government policy toward environmental issues. Rules and regulations were sharpened and extended, and these were not generally favorable to gas transportation or operation of gas stations. Trucks used for transportation of oil products had become extremely expensive because of these new regulations, and large number of small gas stations were closed by government order. The remaining ones had to invest considerably in safer equipment and in the cleaning of polluted soil.

The company's policy was to stabilize business for the next five years. The director intended to invest in current gas stations instead of in new ones. This had implications for the sales group, which was reduced to one employee. The other employee was doing other activities. Nevertheless, business was growing, but more slowly now, which caused a structural overload of work for the clerical group. The manager, in particular, was no longer able to carry out his activities. He later got an assistant, but the assistant's activities are not yet incorporated in the system. It will take some time before this job's content is clear. It is planned, however, to develop ProMES for this job.

Because work overload was continuously high for the manager, it was hard getting data on time. It was decided then to make one of the employees responsible for this, instead of the manager.

With regard to the issue of the application of ProMES in a small and relatively unstructured organization, we consider the implementation to be successful. It helped both the director and the manager to formulate goals and objectives and to be more specific on the kind and the level of performance they expected from their employees. For employees, it was an eye-opener to learn their contribution in terms of the unit's goals. Furthermore, learning about the jobs of others made them aware of interdependencies, the way their performance was related to that of others.

We noticed — a perhaps more general point — when new employees came in, information and explanation of the system helped them to understand the system, but they were not as motivated to perform well and anxious to see the results every quarter as the ones who actually developed the system. Participation in development seems to make much difference. The ones who had been involved in developing the system felt more that it is their system and, therefore, felt committed to make it successful. Furthermore, they were able to make a distinction between effort and effectiveness. They had learned that working right was not just a matter of putting more effort in the same things but to do it in a way that makes it more effective. They made a list, for instance, for all incoming and outgoing phone calls, so they were able to check if phone calls were answered and whether deliveries were made on time.

The second issue — ProMES as a management tool — is related to the first one. ProMES not only facilitated the process of formulating goals and objectives but also made it possible to measure achievements in that respect. Management became aware of weak points that needed attention. Furthermore, it allowed them to assess the performance of each individual employee and to guide and support them. So, indeed, ProMES was very useful as a management tool.

The third issue — ProMES development on a group level and ProMES application on an individual level — did not cause any problems. Especially in units like sales, where employees perform the same activities but are independent from one another, this seems a good solution. In such situations, contingencies are exactly the same, and, therefore, effectiveness scores can be compared easily. However, the system was developed but not implemented for the sales group at the time of this writing, but this was not due to an unsuccessful development of ProMES but to a changed sales strategy.

In this situation, ProMES had to be developed not only in a dynamic organization but also within a dynamic environment. As the bank experience shows (Chapter 11), these conditions are not the most favorable for such a setting. However, the impact of changes for ProMES was not as large as in the bank project. Moreover, management did not oppose to the fact that the system would have to be adjusted according to changes in strategy and, consequently, in jobs. The system was seen as an instrument that allowed them to control their effectiveness and to appraise individual and group performance. Yet, these dynamic factors caused some obstacles. For sales, it meant a considerable delay. For clerical support, the new assistant's job has to be subjected to the system. New employees need special introduction in order to be motivated by the system.

Unfortunately, there are no results yet with regard to the development of productivity over time. Feedback has been given to the clerical support group only two times. For the time being, it remains an open question whether ProMES will enhance productivity in this case.

13

Development of a Productivity Measurement and Feedback System in a Firm of Commercial Painters

Klaus-Helmut Schmidt, Martina Przygodda, and
Uwe Kleinbeck

This chapter deals with the first case study on ProMES carried out in a German work organization. It describes the development and implementation of ProMES in a craft firm of commercial painters.

An essential characteristic of these craft settings is that the real productive work of the employees is performed in groups outside the close organizational boundaries. The company bids on jobs in various locations, and after getting the award, a group is directed to do the work at the site. Under these conditions, the central unit has no direct and immediate control on the work the employees do. As a consequence, the traditional principles of work organization and productivity management, like production scheduling, quality control, and so on, hardly can be applied. Only the group leaders have the chance to supervise the employees' performance. However, because the painters are engaged in different orders at different sites, even the group leaders' influence is limited to some temporary inspections of the work progress at the sites. Furthermore, the employees are often confronted with unforeseen and changing wishes of the customers that call for a high degree of flexibility in following them.

This lack of external structure and control in combination with the changing work demands gives the painters a great deal of autonomy in scheduling their work. On the other hand, however, they have to invest a lot of energy in self-organizing their group activities and in self-managing their individual behavior to bring both in line with the

The research was supported by a grant from the Deutsche Forschungsgemeinschaft (Kl408/10-1). The cooperation and assistance of employees and managers in the firm where the research was done is gratefully acknowledged.

organizational expectations. The requirements of self-organization and self-management are always needed where job scopes offer a high degree of freedom for carrying out the work (Hacker, 1985; Stone, 1985). In order to cope with these requirements, the employees need clear information about what the central organizational objectives are, what is important and what is not so important in their work, and how well they are performing on all important aspects of their responsibilities.

As argued in the introductory chapter, the ProMES approach aims at providing all this information. It can, therefore, be assumed that in such unstructured and changing work situations, ProMES should be a helpful tool for assisting the painters in achieving the organizational goals more effectively.

Based on these characteristics of our setting, the following questions were asked:

Can ProMES be successfully developed in a work situation where tasks are relatively unstructured and changing?

Will the system support work groups in developing more effective self-management strategies and in building up a more effective internal work organization?

At this time, the project is just starting with the feedback and the feedback meetings phase, and, therefore, no hard data on the effects of the system's functioning are available. Thus, the focus of this chapter will be on answering the first question. However, some information is available that also allows for drawing preliminary conclusions relating to the second issue.

ORGANIZATIONAL SETTING AND PROJECT DESIGN

Description of the Organization

The organization where the study was done was an old and well-established family-owned firm located in a large urban area of the midwestern part of Germany. It consisted of four departments with specialized functions. One department was involved in painting and renovating public buildings, churches, and private houses, the second department repaired and installed glass, the third one was engaged in heat insulation, and the fourth was an administrative unit. During our study, approximately 120 persons were employed. Because of its size, the painting department was further divided into four work groups, each of them led by a master painter. The coordination of these groups within the painting department was done by a production manager, who acted as the primary assistant to the owner of the firm.

Because of the small size and the flat hierarchical structure of the firm, the work atmosphere was characterized by a high degree of open communication, familiarity, and trust. In addition, there was a strong commitment between the owner and the employees and good relationships among the employees themselves.

Before ProMES was developed, the organization had no experience with any kind of a productivity measurement system. The only instrument for informing the firm owner about how well the groups were functioning was a monthly computer printout indicating what orders had been finished, what the actual costs to complete each order were, and what price the client actually paid. On the basis of this, the owner was able to recognize whether the groups were just covering costs, if they were profitable, or if they were losing money. This information was also available to every group leader but not to the group members.

This cost accounting, however, provided no opportunity for managing the productivity of the groups in a behavior-oriented manner. Keeping this in mind and remembering the special characteristics of the setting, the firm owner felt a strong need for a behavior-oriented productivity measurement system ProMES. Therefore, he welcomed the development of ProMES very much, giving his complete support.

Description of the Project Units

As mentioned above, the painting department was divided into four work groups. For our investigation, the firm owner selected one of these groups as an experimental group consisting of 15 employees. The members of this group developed the productivity measurement system. They were mainly involved in painting private houses and some public buildings. The employees worked in small subgroups of two to six persons at one site, depending on the volume of work to be carried out. Every participant had served an apprenticeship as a painter. The other groups in the painting department consisted of between 6 and 12 members. One of these groups was selected as a control group; it had ten members.

The selection of the experimental and control groups was determined by the following reasons. Painting department groups were selected because only the painting department groups performed working tasks what were fairly comparable so that a control group design could be applied. Second, these groups were exposed to highly competitive market conditions. In order to award contracts, they had to make estimates that were difficult to meet with an acceptable profit margin. This made productivity extremely critical. In the other departments, productivity was not such a critical issue, because, here, the firm held a less threatened market position. In addition to this, the experimental group in which ProMES was developed had to handle some troubles resulting from a lack of competence and authority in the group leader. The firm owner attributed this to the fact that the group leader was formerly a member of the group. Therefore, the owner hoped that ProMES would help the leader to organize the work within the group more effectively. These problems were not recognized by the research team at first but were later seen as a third selection criterion for this group.

Every group leader in the painting department had to manage several functions. They had to look for new orders from the customers and had to consult with the customer. They also had to calculate the time and material needed to complete an order. This calculation was the basis for the estimates offered to the customers for awarding the contract. Furthermore, they were responsible for the manpower assignment within the group. Finally, they had to supervise the work of the employees. The duties performed by the group members were mainly papering, painting, and plastering walls, doing lacquered work, and, of course, preparing all mixtures they needed.

When we started the project, the initial reactions of the members of the experimental group could be described as reserved. The gains they could earn from developing the system appeared to be not exactly transparent for them. Therefore, they argued that the system would not be very helpful for their work. They gradually changed their opinion, however, as they experienced the process of developing the system and recognized the close connection to their work objectives and their behavior. Questions about why they were selected did not arise.

Project Design and Project Course

For evaluating the effects expected to result from the implementation of ProMES, a control group design was applied with a baseline and a subsequent feedback phase. During the baseline period, the measurement system was used to collect productivity data from both the experimental and the control group but without feeding the data back to the members of either group.

Initially, a period of six months was intended as baseline. However, this schedule was changed because after three months of data collection, the leader of the control group and the production manager left the organization overnight to start their own firm. As a result, the painting department experienced a rather turbulent time until the required new staffing had been accomplished. During this transitional period, the productivity data showed a dramatic decrease in all groups of the department. Therefore, the baseline had to be interrupted for six months until the productivity again reached a level comparable with the one achieved before the shift in management occurred. After that, the baseline period was continued.

Because of this delay, a lot of effort had to be invested in keeping the project in progress. One problem was to enlist the cooperation of the new manager and group leader. This was relatively easy. Far more difficult was to keep the members of the experimental group involved. They had done all the work to develop the system and, therefore, were keen on seeing first results. The delay, however, forced the employees to wait for this longer than expected, and they experienced heavy frustration. It called for a lot of persuasion to gain their understanding for the necessity to extend the time for completing the baseline over one year. At this, the firm owner proved to be a great aid, so that all the difficulties finally could be overcome.

As a supplement to the productivity data, in both the experimental and the control group, several questionnaires were used to evaluate the effects of the ProMES approach. For measuring possible changes in the motivating potential of their jobs, in their job satisfaction and work motivation, the painters were requested to respond to the corresponding scales of a German translation (see Schmidt, Kleinbeck, Ottmann, & Seidel, 1985) of Hackman and Oldham's (1975) Job Diagnostic Survey. Furthermore, a questionnaire was applied specifically developed to assess the experienced level of participation and the level of feedback the group members received about the effectiveness of their performing. Finally, the participants were submitted some subscales from an instrument developed by Pritchard (1990) to rate the clarity of their work roles and objectives. All these questionnaires were applied once before the beginning of the project, once at the end of the baseline period, and will be used further at the end of the feedback phase The number of personnel and hours worked were and will be continuously registered, as well.

DEVELOPMENT OF THE SYSTEM

The design team to develop ProMES consisted of all 15 members of the experimental group, including the group leader, and two members of our research unit as facilitators. For both facilitators, it was the first time that they were involved with implementing ProMES in an organization. However, both had considerable experience in doing field research in many other projects in industry. In addition, a student participated as a facilitator trainee whose role essentially lay in recording the discussions and documenting the progress in developing the system. To develop the system, the researchers met once every two weeks for 1.5 hours with the experimental group at the beginning of their normal workday.

Among the members of the design team, the group leader of the painters had a key function. Only he was provided with information (e.g., about the orders from the customers, the planned time schedule) that was not accessible to the other members but was indispensable for building up a valid and complete productivity measurement system. Therefore, the group leader's opinion carried a little more weight in the process of achieving a consensus on some issues. However, this was accepted by the other participants and did not prevent an open and vivid discussion.

Before starting the development, a half-day meeting was organized to inform the members of the experimental group in detail about the aim of the project, the steps needed to create the measurement system, and the procedure of how to implement it. During this meeting, the firm owner was also present, emphasizing the great importance of the project for the whole organization. In contrast, the control group got only the information that in one unit of the firm an organizational development program would be introduced that, in the case of a success, would probably be expanded to other units.

Identification of Products

Consistent with the steps outlined in the introductory chapter (see also Pritchard, 1990; Pritchard, Kleinbeck, & Schmidt, 1993), the design team started with the development of products. At first, the facilitators gave a short orientation about the exact meaning of products, referring to some hypothetical examples from several other work settings. The necessity was especially stressed to distinguish between products and indicators in order to keep the discussion free from interfering debates on measurement problems.

Subsequently, the painters were asked to describe all activities or objectives the group was expected to perform. This led the group members to begin with enumerating very specific tasks they usually were engaged in during their daily routines. This process continued until no further proposals were brought in. Later, the facilitators encouraged the participants to rephrase their specific statements on a more general level. Asking the question What are the main contributions of the group to the overall organization? turned out to be very helpful in shifting the focus toward this more proper level of product description. After this rephrasing was accomplished, the design team agreed on the following list of four products in all: completing orders on time, quality of order execution, dealing effectively with the painting supplies and materials, and increasing the flexibility of manpower assignment.

The process of identifying the products came off rather smoothly. There was no disagreement that completing orders on time and dealing effectively with the painting supplies and materials represented important aspects of the group's functioning. Depending on the volume of work, which was jointly agreed upon with the customer at the site, the group leader had to calculate the time and the material the employees probably would need to complete the order. The calculation of time and material was the basis for the estimate the group leader submitted to the customer to obtain the contract. Because the customer would not accept a bill for an amount that was higher than the estimate, the firm lost money if the actual time requirements ran longer than estimated or the actual material costs exceeded the estimated ones. On the other hand, in order to get the contract, it was important that the group leader did not overestimate time and material. This made the calculation a risky venture with severe economic consequences.

There was also unanimity on including quality of order execution in the list of products. In discussing this product, however, the facilitators had some trouble with preventing the group members from getting into disagreements on how to measure this product. The facilitators insisted on first clarifying the products before measurement problems would be discussed.

To achieve agreement on product four, increasing the flexibility of manpower assignment, was the most difficult part in establishing the list of products. In view of having served a solid apprenticeship as a painter, the group members complained about a strategy of manpower assignment that, in the past, had led them to become specialists in few aspects of painting while in all the other aspects they would run the risk of losing their practice. The group leader felt these complaints as a hidden attack against his competence of leadership. Therefore, he defended his strategy of manpower assignment, arguing that a specialization in work functions would be the best way for achieving high-quality standards. In contrast, the group members focused more on the negative effects, for example, the extra time the specialists needed to move from one site to another where their specialty was called for.

The discussion on this issue was strongly based on emotion, and the facilitators had to invest a lot of effort to make it realistic again. They finally managed this by pointing out to both parties that their different views had already been incorporated in product one, completing orders on time, and product two, quality of order execution. By this discussion, the group leader and the other group members were led to recognize that the causes of their controversies were essentially a conflict between these two products. After this was understood, both parties realized that an additional important product of their work was to harmonize this trade-off between quality and time requirements. The best way to achieve this was seen in increasing the flexibility of manpower assignment by means of a long-term on-the-job training. This training would enable the group members to carry out all the required work functions and, thus, would make it possible to meet quality standards without losses of time. All participants finally agreed on phrasing this product as "increasing flexibility of manpower assignment."

After the list of products was completed, it was submitted to the firm owner for approval. IIe approved all products and encouraged the design team to continue the good work they were doing.

Development of Indicators

In the next step, the design team had to develop indicators of the products. The underlying concept of an indicator was introduced as "a measure of how well the group was generating each product." The facilitators emphasized the essential criteria for good indicators and illustrated this by some examples from other work settings. In particular, the group members were led to observe that the indicators should cover all products and, above all, should cover each product in all its different aspects. furthermore, the significance of developing indicators that should be controllable by the activities of the group was stressed.

Although it proved rather easy to develop adequate indicators for product one and product three, the initial reaction of the group members on finding indicators for products two and four was "You cannot really measure these facets of our performance."

By discussing the difficulties in getting valid measures for the quality of order execution, the group recognized that this product was multidimensional in nature, covering several distinct subparts. This was a new insight because when the products were identified the focus of the group had been exclusively on technical things like accuracy and tidiness of performing. Now they realized that how well they interact with the customer at the site and how well they serve as good consultants would be of equal or even greater importance for the quality of their work. As consultants, the painters had to advise the customers in selecting the right wallpapers, colors, and so on. However, the group members had no idea of how they could measure all these somewhat ambiguous aspects.

The facilitators tried to promote the problem-solving process by asking the group whose judgment of quality would be the most crucial or the most influential one for the success of the whole organization. Thinking about this, the group finally realized that, above all, the customer's judgment would be decisive, because his judgment would determine whether new customers came to the firm based on, for example, oral recommendations.

After recognizing this, the group decided to measure the quality of order execution by a short questionnaire asking for the customer's satisfaction with the technical performance, the satisfaction with the employees' social behavior and competence, as well as the satisfaction with the consultative performance. This questionnaire should be sent to the customer a short time after the order was finished. For its development, each group member was encouraged to prepare some item formulations for the next meeting. Their proposals were then reviewed within the whole team, and after some minor changes in wording, seven items were selected to be included in the questionnaire. All group members showed a strong engagement in working out the questionnaire and were very proud of their accomplishment.

Finding a valid indicator for product four, increasing the flexibility of manpower assignment, was also a troublesome process. The employees argued that if they wanted to work in a more effective way as a group, it would be necessary to give up the specialization for the benefit of becoming generalists in all work functions. Only then they would be able to meet time as well as quality standards without running the risk of a conflicting trade-off between them.

This judgment met with unanimous approval, but the discussion on adequate measures took a controversial course. The crucial question was how to measure the degree to which the group members were qualified to undertake all job relevant work functions. Some employees argued that it would not be possible to validly assess their individual qualification level. Other group members were afraid of some negative social consequences of such an assessment; they feared that it would bring to light what their different contributions were to the functioning of the whole group.

To keep the discussion in progress, the facilitators suggested that the group members first clarify the most important work functions with which they had to cope at the sites. The group agreed on seven functions in all and finally determined that the group leader would rate each group member monthly on a seven-point rating scale. Because they wanted this rating to be a group-based, not an individual-based, evaluation of qualification, the individual ratings were then transformed for the indicator percentage of group members qualified to carry out all job relevant work functions.

One reason for measuring in this way was that the employees realized that it was the group leader's responsibility to assign the manpower in a way so that all received the chance for broad on-the-job training. Therefore, negative ratings would be more indicative of the group leader's style of organizing their work than reflecting their own deficiencies.

Finding indicators for product one, completing orders on time, and product three, dealing effectively with the painting supplies and materials, turned out to be comparatively easier. At first, the group proposed as a measure for product one the difference between the estimated time of order execution and the time actually needed. In thinking about the consequences of such a measure, however, it soon became clear that the absolute difference did not take into account the different volume of orders. As a result, being a certain number of hours under the estimated time requirements for a small order would receive an equal weight to being the same number of hours under the estimated time of a large order. In a second approach, therefore, the percentage deviation of the actual time from the estimated time was used as the indicator.

However, the facilitators anticipated that even this improved measure would result in problems that would become evident when the data were fed back to the group. To illustrate this, they led the group members to figure out the average score of four hypothetical orders that showed large variations in volume. Using the percentage deviation measure for each order, the group quickly understood that in averaging these measures, the three small orders involved were of greater weight than the one large order. In reality, however, gains and losses in large orders have larger effects than gains and losses in small orders. Therefore, the group understood the necessity to weight the percentage deviation measure with the volume of each order. This was finally achieved by multiplying the percentage deviation by the ratio of the estimated time of order execution to the monthly total working hours of the group. The resulting indicator was then phrased as "weighted percentage deviation of the actual time requirements from the estimated time per order."

The description of developing this indicator might give the impression of a very complicated process. In reality, however, it ran rather smoothly. Obviously, for some of the painters it was a great challenge to demonstrate their problem-solving abilities in circumventing all the difficulties involved. Therefore, they pushed the process ahead until a satisfactory solution was found.

In finding an indicator for product three, dealing effectively with the painting supplies and materials, the same rationale could be applied as for the time indicator. This made its development an easy task. The percentage deviation of the actual material costs from the estimated costs was weighted by the estimated volume of the order in proportion to the total volume of orders per month. With regard to both indicators, it is important to note that before the development of the measurement system, the employees had information about neither the estimate nor the actual results.

After the development of all indicators, a meeting with the firm owner and his production manager was held to review and approve the complete list of indicators. The list was totally accepted, and no suggestions for modification were brought in. On the contrary, the firm owner was astonished at the employees' insights on the functioning of the whole organization. As a businessman, however, he missed a measure for evaluating the profitability of the group's performance. In his opinion, only such a measure would make it ultimately clear to the employees what an essential influence their behavior has on the economic success of the firm.

Although the owner clearly understood that the indicators for products one and three were closely related to what he considered profitability, he believed feedback on the financial gains and losses would provide an additional means for motivating the employees to organize their work more effectively. As a result, the firm owner was invited to the net meeting to inform the group on his proposal. Because the group raised no objections to it, a fifth product, called "profitability of working," was added to the list. To get a measure for this new product, the decision was made to apply the same rationale as before for the indicators of products one and three. The resulting indicator was then phrased as "weighted percentage deviation of the actual costs from the price the customer has to pay."

Table 13–1 presents the final list of all products and indicators. As is easy to see, the indicators for products one, three, and five are all effectiveness measures showing how well the group members are meeting their goals. However, the goals refer to different dimensions, that is, to time in the case of product one and to money in the case of products three and five. In contrast, the indicators for product two and, above all, product four are more measuring the means by which the goals are achieved. Because, for these indicators, no such hard data were available, their measures are essentially subjective in nature. As illustrated before, this made the process of developing adequate indicators a difficult but, nevertheless, a soluble and even challenging task.

Table 13–1   Final List of Products and Indicators

---

1. Completing orders on time
    Indicator 1: weighted percentage deviation of the actual time requirements from the estimated time per order

2. Quality of order execution
    Indicator 2: satisfaction with the technical performance
    Indicator 3: satisfaction with the employees' behavior toward the customer
    Indicator 4: satisfaction with the consultative performance

3. Dealing effectively with the painting supplies and materials
    Indicator 5: weighted percentage deviation of the actual material costs from the estimated costs per order

4. Increasing the flexibility of manpower assignment
    Indicator 6: percentage of group members qualified to carry out all job relevant work functions

5. Profitability of working
    Indicator 7: weighted percentage deviation of the actual costs from the price the customer has to pay

---

Development of Contingencies

In the next step, the design team had to establish the contingencies. The process followed the steps described in Pritchard (1990), except where noted. The facilitators first gave a detailed overview on the process of their development using a hypothetical example. They focused on the specification of the maximum and minimum score and of the expected level of work outcomes. The maximum was defined as the "best possible outcome that the group could achieve on each indicator under optimal conditions," whereas the minimum was introduced as the "lowest level the group could imagine to perform on when everything is running extremely badly." The specific features of contingency functions like nonlinearity and steepness were explained, as well as their consequences upon the functioning of the whole measurement system.

Thereafter, the group started with determining the maximum, minimum, and expected level of each indicator. It soon became clear, however, that this task threw the group into some confusion. For some of the indicators, they had, at best, only vague ideas about the range of possible performance. This was especially true for the three indicators reflecting the deviation of the actual results from the estimated ones. The group had been receiving no information about those measures. Therefore, they asked the group leader what he thought about the range of possible outcomes. Only after he gave the group an orientation could the maximum, the minimum, and the expected level of these indicators be determined.

Because the group members had a lot of experience with the reactions of the customers to their work, it was relatively easy to specify the corresponding levels of the three indicators measuring the customers' satisfaction with the different facets of the group's performance. For anchoring all these indicators, nearly the full range of the underlying questionnaire scales was used, which reached from (1) extremely satisfied to (7) extremely dissatisfied.

It was also easy for the group to commit to the maximum, minimum, and expected level of the indicator covering the flexibility of manpower assignment. They considered as maximum when 100 percent of the group members would be qualified to carry out all job relevant work functions. The minimum was determined on a level of 20 percent of personnel qualified. Table 13–2 presents (among other things) the results of identifying the extreme and expected values of the seven indicators included in the measurement system.

The painters were next asked to rank the maximums of the indicators according to their contributions to the overall effectiveness of the group. The maximum considered as the most important should be given a rank of 1, the one that would contribute the second most to the overall effectiveness should receive a rank of 2, and so on. The discussion revealed astonishing differences in the group members' views on what they believed to be important and not so important in their work. Obviously, the group lacked any common orientation on this. Therefore, considerable discussion took place for them to build up such a common orientation before a consensus on the ranking could be reached. The effectiveness rating that followed the ranking process then ran without severe disagreements.

After that, the ranking and rating procedure was applied to the minimums of the indicators. Here, the same large differences in the painters' views occurred as with the maximums. Furthermore, in order to shorten the troublesome process of finding a satisfactory consensus, some of the participants argued for simply using the same ranks as

Table 13–2 Maximum, Minimum, and Expected Levels, Including Their Ranking and Effectiveness Rating

Indicator	Indicator Values			Effectiveness Scores			
	Minimum Level	Expected Level	Maximum Level	Minimum Ranking	Minimum Rating	Maximum Ranking	Maximum Rating
1. Deviation of the actual time requirements from the estimated time	–20%	10%	25%	1	–100	1	100
2. Satisfaction with the technical performance	7	3	1	2	–90	2	90
3. Satisfaction with the employees' behavior toward the customer	6	3	1	6	–45	3	85
4. Satisfaction with the consultative performance	5	3	1	5	–50	5	50
5. Deviation of the actual material costs from the estimated costs	–20%	5%	25%	4	–70	6	30
6. Percentage of group members qualified	20%	60%	100%	3	–85	4	75
7. Deviation of the actual costs from the price the customer has to pay	–40%	10%	30%	1	–100	1	100

those developed for the maximums. Because this involved the danger of an invalid evaluation of the minimums, the facilitators intervened and suggested thinking at first about the consequence of acting on this advice. They used as an example the indicator for the flexibility of manpower assignment. The maximum of this indicator had received a rank of 4. Would this rank also be adequate for the corresponding minimum? Looking at it this way, the group members realized that the negative effects on the group's functioning resulting from the minimum would be stronger than the positive effects associated with operating at the maximum of qualification level. Therefore, the minimum level received a rank of 3. This example gave the group members an understanding of the issue, and they continued the ranking of the minimums without too much consideration of the maximums' ranks. The rating of the ranked minimums in terms of effectiveness proved again to be fairly easy for the group.

In view of the apparent lack of a common frame of reference for evaluating the different work requirements, the facilitators suspected that the opinion of the firm owner and production manager would also be strongly divergent from the view formed by the group members. Therefore, they interrupted the process before the establishing of the contingency functions and asked for the owner's and manager's opinion on what the group had developed so far. Though this procedure departed a bit from the typical ProMES methodology, it proved to be an effective strategy to foster the process of achieving a consensus.

The expectations of the facilitators were, indeed, confirmed. Although the firm owner and production manager agreed on the determined range for each indicator, they expressed a totally different view on some of the rankings and ratings of the maximums and minimums. For example, they evaluated the maximum of the indicator for dealing effectively with the material as far less important than the group members had done. Hence, the facilitators decided to arrange a meeting with both parties to confront them with the large disparities of their views.

This meeting turned out to be very instructive for all participants. All appeared to realize for the first time what different ideas they had about the concern of the organizational objectives. This experience was confusing but did demonstrate the necessity for developing a common understanding on this. Therefore, the discussion that followed was promoted by the strong need of all to gain such a common understanding. All parties contributed to this process. At the beginning, the firm owner tended to dominate the discussion in a rather dogmatic manner, but later, he developed a better understanding of the view formed by the group. By this, conditions appeared that facilitated an open and vivid exchange of ideas. As a consequence, the final decision on the ranking and effectiveness rating of the maximum and minimum levels of the indicators was more the result of new insights gained in the course of the meeting than a compromise merely combining the different views. After the process was completed, all participants seemed to feel very relieved. Both the group members and the owner seemed to be convinced that the found solutions would make it easier for them to really pull together. Table 13–2 presents the results of this process.

In the next major step of contingency development, the full contingency functions had to be constructed. For drawing the functions, the facilitators first placed the maximum, minimum, and expected values of each indicator as well as their corresponding effectiveness scores on prepared transparencies of blank contingency slides. Then, for each indicator, the size and the number of intervals between the maximum and minimum values had to be determined. Depending on the varying range of the indicators, the design team decided to use between five and eight intervals of equal size in each case. After that, the group members were requested to shape the contingencies, starting from the expected or zero point up to the maximum and down to the minimum.

In the beginning of this shaping process, the group tended to assign to each interval jump an equal increase or decrease in effectiveness. Thus, linear functions did emerge for the section from the expected level to the maximum as well as for the section from the expected level to the minimum. Therefore, the facilitators reminded the group of the possibility to build in the contingencies such features as points of diminishing return or disproportional gains and losses in effectiveness at certain segments of the indicators. For illustration, they confronted the group with a scenario borrowed from the industrial production area. Here, improving quantity often represents only a productive strategy as long as no severe negative consequences have to be faced, like, for example, frequent machine breakdowns due to excessive wear and tear or losses in quality. Further improvements beyond the point, where the risk of such negative consequences is increasing, could be entirely dysfunctional for the productivity of the whole plant. This example gave the group members a better understanding of the issue and led them to reshape some of the contingencies correspondingly.

Especially during this phase of constructing the contingencies, it was sometimes difficult for the facilitators to balance out their roles as ProMES experts on the one side and as promoters of participation on the other. As ProMES experts, they were bound to prevent the group from making decisions that would have threatened the validity of the measurement system. By taking on this role, however, they ran the risk of guiding the process in a too-directive way. As a consequence, the participation of the group members would be restricted. Participation was still a precondition for incorporating the painters' expert knowledge about the reality of their jobs into the measurement system. To cope with these conflicting demands, the facilitators frankly communicated their problematic position to the group and asked for their understanding when they questioned the painters' suggestions or urged the group to reflect the consequences of their proposals more in detail. This proved to be a good strategy to keep the group involved.

The facilitators felt that constructing the contingencies was this part of the development process that gave the group members a full comprehension of the system's functioning. While developing the contingencies, they became clearly aware how and to what extent their own behavior could influence the productivity of the whole firm. It was clear that the contingencies contributed to clarifying the interorganizational rules according to which the employees' performance is transformed into the final outcomes of the organization.

After finishing the contingencies, the opinion of the firm owner and the production manager was asked for. Neither made suggestions for any modifications, and both appreciated the system as a helpful tool for offering the group and themselves a precise orientation on what productivity actually meant in that organization.

Time Needed for Developing the Measurement System

As mentioned before, the researchers met once every two weeks for 1.5 hours with the group to develop the system. The process of identifying the products took no more than three meetings. Five meetings were needed to find indicators for the products. To determine the extreme indicator levels, including their ranking and effectiveness rating, four meetings were required. Finally, two meetings were held for constructing the contingencies. In addition, four separate meetings with the management were necessary to get the approval for the results of all these different steps. The whole development process was completed after about six months.

Further Steps

During the past year, this measurement system was applied to gather baseline data in the experimental group as well as in the control group. In the next few months the feedback period will be set up. In view of the volume of work orders, the decision was made to give a monthly feedback. The data on the seven indicators will then be collected at the end of each month and fed back to the experimental group in the form of a formal feedback report. Besides the indicator scores, this report will contain the resulting effectiveness scores for the indicators, the overall effectiveness, and, finally, its percent of the group's maximum possible overall effectiveness score.

DISCUSSION AND CONCLUSIONS

Despite the above mentioned difficulties resulting from the unforeseen changes in management during the baseline period, the planned design could be maintained, although with some delays. In overcoming these difficulties, it was clear how important it is to have the full support of higher level management. Without the support of the firm owner, it would have been nearly impossible to gain the interest of the new managers in the running project and to convince the group members of the value in continuing the process. In addition, informing the group in detail, in advance, about the whole course of the project, its different phases, and why these phases are necessary has also proved very helpful to manage the rather adverse circumstances. Furthermore, the participation of all group members in developing the measurement system obviously has brought about a strong commitment that made it easy for the participants to tolerate the frustrating experiences with the delays.

Initially, the facilitators had some concerns about including all the 15 groups members into the design team. They feared that this large a group would complicate the development process. These concerns, however, were groundless. The participation of all group members not only guaranteed a strong commitment but also increased the quantity and quality of the ideas invested as input in the development of the system. Furthermore, their participation helped find a sound consensus on some problematic issues. In all, the troubles the facilitators had in moderating the discussion within such a large group were more than compensated by these positive effects.

The steps in developing the measurement system proved very different in difficulty. The development of products was a comparatively easy task. One of the most striking issues was how to shift the focus of the design team from a very specific level of product description to a more general level. This was effectively achieved by directing the attention of the group to the main contributions they provided to the overall organization. Another problem was to the multidimensional nature of some products. For example, the product quality of order execution was first considered as exclusively covering technical performance. Only in finding indicators for this product was it realized that it consisted of two further subparts referring more to the social components of order execution. Therefore, the facilitators have to make the group clearly aware of the possibility of multiple product dimensions.

The process of creating indicators was more difficult to accomplish and needed twice as much time as product development. Two problems were of particular interest. The first one was related to the initial reaction of the group that, for some of their products, it would not be possible to find any adequate measures at all. This reaction appeared not to be caused by a general resistance to measurement but rather by a real lack of ideas on how a measure could be developed. This was most evident for product two, quality of order execution, and product four, increasing the flexibility of manpower assignment.

The main problem was that the group could not imagine using subjective measures. However, after having realized that, for example, in measuring the quality of order execution, the customer's opinion would be crucial, they quickly learned that in some cases, subjective measures were not only unavoidable but also desirable for designing a valid measurement system. This insight was then also applied to measuring product four. It is clear that facilitators should prevent the group from being too closely focused on just developing objective measures. Under some conditions, subjective measures might serve the purpose of a productivity measurement system far better. Furthermore, the development of subjective measures appears to offer the participants a good chance for demonstrating creativity and cleverness. This makes the task a challenging affair.

As a second major issue, it was clear that great care is to be taken in the process of developing good indicators. The different approaches and refinements for creating a measure for product one offer an instructive example. Here, two different indicators were proposed at first that were later recognized as suffering from some severe flaws. These flaws were seen only when the group was urged to rehearse a practical case in which the proposed measures became operational. The final indicator resulting from this iterative process was, no doubt, complex but represented a more adequate solution than its precursors.

Preparing the unit in advance for the possible troubles involved in such an iterative process is important. This makes it easier to deal with the frustration that may occur when only little progress is experienced. Furthermore, rehearsing a practical application allows the group members to identify the deficiencies of their proposals by themselves. This procedure is helpful for motivating the participants to continuously improve their solutions. In addition, it is a good strategy to help the facilitators avoid too much intervention and control.

In the present project, with the improvement of some of the indicators, their complexity increased. However, this was not a problem for most participants. Because of their work, they were fairly familiar with the mathematical operations on which the calculation of these indicators was based.

The most difficult step in developing the measurement system was reaching a consensus on the informational foundations for establishing the contingencies. The reasons for this were twofold. First, for some of the indicators, the group members lacked any information about the potential range of variability in their actual performance. Therefore, to assess the maximum and minimum levels of these indicators, the group was entirely dependent on the group leader, who alone had the necessary information. Second, both within the group and between the group and the management, considerable ambiguity existed on the organizational policy concerning the relative importance of the different activities of the unit, as well as their contributions to productivity. As a result, the ranking and effectiveness rating of the indicator maximums and minimums were a controversial issue.

On the mere procedural level, these circumstances produced some complications. However, it was just these circumstances that offered the ProMES approach an excellent chance to demonstrate its utility. Only by the application of ProMES did both the group and the management become aware what information really is needed for managing the activities of the group in an effective way. Until now, the organization obviously had failed to make this information available to their members. Furthermore, the group and the management realized that ProMES filled this informational vacuum by the resulting measurement system. This system not only informs the group on their actual performance but, in addition, presents a clear orientation on what is important and not so important in their work and how well they are contributing to the productivity of the whole organization.

Based on these existing results, it can be concluded that the ProMES approach was successful in developing a productivity measurement system in an organization where tasks are relatively unstructured and changing. Therefore, question one has clearly been answered. In contrast to this, question two still remains open, because no results on the feedback effects are available yet. However, the selection of some of the indicators and products, such as flexibility of manpower assignment, points out that the employees understood that ProMES presents a good chance to develop more effective self-management strategies and to build a more effective internal work organization. A further indicator for the system's functioning in this way may be the reactions of the management to its development The management agreed on the final system in all its parts and has asked to develop it in other areas of the organization, including the administrative unit.

REFERENCES

Hacker, W. (1985). Activity: A fruitful concept in industrial psychology. In M. Frese & J. Sabini (Eds.), *Goal directed behavior: The concept of action in psychology* (pp. 262–283). Hillsdale, NJ: Erlbaum.

Hackman, J. R., & Oldham, G. R. (1975). Development of the Job Diagnostic Survey. *Journal of Applied Psychology, 60*, 159–170.

Pritchard, R. D. (1990). *Measuring and improving organizational productivity: A practical guide* (p. 248). New York: Praeger.

Pritchard, R. D., Kleinbeck, U. E., & Schmidt, K. H. (1993). *Das Management-system PPM: Durch Mitarbeiterbeteiligung zu höherer Produktivität* [The PPM management system: Employee participation for improved productivity]. Munich: Verlag C.H. Beck.

Schmidt, K.-H., Kleinbeck, U., Ottmann, W., & Seidel, B. (1985). Ein Verfahren zur Diagnose von Arbeitsinhalten: Der Job Diagnostic Survey (JDS) [An instrument for diagnosing job content]. *Zeitschrift für Arbeits- und Organisationspsychologie, 29*, 162–172.

Stone, E. F. (1985). Job scope–job satisfaction and job scope–job performance relationships. In E. A. Locke (Ed.), *Generalizing from laboratory to field settings* (pp. 189–206). Lexington, MA: Lexington Books.

PART III

Other Applications of ProMES

14

Testing the Feasibility of ProMES before Implementation: A Case Study in the Dutch Steel Industry

Jen A. Algera and Annemarie M.C.M. van den Hurk

In this chapter we describe a feasibility study that was set up to test whether ProMES could be implemented in a department of a steel plant at Hoogovens Steel Works in the Netherlands. The main reason for this feasibility study was the very complex environment where ProMES was to be implemented. In this case, the environment was very complex in many aspects: technological (15 different technical operations, e.g., steam production, had to be controlled by the department), organizational (the work is done 24 hours a day in a five-shift system), logistical (the department is part of a very complex logistic network where time is the main parameter), and informational (the 15 technical operations are connected with a number of control and information systems).

The management of the steel plant was interested in implementing ProMES because it fits very well in their management style, which is aimed at delegation of responsibility and the use of bottom up approaches to arrive at new organization structures and management systems. However, there were no examples of ProMES cases in such a complex environment, so, it was decided to set up a feasibility study. Besides the more general conditions, as mentioned by Pritchard (1990), before starting the implementation of ProMES, a number of additional points were to be covered in this feasibility study:

an estimate of how much time and effort would be needed to design a complete ProMES system to be used by all five units

a check on whether the work force really was in favor of having a ProMES system for self-control

a description of the controllability of the work flow coming from other departments.

a description of the control and information systems to get an idea of how much had to be invested to develop an information system to generate ProMES feedback data

the fit between ProMES and two other organizational developments occurring at that time. In one project, each of the five shifts "adopted" some of the 15 technical operations (e.g., high-pressure steam generation) to get at improvements of the working of those operations. This meant that they paid special attention to reasons for any malfunctioning of that operation. The other project aimed at using more uniform work methods among the five shifts.

THE CASE

Task

The task of the department consists of process control and repair of operation breakdowns in a subprocess of steel making. In this subprocess, the pig iron is blown with oxygen to reduce the percentage of carbon. Because of a process of suppressed combustion, carbon monoxide gas is produced and transported to a power plant. In this process the gas is cooled and cleaned. By cooling the gas, steam is also produced, to be used by other operations in the steel plant. The main goals of the work force are process control and repair of operation breakdowns and malfunctioning, to also minimize environmental pollution and safeguard carbon monoxide gas escape.

Method

Start-up

In the start-up of this study, all five shifts got a formal presentation on ProMES and were told of the intention of management to consider the feasibility of ProMES. The main goal of the study, that is, to evaluate whether ProMES could help the department to improve performance, was explained. It was stressed that the opinion of the five shifts would be decisive in this evaluation. One of the researchers (Annemarie M.C.M. van den Hurk, who was a student at the Eindhoven University of Technology at that time) was acting as facilitator. During the three months of this feasibility study, she was often at the site and used document analysis, interviews, and group discussions as main sources of information gathering. In general, the interviews and group discussions were structured but conducted in a rather informal atmosphere in the control room. It can be described as a balanced interaction in which the shifts were informed on the characteristics of ProMES and the researcher was informed on the characteristics of the work.

Design of the Feasibility Study

After the introduction of the idea of a feasibility study into the department, the study itself consisted of seven steps.

Step 1: Analysis of the work of the department in relation to the technical operations. In this step, input-throughput-output analyses were made for each of the 15 technical operations. This analysis was based on a method developed by In 't Veld (1988) and gives a quick view of the flow of material, the relationships between the technical operations within the department, and the relationships between the technical operations and other operations outside the department. Moreover, and even more important, in these analyses, the role of the personnel was described, mainly in terms of their contribution in the input-throughput-output processes. In addition, technical limits for safe operation were listed. These are conditions to be observed by the personnel to prevent possible dangerous situations, for example, exceeding the temperature limits. Finally, on the basis of interviews and group discussions, a more global impression was formed with regard to the responsibilities of the department and the amount in which these responsibilities were divided with other departments in the steel plant.

Step 2: Testing general ProMES criteria. In this step, the nine criteria for implementation of ProMES mentioned in the literature (see Pritchard, 1990) were checked in this specific situation. These criteria pertain to

the dominant attitude in the department on the necessity of improvement of performance,

all people involved endorsing the importance of productivity improvement,

the personnel subsystem being viewed as critical for success,

a minimum level of trust between management and the work force,

stability of management,

willingness to measure performance and to be measured,

visible commitment of management,

minimum knowledge of ProMES, and

no "not invented here" culture.

Step 3: Determining areas of control. In this step, the researchers, on the basis of their knowledge from steps 1 and 2, determined global areas of control. An area of control can be compared with a "product" in ProMES terminology but is much more loosely defined. It is a global indication of the objectives of the department, for example, steam production control. It can be viewed more or less as a global or a priori product.

Next, for each area of control a number of questions were posed: How much influence does the department really have in this area of control? What specific parameters can be influenced and in what way? Is the influence direct or indirect (e.g., by means of communicating with other departments)? Can existing performance levels be identified?

Step 4: Testing defined areas of control. In this step, the globally defined areas of control were checked against the type of criteria as often used for products. Does performance improvement benefit the performance of the whole steel plant? Is the department primarily responsible? What dependence relations exist with other departments? Can unit personnel influence their performance by effort (working harder or smarter)?

Step 5: Determining measurement possibilities. In this step, some preliminary measurement possibilities were explored for each area of control. First, all existing measurements were listed. Second, new ideas on measuring effects in each of the areas of control were gathered.

Step 6: Defining design conditions. In this step, a number of rather specific conditions that had to be met were defined. For example, because of the five shift system, there should be some minimum level of uniformity in way of working to interpret performance differences. Also, as another example, in this situation, some performance indicators will refer to direct controllability by the unit, while others will refer to indirect controllability.

Step 7: Reporting to the department. In this step, the results of the foregoing steps were reported to the department. These results were presented in terms of the opinions of the researchers whether ProMES was feasible in this situation, which design conditions were relevant, and what kind of decisions had to be made, for example, concerning the design team.

RESULTS

The seven steps as described in the previous section led to the following results.

Step 1, which was introduced mainly to give the facilitator a global view of the work processes in the department, also had some very important side effects. Because the personnel were not used to thinking of their own work in terms of input-throughput-output processes, the discussions they had with the facilitator also gave them a much more explicit idea about their real contribution in these processes. As such, it helped to prepare them for the official ProMES design steps in the future. The analyses provided by this step were checked by the worker and the manager of the unit for correctness and made available as a written document.

In step 2, all nine criteria were checked. It turned out that there was broad agreement on the necessity of productivity improvement. This was also reinforced by the fact that in the recent past, some serious problems in process control had occurred. Another reason for the positive attitude toward productivity improvement was that the suppressed combustion process had been installed for only a few years, so the department felt there was still room for improvement. In addition, it was quite clear that the personnel subsystem was a crucial factor in productivity improvement. The shifts also were willing to measure performance. They even pointed out that some new equipment was badly needed to be able to measure a number of parameters that had been measured imperfectly in the past.

Most discussions were on the stability of management and, in connection with this point, the level of trust between management and the work force. The main reason was that in the recent past, some reorganization had taken place in the whole steel plant that influenced this department. The personnel asked for more certainties in the future and consistency of management plans. The responsible manager explained how ProMES would fit in a long-term strategy of the steel plant to develop in the direction of delegation of responsibility and self-management. In general, this explanation was accepted.

In step 3, six areas of control were identified, for example, environmental control (pollution), safety control, economical use of materials (water, energy), and steam production control. A table was produced by the researchers that indicated for each area of control which of the 15 technical operations were involved, how and where the influence of the shifts is visible, and what kind of influence (direct/indirect) and the amount of influence (moderate/high) are present. For example, in steam production control, three technical operations were involved: high-pressure steam cooling, low-pressure steam cooling, and accumulating and transporting steam to other departments.

The result of step 4 was positive, in that all questions concerning the check of areas of control against product criteria were positive. Most questions could be answered by "yes" or "moderate/high" (amount of influence of the shifts). As far as the dependence relations with other departments, the departments and/or specific jobs where such dependencies existed were identified (e.g., logistic planning). The general conclusion from step 4 was that it would be feasible to develop step 1 of ProMES and the resulting products would fit the relevant criteria.

Step 5 pertained to the measurability of performance indicators. The conclusion of the researchers was that, in principle, in all six areas of control, performance indicators could be defined and measured. In addition to this conclusion, for each area of control, it was indicated in a global sense how to measure the performance of the shifts. Specific examples were also provided (e.g., number of alarms, demand of steam production met).

The result of step 6 was a list of conditions that should be considered before starting with ProMES:

uniformity in way of working across shifts;

uniformity in giving feedback across shifts;

minimum level of knowledge within the shifts, that is, at minimum, the required standard level of training in terms of process knowledge; and

development of ProMES as an iterative process, that is, a ProMES system will not be perfect in one design loop but will have to be improved (e.g., some indicators will turn out to be not completely valid and will have to be changed)

In addition, four specific design conditions for this situation were formulated:

The department will not be able to directly influence all performance indicators. Some available indicators (e.g., complaints) are more indications of performance on a longer time basis.

Some operation breakdowns are under direct control of the department. To control some other breakdowns, communication with other departments is necessary, so, there is no direct control. However, this communication is legitimate in terms of responsibilities in the whole steel plant, and other departments are supposed to cooperate.

Some technical operations have contradictory effects on performance. This makes it necessary to look for optimum performance levels in which contradictory effects are taken into account.

In some areas of control, the department divides its responsibility with other departments. This should be taken into account in developing ProMES.

Step 7 was very important and consisted of a formal presentation to each shift on the results of the foregoing six steps. This presentation covered the findings of the researchers and their suggestions how to move on with ProMES if the department was to decide to do so. Because the results of step 4 and step 5 were positive, the researchers stated as their opinion that development of ProMES was possible in this department, provided that the general and design conditions were taken into account. In addition to this conclusion, four other sets of decisions were identified. These decisions would need to be made if the department decided to start ProMES:

1. How to choose the members of a ProMES design team. Four possibilities were presented:
   a. One of the five shifts would be the design team, and the other shifts would comment on their design activities.
   b. The design team would consist of representatives of all five shifts.
   c. Each of the five shifts would design one of the products in ProMES.
   d. Each of the five shifts would design one of the products, preferably related as much as possible to the technical operations adopted by each of the shifts.

For each of the four possibilities, the advantages and disadvantages were mentioned in terms of speed of development, involvement of all five shifts, and coordination needed across the five shifts.

2. Will feedback be given per shift or across shifts?
   In this five shift situation, one can have feedback for each shift or with all shifts combined. Again, advantages and disadvantages were listed in terms of time needed to produce feedback reports for five separate shifts versus one across shifts, the risk of destructive competition among shifts, and the motivating force of feedback per shift compared with feedback across shifts.

3. Cost/benefit analysis, mainly in terms of time needed for development of ProMES and time and money needed for investments in information systems and measurement apparatus.

4. Discussions needed with other departments. Because of the dependability of other departments, discussions would be necessary and agreement on some points should be reached.

After the formal presentation by the researchers, lively discussions on the pros and cons of ProMES in their department followed. Management, which was also present at these presentations, was again questioned on its intentions with ProMES (e.g., is ProMES an instrument for self-management or for tightened control?). In most shifts, the evaluation of the feasibility of ProMES ranged from positive to "give it the benefit of the doubt."

DISCUSSION

The result of the feasibility study was a decision to officially start ProMES development in this department. It took about one year to develop a full-blown ProMES system, which consists of 5 products and 19 indicators. The feedback process had just started at the time of this writing, and no data are available yet.

Looking back at the benefits of the feasibility study in this specific situation, the following observations can be made:

Because of the feasibility study, both management and the work force had a much more realistic idea of exactly what ProMES would mean, compared with previous ProMES projects. This statement is valid not only for the technical aspects, such as time needed, but also for the cultural aspects, such as leadership style. In fact, management was forced to explain their long-term strategies concerning organization structure, management style, and so on.

In this feasibility study, the use of input-throughput-output analyses turned out to be very valuable in the official ProMES development. Because of the work done in the feasibility phase, the remaining development of ProMES could be sped up substantially.

Because of the feasibility study, the knowledge of ProMES was quite sophisticated in the department. Especially in developing indicators, which is the most difficult step, the discussions on valid performance indicators were on a very high level, that is, people came up with some very smart suggestions for performance indicators. This illustrated that they generally understood the difficulties in defining indicators for a valid measure of the performance, taking into account the complex dependencies of other departments in the steel plant.

This feasibility study also contained some problems. The two most important difficulties encountered were:

It is difficult to find a good balance between the right level of abstraction and the required level of detail. In the discussions with the personnel, a great risk is to go into technical details, while the aim of the feasibility study was to give an overall and global evaluation of the possibility to develop ProMES officially.

The check on the product criteria and measurement possibilities (step 4 and step 5) gives only a global impression of final problems to be solved, especially in defining valid performance indicators.

Overall, we feel the feasibility study was very successful. The lessons learned from this experience can be summarized as follows: First, because ProMES was not pushed into the department on the basis of a quick decision, both unit personnel and management got the time to gradually develop the insight on what ProMES really would mean for their way of working. This way of introducing was highly valued. Second, this feasibility study took three months. Most of this time was needed to get all five shifts involved. In a situation that is less complex in this organizational aspect, a feasibility study could be shortened substantially. If other conditions such as technology, logistics, and information systems also would be less complex than in this case, probably two or three weeks instead of three months would be needed. Third, a feasibility study takes time but also saves time and problems for later ProMES development. In this case, the feasibility study took three months and the subsequent ProMES development one year, a total of 15 months. However, we are convinced that, in this case, the whole process would have taken more time if a feasibility study had been omitted, mainly because less support for doing ProMES could have hampered progress in defining performance indicators. Fourth, regarding the position of facilitator in any ProMES project, a minimum knowledge of the technology and so on is needed for the facilitator to be accepted as a serious partner for the unit personnel. A feasibility study like this provides a natural way for a facilitator to learn about the ins and outs of the unit. Fifth, also in much less complex situations, we would advise to do a feasibility study, which would probably take no longer than two to four days, if performed as a "quick scan." It gives all parties involved a more realistic idea of the problems to be solved in the subsequent development of ProMES.

CONCLUSIONS

Evaluating the whole process of the feasibility study and the official ProMES development thereafter, we conclude that the feasibility study turned out to be very effective. Mainly because a great number of problems had been recognized in this phase, the official ProMES development was, in fact, quite smooth if one takes into account the complexities in this situation.

The issue of the five shift system is especially crucial in this case. Without the feasibility study, we believe the development of ProMES would not have gone so smoothly. Probably the most important factor was that the personnel in the department felt they had really chosen to do ProMES and had a fair chance to decide on realistic grounds whether ProMES would fit their needs or not.

ACKNOWLEDGMENT

The authors thank the personnel and management of this department in the steel plant, in particular, Arie Smit, who acted as a manager with a very high commitment to this feasibility study and the subsequent development of ProMES.

REFERENCES

In 't Veld, J. (1988). *Analyse van organisatieproblemen* [Analysis of organization problems]. Leiden/Antwerpen: Stenfert Kroese.

Pritchard, R. D. (1990). *Measuring and improving organizational productivity: A practical guide* (p. 248). New York: Praeger.

15

Development of a New Performance Appraisal Instrument: An Application of the ProMES Methodology

Amie Hedley, John E. Sawyer, and Robert D. Pritchard

This chapter reports an application of the ProMES methodology to individual performance appraisal. The system was designed to measure how well individuals fulfill their roles. This is different from the system used for productivity because when individual performance is measured no interdependencies between individuals are considered (Pritchard, 1990). This application also differs from the standard application of ProMES in that most of the indicators of individual performance in this organization were measured subjectively, as opposed to the objective measures commonly used in ProMES applications.

RESEARCH PURPOSE

One of the major problems encountered with performance appraisal is how to combine the various performance dimensions into a comprehensible composite score. Although most jobs are multidimensional, for many personnel decisions involving comparisons among employees, an overall composite score is indispensable. For example, when determining wage increases, an overall score allows management to assign raises in proportion to the employees' relative merit. An overall score is also needed for promotions, terminations, and deciding who merits special programs. These decisions are very important, so, it is essential to have accurate information from performance appraisals.

Existing methods commonly used for weighting and combining dimensions of performance fail to account for differing importance among the various performance dimensions. The typical performance evaluation instrument includes several dimensions on which an individual is evaluated. Normally, these dimensions are not of equal importance to overall performance. For example, the success with which a person can communicate with his coworkers may be much more important than how neatly he or she fills out paperwork. Also, nonlinear relationships between a particular dimension and overall performance are not accounted for in typical performance appraisals. In the normal linear weighting procedures, an increment of one unit is of equal value, regardless of the individual's standing on the dimension. The problem is that this linear system indicates that the greatest improvement in performance will always occur when improvement is made on the most important dimension, but this is not always accurate. For example, it could easily be that for a health care employee's job, carrying out proper health care procedures for clients is more important than maintaining administrative paperwork. However, if an employee is very good at taking care of the clients but below average at keeping up with normal paperwork, his or her overall performance could be improved more by moving from below average to average on doing paperwork than by improving from very good to excellent on client care. The typical performance appraisal system does not reflect this nonlinearity.

Importance weightings and nonlinearities were addressed by using the ProMES technique. It was felt that if a system could account for these two issues, more accurate overall composites of performance could be produced.

RESEARCH QUESTIONS

This research project was aimed at answering two basic questions. First, can people develop a performance appraisal instrument using the ProMES methodology? In the past, the ProMES system has been used primarily for productivity measurement. In productivity research, almost all of the data are measured objectively. When dealing with performance appraisals, most of the performance measures are likely to be ratings. Can employees differentiate the effectiveness levels of subjectively measured dimensions and successfully generate contingencies?

Second, will use of the ProMES methodology provide overall scores that are different from the traditional combinations such as expert judgments or simple unit weighting?

ORGANIZATIONAL SETTING

This research was conducted in a state government administered organization located in the southwest United States that consisted of two residential facilities. Entry into the organization was through the organization's participation in a research project dealing with satisfaction, climate, and turnover, which was being conducted by the second author. One facility, a state hospital, provided care to the mentally ill.

The other facility, a state school, provided social services to the mentally retarded.

The facility for the mentally ill consisted of a number of smaller subunits. These subunits were wards on which patients lived. The various wards cared for different types of people. For example, there were wards that dealt with people who were newly admitted, while others dealt with patients who were there for extended care. Other wards specialized in cases such as chemical abuse, patients with medical problems, or patients who could not speak English. The school for the mentally retarded was also subdivided into separate buildings in which specific types of patients were cared for; there were buildings for patients who were nonambulatory, those with behavioral problems, and so on.

It was expected at the start of this research that the employees dealing with the various types of patients would have similar job duties and responsibilities but that the relative importance of the various job duties would differ. For example, all employees were responsible for caring for the client's hygiene needs and for keeping the facilities safe and secure. In the buildings with nonambulatory clients, it should be much more important to care for hygiene needs, because these clients have no ability to take care of themselves. On the other hand, the employees dealing with clients who act out and have behavioral problems need to be more concerned that the buildings are secure and the patients will not hurt themselves.

In total, the two facilities employed about 700 mental health workers. These employees were categorized into different employment levels. The levels ranged from the bottom level of aide to service assistant, specialist I, specialist II, and supervisors. The aides and assistants had very similar direct care responsibilities, but aides all had less than six months tenure. Specialists had overall supervisory responsibility for their respective units. The hospital had an additional level of supervisors who were typically registered nurses.

Organizational Climate

Throughout all levels of the organization, the atmosphere was rather unstable. The employees felt they were generally overworked and underpaid. They felt the facilities were greatly understaffed. The pay scales were quite low, and there was a fairly high degree (17 percent per year) of turnover. This turnover percentage would probably have been higher except that the area was experiencing substantial economic depression at the time.

Also, shortly before the project began, management in the state hospital had implemented mandatory transfers for many of the employees. These transfers required many of the employees to be changed to a different ward. The transfers had resulted in a great deal of negative response from employees toward management.

Description of Experimental Groups

The research reported here was done with three units in the client organization. Two of these were made up of employees from the state hospital and one from the state school. These three groups of employees were each working with different kinds of patients. These units were selected because they were representative of the major types of units and provided a reasonable context to conduct the research.

The employees in one of the hospital groups worked in the admitting wards, what was called "acute care" (AC). These employees dealt with the patients who had just entered the facility. These patients were greatly agitated, and their behavior was unstable. The other group of employees in the hospital dealt with patients who had been residents at the hospital for a long time. The behavior of these patients had been stabilized, and, thus, the activities of these employees were more related to daily care and hygiene. This group was called "extended care" (EC).

The remaining group of employees worked at the state school (SC). They worked with clients who not only were mentally retarded but also had behavioral problems. Much of the behavior of these patients was unstable, like that of the AC hospital patients, but these patients also lacked the self-help skills because of their mental retardation.

From each group, a subset of supervisors and employees was selected to comprise a design team. These design teams would participate in the development of the new performance appraisal system. The remaining employees in each group had no direct participation in the project. They were to be the subjects of the new performance appraisal evaluations that were filled out by their supervisors.

METHOD

Research Design

The first step in the research design was to determine which subset of employees would be involved in this research. It was also necessary to identify the performance dimensions to be used for the evaluation. Both of these tasks were accomplished through an interview process.

In order to properly measure the employees, it was necessary to determine how they should be grouped. It was expected that job duties would be similar across levels of employment (such as from aide to specialist I) but that the jobs would differ based on the types of patients being cared for. For example, people dealing with mentally ill, long-term patients were expected to have similar responsibilities to those who cared for the nonambulatory mentally retarded patients, but the importance of various aspects of the work would differ across these units.

An additional part of this first step was to determine what these job duties were and, thus, the indicators that were important in determining the performance of an employee. For example, one dimension of performance might be for an employee to effectively communicate with coworkers. In order to identify these job duties and determine who would comprise the experimental groups, interviews were conducted.

These interviews were conducted with employees at various job levels and from various wards and buildings. The interviews were conducted following a critical incidents interview procedure. Employees were asked to think about a coworker or subordinate they felt was an excellent performer and one that was a poor performer. They were then asked to describe what activities made his or her performance excellent or poor. Approximately 50 people who were felt to be a representative subsection of the work force were interviewed.

Upon completion of the interviews, the researchers met to determine how the employees should be grouped. It was determined that all mental health workers were responsible for the same basic job duties. Thus, it was decided that the lower levels of employees (aides, assistants, specialists I) could be combined and measured by the same performance appraisal dimensions. However, because employees working in different units were dealing with different types of patients, the importance of the dimensions seemed to be different. Thus, the three groups of employees would use the same performance indicators, but each group would develop their own set of contingencies.

The next step taken with the interview data was to produce a suggested list of performance dimensions. From employees' responses in the interviews, 11 dimensions were developed. This list would be used to begin the performance appraisal development process.

It was also necessary to determine a scale that would define the different levels of performance on these 11 dimensions. Because nine of the performance dimensions were characteristics or behaviors that could not be measured objectively, the researchers determined that a subjective rating scale should be used. A one to nine point rating scale was decided upon. A rating of nine would designate the maximum level possible, and a rating of one would designate the minimum level possible (these were defined on the scale as "The most I could ever imagine seeing" and "The least I could ever imagine seeing"). Other anchors were also placed on the scale. The two performance dimensions that could be measured objectively were days absent from work in six months and times late for work in six months. For these two dimensions, each design team would determine objective numbers for the maximum and minimum levels they would ever expect to see. For example, on the dimension of "absences from work," a team might determine that 30 absences would be the most ever possible from an employee in six months and zero would be the least. These, then, become the maximum and minimum levels of the scale for that team.

Developing the ProMES Measurement System

The second step in the research process was to develop the ProMES measurement system. Three groups, one from the state school and two from the state hospital, were selected to develop the system. Each design team was composed of a unit supervisor and three to four specialists who were responsible for first-unit supervision and direct care of clients. These design team members were selected by the personnel supervisor in conjunction with the researchers. Because of the understaffing problems and the demands of their jobs, each design team could meet only for one two-hour session.

The same development process was followed in each design team meeting. This process can be broken down into several parts. First, a short explanation of the process was provided; next, the performance dimensions were reviewed; then, the maximums and minimums were determined; and, finally, the contingencies were drawn.

Process Explanation

Initially, it was necessary to explain the process of what was to happen and for what purposes. The teams were told that the researchers were attempting to develop a performance measurement instrument for research purposes. They were told that the results of this process would provide appropriate scaling of the importance of various dimensions of performance. The results would be used for research and would be fed back to the organizations' administration for their consideration in improving ongoing performance appraisal and feedback procedures. Group members had been informed by personnel directors that this was an organizationally sanctioned project and that the organization encouraged their cooperation. This point was stressed in the introduction.

Performance Dimensions Review

The researchers then outlined the interview procedures that had been conducted earlier and how the initial list of the 11 performance dimensions had been defined. The teams were told that the researchers needed their help in making sure that all important performance dimensions were included and that the wording was appropriate for their work process. They were then told that they would participate in a structured process for determining the relative importance of each performance dimension and for determining an appropriate scaling of each performance dimension to reflect its contribution to overall employee effectiveness.

After approval and consensus were reached concerning the list of performance dimensions, each team developed its set of contingencies. Because this development process followed an identical path for each team, this discussion will focus on only a single team.

Contingency Development

First, the effectiveness values of the maximum and minimum levels of the 11 performance dimensions were established through the following process. The maximum levels for each of the 11 performance dimensions were listed. The team was then asked to rank order these 11 maximums in terms of the contribution of each to the overall effectiveness (or performance) of an employee. The facilitator suggested that the team think that if an employee was average on all of the dimensions and could achieve the maximum on only one dimension, which one would they feel would result in the greatest improvement.

Consensus was reached through discussion, and each maximum was ranked. An effectiveness value of +100 was then given to the maximum that had been ranked most important. The team then rated the other maximums as percentages of the +100 maximum. For example, if the maximum of a given dimension was only half as important to an employee's effectiveness as the most important maximum, it would receive a value of +50. When the maximums were completed, the analogous process was completed for the minimum levels of the performance dimensions. With the minimums, however, the most important (worst) minimum did not have to be given the value of −100. It received the value that the team felt was appropriate. This was because it was not assumed that the degree to which the maximum negative level was *below* expectations was going to equal the degree to which the maximum positive level of the dimension was *above* expectations. If the maximum negative effectiveness value would have been constrained to a value of −100, this assumption would have been made.

After the effectiveness values of the minimums and maximums were established, the zero points were identified. This was done by having the teams decide at what point along the performance dimension an employee would be considered to be neither contributing to nor detracting from effectiveness. In other words, this is the point at which an employee would be considered neutral (neither good nor bad).

The effectiveness values of the remaining points on each performance dimension were also determined through team discussion and consensus. The teams normally focused contingency development on the scale anchors. For example, they determined how much more it should be worth if an employee's performance was "noticeably more than most employees'" (a rating of seven) or how much less it should be worth if an employee performance was "noticeably less than most employees'" (a rating of three). After they had determined the effectiveness values for the anchored dimension scores, they could then fill in the other effectiveness scores to complete the contingencies. By using the anchors to help establish the effectiveness values, the team found it much easier to put a value to a subjectively judged level of performance. For example, by thinking of an employee they were familiar with whose performance on the particular dimension was "noticeably less than most employees'," they were able to determine how detrimental that was to the employee's overall performance. Figure 15–1 shows an example contingency. It indicates that the supervisors decided the maximum rating of nine corresponds to an effectiveness of +98 and a minimum rating of one corresponds to an effectiveness value of –75. The remaining effectiveness values of the contingency were established, and the resulting contingency is shown in Figure 15–1. This contingency indicated that going above the neutral level of four is positive; however, this increase is not linear, because increases beyond a rating of seven do not represent as great an increase in effectiveness. Similarly, going below the neutral level is negative; however, this decrease is not linear, because decreases below a rating of three do not represent as great a decrease in effectiveness.

This instrument development process was used successfully for the other teams as well. Each of the teams determined that the list of performance dimensions that was presented to them did, indeed, cover the important aspects of their work and could be used to develop their appraisal instrument. The teams all differed on the rankings and ratings they produced for their performance dimensions. The shapes of the contingencies also were unique for each team. This was expected because the teams were representing employees who were dealing with different types of patients. This caused the priorities of their performance dimensions to differ.

Performance Data Collection

After the ProMES instruments were developed, the next step in our process was to collect the performance appraisal data on the employees. These data were then used for statistical analyses to answer the two research questions. The next section of this chapter will describe the collection of the performance data and analyses.

Performance appraisal forms were distributed to the supervisors in the designated hospital and school groups. The supervisors were instructed that the ratings were for research purposes only and would not be used for any personnel decisions. They were required to evaluate the workers under their supervision who had previously provided written consent. The supervisors completed the performance appraisal forms considering performance over the past six months. For nine of the performance dimensions the supervisor rated each employee on the one to nine point rating scale. The other two objective performance dimensions required the rater to supply a number of days absent and

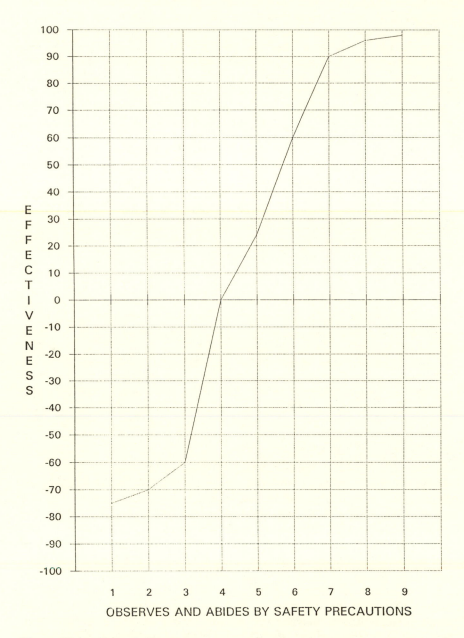

Figure 15–1   Example Contingency

the number of times the employee had been late for work in the past six months. Two other measures required the rater to make an overall judgment of the performance of the employee. The first required the supervisor to mark one of three boxes defined to represent a poor, average, or good performer. The other asked the rater to give an indication of the level of overall performance on a one to nine point rating continuum. The completed performance appraisals were then returned to the researchers in sealed envelopes to protect the confidentiality of the raters.

Measures to be Compared

This research examines the use of ProMES to obtain a measure of overall employee performance. In order to evaluate this new method, the overall performance scores produced by ProMES were compared with other measures of overall performance produced by more traditional methods. How each of the overall measures was obtained is described below.

The first measure of overall performance was based on the ProMES contingencies. Using the contingencies developed in the team meetings, the rating given an employee on each performance dimension was transformed into an effectiveness value. After the effectiveness values were obtained for an employee's 11 dimensions, they were then summed to get the overall effectiveness of that person.

A second measure of overall performance for each employee was obtained by taking the average rating of the raw scores on the 11 dimensions of performance. The rating on each performance dimension for an employee was summed, and the average was obtained (the two objective dimensions, absences and lateness, were adjusted to the same scale length as the nine point rating scales).

For the next overall composite, the raw scores were converted to standard (z) scores. This is a unit weighted composite. All indicators were converted to z-score units based on the group mean and standard deviation for that indicator. An employee's 11 standardized dimension scores were then summed and the mean was computed to produce an overall z-score rating for each employee.

Another overall measure came from the one to nine point overall rating on the performance appraisal sheets. This rating was obtained as an overall judgment given by a supervisor.

Finally, the last two measures to be used for comparison were linear importance weighted performance composites. The first importance weights were determined through statistical regression. Each of the 11 performance dimensions was regressed on the nine point clinical judgment of overall performance mentioned above. This was done for each group separately. This generated beta weights that reflected the importance of each dimension to the overall composite. An employee's score on each dimension was multiplied by the beta weight for that dimension to obtain an overall weighted composite. This procedure reflects a type of policy capturing for the importance of each dimension. This method will be referred to throughout this chapter as the "regression weighted" method.

To produce the second set of linear importance weights, a regression line was fit separately to each of the contingencies. The resulting regression weight reflects the overall linear slope through the points on a contingency. These slopes represent a kind of contingency from which the nonlinearities have been removed. This process preserves the relative importance of the various dimensions because the more important the dimension, the greater the overall slope of its contingency. A separate set of regression weights was developed for each group.

To obtain this composite score, an employee's score on each particular dimension was multiplied by the regression weight for that dimension. This produced dimension scores weighted by importance. The sum of these weighted dimension scores was then computed for each employee to obtain his or her overall composite. This method will be referred to as the "importance weighted" method.

RESULTS AND DISCUSSION

The six sets of overall performance scores were obtained for each group separately as described above, then used in the statistical calculations necessary to answer the research questions. The sample sizes for groups SC, EC, and AC were 37, 35, and 51, respectively. All analyses were computed on each group individually.

Research Question 1

The first question was, Can people develop a performance appraisal instrument using the ProMES methodology? Part of the issue here is whether they can differentiate the effectiveness levels of subjectively measured dimensions and successfully generate the contingencies. The system development process went quite smoothly. The teams were all able to generate their sets of contingencies without much difficulty. They were able to define various levels of performance and determine where those levels would be represented on the subjective rating scale. For example, on the performance appraisal form, the rating of a five had the verbal anchor, "level of performance similar to most employees." The development teams interpreted this to be the level of performance of their average workers. They then decided whether their average workers were failing to meet, meeting, or exceeding the level of performance that they, the supervisors, would expect. This process helped the teams determine the zero points (expected levels of performance). If a development team felt their average employees were just meeting the expected level of performance, the zero point was placed at the rating of five. If they felt their employees were exceeding the expected levels, the zero point was placed lower, at the rating of four. Finally, if the team felt their average employees were failing to meet the expectations of the supervisors, the zero point was placed higher, at a rating of six or seven. After the zero points had been established, the team could fairly easily draw in the rest of the contingencies.

After the contingencies were drawn, each team spent time reviewing their performance dimensions and the corresponding contingencies. At the end of the process, the teams were satisfied that the instruments they had produced would accurately measure the important dimensions of performance. Thus, from the design team's point of view, the systems were accurate.

It is interesting to note that the teams produced several contingencies that did not have the zero point at the middle of the scale (a rating of five). Based on the rating scale anchors, this implies that the average performance of their employees was not the level of performance that was expected. Across teams, 27 contingencies were constructed that used the one to nine point rating continuum (nine by each team). Of these 27 contingencies, 3 had zero points at the rating of four, 17 had zero points at five, 6 had zero points at 6, and 1 had the zero point at a rating of seven. The absence and lateness contingencies were not included in this comparison because they had objectively measured rating continuums that varied among teams.

Two important things can be captured by the use of contingencies. The first of these is the relative importance of the dimensions of performance. This is expressed in the overall slope of the functions. The second is the nonlinear relationships. The contingencies can allow for constant amounts of change in the dimensions to result in differential changes in effectiveness. It was expected that both of these characteristics (differing slopes and nonlinearities) would appear in the contingencies developed for this research. In fact, this was the case.

All of the contingencies produced were nonlinear. In fact, all three teams had within their contingency set a contingency that was actually nonmonotonic. If a contingency is nonmonotonic, this means that as the indicator scores continue to increase, the effectiveness scores will increase to a certain level then will begin to decrease. The contingency appears as an inverted U. This is unusual, but not unrealistic. All of these contingencies were for the performance dimension measuring employee empathy. The teams felt that if a person was too empathetic, it could hurt his or her ability to properly care for and control the patients. All teams independently produced this nonmonotonic contingency for the empathy dimension.

The contingencies for the 11 dimensions also had differing slopes indicating differing levels of importance for the dimensions. The contingencies varied across the dimensions within each group. For example, in group AC, the steepest contingency was for the safety dimension and ranged from +99 to −99 (shown in Figure 15–2). By contrast, the shallowest contingency for this group was on the lateness dimension and only ranged from −10 to +25 (shown in Figure 15–2). This depicts the greater importance placed on the safety dimension. From the information presented above, it appears that the contingencies were able to capture differing importance and nonlinear relationships present in the dimensions of performance.

Another important question is, Were the contingencies really capturing the policies of the groups? It was felt that because all employees in this organization had the same basic job duties and philosophy of care toward the patients, the contingencies would be somewhat similar across groups. However, it was also believed that some differences might be evident in certain areas of performance that depended a great deal on the types of patients with which the employees were working. Although the three teams generally developed contingencies that were very similar in shape and slope, for two performance dimensions, the contingencies had more variation across groups. The largest difference appeared in the contingencies for the dimension, "independently initiates work tasks and asks for additional work" seen in Figure 15–3.

These differences seem to be capturing the variation due to the types of patients being cared for. When examining this contingency for groups SC and AC, it is apparent that they felt this dimension was not highly important, especially if people failed to do it (e.g., group SC in Figure 15–3). This is visible in the contingencies, because the minimums are only −5 and −15. This implies that if a person received a low rating on this dimension, it was not that detrimental. Both of these groups of employees were dealing with patients whose behaviors were very unstable and who often acted out. This required the employees to be much more concerned with things such as safety, and they often did not have time to ask for additional work. On the other hand, group EC produced a contingency that showed greater importance being placed on this dimension. The employees in this group were dealing with long-term patients. They generally knew the patients' behaviors and what to expect. This gave them more time to invest in other things, such as additional work tasks that needed to be completed. For this group, it was important that they initiate work or ask for additional tasks.

These results indicate that the teams were able to construct contingencies that captured the differing slopes and nonlinearities that existed in the performance dimensions. Also, because the contingencies were very similar with differences observed only for dimensions where a difference was appropriate, there is some evidence that the contingencies were capturing the policy of the individual groups and of the organization as a whole.

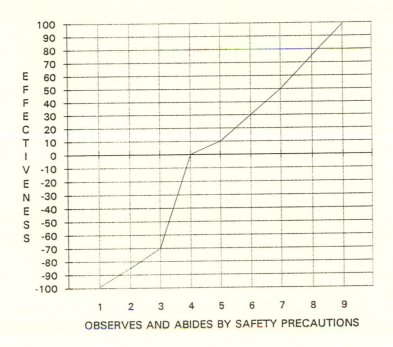

OBSERVES AND ABIDES BY SAFETY PRECAUTIONS

TIMES LATE FOR WORK (MISSING REPORT)

Figure 15–2   Sample Contingencies Showing Differing Importance

GROUP SC

GROUP EC

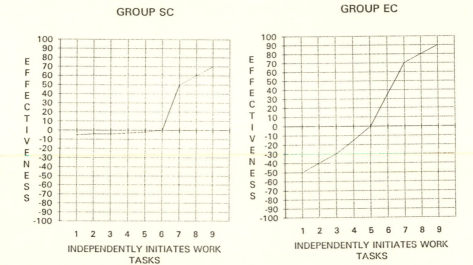

GROUP AC

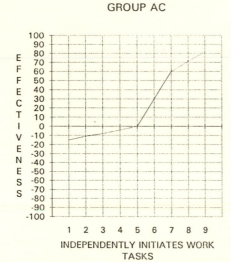

Figure 15-3   Sample Contingencies Showing Differences across Groups

Research Question 2

This question dealt with whether the use of the ProMES approach would provide overall scores that were different from those produced under more traditional methods. Results from correlations that were calculated between the various overall scores and ProMES would suggest that the scores were not much different. The correlations ranged from a low of .73 to a high of .99. The majority of the correlations were .95 or above. The details of these and the other analyses can be found in Sawyer, Pritchard, and Hedley (1992). An overall mean was calculated across all groups and all methods. This overall mean correlation with ProMES was .93. Because the correlations among the composites were so high, one might conclude that nonlinearities were not adding any meaningful amount of unique information. However, as Pritchard and Roth (1991) have shown, other analyses need to be explored before this conclusion is made.

Employee Rankings

Because many organizational decisions involve the employees at the extremes (hiring, promotions, who gets merit raises, terminations, and so on), looking at the extremes is one way to evaluate the similarities in the actual decisions that would be made. To investigate the impact of using a linear method versus a nonlinear method on the decision that would be made about employees, we looked at the proportion of times the top and bottom ranked employees differed using the ProMES contingencies compared with the linear weighting models. The percentage of change in membership in the top and bottom 15 percent of employees on overall effectiveness was examined.

It was determined that as many as 33 percent of the people in the top 15 percent and as many as 60 percent of the people in the bottom 15 percent were different with ProMES compared with the various linear weighting methods. On average, 21 percent of the top 15 percent and 25 percent of the bottom 15 percent were different. Thus, using ProMES would result in considerably different decisions about employees than the other systems.

Evidence from Priorities for Performance Improvement

If performance assessment is to be used to provide guidance for employee improvement, it is necessary that the appraisal system provide guidance as to which indicators of performance the person needs to work on the most. In a linear model, the indicator with the highest linear weight should always receive the highest priority. However, nonlinearity suggests that priorities for change depend on current standing on that indicator. In the health care employee example presented earlier, the employee may benefit more by improving his or her paperwork than by improving client care practices, even though client care is the most important dimension.

Priorities were determined by treating the indicator with the largest linear weight as the highest priority and the three indicators with the largest linear weights as the top three priorities for each employee. The priorities from the ProMES contingencies were determined by locating each employee on each contingency for that employee's group and determining the top priorities by the greatest gain in effectiveness produced by one increment of increase on each indicator. For example, in Figure 15–1, if an individual was currently performing at the level of six and could increase his performance to a seven, he would gain 30 effectiveness points.

The percentages of times the top one and top three priorities differed from ProMES using each of the two linear importance weighted methods were calculated. These percentages all ranged from 59 percent to 100 percent and averaged 89 percent for the top priority and 94 percent for the top three priorities across the three groups.

The evidence shows that a large percentage of employees would be counseled to focus attention on improving different indicators of performance if the ProMES contingencies were used to provide feedback compared with the various linear weighting models.

Summary of Results

Taken as a whole, these results suggest that the answer to the first research question is that ProMES can be used to develop a performance appraisal system. All the design teams were able to generate what they believed to be an accurate set of contingencies for the dimensions, even though most were subjective in nature. The contingencies seemed to be sensitive to differences in expectations, all were nonlinear, and substantial differential importance across dimensions was present. In addition, the contingencies developed by the different design teams were very similar where policies were similar and seemed to capture differences when differences in policy existed.

The second research question was whether scores produced by ProMES would be different from those by more traditional systems. The results indicate that although the correlations of the ProMES composites with those developed by other methods are high, ProMES puts different people at the top and bottom of the performance distribution, resulting in very different priorities for improving performance. Thus, in some important ways, ProMES gives quite different results than the traditional approaches.

GENERAL ISSUES RAISED DURING
THE DEVELOPMENT PHASE

Some interesting issues arose during the instrument development process. This section will be separated into four areas: group dynamics, product stage, indicator stage, and contingency stage.

Group Dynamics

Several issues dealt with the interactions within the design teams. First, a problem arose with one team because the team was composed of four employees who worked directly with each other and one employee who worked in a different building. They were all working with the same types of patients, but the four employees from the same building were used to working and communicating with each other. As the system was being built, those four employees saw things in very much the same way and were thinking on the same wavelength. The lone employee could not as easily communicate her opinion to the others. At the beginning of the meeting this woman spoke up, but as the other four members began to agree among themselves and not listen to her comments, she became very withdrawn. To resolve this problem, the facilitator had to make a special point to try and elicit the woman's opinion so she did not feel totally alienated from the development process. This effort was made but was not totally successful.

This issue makes it clear how important it is to be very careful in the selection of the design team. The team should be composed of people who can work together. If people are going to be working together who do not normally do so, try to have an equal number of them so that any one person does not feel outnumbered during the meetings.

A second issue centered around the fact that the team members had varying levels of education. Most of the employees in this organization had a relatively low level of education (high school diploma). Most higher level supervisors gained their positions not because of more education but because of more experience. There were, however, a few positions, such as the professional nurses, that did have more education. Because their levels of education were different, it caused different levels of understanding of the development process. This required the facilitators to adjust how the development process was conducted to meet the needs of the various teams.

It was easier to develop the instruments in the teams that had members with more education. They caught on more quickly to the process and began to produce good information for the development. These team members also raised more questions about the specifics of how the system would work. Lower level employees without as much education had a more difficult time understanding the process and what the team was to accomplish.

To deal with this problem, the facilitators tried to be receptive to the types of employees with whom they were working. The facilitators then adjusted their method of facilitating depending on the composition of the team. For the people with a lower level of education, it was necessary to break the development down into very small, basic steps. The facilitators also did more guiding of the process by reminding the group often of what they were suggesting and what that would mean to their completed instrument.

A third issue became apparent in one team because of the inclusion of both incumbents and supervisors. When there was disagreement in the discussions, the supervisor would step in and make the point that she was in charge and this is how it should be. The team would then basically concede to her position. This would sometimes stifle team discussion and consensus. Because it is ideal for various levels of employees to be involved in the development phase, this problem must be dealt with.

Under normal conditions, this situation might be avoided before it arises. Normally, the selection of the personnel who would be involved in the development team would be done very carefully so as to avoid selecting people who would try to dominate the team. If it does happen as the development is being done, it might be beneficial to discuss the issue with the supervisor. It would be important to point out to him or her how important it is to gain team consensus. This team consensus will facilitate the employees' acceptance of the system when it is complete. If the employees feel that their opinions have not been considered, they will not like or accept the system. If this happens, it is very unlikely that the system will be as successful.

In this particular research project, the facilitator did not have the opportunity to discuss the problem with the supervisor. The facilitator's only option was to curb the action as it was happening. The facilitator made an effort to reiterate the opinions of the other team members. Also, she directly asked the supervisor to more carefully consider the suggestions made by the other team members. These actions were carried out very carefully by the facilitator so as not to offend the supervisor.

Product Stage

In this setting, products were the long-term effects of client treatment, the extent to which dangerous incidents were prevented, and maintenance of proper care of clients. If the goals of this project were to measure unit level productivity, indicators of these would be produced. However, although individual performance may contribute to unit level productivity, performance and productivity are different constructs. In this context, our concern was with determining indicators of individual performance. Additionally, in this context, the products of individual performance are mostly intangible, and objective measures are either unmeasurable or measurable only in the long term. Thus, our development began with the development of indicators of individual performance.

Indicator Stage

In this project, the indicators were the performance dimensions on the appraisal instrument. Because of the time limitations of the organization, the performance dimensions were initially developed by the research team. Through interviews with the various levels of employees, the facilitators were able to construct a list of possible performance dimensions. These were then presented to each team for review and approval at the beginning of the development process.

By using this method, the teams did not get to participate in the actual thought process of coming up with the dimensions. In a normal ProMES development, this participation is important, because it helps facilitate acceptance of the new system. Normally, the indicator stage is the most difficult for a development team. By just giving them a list to review, much of the discussion was eliminated and agreement on the list came very quickly. Although we did ask the teams to determine if the dimensions covered all aspects of job performance completely, it is not known how much was lost or how different the list would have been if the normal ProMES development process would have been followed.

Contingency Stage

Thsi was the only step in the process that followed the typical ProMES development. It basically went quite smoothly except for one point. A difficulty arose in the process of ranking and rating the maximums and minimums. The first team found this rather difficult. They did not have a great deal of trouble ranking the dimensions, but they experienced difficulty with the ratings. Team members had a hard time understanding what the ratings meant or how they should determine them. Rating the top and bottom dimensions was not as difficult as rating those dimensions in the middle. The team could not differentiate the ratings of those dimensions in the middle range. The facilitators initially asked the team to start with the top ranked dimension and rate the dimensions from the top to the bottom. This proved to be difficult, because the teams felt the dimensions were all close. The ratings were all falling in a range from only 100 to 80, for example. A new method was then tried. The team rated the top dimension, then they rated the bottom dimension. They could more easily think of what percentage of importance the last place dimension had in relation to the first ranked dimension. For example, was it 50 percent as important or maybe only 25 percent as important? They then had established ratings for the extremes and could base their other judgments on them. This proved to be the better way to rate the maximums and the minimums, so, this technique was used for the remainder of the teams.

Actual Implementation

This project did not actually use the instruments to appraise performance. The study was designed only as an experiment with the new system. However, a very similar procedure could be followed if one wishes to develop and use a performance appraisal system utilizing ProMES. If the system is to be used, a number of points need to be considered.

The normal development of a system that will be used to evaluate performance would require more time. It is necessary that all members of the design teams understand fully how to develop the system. Careful explanation is required from the facilitators, and time needs to be allotted for answering questions or concerns that arise.

In the development process itself, it would be advantageous to have the design team develop the indicators of performance. This helps clarify the goals and policies of the organization. It also leads to greater acceptance by those who will be evaluated with the new system because they know their fellow coworkers helped develop all aspects of the new system. It would also be important to have more than one two-hour session to develop contingencies. Design team members need time to review their decisions. With a normal development process, it is also necessary to allow time for upper level management to examine and approve the indicators and the contingencies. Having more members on the design teams might also be helpful. Normally, five to nine members is a good size for a design team.

ProMES SYSTEM ADVANTAGES

Several important advantages would be achieved by using ProMES for performance appraisal. As was seen in this project, by allowing for differing importance between dimensions and for nonlinear relations between a particular dimension and overall performance, the system produced different and potentially more usable information. There are many other advantages that could be achieved by using this system, as well.

Henderson (1984) provides a large list of human and technical problems that block successful appraisal of performance. The ProMES system of measuring performance does provide techniques that could alleviate some of these problems. In the following section, many of the common performance appraisal problems will be described and the solutions that might be produced by using this new system will be suggested.

Performance Appraisal Problems and Solutions

Employees being appraised often feel raters do not know the job requirements, recognize the standards to measure job performance, or have the opportunity to observe many of the behaviors on which the appraisal is being done. As a result, it is often felt that appraisals are made on the basis of things other than job performance (e.g., sex, age, race).

This new approach provides ways to solve this problem. Because the supervisors themselves, along with some of the job incumbents, develop the appraisal instrument, they will have determined and better understand the job requirements and standards. This is the process of role clarification. If there are any disagreements between the supervisors and the incumbents, they will surface and can be resolved. The system is also reviewed by the upper management in a normal application. When this is finished, all levels of workers involved will have a much clearer picture of the job and what the objectives of performance should be. This helps the supervisors when doing the ratings. It also helps give more credibility to the ratings in the eyes of the employees being rated.

Another problem concerns giving people average ratings. When performance is described, being average has a negative connotation that implies mediocre performance. To avoid this, many raters rate their average employees higher than they truly deserve (Henderson, 1984). The result is biased ratings. With the ProMES method, the zero point is defined, and this is the neutral or expected level. By defining the zero point clearly in the development process, the raters may be more likely to give average ratings when observed.

One subset of halo error is called logical error (Cascio, 1987). This error occurs when one performance dimension is confused with another because they are not clearly defined. This can cause incorrect ratings on some of the performance dimensions. Through the process of ProMES development, the dimensions are accurately and clearly defined by the raters themselves. Further, because they have discussed them and defined them in their own words, this problem should be less likely to occur.

Another concern is that raters often feel the appraisal system they use fails to really describe the policies of their organization. As a result, they do not have much acceptance of, or commitment to, the system. Again, because of the involvement of the raters in the development process of the ProMES instrument, these feelings should be minimized.

Many supervisors know the behaviors on which they are appraising an employee, but they do not know which ones are more important. This often causes raters to weight all things equally or to weight them based on their own personal value systems. The ProMES method accounts for the differing importance weightings in the development of the contingencies. This allows the raters to determine the various levels of importance when they develop the system.

Managers also have many concerns about the performance appraisal tools being used in their organizations. They often lack trust in the system because they feel the accuracy and effectiveness of the system probably are not good. The lack of trust from management can promote a credibility gap throughout the whole organization. The management sometimes feels that some performance dimensions and information on standards have been left out. Using ProMES, managers are included in reviewing the system and approving it. Because of this involvement, these negative feelings should be reduced. Also, the credibility of the system should be greatly increased.

Feedback

Many problems have been encountered when attempting to provide performance feedback. The ProMES instrument could prove helpful in this area. In most organizations, some form of a feedback process is engaged in between supervisors and employees (Field & Holley, 1975; Lacho, Stearns, & Villere, 1979). This feedback to employees is usually intended to serve three main purposes (DeVries, Morrison, Shullman, & Gerlach, 1981). First, it is used to establish performance goals, expectations, and standards to improve or maintain performance. Second, it is a time to review progress and solve problems. Finally, overall performance is examined and things such as raises or promotions may be discussed.

There are some important guidelines one should follow when hoping to produce effective performance feedback. An important aspect of performance appraisal and feedback is that specific goals and objectives need to be present, as well as the standards of performance if employees are expected to improve. These goals must be clearly communicated and understood by the employees (Erez, Earley, & Hulin, 1985; Ilgen, Fisher, & Taylor, 1979; Latham, Mitchell, & Dossett, 1978; Latham & Wexley, 1981). In a similar nature, the feedback should be specific (Stone, Gueutal, & McIntosh, 1984). However, when performance feedback sessions are conducted, Carroll and Schneier (1982) have shown that rarely are developmental plans to improve job performance ever established. Another important aspect of feedback is giving positive support and constructive criticism (Burke & Wilcox, 1969).

The system presented here would help meet these guidelines. The system itself has the ability to communicate what is important, what is less important, and the expected level of performance on each dimension. What areas the person performed well on and those he or she did not perform so well on are indicated. This facilitates specificity when giving feedback. By producing priority information, the system provides a basis for performance counseling by the supervisor (Pritchard, 1990). This helps the supervisor provide positive and constructive feedback on how the employee can improve performance.

Other Advantages

Some other advantages also exist with this new approach to performance appraisal measurement. Often, on performance appraisals, raters are required to make one overall judgment of a person's performance. Better prediction should be achieved if the data are combined statistically (Blenkner, 1954; Meehl, 1954; Sawyer, 1966). Using the ProMES method to form a composite score allows the rater to make several molecular judgments that then get combined mechanically. This overall rating of performance should be much more accurate than an overall judgment arrived at in a clinical fashion by the rater.

The ability of the system to produce both the overall evaluation and evaluations on the multiple dimensions is also very important. On one hand, multiple criteria are very helpful for providing feedback. However, for many personnel decisions, it is also necessary to obtain an overall measure of performance for each employee to determine how much he or she is contributing to the organization. This system has the ability to produce an overall composite that is representative and meaningful.

CONCLUSIONS

This research has shown that the ProMES methodology can be used to develop a performance appraisal instrument. Once developed, this new method can produce new and different information that could be very helpful to an organization.

A performance appraisal instrument needs to be not only psychometrically sound but also acceptable to the people involved if it is expected to produce accurate and usable data (Cascio, 1987). This new approach for appraising performance shows promise in both of these areas. Because it suggests advances in both measurement techniques and personnel involvement, it is felt that this method of performance appraisal could prove very valuable in the future.

REFERENCES

Blenker, M. (1954). Predictive factors in the initial interview in family casework. *Social Services Review, 28,* 65–73.

Burke, R. J., & Wilcox, D. S. (1969). Characteristics of effective employee performance reviews and development interviews. *Personnel Psychology, 22,* 291–305.

Carroll, S. J., & Schneier, C. E. (1982). *Performance appraisal and review systems.* Glenview, IL: Scott, Foresman.

Cascio, W. F. (1987). *Applied psychology in personnel management* (3rd ed.). Englewood Cliffs, NJ: Prentice-Hall.

DeVries, D., Morrison, A., Shullman, S., & Gerlach, M. (1981). *Performance appraisal on the line.* New York: John Wiley.

Erez, M., Earley, P. C., & Hulin, C. L. (1985). The impact of goal acceptance and performance: A two-step model. *Academy of Management Journal, 28,* 50–66.

Field, H. S., & Holley, W. H. (1975). Performance appraisal — an analysis of state-wide practices. *Public Personnel Management, 7,* 145–150.

Henderson, R. (1984). *Performance appraisal.* Reston, VA: Reston Publishing Company.

Ilgen, D. R., Fisher, C. D., & Taylor, M. S. (1979). Consequences of individual feedback on behavior in organizations. *Journal of Applied Psychology, 4,* 349–371.

Lacho, K. J., Stearns, G. K., & Villere, M. F. (1979). A study of employee appraisal systems of major cities in the United States. *Public Personnel Management, 8,* 111–125.

Latham, G. P., Mitchell, T. K., & Dossett, D. L. (1978). The importance of participative goal setting and anticipated rewards on goal difficulty and job performance. *Journal of Applied Psychology, 63,* 163–171.

Latham, G. P., & Wexley, K. N. (1981). *Increasing productivity through performance appraisal.* Reading, MA: Addison-Wesley.

Meehl, P. E. (1954). *Clinical vs statistical prediction: A theoretical analysis and a review of the evidence.* Minneapolis: University of Minnesota Press.

Pritchard, R. D. (1990). *Measuring and improving organizational productivity: A practical guide* (p. 248). New York: Praeger.

Pritchard, R. D., & Roth, P. J. (1991). Accounting for non-linear utility functions in composite measures of productivity and performance. *Organizational Behavior and Human Decision Processes, 50,* 341–359.

Sawyer, J. (1966). Measurement and prediction, clinical and statistical. *Psychological Bulletin, 66,* 178–200.

Sawyer, J. E., Pritchard, R. D., & Hedley, A. (1992). *Comparison of non-linear ProMES versus linear procedures for obtaining composite measures in performance appraisal.* Unpublished manuscript.

Stone, D. L., Gueutal, H. G., & McIntosh, B. (1984). The effects of feedback sequence and expertise of the rater in perceived feedback accuracy. *Personnel Psychology, 37,* 487–506.

16

Linking Training Evaluation to Productivity

Steven D. Jones and Lynn Ourth

Although ProMES has been most often used as a method to enhance productivity through providing a comprehensive and integrated feedback system, there are other possible uses. One such use is that of a criterion for evaluating organizational improvement efforts. Supervisory training and organization development are improvement efforts that we often find are in need of an adequate system for evaluating their effectiveness.

It has been estimated that companies spend upward of $30 billion per year on training (Bernhard & Ingols, 1988), but the evaluation of training remains a perennial problem. In fact, considering the expenditure levels, it is astounding that only a small percentage of training is evaluated (Bell & Kerr, 1987). The purpose of this chapter is to describe a demonstration project where ProMES was used to evaluate an organization development program consisting primarily of supervisory training and to link that program to productivity improvement. The primary focus of the organization change effort was to empower supervisors, and the major vehicle for this change was a formal supervisory training program.

TRAINING AND TRAINING EVALUATION

In the area of training evaluation, several authors have emphasized the increasing importance of relating training outcomes to productivity and organizational effectiveness criteria (Bell & Kerr, 1987; Chapados, Rentfrow, & Hocheiser, 1987; Dopyera & Pitone, 1983; Phillips, 1983). These authors argue that training is an accountable function that must show results like any other function in the organization. In turn, these results strengthen the viability of the training function in the organization. As Swanson (1989) has noted, top managers in business and industry look at training through an "economic lens." If they are not given sufficient data to make an economic evaluation of training, they will fill in the blanks themselves, often to the detriment of the training program. Providing productivity and organizational effectiveness related measures of training gives training more of an operational role, makes it a stronger force in strategic planning, and makes it less of a target for cutbacks.

Therefore, the evaluation of training in terms of productivity and effectiveness becomes more of a central issue. In his text on training, Phillips (1983, Chap. 4) recommends that the indicators and methods of training evaluation be developed even before training objectives are determined and the training program is developed. As the author states, "It is useless to set an objective in an area for which there is no way of gathering information" (Phillips, 1983, p. 53). Phillips cites examples of productivity and effectiveness indicators for training evaluation such as reduction in the time to reach a standard proficiency level, improvement in the scrap rate, reduction in turnover, improvement in safety record, and reduction in equipment maintenance after training.

The well-known four level training evaluation model first proposed by Kirpatrick (1959a, 1959b, 1960a, 1960b) looks at the affective reactions to the program (Level one), the resultant learning (level two), the degree to which information learned is utilized (level three), and the results of the program on organizational goals or productivity (level four). Although all of these levels of evaluation are important, it has been argued that evidence of positive impact on levels one to three only complicates the picture and may be of little consequence unless an impact at level four may be shown (Newstrom, 1978). More recently, Alliger and Janak (1989) have argued that the four levels of the Kirpatrick model are not necessarily positively correlated nor is there necessarily a clear causal relationship among the four levels.

Thus, if one wants to argue that training programs affect the productivity of the organization, then training evaluations need to have been done in terms of productivity indices, rather than inferred from evaluations of levels one to three. Consider, for example, the following quote:

We also insist that training be realistic and results oriented. We don't have training merely because it's fashionable . . . but because it is a good dollar investment. We measure training with control groups where we can, comparing those that have been trained with those that haven't, and by arriving at baseline data for productivity in the past and comparing it with what happens after an educational and training process has been applied. . . .

It is simply another area of investment and we are willing to invest to the degree that it seems to us to be wise. (Phillips, 1983)

One suggested method for level four evaluation of a training program compares the cost of the training program with the value of the improved productivity and effectiveness resulting from the training. To this end, recent articles and book chapters have demonstrated how to establish a return on investment of training costs relative to the estimated benefit in dollars of solving specific effectiveness and productivity problems (c.f. McCullough, 1984; Phillips, 1983). Return on investment calculations for training evaluation have not become well-accepted, possibly due to the assumptions that must be made to estimate the value of the improvement in productivity and effectiveness, which is rarely actually measured.

Level four training evaluations are rarely reported. When they are reported, we typically see level four training evaluations in terms of organizational and individual level outcomes such as production records, customer satisfaction ratings, supervisor ratings and ratings on surveys designed to measure changes in outcomes, and observations of behaviors targeted for training.

One feature that these evaluations have in common is that, from a productivity measurement perspective, they are partial measures, that is, the focus on only those dimensions of performance that are targeted by the training program. This is understandable for two reasons. One is the time investment to comprehensively measure productivity. The second reason is to reduce the measurement error by evaluating only outcomes that the training program can affect. In their text on productivity in organizations, Campbell and Campbell (1988, Chap. 8) make the point that individual performance is only one contribution to productivity and that training is only one contribution to individual performance; therefore, training should not be evaluated by overall performance or by overall productivity.

However, partial measurement leaves open the nagging question of what happened to the unmeasured dimensions of performance. Would the training program be considered effective if it traded off improvement in one area of performance at the expense of another? Suppose a training program reduces absenteeism, but, at the same time, turnover increases and quality decreases. Was the training program well designed and executed? Was the improvement in absenteeism offset by the losses in the other two areas? Obviously, other causes could affect these outcomes, but training does not operate well in a vacuum, nor should it be inconsistent with other organizational changes.

To answer these kinds of questions requires a comprehensive productivity measurement system that integrates all measures into a composite. To relate the changes in productivity more specifically to training, several levels of training evaluation are needed. This multilevel evaluation provides the information to assess the effects of training on the individual participants and on the organization as a whole.

ORGANIZATIONAL SETTING AND
THE TRAINING PROGRAM

The project was conducted in a textile manufacturing plant in the southeastern United States. This facility was one of a chain of plants, each of which performed certain steps in the manufacturing process and passed their semifinished product on to the next plant in the manufacturing chain. This particular plant was the second link in the chain.

The project began following a turnover in plant management. The previous plant manager had a benevolent autocratic style in which all decisions and power were controlled by him. Under this manager, supervisors acted as quality control inspectors and skilled technicians; virtually all supervisory actions were taken by the previous plant manager. It was also rumored that the previous plant manager worked long and hard hours but had somewhat low expectations of workers and supervisors. In spite of this, the plant reportedly had the highest efficiency rates (units per man-hour) of any similar plant in the industry.

The impetus for this project came from the new plant manager with support from the human resources department. The new plant manager had both a participative management style and high expectations of workers and supervisors. His top agenda was to empower the supervisors so that they could supervise rather than inspect. Although this was done primarily through the supervisory training program, it was reinforced by other changes, such as, changing job responsibilities to remove the inspector parts of the job and to enlarge the supervisory responsibilities, making supervisors more accountable for reporting results in their areas, increased support for supervisory decisions, and directing employees' concerns to supervisors rather than to manager. Although it was impossible to separate the effects of supervisory training from other changes, it was unnecessary in this case, because the supervisor training program was a part of a larger, planned organizational change directed by the plant manager. Therefore, the third level of evaluation was thought of as an evaluation of the entire change effort that principally comprised the supervisory training program.

To this end, a supervisory training program, including training evaluation, was designed for approval by corporate management. The supervisory training program consisted of modules presented to supervisors in formal, bimonthly training sessions lasting six months. This program focused on supervisory skills such as giving feedback on performance, listening, giving instructions, coaching employees, confronting conflicts, and using progressive discipline. The training program was designed to be part of a larger effort to empower managers, supervisors, and employees.

TRAINING EVALUATION

The design of training evaluation was to measure training at three levels. The levels were: level 1 — reactions to training in terms of training procedures, suitability of materials, interest level, relevance of the topics, and so on; level 2 — desirable supervisory behavior in terms of job performance items keyed to training objective; and level 3 — plant productivity figures as assessed by ProMES. Thus, our levels one, two, and three corresponded to Kirpatrick's levels one, three, and four, respectively. Kirpatrick's level two, learning, was not assessed because of the supervisor's stated aversion to the training program becoming like school and to the plant manager's intent not to use the training program to evaluate the supervisors.

Level One Evaluation

It was decided to take the level one evaluation midway through the training program to allow for midterm corrections to be made if the training program was not meeting the needs of the supervisors. It was also thought that this midterm evaluation would allow the supervisors enough experience with the training program to make an informed evaluation.

The training reaction form was designed by selecting and modifying items from published training reaction questionnaires. In it, the trainers are rated by each supervisor on a one to five scale across 15 items. To get a score for this level, the ratings were averaged across supervisors and across items that could then be placed on a one to five scale, with one being the most negative reaction and five being the most positive reaction.

Level Two Evaluation

The level two evaluation focused on changes in supervisory behavior in specific skills that were expected to be impacted by the training program. Because the supervisors had not been allowed to fully supervise by the previous plant manager, the overriding goal of the training program was for the supervisors to become more comfortable with their role as supervisors. To make this evaluation, four managers evaluated the supervisor's behavior on a 39 item questionnaire. The 39 items were tied to training objectives, such as giving feedback, dealing with absenteeism, using listening skills, and encouraging teamwork. Responses were on a one to five scale, with one being very uncomfortable and five being very comfortable using this skill. Two responses were required for each item, one response asked for a rating of that behavior prior to training followed by a rating of that supervisor's present behavior. Thus, training was evaluated at this level by looking at change score from pretraining to the present. An average change score was calculated for the ratings on all 39 items.

It was decided to administer the level two evaluation twice, once at the midpoint of training and once six months after the completion of training. It was felt that the follow-up evaluation was most important because it would indicate whether the training was being put to use. The midterm evaluation, on the other hand, would give the trainers some feedback about the immediate impact of the training.

Level Three Evaluation

A major concern at this third level of evaluation was not to create additional work for managers or supervisors, because both groups were already filling out evaluation questionnaires. In order to streamline the ProMES development process, three decisions were made: to use only indicators on which data were already being collected; to develop the measurement system through meetings with only the plant manager (although other managers were appraised of the evaluation effort); and to simplify contingency development so that only relative importance ratings, maximum and minimum values, and zero points would be required. These three decisions dramatically reduced the development time, so that the entire ProMES was developed in just four meetings of about one hour each.

In the first meeting, we became familiar with the goals of the plant, took a tour of the various departments, and became familiar with the terminology of the operations. In the second meeting, we became familiar with all of the plantwide indicators that the plant collects and reports to corporate management. A third meeting was required to answer our questions about these indicators and to make decisions about which ones would be appropriate for evaluation. As a result, a subset of seven indicators was chosen, which, when taken together, should show improvement if the training program and the other organizational improvement efforts were being effective. The key question we asked here was, Of all the measures that you now collect, which would you expect to show some improvement if the training program is successful?

At the end of the third meeting, we had selected seven plantwide indicators. These indicators and their definitions were as follows:

1. Absenteeism — number of absences per man-hour worked
2. Direct labor — actual cost minus budgeted cost per month
3. Indirect labor — actual cost minus budgeted cost per month

4. Cost per pound — cost of labor, supplies, and overhead per total pound of product produced
5. Seconds — pounds of seconds per thousand pounds of product produced. This is product that does not have to be scrapped but is sold at a lower value as second, or lower, quality.
6. Waste — dollar value of scrap produced per month
7. Safety — number of injuries per total hours worked

Note that many of these indicators are in relation to goals set by corporate management. Thus, an indicator could have a plus or minus value if it is above or below its goal.

By examining past data and asking management, we determined the maximum and minimum (best and worst possible) values for each of the seven indicators. Then, in the fourth meeting, the maximum and minimum values of the seven indicators were ranked and rated for importance using standard ProMES methods (Pritchard, 1990; Pritchard, Jones, Roth, Stuebing, & Ekeberg, 1988, 1989). Also in that meeting, zero point, or the level of minimal acceptable performance, was established for each indicator. This information then allowed a simplified contingency to be created for each of the indicators. The contingency was formed graphically by establishing the horizontal and vertical axis, then connecting the maximum and minimum points with the zero point.

An example is given in Figure 16–1 for the indicator of absenteeism. Note that it is two straight line segments with the minimum at 3.5 percent, the zero point at 1.2 percent, and the maximum at 0.5 percent absenteeism. On the positive side, this indicator was rated 95 of 100 in importance, indicating that when the plant's performance is at its best on this indicator, it is very important. On the negative side, it is much less important, getting a rating of –25 out of 100.

A simplified contingency was developed for each indicator. Of the seven contingencies, three turned out to be straight lines. Although something was undoubtedly lost in accuracy of the contingencies compared with the usual ProMES methodology, the savings in time was significant. The entire contingency development process took approximately one hour.

Following contingency development, a spreadsheet program was written to computerize the measurement system. This program also produced the feedback report and graphs. Formulas were written in the program to convert the indicator scores into effectiveness scores that could then be summed to get the overall effectiveness score. Because the contingencies consisted of one or two straight line segments, only one or two formulas were necessary to describe each contingency. This also made the spreadsheet program much faster to write than if the contingencies had been true curves.

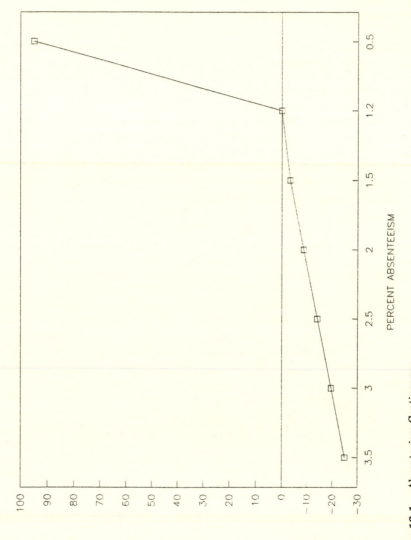

Figure 16-1　Absenteeism Contingency

Referring to Figure 16–1, notice the lower half of the contingency as absenteeism improves from 3.5 percent to 1.2 percent. The formula for this segment is as follows:

@IF(AC4<=3.5#AND#AC4>1.2,(10.87*(3.5-AC4))-25,AF4).

Although this may perhaps be an imposing formula to those not familiar with spreadsheets, it is a function describing the slope of a line. It reads as follows: If the value in cell AC4 (which contains the raw indicator value for absenteeism) is between 3.5 and 1.2, then multiply 10.87 (the slope that is the rise over the run or 25/2.3) times the difference between 3.5 (the starting point on the horizontal axis) and the raw indicator value for absenteeism and subtract 25 (the value of the starting point on the vertical axis); then, if the raw indicator value for absenteeism does not fit into this range (is not between 3.5 and 1.2), move to the second equation, which is in cell AF4. The second equation uses the same logic and is as follows:

@IF(AC4<=1.2#AND#AC4>.5,(135.71*(1.2-AC4))-0,@ERR).

The ERR statement means that if the raw indicator value does not fit into either of these two equations, there is an error somewhere.

With these two formulas, the spreadsheet program converts the absenteeism values for a given month into an effectiveness score. If we had an absenteeism rate of 3 percent, we would plug this number into the first formula. The program would calculate the following: (10.87*(3.5-3))-25 = −19.56. So a 3 percent absenteeism would produce an effectiveness score of −19.56. Likewise, each of the indicators had a contingency and formulas to convert the raw indicator values into effectiveness scores. The program then summed these effectiveness scores to get an overall effectiveness score for a given month.

For each month, the program calculated an overall effectiveness score for the plant's productivity. To evaluate the effectiveness of the training program and the other management changes, we could compare the overall effectiveness score during the months prior to the training program with that in the months during and following training.

RESULTS OF TRAINING

Level One

The level one evaluation consisted of the supervisor's reactions to the training program at the midterm of the training sessions. The average rating on the one to five scale was a 4.55, with a five being the most positive reaction. Across the 15 items on the scale, the average reactions ranged from a low of 4.00 to a high of 4.88. The results indicate a strong positive reaction by the participants to the training program.

Level Two

The level two evaluation consisted of ratings by management of the supervisors' behaviors that were targets of the training program. These ratings were made at two times, the first rating being at the midterm of the training program. The ratings provided a change in score, because the managers made a rating of pretraining behavior and present behavior. The change score was calculated by subtracting the pretraining from the present score, so that a positive score would indicate improvement. The scales called for a one to five rating with five being the highest possible score; the maximum possible improvement was a difference between five and the pretraining average of 2.2. Therefore, the maximum possible improvement was a difference score of 2.8.

At the midterm rating period, the average change across all 39 behaviors and across all raters was +1.39, indicating that the supervisors improved 1.39 on a 0 to 2.8 scale, or an improvement of 50 percent. The changes ranged from a low of −1 to an improvement of 3 points.

Level Three

The data for the level three evaluation are shown in Figure 16–2. This graph is a plot of the overall effectiveness scores as calculated by the spreadsheet program from the plant's seven indicators. The graph shows baseline data beginning ten months prior to the training program. The graph also shows the overall effectiveness scores for seven months during and subsequent to the training program. The average overall effectiveness score for the baseline period was 15.8, and for training, it was 125.8, indicating an improvement of 29 percent on a 0 to 100 percent scale. (This calculation was made by dividing the improvement of 110 points by the maximum possible improvement of 379 effectiveness points.) In addition, if trend line were fit to the data points in Figure 16–1, the slope during baseline would be downward, and the slope during and subsequent to training was positive, indicating a marked improvement in the trends.

DISCUSSION

These results indicate that a simplified ProMES can be used to evaluate a training program, especially in situations where the training program is part of a larger organizational change effort. It is less likely that a ProMES evaluation would be appropriate for training programs

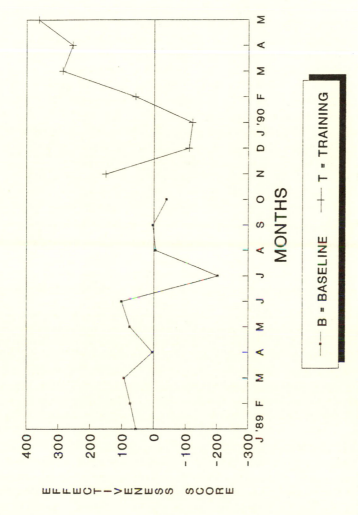

Combines 7 measures of productivity

Figure 16-2 Overall Effectiveness

that are not part of a larger organizational change effort. In these more limited training situations, the point made earlier by Campbell and Campbell (1988) that the effects of training are too specific to be evaluated at the level of organizational productivity and effectiveness is a good one. However, often a training program is nested within and consistent with larger change efforts, where it does make sense to evaluate in terms of productivity and effectiveness measures.

On this project, we found it was feasible to develop the measurement system in four one-hour meetings with just the plant manager. This short development time was feasible because the measurement system was to be used as a criteria rather than as a feedback system. When ProMES is used as a feedback system, it has typically required extensive participation by managers, supervisors, and employees so that the system is understood and accepted by those who will be receiving the feedback. In this case, because ongoing feedback was not a purpose, this extensive participation was not appropriate.

In addition to the four hours of meeting time, the Steven D. Jones spent roughly six hours writing the spreadsheet program and entering data, resulting in 14 man-hours for the entire process, including making the graphs in Figures 16–1 and 16–2. Certainly, this does not seem an excessive effort to evaluate a training program. Thus, it seems feasible to use ProMES to evaluate training where that training is within the context of an organizational improvement effort.

The results indicate that the reaction (level one) to the training program was highly positive, the extent of utilization (level three) showed an improvement from baseline through training, and the plant showed a strong overall effectiveness improvement from baseline through training. The consistency of these results indicates that the supervisory training program was effective within its context of an overall empowerment effort engineered by the new plant manager. We cannot isolate the effects just due to the training program. We can conclude that the training program worked, because of the consistency of the three levels of evaluation and that the training was synchronized with other changes in the organization.

If we had only the level one and level three evaluations to rely on, there would have been some concerns as to the effectiveness of the training. Also, if we had only a partial productivity measurement system, there might still be concerns about overall impact. ProMES can combine with other levels of evaluation to successfully address these concerns.

REFERENCES

Alliger, G. M., & Janak, E. A. (1989). Kirpatrick's levels of training criteria: Thirty years later. *Personnel Psychology, 42,* 331–342.

Bell, J. D., & Kerr, D. L. (1987, January). Measuring training results: Key to managerial commitment. *Training and Development Journal*, pp. 70–73.

Bernhard, H. B., & Ingols, C. A. (1988, September-October). Six lessons from the corporate classroom. *Harvard Business Review*, pp. 40–47.

Campbell, J. P., & Campbell, R. J. (1988). *Productivity in organizations*. San Francisco: Jossey-Bass.

Chapados, J. T., Rentfrow, D., & Hocheiser, L. I. (1987, December). Four principles of training. *Training and Development Journal*, pp. 63–66.

Dopyera, J., & Pitone, L. (1983, May). Decision points in planning the evaluation of training. *Training and Development Journal*, pp. 66–71.

Kirpatrick, D. L. (1960a, January). Techniques for evaluating training programs, Part 3: Behavior. *Training and Development Journal*, pp. 13–18.

Kirpatrick, D. L. (1960b, February). Techniques for evaluating training programs, Part 4: Results. *Training and Development Journal*, pp. 28–32.

Kirpatrick, D. L. (1959a, November). Techniques for evaluating training programs, Part 1: Reaction. *Training and Development Journal*, pp. 3–9.

Kirpatrick, D. L. (1959b, December). Techniques for evaluating training programs, Part 2: Learning. *Training and Development Journal*, pp. 21–26.

McCullough, J. M. (1984, June). To measure a vacuum. *Training and Development Journal*, pp. 68–70.

Newstrom, J. W. (1978, November). Catch-22: The problems of incomplete evaluation of training. *Training and Development Journal*, pp. 22–24.

Phillips, J. J. (1983). *Handbook of training evaluation and measurement methods*. Houston, TX: Gulf.

Pritchard, R. D. (1990). *Measuring and improving organizational productivity: A practical guide* (p. 248). New York: Praeger.

Pritchard, R. D., Jones, S. D., Roth, P. L., Stuebing, K. K., & Ekeberg, S. E. (1989). The evaluation of an integrated approach to measuring organizational productivity. *Personnel Psychology*, *42*, 69–115.

Pritchard, R. D., Jones, S. D., Roth, P. L., Stuebing, K. K., & Ekeberg, S. E. (1988). The effects of group feedback, goal setting, and incentives on organizational productivity. *Journal of Applied Psychology Monograph Series*, *73*, 337–358.

Ross, J. E. (1981). *Productivity, people and profits*. Reston, VA: Reston Publishing.

Swanson, R. A. (1989). Everything important in business and industry is evaluated. In R. O. Brinkerhoff (Ed.), *Evaluating training programs in business and industry*. New Directions for Program Evaluation, No. 44. San Francisco: Jossey-Bass.

Tuttle, T. C. (1983). Organizational productivity: A challenge for psychologists. *American Psychologist*, *38*, 479–486.

17

Identifying Strategic Objectives in Productivity Management: Combining Features of HISYS and ProMES

Ingwer Borg, Thomas Staufenbiel, and Robert D. Pritchard

Any behaviorally based productivity enhancement system requires clarifying the objectives that characterize a particular job or work assignment. These objectives serve as the criteria for performance appraisal, feedback, and goal setting. To derive such objectives, structure them, and link them to measures is not an easy task. The approach used by ProMES as described in the majority of the chapters in this book is to have the group develop these objectives in the form of ProMES products. These products, along with their indicators, are then approved by higher level management. This results in a bottom-up strategy, which has a number of advantages, including the participation and ultimate feeling of ownership of the system by those who will be measured by it.

However, one concern is that the products generated by the group are, in fact, consistent with the overall strategy of the broader organization. It is essential that the group be working in such a way as to maximize the objectives of the broader organization. Hopefully, the approval process will insure that this consistency between the group's products and the overall organizational objectives exists, but there are some situations where this may be a problem. The most obvious case is where the broader organizational goals are themselves not clear. If higher management is not clear on their goals, it will be difficult for them to assess whether the group's products are consistent with these broader goals.

This suggests that in some situations a top-down approach can be a valuable addition to the standard ProMES approach. Another situation where a top-down approach may be valuable is where management itself is not comfortable with the typical ProMES bottom-up approach.

They may not have enough trust in the lower level groups to develop appropriate products, or they may want to initiate some changes in the former business strategy and want to use the top-down approach to help communicate these changes. In such a situation, starting with a top-down approach as a framework in which the bottom-up ProMES approach is done may be beneficial.

The purpose of this chapter is to describe such an approach that has been developed by Staufenbiel and Borg (1994), show its application in a German organization, and describe how this approach might be integrated with ProMES.

THE SETTING

The application started when a major computer manufacturer asked Ingwer Borg and Thomas Staufenbiel to help strengthen what they called the "change mentality" of the district managers (DMs) of the service support organization (SSO) of its German subsidiary. The senior management felt that DMs were not as open to change as they would like them to be. As a first step in the project, an attitude survey was carried out that addressed a wide spectrum of issues, such as the work itself, working conditions, and communication. Action plans that focused on technical, organizational, and social problems identified by the DMs were designed and implemented. This helped to improve the situation greatly from the DMs' perspective, but higher management felt that the actions were one-sided in the sense that much was done for the DMs but little was done by them with regard to management's main concern, that is, improving willingness for change.

One central concern of the DMs was that the objectives their managers had for them were not clear. It was proposed that this request from the DMs for clearer objectives be used as a basis for bringing the SSO management team's priorities to the DM group. The DMs had said that they were confused about their performance criteria, especially with respect to "new" objectives, such as selling repair contracts and site consulting. The existing performance appraisal system was considered useless in this regard.

Hence, we suggested to first explicate the DMs' work objectives and link these objectives to very concrete behavioral measurement scales. Then, after agreements were reached on this system, it would be used for regular performance assessment and feedback in order to guide development in the desired directions.

Such a recommendation meant that the objectives of the DMs' work must be clearly identified and then linked to specific expected behaviors on the part of the DMs. The idea was that this would be done by the senior SSO managers and then communicated to the DMs.

THE APPROACH

The method we will discuss combines features of HISYS (Staufenbiel & Borg, 1992) and ProMES (Pritchard, 1990) and will, thus, be referred to as "ProSys." We will present ProSys in the context in which it was developed. This should help better understanding of ProSys and, in particular, the process in which it is embedded in an organizational context.

The Existing System of Objectives

The SSO management team had, on its own, worked out a system of objectives for the DMs. There were five such objectives: leadership, development of business, management skills, district performance, and knowing the business. Each of the five had three or four short phrases defining it. For example, under leadership was coaching, personnel selection, and develops subordinates. Each of the five major areas had an importance weight associated with it, ranging from three to seven.

This approach to defining objectives is typical of what exists in many companies: a listing of a few objectives and their facets, together with simple importance weights. Such a system has a number of problems:

1. Conceptually, one can question whether the system of objectives is really that simple. Objectives typically are interconnected. Moreover, they usually form a hierarchy of superobjectives and subobjectives.
2. The list of objectives is incomplete: in further interviews, many more objectives surfaced easily. Some of them had been left out because they seemed too "subjective" to the SSO managers. Others were deemed to be already "somehow covered" by the objectives on the list, but on closer inspection, that proved incorrect.
3. The weights are essentially arbitrary. Their scale level is unknown. Hence, it is difficult to convince the users of the validity of the system.
4. Practical measurement issues are not addressed. How should an employee actually be assessed on these criteria? If one uses, for example, a good-to-bad rating, what exactly is "good," what is "bad"?
5. Feedback issues are not addressed. In particular, the list does not specify how one should compute a global performance measure for an individual person or a work team.
6. Finally, no process on how to use this system of objectives to enhance productivity is offered.

Such issues make any resulting measurements dubious — both for management purposes, as well as for self-monitoring. Consequently, it is hard to convince the users of the system, the DMs, of the utility of the system.

Setting up a System of Objectives Using HISYS

As a first step in arriving at a more complete and refined system of objectives, the list of objectives described above was supplemented with all other objectives that were found in the individual interviews with the members of the SSO management team. The management team then worked as a group to conceptually sharpen and structure this set of objectives. After some reduction of the list of objectives into clusters of synonyms, the formal process involved the following series of steps. These steps were supported by a computer program that generates graphic displays for overhead projection, stores the results, and computes statistics (Staufenbiel & Borg, 1992).

Step One: Stratifying the Objectives in Terms of Lower Level and Higher Level Objectives

This is done by specifying a starting value for the number of levels of objectives that will be used, usually three to five. The overall objective, in this case, the performance of DM, is placed in the top level, and then the other subordinate objectives are sorted into the levels below in terms of logical dependency (causality) or semantic overlap (containment). For example, the managers thought that the overall performance of a DM rests, so to speak, on three columns: trade performance, customer satisfaction, and keeps within budget. Hence, they put these criteria in the level just below overall performance.

Deciding on these major objectives usually leads to considerable discussion of the concepts themselves. This leads to a significant sharpening of the formulations and a clarification of the objectives in the minds of the managers. Semantic vagueness is decreased, and this helps the process of obtaining agreement.

Step Two: Building a Qualitative Hierarchy by Connecting Lower Level to Higher Level Objectives

The specific relationship between different levels of objectives is next discussed and agreed upon. Each objective on a given level is connected to at least one objective on the level below it. This also involves possible shifting upward or downward of specific objectives in the hierarchy and further clarifications of the meaning of some of the objectives. In this situation, the process led to the hierarchy of objectives shown in Figure 17–1. Note that "trade performance" and "keeps within budget" cover the same subobjectives, while "customer satisfaction" depends only on "develops resources" and "utilizes resources." Hence, we obtain a hierarchy that is not a tree but, rather exhibits conceptual overlaps.

Step Three: Quantifying the Hierarchy

All objectives on a given level of the hierarchy that contribute to a higher level objective are next compared pairwise with respect to the

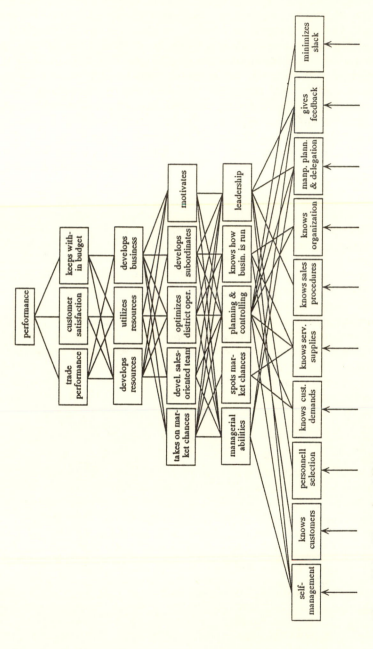

Figure 17-1 Hierarchy of Objectives

ratio of their contribution to that objective. Building on work by Borg and Tremmel (1988), this is done with computer aid on a projection screen by splitting a beam that expresses the ratio of the two subobjectives to the higher level objective.

The observed ratios can be checked mathematically for logical inconsistencies. For example, looking at Figure 17–1, assume that the managers said that "trade performance" contributes twice as much as "customer satisfaction" to the overall objective: "performance." Assume further that they also said that "customer satisfaction" is three times as important for "performance" as "keeps within budget." Then, "trade performance" must be six times as important as "keeps within budget" for perfect consistency, and any answer that differs from six means inconsistency. The mathematics for doing this can be found in Borg and Staufenbiel (in press).

The computer program that is used with this process calculates these inconsistencies, and they are immediately available for the managers to see. Finding such inconsistencies provides useful feedback to the managers. The managers wanted to be consistent, and inconsistencies, once identified, served as a powerful motivator. The SSO management felt that it had to sharpen the semantics of the objectives or reconsider the qualitative hierarchy and its path connections so that it would be possible to come up with essentially consistent weight assignments. Consistency was deemed important, because an inconsistent system of objectives would be difficult to communicate and to control. Moreover, it was felt that if the SSO management team did not agree on what it wanted, it would be hard to give clear-cut expectations to their subordinates.

In any case, a best-fitting (ratio) scale of contribution weights can be derived mathematically from the paired-comparison data collected with respect to each higher level objective (Borg & Staufenbiel, in press; Saaty & Vargas, 1981). Hence, for the hierarchy in Figure 17–1, one can compute how much each lower level objective contributes to any higher level objective at any level in the hierarchy. For example, in this set of objectives, "self-management" contributes or determines 29 percent of "managerial abilities." In turn, "self-management" contributes 19 percent to "performance." The same type of calculation can be done for any lower level objective to any objective higher in the hierarchy. The contribution is 0 if there is no path connecting the two objectives.

Step Four: Exploring the Hierarchy of Objectives

Constructing a hierarchy of objectives is similar to solving a jigsaw puzzle: one successively looks at just a few individual pieces and tries to fit them together. The complete picture arises in the background. When completed, this final picture can be studied for its features. They are not all obvious from the construction process. Some of them can be seen only through computation. Consider Figure 17–1 and assume that the design team wants to know the contribution of "motivates" to the overall criterion "DM performance" and the constituents of "motivates" (i.e., its lower level). Such questions are answered by the computer. With the computer program used, one only has to click on the "motivates" box on the computer screen, and it presents all paths leading to and leaving from "motivates"; a toggle switch is also available that shows the path weights for each connection. Additional tables available in the program show the contribution weights of every objective on a given level to those on higher levels. For a given objective, these weights are computed by first multiplying the percentage contribution weights over each path leading upward from that objective and then adding these products over all paths.

Exploring the hierarchy leads to further discussion. For example, the design team sometimes notices that a given objective makes a substantially greater contribution to the overall objective than had been estimated previously by direct rating. The typical reason is that such an objective has many paths leading upward, and this leads to an accumulation of weights. The converse is true, of course, for objectives with relatively few connecting paths. (Indeed, the number of different paths leading to a higher order objective usually correlates highly with the objective's weight derived via the pair comparison process [see Borg, 1987; Borg & Staufenbiel, 1991].)

The design team may also notice that some paths in the hierarchy are missing or that other paths should be deleted. If so, they go back to step three and make the revisions and then study the result. One may even be forced back to step two if the design team feels that there is still too much inconsistency and too little agreement.

The Assessment Scales: Bars and Effectiveness Scores

The quantified hierarchy defines the system of objectives. It shows how different levels of objectives are related to each other and gives importance weights for the contribution of objectives to overall performance. However, this is only the first part of the process. In order to assess a DM's performance within this system and use that as feedback, one needs measurements of the final, lowest level objectives. There are the "boxes" at the roots of the hierarchy. This need for more specific measurement is suggested by the arrows that point into the hierarchy from below in Figure 17–1.

The root objectives in Figure 17–1 are, however, not concrete enough for practical purposes. For example, what exactly is good or poor self-management? Obviously, this has to be defined. One can think of the lowest level boxes as the products in ProMES. It was necessary to be more specific by developing indicators. We decided to set up behaviorally anchored rating scales for measuring these root objectives. This part of ProSys proceeds in four steps.

Step One: Clarifying Facets of Root Objectives

For each root objective or product, one first needs to clarify to what it refers in terms of concrete behavior. Table 17–1 shows an example of this for the root objective self-management. There are seven facets of behaviors that define self-management. Each row of the table is one of these facets of behaviors, such as "keeping appointments and deadlines under control," "explicit goal setting," "ordering one's work in terms of priorities."

Table 17–1   Rating Scale for Self-Management

Minimum Level	Expected Level	Maximum Level
Keeps most important deadlines and appointments under control	Does clear planning job on deadlines and appointments	Keeps deadlines and appointments under control
Sets vague personal goals	Sets clear personal goals	Sets aggressive personal goals
Prioritizes work activities minimally	Pritorizes work activities clearly	Follows work priorities in a disciplined manner
Roughly knows how well goals are achieved	Regularly checks on goal achievement	Makes sure goals are achieved
Is willing to deliver "normal" performance	Motivates himself or herself for high performance	Is highly achievement oriented and ambitious
Does technically correct work but does little to assure interests of SSO against outside pressure	Technically correct work and assertively assures interests of SSO vis-à-vis internal and external customers	Technically correct work and assertively assures interests of SSO vis-à-vis internal and external customers
Hardly ever risks anything without reassurance	Takes calculated risks	Takes calculated risks and documents reasons for decisions

Note: The seven facets of this objective are graded on a rating scale ranging from minimum acceptable level (–8) to expected level (0) to maximum attainable level (+6).

Step Two: Defining Behavioral Anchors

Three behavioral statements or anchors are defined for each of the behavior facets in a process similar to ProMES. First, the expected level is specified. This is defined as it is in ProMES as the level of performance that is neither especially good nor bad. For example, the fourth row of Table 17–1 deals with goal setting. It shows that SSO management believes that for a DM to "regularly check on goal achievement" meets but does not exceed expectations. Next, having defined the expected behavior, the design team describes the maximum performance, that is, what can be optimally achieved under the existing circumstances. This is what ProMES would term the "maximum level of the indicator." Also, as in ProMES, a minimum level is specified that indicates what level of behavior is the very least that can be accepted. Performance below this level for an extended period cannot be tolerated. As shown in the first column of Table 17–1, the SSO managers expect the DM always to have at least a rough awareness of goal achievement.

Step Three: Scaling the Expected Level

Proceeding as in step two and defining minimum, maximum, and expected behaviors has the consequence that the expected behavior may not be in the middle between the minimum and the maximum. Table 17–1 shows, for example, that the expected level of behavior on the second facet from the bottom ("technically correct work and assertively . . .") is both the expected level and the maximum level. Generally, the design team decided that the expected level of self-management behavior was a little closer to the maximum than to the minimum. If one wants to rate expected behavior as 0 — a preferred choice to avoid notions of complacency for the "average" performer — one, thus, has to shift the rating scale to the left so that the maximum category gets closer to the zero point. With our original plus/minus seven scale, this resulted in a rating scale ranging from –8 to +6.

Step Four: Establishing Effectiveness Scores

As in the contingencies in ProMES, behavioral ratings may be nonlinearly related to satisfying the objectives. Thus, rather than using scores of scales like the one in Table 17–1 directly as inputs into the quantified hierarchy of objectives, one should first transform them into effectiveness scores. In our system, this is done as follows. First, minimum, expected, and maximum levels are mapped into –100, 0, and +100, respectively. Second, for ratings between these categories, the mapping is done by linear interpolation. If the expected level is not exactly in the middle of the rating scale, this automatically induces a nonlinear (although locally linear) function of rating scores to effectiveness. (In case of the rating scale for Table 17–1, the function is slightly concave upward, because the position of the expected category lies to the right of the middle of the scale.) The function can then be modified "by hand" (i.e., again, graphically on a computer display).

Other Issues in ProSys

Not all behaviors subsumed under a root objective are monotonically related to the objective in terms of effectiveness. This is easiest to see by example. The design team wanted to stress that DMs should be more willing to take risks. Of course, more risk is not always better, and risk taking should not become unreasonable. In a case like this, we suggest changing the wording of the behavior scale rather than allowing for U-trends. Such changes have to be done by appropriate choice of semantics, not by mathematical means, because, by avoiding mathematical tricks as much as possible, the model stays simple, and higher ratings always mean better performance.

Another issue is that, in practice, it sometimes happens that in one or more indicators, the expected level of performance is equivalent to the maximum level. This is similar to a ProMES contingency that is flat from the expected level to the maximum. This case is actually not as unrealistic as it may seem at first. In Table 17-1, we see an instance on the sixth behavior facet, where the management team specifies that the expected level of performance is indeed nothing short of the maximum one. This leads to a formal complication, because when expected approaches maximum, assigning an effectiveness score of 0 to expected and +100 to maximum gets increasingly problematic, because small behavior improvements then become related to excessive (and, in the limit, infinitely large) effectiveness growth. (The analogous is true for expected to minimum.) How should one handle this problem? One possibility is to give up the notion that the effectiveness function must range from −100 to +100. However, this solution brings in further problems, for example, the fact that the best possible total performance score is less than 100. Furthermore, if one modifies the effectiveness functions (and constructs "contingencies" as in standard ProMES), an implicit weighting is introduced that is difficult to bring into agreement with the weights derived previously for the hierarchy.

From a practical point of view, however, the problem is not likely to occur for a root objective as a whole, but only for one or a few of its behavior facets. Indeed, it seems hardly conceivable that root objectives become so monolithic that there would not remain a substantial proportion of facets for which the expected level lies clearly below the maximum.

Using Objectives and Behaviorally Anchored Rating Scales in the Feedback Process

ProSys not only is a measurement model but also includes a formal feedback process. These options essentially correspond to ProMES and, thus, need not be explicated here in detail. A few comments should do.

Feedback systems are designed to provide individuals or units with frequent assessments on their performance. The assessments have to be made on criteria that are clear, accepted, and closely related to behavior that is under the control of the individual. The scores serve to guide change efforts.

The process set up with ProSys is to provide each DM with feedback once a month, discuss his performance in general and with respect to the root objective facets, and explore possibilities for most effective improvements. A rating is made on each of the ten root objectives. These ratings are then used to calculate the degree of goal achievement on each objective, including overall performance, using the weights established for the hierarchy of objectives. A relatively frequent feedback (e.g., monthly or bimonthly) seems necessary to guarantee a reasonable degree of contiguity of the appraisals to the DM's behavior. Also, performance below the minimum level cannot be compensated by even brilliant performance on all other objectives, and, thus, a minimal level of performance on all relevant behaviors must be closely checked.

DISCUSSION

We found it useful to work with the design team using our computer-aided design method for several reasons. It involves no paperwork, and, thus, the team can sit back and concentrate on results. Printouts, graphics, and screen-dumps are available at any time and help to develop the model in a spirallike fashion. What proved most effective was the possibility to check the internal consistency of the judgments. Inconsistencies always led to discussions and motivated the team to work hard on a common understanding and better wordings for the objectives.

A system that can be shown to be internally consistent is also easier to "sell" to employees on lower levels. In the above case, the DMs were first critical about what the management team had worked out for them. However, the result could be explained to them as a nonarbitrary, internally consistent system, where one cannot easily change individual weights without affecting everything else. The DM team, then, tested out a number of weight assignments by going through the respective pair comparisons themselves and arrived at almost exactly the same weights, with almost perfect consistency. This led them to understand the jigsaw-puzzle logic behind the system and to quickly accept the entire hierarchy.

For the measurement scales, we found that behaviorally anchored rating scales anchored at expected, minimum, and maximum values were easiest to set up. A procedure that forces the design team to specify the meaning of the end points and the middle category of a given schematic scale proved to be unnatural.

Although ProSys and standard ProMES have many things in common, there are also a number of major differences. It is valuable to explore these and consider how they could contribute to each other.

The major thing that ProSys offers is a method for capturing the complexities of broad and sometimes vague sets of objectives. The hierarchical approach provides a tool to organize and discuss rich sets of objectives systematically. It also allows for "overlap" of the classes of objectives. Only the objectives are, as the basic building blocks, assumed to be independent of each other. Thus, ProSys acknowledges the complexity of such sets of goals and offers a methodology for managers to develop these sets of goals in a way that can be communicated and tied ultimately to specific behavior. In addition, it is a top-down approach that can be useful when overall strategic objectives are not clear.

However, one of the key aspects of ProMES is the contingencies and, especially, the nonlinear aspect of contingencies. Design teams working with ProMES describe this as one of its most compelling features. ProSys, in the above application, did not utilize nonlinear contingencies within the objective hierarchy. The ProSys weights correspond essentially to the slopes of linear contingencies functions relating the root objectives to the global objective. In addition, the scaling of the behavioral rating scales into effectiveness scores does not contain all the features of normal contingencies. These behavioral rating scales are analogous to ProMES indicators. In ProMES, they would be represented by contingencies. In its present form, ProSys does not allow the different behavioral scales within one root objective to differ in importance. For example, in Table 17–1, all minimums receive a score of –8, all maximums +6. If these are the behaviors in which personnel are expected to engage it could be useful to add information on the relative importance of such behaviors.

It would be possible to utilize contingencies more fully in ProSys by having the managers do full nonlinear contingencies within the objective hierarchy. However, although this has conceptual advantages, there are practical problems. It already takes considerable time to do ProSys, and adding more time to deal with nonlinearities may not be practical. In addition, the mathematics in ProSys are not compatible at this time with nonlinearity. However, it would be possible to do more typical contingencies with the behavioral rating scales, as was done in the case by Hedley, Sawyer, and Pritchard in Chapter 15.

Another difference between ProSys and standard ProMES is that the former relies very much on ratings of behavior rather than on the outcomes of behavior such as units produced or times when deadlines were met. In this sense, it is like a ProMES application for performance appraisal such as that described in Chapter 15. However ProSys, in principle, could also be set up with other measures that assess outcomes or a mix of behavioral and outcome measures.

Typically, ProSys would be used in a top-down approach similar to the case discussed above. However, a traditional ProMES approach would suggest that the development of objectives and measures of these objectives might profitably be done with participation on the part of those that will be affected by these decisions. In this case, that as not deemed appropriate by management, but in other settings, it might be explored.

One could combine ProSys with ProMES in a situation where management feels that it should first clarify what it wants or where the system of objectives is sufficiently complex or subject to changes. Management might choose first to build a ProSys hierarchy of objectives. If appropriate, this could be done with the participation of lower level managers. Ideally, such a set of objectives should include the outcomes of behavior such as is found in a typical ProMES case. This hierarchy of objectives could then be handed down to the work units as a guideline and as a start for a ProMES design that essentially concentrates on translating the root objectives into things under the control of the work unit. When products and indicators are developed by the work group, they can then be checked by management against the ProSys hierarchy. This way, management can stress its leadership function and still maintain involvement of employees in areas where they have an edge on expertise. Moreover, commitment through ownership is neither at risk for the employees, like it might be in a pure top-down approach, nor for the managers, because it is they who define the initial map.

REFERENCES

Borg, I. (1987). Arbeitszufriedenheit, Arbeitswerte und Jobauswahl: Ein hierarchischer, individuen-zentrierter Ansatz. *Zeitschrift für Sozialpsychologie*, *18*, 28–39.

Borg, I., & Staufenbiel, T. (in press). Zur statistischen Bewertung der Konsdistenz paarweiser Verhältnisurteile. *Archiv für Psychologie*.

Borg, I., & Staufenbiel, T. (1991). Ein idiographisches Modell und Meßverfahren zur Analyse von Arbeitswerten und Arbeitszufriedenheit. In L. Fischer (Ed.), *Arbeitszufriedenheit* (pp. 157–175). Stuttgart: Verlag für angewandte Psychologie.

Borg, I. & Tremmel, L. (1988). Compression effects in pairwise ratio scaling. *Methodika*, *2*, 1–15.

Pritchard, R. D. (1992). Organizational productivity. In M. D. Dunnette & L. M. Hough, (Eds.), *Handbook of industrial/organizational psychology* (2d ed.). Palo Alto, CA: Consulting Psychologists Press.

Pritchard, R. D. (1990). *Measuring and improving organizational productivity: A practical guide* (p. 248). New York: Praeger.

Saaty, T. L., & Vargas, L. G. (1981). *The logic of priorities*. Boston, MA: Kluwer-Nijhoff.

Staufenbiel, T., & Borg, I. (in press). Computer aided design of productivity measurement and enhancement systems. In F. Faulbaum (Ed.), *Softstat '93*. Stuttgart: Fischer.

Staufenbiel, T., & Borg, I. (1992). HISYS, a program for the scaling and measurement of hierarchical systems. In F. Faulbaum (Ed.), *Softstat '91* (pp. 161–166). Stuttgart: Fischer.

18

Lessons Learned about ProMES

Robert D. Pritchard

Now that each of the 16 cases has been described, it is time to look at what we have learned from them about ProMES and productivity improvement in general. The discussion in this chapter will focus on several questions.

Can ProMES be developed in different settings?
Does ProMES improve productivity?
What factors seem to be important for making ProMES successful?
How long does it take to do ProMES?
What improvements in the process of doing ProMES have been developed?
What are some of the other effects of ProMES?
For what other applications can ProMES be used?
What have we learned about why ProMES works?
What do we still need to know about productivity and ProMES?

CAN ProMES BE DEVELOPED IN DIFFERENT SETTINGS?

When the original ProMES project was done with the Air Force, it was clear that ProMES could be developed in an ongoing organization and that it improved productivity substantially (Pritchard, Jones, Roth, Stuebing, & Ekeberg, 1988, 1989). However, the next questions were, first, whether the system could be developed in other settings and, second, whether it would prove an effective method of productivity improvement in these other settings.

As for the first question, the chapters in this book describe ProMES development in 45 different groups. In each case, the system was successfully developed.

Variation in Settings

This is particularly important when we consider the great variety of settings represented by these cases. ProMES was developed in organizations in four different countries on three different continents. The applications were done in different types of industries, such as electronics, electrical components, office equipment, banking, education, distribution, and public service. The technologies also varied greatly and included personal service, high and low technology manufacturing in individual, team, and assembly line settings, technical repair, and professional service. The jobs themselves also varied greatly. There were various types of assembly and testing jobs, technicians of various sorts, clerical jobs, sales jobs, process control jobs, mental health and mental retardation care giving jobs, and college professor jobs. These jobs varied in many dimensions. For example, on degree of autonomy, there were jobs where control was very close, such as some assembly jobs, and others where high degrees of autonomy were present, such as commercial painters and college professors.

ProMES was also developed with quite different types of people. There were large differences in education level, ranging from people with less than a high school education to college professors. In Chapter 11, "ProMES in a Bank," Miedema and Thierry developed the system with individuals, where each person had his or her own products, indicators, and contingencies. It was also developed with individuals where each person got feedback on his or her own individual productivity but where the system was the same for all the individuals. It was developed on small and on fairly large groups. For example, Watson, Hedley, Clark, Paquin, Gottesfeld, and Pritchard found in Chapter 10, "Using ProMES to Evaluate University Teaching Effectiveness," that some of the academic departments contained more than 50 people. ProMES was also developed where the system contained a combination of individual indicators and group based indicators, for example, Kleingeld and van Tuijl's chapter on "Individual and Group Productivity Enhancement in a Service Setting."

The systems developed also used many different types of measures. An interesting finding was that it was not uncommon for subjective measures to be used. In Chapter 15, "Development of a New Performance Appraisal Instrument: An Application of the ProMES Methodology," Hedley, Sawyer, and Pritchard combined subjective measures with objective measures while working with mental health staff. Schmidt, Przygodda, and Kleinbeck utilized the same system with painters in Chapter 13, "Development of a Productivity Measurement and Feedback System in a Firm of Commercial Painters." In other cases, the entire system was based on subjective measures only.

One of the major factors for ProMES development in different settings was the contingencies. Contingencies are one of the key factors in ProMES and the feature that most separates it from other approaches to measuring productivity. They are also the most conceptually complex part of the system. Our biggest concern when ProMES was first tested in the Air Force was whether people could actually do the steps necessary to develop the contingencies. As the project progressed, it became clear that people could develop the contingencies in that setting. The cases in this book confirm this finding in that it was possible for people in many different types of organizations to develop the contingencies, regardless of their education level. The contingencies they developed were mostly nonlinear, and people were able to develop contingencies for purely subjective measures, even when they had no prior experience with these measures.

ProMES Flexibility

It is clear from all these applications that ProMES can fit differing circumstances. One of its features is its flexibility. This is seen in its adaptation to different countries. Clearly, the United States, western Europe, and Australia have many more things in common than they have differences, but, still, differences do exist. One of the clearest examples is the importance of participation in Europe, especially Germany. Because of this importance, the participative features of ProMES could be especially emphasized in Germany. The name "ProMES" has even been changed in the German adaptation to "PPM" or (as a rough translation) "Participative Productivity Management" (Pritchard, Kleinbeck, & Schmidt, 1993) to reflect this emphasis on participation.

Another aspect of this flexibility is the ability of the system to capture differences in policy within the same organization. This was best illustrated in the teaching effectiveness case in Chapter 10. Here, different academic departments had different policies about the importance of different indicators. For example, the basic science departments emphasized understanding large amounts of subject content, while the clinical departments, where the more advanced students were actually treating animals, emphasized problem solving. By changing the shape of the contingencies, the various departments were able to capture these differences.

Thus, we have a clear answer to the first question. It is clear that ProMES can be successfully developed in different settings. In fact, as these cases and other applications of the system have shown, we have not yet found a setting where the system cannot be developed so that it measures productivity. This is not to say that such settings do not exist; I am sure that they do, but they seem to be rare.

DOES ProMES IMPROVE PRODUCTIVITY

Just because ProMES can be developed in a given setting does not mean that it will improve productivity in that setting. The effects on productivity in the original Air Force study were quite positive, but we still needed to know whether ProMES would improve productivity in other settings. In this section, we will review what we have learned from the cases about the effects of ProMES on productivity.

Effects over Time

In all, there have been 26 units from which we have productivity data. Five are from the original Air Force project; 21 are from groups in this book. The first way of summarizing the data is to look at the effects of productivity over time. In each study, there is a baseline period that shows productivity data before ProMES feedback and a feedback period that shows productivity data after feedback was started. Thus, we can summarize the data by looking across studies at the productivity data during baseline as compared with the productivity data during the feedback period.

To put all these data together into a meaningful summary is a task that requires a series of somewhat arbitrary decisions. The first has to do with what time periods to include. A time period could be a week, month, a quarter, or a semester; its length depends on the time interval used for giving feedback in that project. In some cases, baseline data are available for up to 22 time periods; in other cases, the baseline is only one period. Likewise, in some cases, we have productivity data for feedback spanning 24 time periods, and at the other extreme, there is one case with data from only one feedback period. This means that for each of the 26 groups, we have data from at least one period of baseline and at least one period of feedback. However, as we extend the baseline period back in time to include more periods, the number of groups with data for that time period decreases. For example, we have baseline data on all the 26 groups for one period, data for 81 percent of the groups going back four periods, 69 percent of the groups back eight periods, and 54 percent of the groups back nine periods. For ten periods, the percentage of groups with data decreases substantially to 38 percent and decreases further as we go back more periods. A similar situation exists for feedback, where we have 100 percent of the groups with 1 period of feedback, 85 percent with 3 periods, 77 percent with 5 periods, and 54 percent with 10 periods, 46 percent with 11 periods, and 42 percent with 12 periods. After 12 periods, the percentage drops to 27 percent and continues to decrease as the number of periods increases.

Based on these percentages, the decision was made to include the data back into the baseline for 9 periods and to use 12 periods of feedback data. Thus, the minimum percentage of groups represented in the baseline period is 54 percent, and the minimum for feedback is 42 percent. For each period of baseline and each period of feedback, we can take the average productivity score for that time period across the groups for which we have data. This gives us a mean score for each of the 9 periods of baseline and each of the 12 periods of feedback.

Two other decisions involved what data to include. Some projects have clear results indicating that productivity improved substantially during the development of the system, for example, Chapter 7, "ProMES and Computer Service Technicians: An Australian Application," by Bonic and Chapter 3, "ProMES as Part of a New Management Strategy," by Janssen, Berkel, and Stolk. In the typical way the data are analyzed, this improvement in productivity occurs during the baseline. If the development period is included in the baseline, the difference between baseline and the feedback period is decreased, potentially underestimating the size of the difference between baseline and feedback. However, the decision was made to include all data before feedback as part of the baseline, even if there were clear data that productivity improved during the baseline period. In this way, the improvements shown would be conservative.

Another complicating factor is the presence of a goal-setting intervention. In some groups, goal setting was added to feedback. The ProMES intervention consist of a productivity measurement process and a feedback process. Formal goal setting, where people set public goals, is not part of ProMES. When it is included, it is an additional intervention beyond ProMES. Thus, from one point of view, any productivity results that include goal setting should be excluded. However, this was not done. In all cases, the primary intervention was ProMES feedback, that is, the majority of the time and effort went into developing the productivity measurement system and giving feedback. In addition, simple inspection of the data indicates that the conclusions would not be different if the goal-setting data were omitted. It seems that there were too few such cases, and the data were not typically clear that goal setting had any additional effect.

Having made these decisions, the data were analyzed and are shown in Figure 18–1. The horizontal axis is time period, showing the 9 periods of baseline and the 12 periods of feedback. The vertical axis is the ProMES overall effectiveness score, as reported by the individual cases. In some cases, the chapters reported averages across more than one group. In other chapters, just the two average overall effectiveness scores, one for baseline and one for feedback, were reported for some groups. Thus, some of the individual time period data points were not reported in the chapters. These individual data points for each period for each group were obtained from the chapter authors.

The results presented in Figure 18–1 are quite compelling. They show that across these 26 units, productivity during the baseline started out just slightly above the expected level. There is some

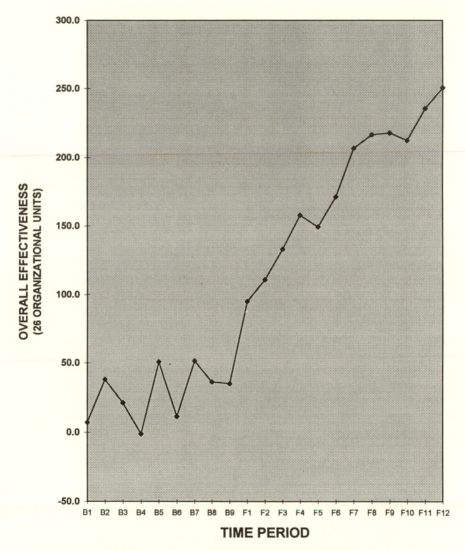

Figure 18-1   ProMES Productivity Effects over Time

evidence of an improvement in productivity toward the end of baseline. For example, the mean overall effectiveness for the first six periods of baseline is 21.1, while the mean for the last three periods is 40.1. If we look at only the cases where we have data for a considerable period of baseline, the difference is even stronger. There were 18 of the 26 units where we had full baseline data for at least eight periods. Looking at those 18 units, the mean during the first five time periods of baseline was 26.1, while the mean for the last three time periods of baseline was 50.2. These results suggest that productivity was increasing toward the end of baseline. I will have more to say about this issue later in this chapter.

The most powerful findings in Figure 18–1 are the large positive changes in productivity when feedback started. The figure indicates that when the first period of feedback started, there was an immediate improvement of substantial magnitude. In fact, this first period improvement was the largest improvement of any single feedback period. After this initial improvement, productivity continued to improve substantially over the remainder of the time period.

These results indicate a powerful effect of ProMES feedback on productivity. The initial large improvement suggests a rapid and significant change in how the work is being done. This rapid change is followed by a continued, long-term, more gradual improvement. The results from cases with more than 12 periods of feedback data suggest that productivity continues to improve even after 12 periods, which in most cases is 12 months.

The data in Figure 18–1 include units with varying possible overall effectiveness scores, and different numbers of units are present at different time periods. This opens the possibility of potential confounding of the results. To check this, another analysis was run on those cases where there were substantial baseline and feedback data. There were 12 such units where each unit had at least eight periods of baseline data and ten periods of feedback data. The data from these units were analyzed separately. The results were identical to those shown in Figure 18–1. The baseline was slightly above the expected level; it increased slightly prior to feedback; there was an immediate and very large increase in productivity when feedback started, followed by a slower increase over time. Thus, the results in Figure 18–1 are representative.

Effect Sizes

Another way to look at the magnitude of the improvements is to look at effect sizes. Effect sizes are a way to compare the magnitude of changes across different studies. The basic idea is to compare the amount of difference between baseline and feedback in terms of the number of standard deviations of difference between the baseline mean and the feedback mean. This d-statistics approach (Hunter, Schmidt, & Jackson, 1982) was used with the Air Force data (Pritchard, Jones, Roth, Stuebing, & Ekeberg, 1988, 1989) and here as well. To calculate the effect size, the mean difference between feedback and baseline was calculated. This difference was then divided by the pooled standard deviation. This pooled standard deviation was calculated by getting the sum of the squared deviations of the baseline data points around the baseline mean, adding this to the sum of the squared deviations of the feedback data points around the feedback mean, dividing the sum by the combined degrees of freedom, and taking the square root of the result. An effect size was calculated for each of the 26 groups.

One decision had to be made on how to treat the effect sizes in the university teaching application in Chapter 10. The data reported in the chapter are based on three separate departments where there were sufficient data to do this analysis over time. Because there were three separate groups with separate contingencies and feedback reports, the normal procedures would have been to calculate the effect sizes for each group separately. However, with this approach, the three effect sizes were .63, 5.03, and 16.5, with an average of 7.39. These are highly variable, and the higher values are probably not realistic. These extreme values probably occurred because of the small samples involved. The other approach would be to combine all three groups together and then calculate one effect size. When this is done, the effect size is 4.8. However, reporting only one effect size of 4.8 seems inappropriate, because there were actually three groups. As a compromise, an intermediate strategy was used. The more conservative average value of 4.8 was used, but it was entered into the calculations and the figure three times, once for each group. Had only one value of 4.8 been entered, rather than the three, the average effect size drops from 2.3 to 2.1. Thus, whether this effect size is added once or three times has no meaningful effect on the conclusions.

The resulting effect sizes are presented in Figure 18–2. The effect size for each group in each chapter where productivity data were presented is shown in order of increasing size. The groups are identified by which chapter they are in, for example, C3 (Chapter 3). If a chapter describes data on more than one group, this is indicated by a group designation. Thus, the first entry at the bottom of the figure is C6Gp2, indicating that the effect size is for the second group described in Chapter 6. The group number is based on the order in which the group was described in the chapter. For example, the first group described gets the Gp1 designation; the second that is described, Gp2; and so on. The results from the five Air Force groups are AFGp1–5.

The average effect size across these 26 groups is 2.3. This means that, on the average, productivity under ProMES feedback is 2.3 standard deviations higher than productivity during baseline. Typically, an effect size of .5 is considered a meaningful effect that has practical

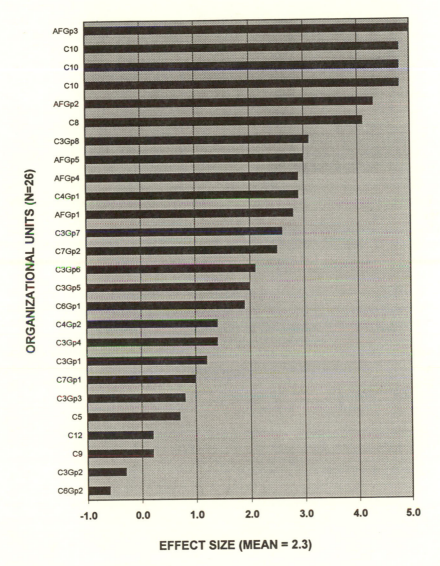

Figure 18–2   ProMES Effect Sizes

consequences. Cohen (1977) indicates that an effect size (d-statistic) of .2 is small, .5 is medium, and .8 is large. Clearly, our mean effect size of 2.3 is a very strong one. Even without the strong Air Force results, the mean effect size is still very large, a value of 2.0.

Another way to compare this mean effect size is to look at the effect sizes that have been reported for productivity improvement interventions in the literature. Guzzo, Jette, and Katzell (1985) reviewed this literature and calculated effect sizes. The mean effect size they found for using feedback to improve productivity was .35 for all criteria and .41 for output. The average effect size for all interventions on output was .63. Thus, the average effect size using ProMES is over five times larger than the average effect size for other feedback studies and over three times larger than the average effect size for all interventions they report. Clearly, the size of the productivity improvements using ProMES are very strong and much stronger than typical interventions found in the literature.

One way to interpret these findings is to look at the impact of a change of 2.3 standard deviations in other settings. For example, the mean IQ of adults in the United States is normed to be 100, and the standard deviation on most measures is about 15. Thus, if you could improve a person with an average IQ by 2.3 standard deviations, you would move him or her from an IQ of 100 to an IQ of 135.

Yet another way to appreciate the magnitude of an effect size of 2.3 is to think about percentiles. If we took the overall effectiveness score over a unit for a large number of time periods, we could plot these overall effectiveness scores into a distribution. The mean of this distribution would be the mean overall effectiveness across the many periods. Let us assume that this distribution was formed by taking overall effectiveness scores without ProMES feedback. In other words, this is a distribution of productivity scores that corresponds to the baseline. The question is what the amount of change would be if ProMES was introduced and there was an effect size improvement of 2.3 in productivity, the average improvement shown in our cases. If we assume that the baseline distribution was close to normal, a change in productivity of 2.3 standard deviations would mean that the unit went from their average productivity being at their fiftieth percentile in baseline to their new average being at their old ninety-ninth percentile. They would now be averaging what in the past they were able to achieve only 1 period out of 100.

Other Issues

Although the effects of ProMES feedback have been generally very large, in 2 of the 26 groups productivity decreased during feedback. The first was one of the groups reported in Chapter 3; the other was one of the groups described by Jones in Chapter 6, "ProMES with Assembly

Line Work Groups: It Is More than Just a Technology." In both groups, a significant number of experienced personnel were removed from the group just when feedback was starting and were replaced with new people. These new personnel were new to the job and had not been involved in the development of ProMES. Thus, it is not surprising that productivity decreased during this period. In addition, in Chapter 3 there was an accident during feedback, which had a major negative effect on their effectiveness scores. This was a rare event that did not occur again.

Another issue is how long the effects of ProMES will last. We do not have a clear answer to that question yet, because we do not have enough groups who have used ProMES for a long period. Figure 18–1 indicates that improvements are continuing for at least 12 periods (typically, a year). The longest ProMES project is the original group in Chapter 3 where the group started with ProMES feedback in 1989 and in 1994 are still maintaining the gains they have made.

Another interesting finding is the effects of removing ProMES. In Chapter 3 the computer system was not operational for four months, and it was not possible to get the data for the ProMES feedback reports. When the computer was again functioning, it was possible to go back and reconstruct the data. They found that without ProMES feedback, productivity had decreased dramatically When feedback was reinstated, productivity improved very quickly again.

Chapter 3 formally analyzed the cost savings with ProMES. This analysis indicated that the improvements in overall effectiveness resulted in an increase in $8,200 per month, assuming that the extra production generated by the group did, in fact, lead to that amount of revenues. Considering that this was only four people, this is a considerable savings. Even if the facilitators are consultants with high hourly fees, the cost of a ProMES project could be recouped very quickly, making the return on investment substantial.

More analyses of this type are needed to get a better picture of the cost effectiveness of ProMES interventions. However, it is also worth noting that the effect size for this group was only 1.2. Thus, the improvement in effectiveness was much less than the improvement of the average ProMES group (2.3). This suggests that the savings might be expected to be even larger in many settings.

In summary, the answer to the second question is that ProMES does improve productivity. Developing the system seems to have a positive effect on productivity. Productivity improves dramatically from baseline to feedback, and the size of the improvement is much larger than with other interventions that have been reported in the literature. Improvements in productivity continue to occur over time, and the limited data we have available indicate that improvements are maintained for years.

WHAT FACTORS SEEM TO BE IMPORTANT FOR MAKING ProMES SUCCESSFUL?

Clearly, ProMES is a powerful way to improve productivity. However, there is clear variation in the degree of success for different projects. A number of important lessons have been learned about the factors that make a project successful or not so successful. Most of the cases discuss the factors that the authors feel were important in that application. This next section summarizes what we have learned from the cases overall.

Management Support

One of the most important factors in making a project successful is strong management support. A considerable amount of resources are needed to do a ProMES project successfully. This means a significant investment in time from the unit's personnel and their managers and supervisors. It also means support in the form of a quiet place to meet, time to review feedback reports, and so on. If these resources are not clearly available, problems will result. An example of this is in Chapter 6, where lack of proper support in the second group was probably a factor in the lack of success of that case.

Top management support is also essential when problems develop. One outcome of doing ProMES is that underlying conflicts in policy and procedures become apparent. This creates discomfort, and one way to relieve this discomfort is to discontinue the project. Management support is necessary at this time to give the impetus to continue on and resolve these conflicts. Another example of a problem is that people generally do not want to be evaluated. This resistance to evaluation can take the form of resistance to the project. Again, management support is essential at this time. We saw this phenomenon in the project on teaching evaluation in Chapter 10.

Finally, management support is necessary when organizational changes threaten the ProMES project. For example, in Chapter 2, "ProMES in an Electronic Assembly Plant," by Roth, Watson, Roth, and Pritchard, the ProMES project was viewed as a pilot study. We did not seek the direct support of the senior management of the plant. When changes in the structure of the work were made from the central office in another state, the work of the group that had done ProMES was redistributed and the personnel in the group were reassigned to other work groups. With support of senior plant management from the beginning of the project, there might have been more loyalty to the project, and it might have been continued.

Organizational Stability

Changes in the organizational structure can be serious problems for the success of a product. In Chapter 2, an organizational change caused the loss of a project after most of the work was finished. In Chapter 9, "ProMES in a Service Setting," Howell, Jones and Hood also had problems when a restructuring led to making the feedback less meaningful.

It is neither possible nor desirable to keep organizations from making structural changes. However, it is a good idea to assess the chances for structural changes before starting a project and to do projects in those parts of the organization where such changes are least likely. Another approach is to get a commitment from the organization to try to keep the ProMES unit intact until it is possible to evaluate the success of the project. If structural changes must be made, they could be made after experience with ProMES.

A second aspect of organizational stability is the stability of the work group. Normal or even considerable turnover in the unit does not seem to be a problem for maintaining productivity gains. In the Air Force project, there was a 30 to 50 percent turnover rate each year because of normal reassignment, and, yet, the gains were maintained. In Chapter 3, assimilating new workers was not a problem. In Chapter 7, Bonic found that new workers were assimilated but this led to lowered expected levels for a time. Normal turnover presumably was present in the other cases as well.

The only exception to this seems to be when a substantial influx of new personnel occurs just at the start of feedback. In one of the groups in Chapter 3 and in Chapter 6 there were examples where a substantial number of the personnel who developed the system were replaced at the start of feedback by people new to the work and to ProMES. In both of these cases, productivity decreased.

The conclusion seems to be that normal or even fairly high turnover is not a problem for ProMES units as long as there is not a big change just as feedback is started. It seems that the new people are quickly assimilated into the ProMES approach and are largely trained by their peers and the supervisor of the group. In most cases, there was no formal attempt to train the new people in ProMES, although this could be done without much difficulty.

The final aspect of stability is technological stability. Lack of technological stability can be a serious problem, especially at the beginning of a project. A significant change in technology typically means a major change in the measurement system. This could mean new indicators and will almost always mean a change in the contingencies.

If the group has significant experience with ProMES, a change in technology should not be a problem. The group should be able to revise the system rather easily. In fact, ProMES could help them work out procedures for using the new technology. Chapter 3 illustrates an example where a change in the equipment the group used was made easily.

However, if the change is frequent or it occurs during the development of the system, this can be much more serious. The case in Chapter 11 gave an example in a bank where, after much of the work to develop the system was done, the technology changed substantially. This leads the employees in the design team to feel that their work has been wasted and could easily make them doubt the value of doing more such work, because things could change again. If the setting is one where the technology changes frequently in such a way that the ProMES system would need to be revised every few months, it is usually not going to be cost-effective to use ProMES. However, settings where there are frequent changes of that magnitude are rare.

Issues for the Unit's Personnel

A very critical factor seems to be the willingness of unit personnel and their supervisors to do the project. This means that they understand the process that will take place, see the advantages and disadvantages, have their concerns addressed, and have some say in whether the project is done with them. One basic issue is that a new approach such as ProMES is typically going to be met with skepticism by the members of the group. They need to be convinced that the process makes sense and that it will not be more trouble than it is worth.

Another basic issue deals with the underlying philosophy of ProMES. In ProMES, the members of the unit have a significant say in how their success is measured and participate directly in both the measurement process and deciding what to change to improve things. It is important that this philosophy be implemented from the start. That means that the group should have some say in whether they participate in ProMES or not. Giving them some decision-making authority from the start is a way to give them power over the system and help them to accept it when developed. It also makes it easier to deal with the inevitable problems that come up in developing ProMES, because the group had a choice in starting the system and, thus, feel more committed to it.

A number of the chapters make a point of these issues, and in many, steps were taken to establish rapport and help the group understand what the project was to be about, and some had the groups decide whether to start the project at all. The chapter by Algera and van den Hurk, Chapter 14, "Testing the Feasibility of ProMES before Implementation: A Case Study in the Dutch Steel Industry," is the best example of this. They did a formal feasibility study that included substantial work with the group on understanding and making decisions about using ProMES before a decision was made to start the system. The converse is also true. In cases where there was less participation (e.g., Chapter 6) and where there was less clear understanding of the system at the start (e.g., Chapter 8), these factors seemed to cause problems.

Another issue with the unit personnel is the level of agreement between personnel and management about the organization's goals. In most cases, this is not a problem. However, there were two examples where this issue came up. In Chapter 9 the service technicians who repaired photocopiers felt that their job was to repair and maintain the equipment. Management wanted them also to be responsible for generating revenues from new business, for example, getting existing customers to buy additional service contracts. The technicians felt uncomfortable about this dual role. A similar situation occurred in Chapter 8. Interestingly, both cases involved the same jobs in different countries (the United States and the Netherlands), but both groups had the same disagreement about doing both repair and sales.

Such differences in goals will be identified by developing the system, if they are not already apparent. It is important that such differences be confronted directly and resolved. To go on using the system without such a resolution merely perpetuates the problem and can make it even worse. Taking the time to fully discuss the issues and for both sides to constructively communicate why they take their positions can go a long way to finding some compromise with which both sides can live. A good ProMES facilitator can be a big help in keeping this process constructive and moving forward.

Structural Characteristics

Other lessons learned about making projects successful have to do with structural factors in ProMES. The first is the quality of the indicator data. It is essential that the indicator data be valid before being used for feedback. There are two issues here. The first is the accuracy with which the indicator data are collected. A good example of this issues was seen in Chapter 8. In this case, some of the indicators were not being measured accurately. This became apparent only after the technicians began to complain that their feedback data were not correct. After looking into this, it became clear that the reports contained some incorrect data. In that case, steps were then taken to correct the problem. However, the damage had already been done. The lack of valid data caused the technicians to lose faith in the accuracy of the system, and it took some time to regain this trust.

The second issue has more to do with the validity of the measure. It is not uncommon for a measure actually to be measuring something other than what personnel, including management, think it is measuring. For example, it could be that the measure was developed some time ago by people who are no longer in the unit. Over time, an inaccurate understanding of how the measure is calculated develops.

The lesson from both of these types of problems is that the design team should take the time to go through how each indicator is collected, defined, and reported. They should also get samples of the indicator and check them for accuracy. This not only increases the confidence of the design team in the resulting feedback but also avoids the problem of loss of trust in the system if it is discovered later that the feedback has been inaccurate. A next best strategy is the one used by Jones in Chapter 5, "ProMES in a Small Manufacturing Department: Results of Feedback and User Reactions." After the first feedback report, the group was asked their perceptions of accuracy, and any needed revisions were made to the system before further use.

A second structural issue is the time between the start of the project and feedback. Several cases have pointed out the problems created when this time period is too long. There are two situations where this is most likely to occur. The first is where it simply takes a long time to develop the system, for example, more than seven to eight months. This can come about when the facilitators are new to ProMES and, thus, not highly experienced or when the work setting itself is very complex.

Although this can be a problem when the development time becomes long, it is not nearly as much of a problem as the second type of situation. This second situation is where the design team has developed the system but does not start to give feedback in order to establish a baseline. In such a situation, there is a dilemma between good research design and a successful implementation. Good design calls for a baseline period long enough to get a stale estimate of the level of productivity before the start of feedback. However, after the system is developed, the group has done the work to design it and now wants to see their feedback. In addition, management has made the investment in the project and wants to see a return for this investment as soon as possible. If the delay is too long, the unit personnel begin to lose interest, and management may begin to question the utility of the project. A long delay of this type occurred in the case with the commercial painters in Chapter 13 and in the bank project in Chapter 11. In both cases, the authors pointed out the problems this delay produced.

It is clear that properly evaluating the effects of ProMES on productivity is important, and a good baseline is a valuable aid to that process. However, if the baseline is extended too long, the intervention itself is affected in a negative way. Thus, a long baseline can have a direct effect on the results. This means that the ability to accurately evaluate the effects of the system become compromised.

A solution to this dilemma could be in the timing of the work of the design team. Normally, the design team does products, indicators, and contingencies and then designs the feedback reports and begins collecting the indicator data. As an alternate strategy, after products and indicators are developed and approved, the design team could turn its attention to the problem of how the indicator data will be collected and actually start the process of collecting it. This can be done in the context of making sure that obtaining the data is feasible and that proper procedures be worked out for gathering it. After this process starts, these data become part of the baseline. However, it easily can be justified that these data not be given to the group, because the system is not yet finished.

After the data are being collected and the problems of feasibility and accuracy of the data are worked out, the design team can then start contingencies. It will take some time to develop the contingencies, have them approved, design the feedback report, and train the supervisors to conduct feedback meetings. By the time this work is done, there should be a reasonable amount of indicator data available for the baseline. Feedback itself can then be started as soon as the steps in designing it are finished. This approach will avoid the problem of a long period of no feedback after the system is developed.

A final structural issue is the amount of feedback in the setting before ProMES. One concern has been over how much feedback is available in the work setting to start with. If personnel already get a substantial amount of feedback, can ProMES really add anything? This was a concern in the original Air Force project for one unit, but this group showed a substantial improvement in productivity with ProMES. A number of the cases here also speak to this issue. For example, when we toured the German plant used by Przygodda, Kleinbeck, Schmidt, and Beckmann in Chapter 4, "Productivity Measurement and Enhancement in Advanced Manufacturing Systems," we were concerned because the personnel got daily feedback on number of units produced and other measures. However, when ProMES was implemented here, substantial improvements occurred. In fact, the average effect size for the improvement in productivity over the two groups from this case was 2.2, very near the 2.3 average across all studies. A similar concern was raised in chapters 6 and 7, yet, large productivity increases occurred.

Most of the feedback typically given to personnel, at least in our experience, is on measures over which the people do not have a substantial amount of control. Thus, they do not find such feedback particularly motivating. In addition, the fact that these pieces of feedback are not integrated as they are in ProMES seems to be a factor in the superiority of ProMES. Finally, because in ProMES the personnel are actively involved in the development of the measures and understand them better, they seem to have more impact.

HOW LONG DOES IT TAKE TO DO ProMES?

ProMES is a fairly labor-intensive intervention. It requires the time of the design team, the facilitators, and the managers. It is useful to be able to predict how much time it will take to do a ProMES project, and the cases in this book give us a way of estimating this.

The largest amount of personnel time is the work done by the design team. It is here we have the facilitator(s) and a group of supervisors and incumbents who are being paid but are not directly producing. This group typically ranges from five to ten people. Thus, the time taken by the design team is most important, because it is here that the largest number of personnel hours are used. There were a total of 37 units in this book where we have clear time data on design team activities for ProMES projects dealing with productivity. For each unit, the time for the design team to develop the system was determined. This includes initially meeting with the unit personnel to explain the system; doing products, indicators, and contingencies; getting approvals; and designing the feedback report.

The average time to design the system was 20.7 hours, the median was 17.0. Times ranged from 8 to 60 hours. Two of the 37 units took less than 10 hours, 17 took between 11 and 20 hours, 14 took 21 to 30 hours, 3 took 31 to 40 hours, and 1 took more than 40 hours.

In addition to these times, there is also the time required of the facilitators outside of design team meetings. This includes preparing for meetings, preparing summaries of the meetings, working with personnel to identify indicator data and solve problems of various types, and training the supervisors in conducting the feedback meetings. This typically takes 40 to 50 hours for an experienced facilitator in addition to the design team meetings.

Finally, there is some management time involved to approve the system as it is developed and to deal with problems that come up. This is typically three to six hours.

Factors Affecting Time to Do ProMES

When one considers the high degree of variability in type of work, technology, level of personnel, and setting, the amount of time to do ProMES is rather consistent. The data show that 84 percent of the design teams took between 11 and 30 hours.

However, there are some factors that seem to be related to the amount of time taken. One factor that does not seem to be related is the experience of the facilitator. I had expected that a new ProMES facilitator would take longer to guide the design team in developing the system than would a more experienced one. This does not appear to be the case. There is no appreciable difference in the average time it takes an inexperienced facilitator over an experienced one. However, in almost all cases, the inexperienced facilitator had a person more experienced with ProMES available to guide their work and answer questions.

What seems to make a much greater difference is experience with the organization. ProMES projects in a given organization after the first one take significantly less time. This is probably because the facilitator knows the technology and how the facility operates and knows many of the people involved and because a level of trust in ProMES and the facilitator has developed.

The other major effects on system development time seem to be structural ones. The size of the unit is a factor. Larger units take more coordination time and more time to communicate to the rest of the group the decisions being made in the design team. The complexity of the task is also a factor. Jobs where it takes the facilitator a good deal of time to really understand the task take more time. Finally, the complexity of the group structure influences the amount of time. If the unit has multiple shifts and all shifts are developing the system, this takes longer than if it is a single shift.

Calendar Time to Do ProMES

In addition to the amount of personnel time to do ProMES, it is also instructive to look at the amount of calendar time it takes to do the system. This varied widely in the applications in the chapters. The variation seems to be a function of the frequency of meetings, experience of the facilitators, and complexity of the setting. There does seem to be general agreement that meetings every week of about 1.5 hours are probably optimal in the typical setting.

Because the average time taken to develop the system is about 21 hours, if a design team meets once a week for 1.5 hours, it will take 14 meetings to develop the system in the average application. The design team will occasionally not be able to meet because of scheduling problems, vacations, work load, and so on. Thus, one should expect it to take 18 to 20 weeks in the average application. If the particular setting is more or less complex than average, this expected time should be adjusted. The factors that will make the development of the system take more or less time were discussed in the previous section.

WHAT IMPROVEMENTS IN THE PROCESS OF DOING ProMES HAVE BEEN DEVELOPED?

In the various projects using ProMES described in this book, a number of procedures have been tried that differ from the original steps described in Pritchard (1990). Many of these have been improvements over the original technique, and their applications have been quite successful. We now turn to a summary of these improvements.

Introduction of the System

Many of the projects in this book used one method or another at the start of the project to allow for rapport to be built and for the facilitators to learn about the work. For example, Janssen, van Berkel, and Stolk (Chapter 3) started with a problem-solving phase; Kleingeld and van Tuijl (Chapter 8) started with a series of meetings with the whole work group; Jones (chapters 5 and 6) did a type of organizational analysis; and Bonic (Chapter 7) and Miedema and Thierry (Chapter 11) did an analysis of the functioning of the work group. The authors feel that these steps allowed for gaining initial commitment, led to better acceptance, and increased the speed of system development because facilitators knew more about the job.

The most extensive approach of this type is the work by Algera and van den Hurk (Chapter 14), where a formal feasibility study was done. I found this a very convincing approach and feel it should be a part of future ProMES projects, at least in an abbreviated form. Because we know a good deal about the factors affecting the success of a ProMES project, it seems that a formal feasibility study could be done that assesses the organization on these factors and, at the same time, works with the proposed groups directly. The idea would be to do the type of feasibility study activities with the group described in Chapter 14 but in a shorter time period. The facilitators could meet with the group, explain the system, have them do some preliminary work on developing products and indicators, and identify the decisions to be made, such as who should be on the design team. Then, the groups could be asked whether they were willing to participate.

This would result in two sets of information: one about where the organization falls on the factors that influence success (such as, management support, organizational stability, and so on) and the other about feelings of the groups that might be involved. Together, this information should give one a good idea about the ultimate success of a ProMES project. The information could then be used to decide whether a project should be undertaken and, if so, with which groups.

Another more general issue in starting ProMES is the idea that developing the measurement system is a continuous process. As it was originally formulated, the idea was that one did the work to develop the measurement and feedback system and then started feedback. When feedback was started, the measurement system was finished. Admittedly, there was a necessary place for regularly reviewing the system for accuracy, but the sense was that one had "finished" the system when feedback started.

A number of the cases have made the point that there should be a more continuous process for developing and refining the system. This point is made clearly in chapters 5 and 14. The argument is that one should develop the first variant of the system, have the personnel get some experience with it, get feedback from the group, and revise the system as necessary. Furthermore, the expectation that there will be revisions until the system is acceptable should be communicated from the start of the project.

Ways to Speed ProMES Development

Developing the ProMES measurement system is labor-intensive and can take a fairly long time. There were a number of procedures tried that would help reduce this time. The authors describe some of these as being quite successful. Bonic (Chapter 7) started by having the groups do products and indicators by questionnaire prior to starting formal meetings as a way to get them thinking about the system. Howell, Jones, and Hood (Chapter 9) did not meet with the design team as a group but did individual interviews and had the unit personnel review the results. Kleingeld and van Tuijl (Chapter 8) had a situation where the members of the group worked in geographically separate areas, so, it was difficult to get them together for meetings. They used to deal with this problem was nominal groups and Delphi techniques. They also used a type of paired comparison to generate contingencies.

Other approaches to speed the process have included giving the design team lists of possible products and indicators, such as was done with the university faculty in Chapter 10. If such lists are available, they could speed the process. Another approach that was mentioned is to do indicators and then contingencies for just a few measures at a time rather than do all the indicators and then all the contingencies. Using this approach, the design team develops one or two indicators and then does the contingencies for those. Then they go back and repeat the process until all are finished. Miedema, Theirry, and van Oostveen, in Chapter 12, "ProMES in a Small Oil Distribution Company," did something like this. This has the advantage of helping the group see how the whole process will go together. However, we do not know if it would have any impact on speeding the process.

Another issue that has been addressed is the idea of doing the system in multiple groups that do similar work. The project described by Kleingeld and van Tuijl (Chapter 8) has been expanded to other regions where different groups of photocopier technicians work. They have tried different degrees of participation in the development of the measurement system by these different groups. Preliminary results suggest that if the group does not participate in all the development steps, productivity after feedback still increases but not as much as when they are involved in all the steps. In Chapter 10, Watson, Hedley, Clark, Paquin, Gottesfeld, and Pritchard used another approach. Here multiple academic departments were doing very similar work. To speed the process, a design team was formed of representatives from all departments, and this team did products and indicators. After this was finished, separate design teams were formed in each department to do contingencies. The original representative to the product and indicator design team was part of the contingency design team in his or her department. Thus, the products and indicators were identical for each department, but the contingencies were developed separately. This seemed to work fairly well.

Admittedly, we do not have enough data on these potentially time-saving procedures to know if they are generally effective. Although most should speed the process, we do not know if there will be some loss in acceptance of the system or in ultimate productivity improvement. As the number of applications increases over the years, we should know more about this.

Structural Characteristics

A third category of improvements to the system deals with structural characteristics, such as how to develop contingencies and design feedback reports.

The chapters by Jones add a step in the development of contingencies. He argues that it is important to maintain the relative importance of the different products and that having differing numbers of indicators for the products could lead to a situation where, for example, the effectiveness points for a product with many indicators could be greater than it should be. His solution is to determine the relative importance of each product and then express each as a type of percentage of the total. He then constraints the effectiveness points in the contingencies so that the indicators for a given product reflect the appropriate percentage of effectiveness points for that product.

I have checked for this potential problem in doing the cases in Chapter 2 and Chapter 10 and found that the total points for a given product did, in fact, very closely match the overall relative importance of that product. Thus, in my experience, the additional step proposed by Jones is not necessary. However, there easily could be other situations where it is necessary, and a procedure like Jones uses could be valuable there. At the very least, the issue raised by Jones should lead to the facilitator checking for this issue in developing any system. This can be done when the group is finished developing products and indicators. The facilitator should ask them to consider the amount of effectiveness points that they have allocated to each product and to make sure that they are comfortable with those decisions. If they feel a product has too many points associated with it, they can adjust the contingencies.

Several cases developed creative procedures for the situation where the design team does not have enough information to do contingencies. This most often comes about when the group has not seen any data on a given indicator in the past and has no way to meaningfully make contingency decisions. Several projects (chapters 3, 8, and 13) gave the design team past data to help them to do contingencies with the understanding that these were merely best estimates. After some data were collected, the contingencies were revised.

A very useful technique to deal with the situation of seasonal variations in expected performance on indicators was developed by Miedema and Thierry in Chapter 11. Their "compensators" were special contingencies that reflected the seasonal variation by giving the unit extra effectiveness points for times when output was expected to be lower. This not only made the system more accepted but also probably improved validity.

Another innovation in developing contingencies was discussed by Borg, Staufenbiel, and Pritchard in Chapter 17, "Identifying Strategic Objectives in Productivity Management: Combining Features of HISYS and ProMES." Borg and Staufenbield developed a computer program where design team members could do contingencies on the computer screen by moving points with a mouse. For example, if the effectiveness score for a given level of an indicator is to be reduced, one puts the mouse pointer on that point and drags it to the new location. The new contingency is then immediately drawn on the screen and can be printed out for inspection and comparison with others. This seems like a valuable approach.

One of the things that has become clear is the importance of using graphics for reporting feedback. People sometimes have trouble with feedback that is only numeric and seem to understand graphics more easily. One of the most effective techniques I have seen for reporting feedback graphically is the approach developed in Chapter 12. Here, the feedback report, Figure 12–1, showed the effectiveness score for each indicator as a bar going above the horizontal axis for a positive effectiveness score and below it for a negative one. In addition, the maximum and minimum possible effectiveness scores also are shown as points on the graph.

WHAT ARE SOME OF THE OTHER EFFECTS OF ProMES?

The evidence is clear that ProMES feedback has a strong positive effect on productivity. However, ProMES is a complex intervention that has effects on a number of other things. We will examine these effects in this section.

The first effect is one mentioned briefly in the section on productivity improvement: productivity effects during ProMES development. There was evidence in the original Air Force project that productivity was increasing during the development of the system. This caused us some concern, because improvements that occurred before or during baseline would reduce the effects of feedback, because some of the improvement would have already occurred. As it turned out, this was not a problem, in that there were large productivity improvements during feedback.

There are other findings that indicate the same effect. The plot of productivity over time shown in Figure 18–1 indicated some evidence of productivity improvement toward the end of baseline. In addition, a study by Paquin, Jones, and Roth (1992) looked at the data from several early ProMES studies in the United States and found clear evidence that productivity was improving during the development of the system. The productivity improvement just during development had an average effect size of .7. Similar results were found in Chapter 7 by Bonic in an Australian application and in Chapter 3 by Janssen and van Berkel in the Netherlands.

Thus, there is considerable evidence that the process of developing ProMES has a positive effect on productivity in and of itself. The process of going through the steps in developing the system causes unit personnel to get clear among themselves and with management what their objectives are, produces joint decisions about what measures should be used to assess how well these objectives are being met, and gives them clear information on the relative importance and expected levels of output on the measures. This also leads to a reexamining of the unit's activities and produces changes even before feedback starts.

Another implication of these results is that even though the effect sizes obtained in the cases in this book are very large, in one sense, they are underestimates of the overall impact of ProMES. With the type of analysis I used to report effect sizes, any improvements during development are counted as part of baseline, not as part of feedback. A more accurate approach may be the one used by Bonic in Chapter 7. He separated the productivity prior to system development, during system development, and during feedback. It is interesting to note that when the development period is included in the baseline, as was done for the effect size calculations earlier in this chapter, the effect sizes for productivity improvements during feedback for his two groups were 1.0 and 2.5. If the development period is excluded from the calculations in baseline and only the predevelopment period is used for baseline, the respective effect sizes increase to 1.6 and 3.6. Thus, with the development period removed from baseline, the effect sizes comparing baseline to feedback increase considerably in this study. It is interesting to note that across Bonic's two groups, the difference in the effect sizes with and without considering the development period is .85, very close to the average effect size due to development of .7 found by Paquin, Jones, and Roth (1992). This adds further evidence that the effect size for simply developing the system is approximately .75.

This approach of separating development from baseline is limited to situations where data exist prior to the start of the development of ProMES. If new measures are developed by the design team or there are no earlier data available, this approach cannot be used. However, it is common for at least some of the indicators to be available from before the start of the project, and these could be used to get a partial idea of the effects of system development by examining this subset of the data for predevelopment, development, and feedback periods.

It is also interesting to note the effect of ProMES on attitudes. This issue can be looked at in two ways. The first is the effects of ProMES on attitudes such as job satisfaction, morale, and role clarity. The original Air Force study found that attitudes either stayed the same or improved during ProMES. Although not discussed in Chapter 4, Przygodda, Kleinbeck, Schmidt, and Beckmann found similar results in their project. Most of the chapters do not speak to this issue directly, so, we do not have a great deal of research to examine the effects of ProMES on attitudes.

The second way to look at attitudes is to examine peoples' attitudes toward ProMES itself. Here we have considerable information from the chapters, because many of them discussed this issue. It is very clear that, although ProMES has a strong positive effect on productivity, peoples' attitudes toward it are clearly mixed, during both development and feedback. The clearest example of this comes in Chapter 5, where Jones did a systematic evaluation of attitudes toward the system. Although he found the overall attitudes more positive than negative, there were a significant number of negative reactions.

Considering the cases together, there seemed to be a fairly consistent picture of the positive attitudes toward the system. In general, people like the participation provided by ProMES, especially because they are participating in something that is really important. Some attempts at participation involve participation on issues that have no real consequence for the organization, and it is not too surprising when the participants do not take this too seriously. People also like the self-determination that ProMES brings. The idea of determining, in large part, how they will be evaluated seems positive to them. It is interesting that there has been no evidence of which I am aware where a design team has attempted to "game" the system by intentionally picking measures or setting the contingencies in a way that will make them look good. One reason for this may be because they know their decisions will have to be defended to and approved by management. However, I think a significant factor is that they take the process of developing the system very seriously and want to do it accurately.

Another thing people like is being taken seriously by management. Having made a serious attempt to identify objectives, develop measures, and establish contingencies makes them more credible to management. Successfully selling their ideas to a management that is truly listening also adds to their feeling of being taken seriously. People also like the system because it helps them fix what is wrong. Frequently, personnel get the message that something is wrong but do not know what they can do to change things. Through the feedback reports, ProMES very quickly gives them the information if something is wrong, usually before anyone else knows about the problem. It also gives them the mechanism to fix the problem through the feedback meetings.

One of the most interesting attitudes is peoples' reactions to the quantitative aspect of ProMES. Most people appreciate the quantification of policy that ProMES does. They feel it reduces ambiguity and causes a formal discussion of policy that could not be done without quantification. They also like feedback in quantitative form because of its clarity. However, some people simply do not like attempting to quantify complex concepts like objectives and expectations. They feel that much is lost by doing this and that this loss of richness makes the resulting numbers, at best, incomplete indications of a much more complex phenomenon. This latter type of person is the minority but is clearly present in many situations.

On the more negative side, peoples' first reaction to ProMES is to have doubts about its ultimate accuracy. A good deal of this doubt is decreased as they see how the process is actually done. However, for many, it is still present. This is especially true if the feedback is not particularly positive. People would rather doubt the validity of the measures than admit that their productivity was not up to expectations. This naturally occurring doubt makes it especially important that the measures be accurate before feedback starts. Finding that the data are, in act, inaccurate after feedback starts feeds into this skepticism and is very difficult to overcome later.

Probably the most pervasive cause of negative attitudes toward the system is that people simply do not like to be evaluated. This is human nature. What we all want is to have perfectly valid feedback given to us on a regular basis in a totally private way. If the feedback is less than optimal, we want it kept private. If it is outstanding, we want it published in the newspaper. Unfortunately, life is not like that, and we must be evaluated, and in a semipublic way. This sort of accountability is not desired, and because it is one of the effects of ProMES, it produces some negative reactions.

Another source of negative reactions to ProMES is the time it takes to develop and maintain the system. Development time takes away from work, and even if the people developing the system are being paid and the development time has no effect on their work load, the supervisors and management become concerned about the time spent. If work done during development time must be somehow made up by the members of the design team, they also become concerned about the time. It also takes time to collect the indicator data and put the feedback reports together for every report period. This effort is sometimes a strain on people already working hard.

Another class of effects of ProMES is on conflicts. ProMES brings out existing conflicts, which can be of many types. They can be problems of a broad nature dealing with the relationships between groups of people. For example, if there is distrust between workers and management, this will surface in system development. There was some evidence of this in Chapter 6. Other conflicts could be between specific individuals. The system can bring out existing conflicts between different shifts doing the same work. Other types of conflict over policies and procedures will also become apparent. This could be in the form of disagreement about goals, such as in Chapter 7 and Chapter 8, where service technicians did not want to be responsible for developing new business but management did want this. There can also be conflicts between quantity and quality issues or about what should be expected on an indicator.

The point is that ProMES does bring out these conflicts. It does not create them, but it does make it apparent when they exist. The negative side of this is that there is more observable conflict that is not generally pleasant and sometimes is quite aversive. The positive side is that it is far better to deal with the conflict directly rather than either pretend it does not exist or try to work around it. Both result in a loss of energy and personal resources. ProMES highlights the conflict and legitimizes working to solve it. This legitimation is that the development of the system requires that these issues be resolved, and because of this requirement, all parties are given both the motivation and the setting where these issues can be worked out.

Another major effect of ProMES is that units become aware of their interdependency. After developing and using the system, it is very clear to the unit that they cannot do their work really well without cooperation from other units. This dependence on other units could be because they need quality raw materials, a predictable flow of another group's output, or information of different types in a timely manner to do their own work. This has generally resulted in a positive effect. Chapters 3, 5, and 12 all noted the effect of increased awareness of interdependency. The general effect seems to be to make the unit personnel more aware of what they need from other units and how their work affects other units.

FOR WHAT OTHER APPLICATIONS CAN ProMES BE USED?

The cases in this book have also highlighted some of the other applications where ProMES could be used. One such application is using ProMES to tie rewards to performance, especially pay. One of the most difficult things about tying pay to performance is getting a good measure of performance when people are doing work involving multiple activities. Work where such multiple activities are being done is by far the norm in most organizations. ProMES offers a way to measure all the important things personnel do and combine them into a single index,overall effectiveness. Pay can then be tied to this overall index.

There were several examples of this type of problem in cases. In Chapters 8, 11, and 12, tying pay to performance was part of the motivation for doing the ProMES project. These chapters highlight that it is possible to measure effectiveness in such settings, that one can combine individual and group measures into one ProMES score, and that ProMES information can be combined with more typical performance appraisal measures.

Another application is the use of ProMES for performance appraisal. The best example was the case by Hedley, Sawyer, and Pritchard (Chapter 15), where ProMES was used directly to develop a potential performance appraisal instrument. The idea is to take the typical dimensions that are rated in a performance appraisal and add contingencies. A contingency is developed for each dimension that is rated. The quantified rating anchors, (e.g., 1–7) are the levels of the indicator, and the contingencies are drawn using the same procedure as is used in a typical ProMES application.

There are several advantages of adding contingencies to performance appraisal. One advantage is that a more valid overall score is generated, because the ProMES overall score includes differential importance and nonlinearities. With contingencies, ratees can see what level is expected and how good the different levels of the ratings are in absolute, or criterion referenced, terms. Feedback using the contingencies allows the identification of priorities for improving performance so that the person has a more accurate picture of where to focus efforts to improve. Finally, using contingencies allows different parts of the organization to reflect their own policies for performance even though the same rating dimensions are used for the different jobs. For example, if a particular dimension of performance is particularly important for some jobs in some parts of the organization, the contingency for that dimension can be made more steep for those jobs.

Another interesting application of ProMES came out of Chapter 16, "Linking Training Evaluation to Productivity," by Jones and Ourth and addressed using the system to evaluate training. This was a creative application that brings up the broader issue of using ProMES as the basis for a management information system. The typical ProMES application is designed to improve productivity at the level in the organization where the work is directly done. However, the system also can be used at a much higher level in the organization. In such an application, the products and indicators are much broader measures that require many more people in the organization to change. Examples would be time to develop a new product, percentage growth of customer base, and level of overall customer satisfaction.

Using ProMES to evaluate the effectiveness of broader levels of the organization should, presumably, have the same advantages as developing it at lower levels. Designing the system should help clarify the objectives of the broader organizational unit, identifying indicators should help to focus attention on those measures that are most important, and feedback from the system should aid in assessing current functioning and planning improvements. What is not known is whether feedback on such broad measures would have the motivational impact that the typical ProMES application seems to have. Because the measures are much broader and are influenced by so many people, it could be that feedback on them would not have as much impact. However, this remains to be seen from future research. Even if no motivational impact was found, such an approach should still help clarify objectives and serve as a more accurate assessment device for overall functioning.

Taking this argument a step further is the idea of using ProMES as a mechanism for strategic planning. Chapter 17 describes an approach that combines ProMES with work by Borg and Staufenbiel to try this. The ProMES approach is to argue that strategy development is essentially the process of developing ProMES products at the level of entire organization. We could then add the other steps in ProMES by identifying indicators and contingencies. Going through the process of developing the system should help top management refine their thinking about the nature of the strategic plan, which should result in a better plan.

In addition, the completed ProMES system would be a way to more clearly communicate to lower management what the strategy developed by top management really means and how they should adjust their priorities to implement this plan. For example, when many organizations do a strategic plan, it tends to include all good things the organization could do: increase revenues, increase market share, improve customer satisfaction, empower employees, and so on. However, it is not clear to the middle managers what they should do to implement this plan. For example, what is the relative importance of increasing revenues as compared with increasing market share? Resources directed at one goal usually cannot be used for the other. How much improvement in customer satisfaction is worth how much decrease in revenues? Without knowing this, it is difficult to make the type of trade-off decisions needed. Finally, what does a strategic goal of empowering employees mean, and how do we know when we are achieving it?

These are all questions that would be answered by adding indicators and contingencies to the products in strategic planning. The indicators identify what measures define achieving that objective. Top management would have to define what the indicators of, for example, employee empowerment are in a way that they could be measured. This tells middle management on what they should be focusing. The relative priorities among the objectives could be directly assessed by studying the contingencies. The contingencies define policy and indicate in quantitative terms the relative gains in overall effectiveness that will occur with changes in different indicators. Finally, ProMES defines for middle management how they will be evaluated, because improvement in overall effectiveness would determine how well their parts of the organization are functioning.

WHAT HAVE WE LEARNED ABOUT WHY ProMES WORKS?

It is clear that ProMES has a very powerful effect on productivity and that this effect is much larger than the typical interventions we use to improve performance and productivity. It is useful to speculate on why these large effects occur and why they are so much larger than what has been used in the past. The cases in this book give us some insight into these questions, and we now turn to a discussion of what we have learned.

In simplest terms, I believe ProMES works so well because it impacts all the major variables influencing the motivational process. The development of ProMES and the use of ProMES feedback seem to have effects on all these variables, essentially at the same time. In contrast, the effects of most interventions is on only a subset of the motivational variables. This part/whole difference is why ProMES seems to be so much more powerful than other interventions.

The Motivation Theory

This issue can be clarified by considering the major variables in the motivational process. The framework to be used is the Naylor, Pritchard, and Ilgen (1980) theory of behavior in organizations, sometimes called "NPI theory." In this view, motivation is the allocation of time and effort to tasks. It is the amount of time and effort and how this time and effort is distributed across the possible behaviors that could be emitted in that setting. The amount of time and effort and how those personal resources are distributed across tasks is determined by a series of motivational variables. These are shown graphically in the top section of Figure 18–3.

The boxes in the figure show the major variables. People emit behaviors (acts) that result in consequences (products). Thus, as I sit here typing (an act), I generate the chapter (a product). When finished, the chapter is evaluated by me, people who read the draft, and people like you who read this book. This results in evaluations, which can be thought of as measures of performance. After evaluations are made, outcomes occur. These will be intrinsic, such as a feeling of accomplishment I get when I feel I have written a good chapter, or extrinsic, such as forms of recognition or pay raises for doing scholarly work.

NPI MOTIVATION THEORY

LOCUS OF MAJOR INTERVENTIONS

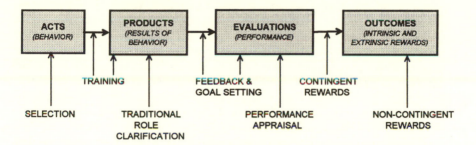

LOCUS OF PROMES INTERVENTIONS

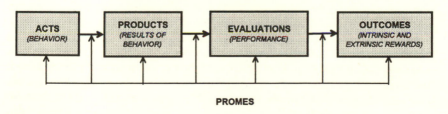

Figure 18–3   Motivational Impact of ProMES and Other Interventions

Between each of these major variables (boxes) in the figure are connecting arrows. The first is the arrow between acts and products. This is meant to convey that there are contingencies between acts and products. These are conceptually the same type of contingencies as are done in ProMES. In fact, this theory is where the contingencies in ProMES came from. Act-to-product contingencies describe the relationship between the amount of personal resources (time and effort) that is emitted and the amount of the product that results. The contingency may be quite steep, indicating that there is a strong tie between the amount of the act done and the amount of the product produced. The contingency will be less steep when there is less of a relationship or connection between the amount of the act and the amount of the resulting product. When I weed the garden, there is a strong positive contingency between time and effort weeding and amount of the garden weeded. When I work on this chapter, there is a less strong relationship between time and effort and pages completed. At the extreme, if I really do not know how to do a task, the relationship between time and effort and the amount of product produced is quite small. For example, because I know little about car repair, such a contingency would exist for me if I was trying to repair the oil pump on my car. These contingencies may also be nonlinear, when, for example, there is a point of diminishing returns such that further amounts of time and effort devoted to the act do not result in any increase in the amount of the product. If I keep working on this chapter beyond the point where I am tired, additional amounts of time and effort result in progressively less and less of the chapter being finished.

Between products and evaluations, there is another set of contingencies. These are the most similar to ProMES contingencies in that they define the relationship between how much of the product is done and how that level of the product is evaluated. In ProMES, the terminology is a bit different, but the idea is the same. The indicators in ProMES are how the product is measured, and the contingency is the relationship between amount of the indicator and the evaluation (overall effectiveness). Finally, there is another set of contingencies between evaluations and outcomes that define the relationship between how favorably one is evaluated and the level of outcome that follows. For example, in a strong merit based pay system there will be a fairly steep contingency between level of evaluation and size of pay raise. Where pay raises are given across the board, the contingency between evaluation and size of pay raise will be flat.

In the full NPI theory, there are additional variables involved and feedback loops exist between many of the variables. These are important to the theory, but to keep the discussion more manageable, I will focus only on the key variables and contingencies.

According to the theory, motivation is maximized when the person is able to do the acts required, all the contingencies are clear and have strong slopes, and the outcomes available are valuable to the person. The more of these conditions that are met, the stronger is the motivation. Furthermore, for motivation to be high, all the components must be at least somewhat present. It could be that available outcomes are highly valued and are dependent on evaluations, there could be clear connections between products and evaluations, and the person could be ale to emit the acts. However, if there is not a clear connection (contingency) between acts and products, motivation will be low. For example, if the person did not know what products were expected or what strategy to use to produce the products, motivation in the form of the amount of time and effort devoted to the task would be low.

Traditional Interventions

The primary lesson from this theory is that all of the motivational components must be high for motivation to be maximized. With this in mind, let us look at some of the typical interventions used to improve motivation, performance, and productivity. The middle section of Figure 18–3 shows some of the most common interventions used for this purpose. It also shows where in the motivational process these interventions are likely to have their effects.

For example, personnel selection is designed to hire people who have the best ability to do the job. In NPI terms, this mean that people are hired who can best do the acts or behaviors required by the job. Training is geared to taking that raw talent and teaching the person how to use it to produce products that are desired by the organization. Thus, training affects act-to-product contingencies and helps clarify what the expected products are. Traditional role clarification does much the same thing. It makes explicit the products the person or group is expected to generate for the organization. Typical feedback and goal-setting interventions help define the product-to-evaluation contingencies and clarify what is being evaluated. For example, goal setting defines the point (the goal) where the evaluation increases dramatically, that is, where it is defined as good or outstanding performance. Performance appraisal makes evaluations clear and, if tied to outcomes such as pay or recognition, influences evaluation-to-outcome contingencies. Contingent reward systems make the contingencies stronger between the organization's evaluation and obtaining organizationally controlled rewards such as pay, promotion, and recognition. Noncontingent rewards such as benefit packages or working conditions that are not determined by level of performance affect the total amount of outcomes but, according to the theory, should have little relationship to motivation.

Clearly, some applications of a given intervention could have more effects than just those identified above. For example, a traditional performance appraisal intervention could be broadened to include discussions about reasons for the evaluation (product-to-evaluation contingencies) and could lead directly to pay raises (evaluation-to-outcome contingencies).

However, whether done in their traditional form or broadened to include more motivational factors, what is most important about this discussion is that each of these traditional interventions affect only a subset of the motivational process. As can be seen in Figure 18–3, they generally tend to be quite localized in their effects. If the other motivational variables happen to be sufficiently high, increasing the one or two toward which most of these interventions are geared will have a positive effect on motivation and, ultimately, productivity. However, if any of the other variables are low, improving one or two in isolation will have little effect. For example, hiring people with higher ability will have little impact if the people do not know clearly on what products to focus their energies.

ProMES and Motivation

The difference between ProMES and these traditional interventions is that ProMES has at least some effect on all the aspects of the motivational process at essentially the same time. This is characterized in the bottom third of Figure 18–3, where the impact of ProMES effects is shown graphically. If there is evidence that ProMES does, indeed, affect all these aspects of the motivational process, it becomes clearer both why ProMES has such a large impact and why the size of this impact is larger than traditional interventions. In this next section, these effects will be discussed in relation to what the cases in the book have found.

The first effects are on acts and act to product contingencies. There are clear indications that these variables are affected by ProMES. The feedback meetings produce suggestions for improved work methods. This was mentioned in Chapter 3, occurred in the Air Force project, and is mentioned at least in passing in many of the chapters. Improved work methods means doing different behaviors (acts) and knowing more clearly what behaviors will result in the desired end states (products) and which will be less effective. This is essentially the process of defining and clarifying act-to-product contingencies. At a broader unit of analysis, we see the same phenomenon when the group understands its interactions with other groups more clearly. This finding was discussed above, and a good example of it is in Chapter 12, where, as a result of doing ProMES, the groups seemed to be able to see what they should do differently to relate well to other units. This is the process of clarifying acts and act-to-product contingencies at the group level.

ProMES seems to have a powerful effect on clarifying products and product-to-evaluation contingencies. ProMES contingencies are essentially the product-to-evaluation contingencies in NPI theory. The terms are a bit different, but the idea is exactly the same. Developing the system clarifies what the products are and how they are to be measured, and the contingencies define how these measures are combined to form evaluations. Furthermore, the process of development by the group and approval by the management insures that the products and these contingencies are agreed on by all. This reduces role ambiguity and role conflict. If all the evaluators in a setting (self, peers, other groups, supervision, management) use the same criteria (product-to-evaluation contingencies), the motivational forces generated from the evaluations of these different sources all are directed toward the same products, and this increases overall motivational force.

A number of the cases discussed these effects. One type of effect is for personnel to learn how to measure their work. Most groups start the ProMES process believing that one cannot measure how well they do their work. However, by doing the process, they learn that they can measure it. This is an example of going from very vague product-to-evaluation contingencies and levels of evaluation to quite clear ones. Another type of effect on the same motivational variables was discussed in Chapters 4, 7, 12, and 13. Each author discussed how the unit's objectives and its role were made clearer with ProMES. This occurred both during development of the system and during feedback. The system also seems to stimulate thinking about priorities during both development and the feedback phase. This occurred in the Air Force project and was mentioned in Chapter 3. Priorities come directly from knowledge of product-to-evaluation contingencies.

There also seems to be a direct effect on knowledge of evaluation, particularly the evaluation of the unit by management. In the case of the commercial painters in Chapter 13, doing ProMES enabled the work group to know much better how they were being evaluated by management. According to the theory, this knowledge of evaluation is needed for the motivational process to be maximized.

The final links in NPI theory are evaluation-to-outcome contingencies and the value of the outcomes themselves. The most direct ProMES effect here is probably on intrinsic rewards. With good feedback, there is a sense of pride in a job well done. However, there is also increased recognition when the unit is effective. A number of the chapters (e.g., Chapter 1, Chapter 8, and Chapter 10) mentioned that management was giving recognition to unit personnel during the development of the system and that they got more recognition during feedback. Thus, unit personnel received more outcomes and also more clearly saw a tie between the evaluations and these outcomes.

Clearer evaluations also allow for adding more formal extrinsic rewards, such as pay raises or bonuses. If such rewards are added, the fact that additional outcomes are available and their tie to evaluations is very clear adds to motivation. An example of this was the case with the Dutch photocopier technicians in Chapter 8.

It seems clear that there is considerable evidence that ProMES does impact the entire motivational sequence. Much of this evidence is anecdotal and needs to be more formally explored in future projects. However, it certainly suggests that an explanation of why ProMES works so well and why it seems to work so much better than traditional interventions is that it impacts the entire motivational process, not just a subset of it.

WHAT DO WE STILL NEED TO KNOW ABOUT PRODUCTIVITY AND ProMES?

Although we have learned much about ProMES in these applications, there is still much to be learned. In this final section, future research needs will be summarized.

Psychological Processes in ProMES

The section above on why ProMES works is an excellent start to identifying the mechanisms for why the system has the effects it does. There have been a number of efforts to do this starting with the first Air Force project (Jones, 1985), but we still have much to learn. The cases in this book have generated a large number of ideas on why the system works, and others have been hypothesized in other places (Pritchard et al., 1989; Pritchard, 1990). It is now time to devote increased attention to this issue.

The basic approach should be to develop a comprehensive list of variables that could be affecting the process. Next, good measures of these variables need to be developed. Good measures exist for a few, but for only a few. Then, data on these measures need to be collected during ProMES projects. The most difficult part is developing a measurement strategy that is able to detect changes in these somewhat subtle variables over the long periods of time involved in ProMES projects.

Such research has important theoretical and practical significance. It is important theoretically because determining exactly the mechanisms operating that make ProMES so successful can teach us a great deal about how these variables operate both singly and in combination. The research is important from a practical standpoint because a better knowledge of the causal mechanisms can lead to making ProMES stronger and being able to identify in advance how much a given unit is likely to benefit from the intervention.

Making ProMES Efficient

One of the disadvantages of ProMES is that it is labor-intensive and takes a considerable amount of calendar time to do. Thus, it is important to look at ways to make ProMES as efficient as possible. A number of ideas were raised in this book, but we need more work to determine the effects of some of these strategies. For example, is it cost-effective to do an abbreviated form of ProMES to get a system started and then refine it over time? Would any immediate improved productivity and other immediate positive and negative reactions be worth starting with an imperfect system? Another example is doing some work on developing products and indicators before the group started meeting. Will such a procedure speed the development process, and will there be any loss of positive effect from this strategy?

An interesting aspect of efficiency is the number of ProMES facilitators used. Ideally, there is a facilitator and a second cofacilitator to help in the process. It is common for additional people to be there as facilitators in training. Facilitators tend to be costly personnel, and one way to make ProMES more cost-effective is to use just one facilitator. The question becomes whether or not a single experienced facilitator can do the work.

A related point is how to train facilitators. The current process is, typically, for a trainee to observe a design team doing ProMES, then move to a cofacilitator role, and then take over as facilitator with an experienced facilitator present. However, it would cut costs if some of the training process could be done more efficiently with simulations, exercises, and so on.

Another issue in making ProMES more efficient is a determination of how much participation is needed in doing the system. How much is lost when full participation is not used? A number of alternatives were described in the chapters, especially with larger groups. As these techniques are tried in more projects, we will have better data on their success.

ProMES throughout the Organization

As successful as ProMES has been, we are starting to see situations where there is an attempt to install ProMES throughout the organization. For example, the company described in Chapter 3 by Janssen, van Berkel, and Stolk is doing this. Broad-based applications of the system bring up a series of new challenges that future research needs to address.

One challenge is related to the efficiency idea in the previous section. How can an organization install this system in a timely and cost-effective manner in large parts of the organization? If the organization is small, like the one in Chapter 3, it can be done over time with a single pair of facilitators. However, if the organization has dozens or hundreds of groups, the problem becomes much more complex.

One issue to be addressed is whether the organization chooses to use internal or external facilitators. There are advantages to both. Internal facilitators are typically cheaper, and there can be a large number of them if the organization so chooses. However, ProMES projects take them from their existing work, and the organization must pay for a fairly involved training program. Almost all of the organizations we have worked with so far that have wanted to expand ProMES have chosen an external facilitator. A major argument by these organizations has been that people in the organization will respond more favorably to an external person. An external person does not represent management and, thus, should not be perceived as taking management's side of things. This leads to higher credibility and greater trust.

If the organization chooses external facilitators, it is simply a problem for the university, consulting firm, or whoever is doing the project to get enough facilitators trained to do the work. Although this takes time and resources, it is not difficult conceptually, only logistically. If the organization chooses to use internal facilitators, one can have full-time or part-time facilitators. Full-time people do nothing but ProMES; part-time do ProMES and some of their regular job. These internal facilitators can be trained by starting them with a formal training program where they learn about ProMES and then have them observe ProMES being developed. Next, they would participate in facilitating a group, then lead a group while being observed by an experienced facilitator. If four or five such people are trained and each of them trained several others, a great deal of ProMES work could be done in a fairly short time.

Aside from the logistics of getting the system developed throughout the organization, there are conceptual problems to be addressed as well. The most important is the issue of vertical integration of the system across levels. Earlier in my work on ProMES, I believed that if you could develop a way of aggregating the productivity measures of different units into a broader measure that would solve the problem of vertical integration. For example, suppose there was a maintenance department with five separate units, where each unit maintained different types of equipment. If you could get a measure of productivity on each of the five units and combine them, taking into consideration the relative importance of each unit, I thought you would have a good measure of the productivity of the entire maintenance department. In fact, I described a technique for doing this in my 1990 book.

I no longer believe that such a strategy will work. It is certainly possible to aggregate measures, and such aggregated measures can give you an index of the average or total productivity of the five units. Such a measure could be useful for a number of purposes, especially in getting an overall picture of how those units are doing as a group. However, this is not the whole picture. There are important things the overall maintenance department does that are not contained in the measurement systems of the five separate units. For example, the overall maintenance department might have to coordinate with purchasing to make sure enough new pieces of equipment were being purchased to replace worn-out items. Other examples of things the maintenance department might have to do for which the individual departments were not responsible would include staffing and long-range projections of maintenance needs.

To the extent that each new level in the organization adds new tasks and responsibilities that are not included in the work of the units below that level, their work is not simply the sum of those lower level units. This addition of new tasks will almost always be the case. For example, there will almost always be types of coordination with other units that the broader department must do but that the subunits are not responsible for. Thus, it is not appropriate to simply sum or average the productivity of the units below. The presence of these additional tasks and responsibilities suggests that new products and indicators must be added to get an accurate picture of the functioning of the broader department. Therefore, a complete productivity measurement system for the higher level must include both measures of units below that level and some measures that are unique to that level.

Exactly how this combination should best be done has yet to be worked out. On the surface, it seems simple enough. In addition to developing ProMES at the lower level units, one should also develop a measurement system at the higher level. Some products and indicators will be the same as for the lower level units; some will be new. The basic idea is quite simple, but it will be interesting to see how future projects actually implement the idea and how it works.

This idea of vertical integration leads to another issue, the relationship of ProMES to strategic plans. One fear that some of us have had is that the bottom up approach of ProMES could lead to a situation where the units were setting priorities that were inconsistent with the broader strategic objectives of the organization. Hopefully, the process of obtaining management approval would minimize the chances of this being a problem. However, if the management who approve ProMES are not clear on the strategic objectives, there still may be a problem.

This is not specifically a ProMES problem. If middle management does not know or understand the strategic plans, this will have a negative effect in general, not just on ProMES. However, if the system is to be effectively implemented, especially in broad sections of the organization, it is an issue that should be addressed. This point was made clearly in Chapter 17 by Borg, Staufenbiel, and Pritchard, when they discussed the issue of determining policies at high levels of management.

One approach that is appealing is the one described in the previous section where using ProMES for strategic planning was discussed. One could start with ProMES at the highest level and communicate the overall policy down the organization. The system developed by top management would be presented as a more formally stated set of strategic goals. Then, as ProMES projects were started at lower levels, products and indicators could be examined for their consistency with the overall plan. Hopefully, this approach would not only improve strategic planning but also increase the likelihood that ProMES systems at lower levels in the organization would be consistent with the overall strategic objectives.

ProMES Feasibility Study

Another area of future research is to expand on the work of Algera and van den Hurk (Chapter 14) to develop a formal mechanism for doing ProMES feasibility studies. This was discussed earlier in this chapter. I think the idea of a feasibility study is an excellent one. What I envision is a formal mechanism of collecting specific data using prescribed data collection formats such as structured interviews and questionnaires that would lead to quantitative predictions on the likely success of a ProMES project in that setting. I believe we have the information to develop such a set of instruments and a mechanism for how the data could be combined. It would be quite useful to develop such a procedure and begin to evaluate it in future ProMES projects.

CONCLUSION

It is always hard to end a major piece of work like this. You feel like you should make some sweeping overall statements, but, at the same time, you feel like you have said everything you want to say already. So, let me conclude with some personal observations. Working with ProMES and the people who have been involved with it has been a true high point in my career. To have developed a technique that seems to work quite well in organizations is a source of great pleasure to me. It is also a real joy to have gotten to know the people who have written these chapters, and many of them have become close friends. I hope that others will try ProMES. I will be happy to help others in their exploration, and I expect this to lead to even more of the kinds of fulfilling personal relationships to which ProMES has led me already.

REFERENCES

Cohen, J. (1977). *Statistical power analysis for the behavioral sciences* (rev. ed.). New York: Academic Press.

Guzzo, R. A., Jette, R. D., & Katzell, R. A. (1985). The effects of psychologically based intervention programs on worker productivity: A meta-analysis. *Personnel Psychology, 38*, 275–291.

Hunter, J. E., Schmidt, F. L., & Jackson, G. B. (1982). *Meta-analysis: Cumulating research findings across studies.* Beverly Hills, CA: Sage Publications.

Jones, S. D. (1985). *Mediating mechanisms of the feedback-performance relationship.* Unpublished doctoral dissertation, University of Houston.

Naylor, J. C., Pritchard, R. D., & Ilgen, D. I. (1980). *A theory of behavior in organization* (p. 299). New York: Academic Press.

Paquin, A. R., Jones, S. D., & Roth, P. L. (1992, April). *The Hawthorne effect when evaluating productivity gains.* Paper presented at the meeting for the Society for Industrial-Organizational Psychology, Montreal.

Pritchard, R. D. (1990). *Measuring and improving organizational productivity: A practical guide* (p. 248). New York: Praeger.

Pritchard, R. D., Jones, S. D., Roth, P. L., Stuebing, K. K., & Ekeberg, S. E. (1989). The evaluation of an integrated approach to measuring organizational productivity. *Personnel Psychology, 42,* 69–115.

Pritchard, R. D., Jones, S. D., Roth, P. L., Stuebing, K. K., & Ekeberg, S. E. (1988). The effects of feedback, goal setting, and incentives on organizational productivity. *Journal of Applied Psychology Monograph Series, 73,* 337–358.

Pritchard, R. D., Kleinbeck, U. E., & Schmidt, K. H. (1993). *Das Management-system PPM: Durch Mitarbeiterbeteiligung zu höherer Produktivität* [The PPM management system: Employee participation for improved productivity]. Munich: Verlag C.H. Beck.

Bibliography

Alliger, G. M., & Janak, E. A. (1989). Kirpatrick's levels of training criteria: Thirty years later. *Personnel Psychology, 42*, 331–342.

American Productivity and Quality Center (1986). *White collar productivity improvement*. Houston: American Productivity and Quality Center.

Balcazar, F., Hopkins, B. L., & Suarez, Y. (1986). A critical, objective review of performance feedback. *Journal of Organizational Behavior Management, 7*, 65–89.

Bandura, A. (1982). Self-efficacy mechanism in human agency. *American Psychologist, 37*, 122–147.

Belcher, J. G. (1986). *Productivity plus*. Houston: Gulf.

Bell, J. D., & Kerr, D. L. (1987, January). Measuring training results: Key to managerial commitment. *Training and Development Journal*, pp. 70–73.

Bernhard, H. B., & Ingols, C. A. (1988, September-October). Six lessons from the corporate classroom. *Harvard Business Review*, pp. 40–47.

Biessen, P. (1992). *Oog voor de menselijke factor: Achtergrond, constructie en validering van de Basisvragenlijst Amsterdam* [Taking account of the human perspective: Background, construction and validation of the basic questionnaire Amsterdam]. Amsterdam: Swets & Zeitlinger.

Blackburn, R. T., & Clark, M. J. (1975). As assessment of faculty performance: Some correlations between administrators, colleagues, students, and self-ratings. *Sociology of Education, 48*, 242–256.

Blenker, M. (1954). Predictive factors in the initial interview in family casework. *Social Services Review, 28*, 65–73.

Bonic, I. D. (1992). *ProMES: The use of group-based feedback and goal setting interventions in enhancing productivity*. Unpublished master's thesis, University of New South Wales, Sydney, Australia.

Borg, I. (1987). Arbeitszufriedenheit, Arbeitswerte und Jobauswahl: Ein hierarchischer, individuen-zentrierter Ansatz. *Zeitschrift für Sozialpsychologie, 18*, 28–39.

Borg, I., & Staufenbiel, T. (in press). Zur statistischen Bewertung der Konsdistenz paarweiser Verhältnisurteile. *Archiv für Psychologie*.

Borg, I., & Staufenbiel, T. (1991). Ein idiographisches Modell und Meßverfahren zur Analyse von Arbeitswerten und Arbeitszufriedenheit. In L. Fischer (Ed.), *Arbeitszufriedenheit* (pp. 157–175). Stuttgart: Verlag für angewandte Psychologie.

Borg, I. & Tremmel, L. (1988). Compression effects in pairwise ratio scaling. *Methodika, 2,* 1–15.

Braskamp, L. A., Brandenburg, D. C., & Ory, J. C. (1984). *Evaluating teaching effectiveness: A practical guide.* Beverly Hills, CA: Sage.

Brief, A. P. (Ed.). (1984). *Productivity research in the behavioral and social sciences.* New York: Praeger.

Burke, R. J., & Wilcox, D. S. (1969). Characteristics of effective employee performance reviews and development interviews. *Personnel Psychology, 22,* 291–305.

Cameron, K. S., & Whetten, D. A. (Eds.) (1983). *Organizational effectiveness: A comparison of multiple models.* New York: Academic Press.

Campbell, J. P., & Campbell, R. J. (1988). *Productivity in organizations.* San Francisco: Jossey-Bass.

Campbell, J. P., & Pritchard, R. D. (1976). Motivation theory in industrial and organizational psychology. In M. D. Dunnette (Ed.), *Handbook of industrial and organizational psychology.* Princeton: Van Nostrand.

Carroll, S. J., & Schneier, C. E. (1982). *Performance appraisal and review systems.* Glenview, IL: Scott, Foresman.

Cascio, W. F. (1987). *Applied psychology in personnel management* (3rd ed.). Englewood Cliffs, NJ: Prentice-Hall.

Cashin, W. E. (1988). *Student ratings of teaching: A summary of research.* IDEA Paper No. 20, September. Manhattan: Kansas State University, Center for Faculty Evaluation and Development.

Centra, J. A. (1980). *Determining faculty effectiveness.* San Francisco: Jossey-Bass.

Centra, J. A. (1979). *Determining faculty effectiveness: Assessing teaching, research, and service for personnel decisions and improvements.* San Francisco: Jossey-Bass.

Centra, J. A. (1975). Colleagues as raters of classroom instruction. *Journal of Higher Education, 46,* 327–337.

Centra, J. A. (1973). Self ratings of college teachers: A comparison with student ratings. *Journal of Educational Measurement, 10,* 287–295.

Chapados, J. T., Rentfrow, D., & Hocheiser, L. I. (1987, December). Four principles of training. *Training and Development Journal,* pp. 63–66.

Chhokar, J. S., & Wallin, J. A. (1984). A field study of the effect of feedback frequency on performance. *Journal of Applied Psychology, 69,* 524–530.

Cohen, J. (1977). *Statistical power analysis for the behavioral sciences* (rev. ed.). New York: Academic Press.

Connolly, T., Conlon, E. J., & Deutsch, S. J. (1980). Organizational effectiveness: A multiple constituency approach. *Academy of Management Review, 5,* 211–217.

Costin, F. (1968). A graduate course in the teaching of psychology: Description and evaluation. *Journal of Teacher Education, 19,* 425–432.

Deming, W. E. (1982). *Out of the crisis.* Cambridge, MA: Massachusetts Institute of Technology.

DeVries, D., Morrison, A., Shullman, S., & Gerlach, M. (1981). *Performance appraisal on the line.* New York: John Wiley.

Dopyera, J., & Pitone, L. (1983, May). Decision points in planning the evaluation of training. *Training and Development Journal,* pp. 66–71.

Edwards, A. L. (1957). *Techniques of attitude scale construction.* New York: Appleton-Century-Crofts.

Edwards, M. R. (1983). Productivity improvement through innovations in performance appraisal. *Training and Development Journal, 12,* 13–24.

Erez, M., Earley, P. C., & Hulin, C. L. (1985). The impact of goal acceptance and performance: A two-step model. *Academy of Management Journal, 28,* 50–66.

Field, H. S., & Holley, W. H. (1975). Performance appraisal — an analysis of state-wide practices. *Public Personnel Management, 7,* 145–150.

Goodman, P. S., & Pennings, J. M. (Eds.) (1977). *New perspectives on organizational effectiveness.* San Francisco: Jossey-Bass.

Guion, R. M. (1965). *Personnel testing.* New York: McGraw-Hill.

Guzzo, R. A., & Bondy, J. S. (1983). *A guide to worker productivity experiments in the United States 1976–1981.* New York: Pergamon Press.

Guzzo, R. A., Jette, R. D., & Katzell, R. A. (1985). The effects of psychologically based intervention programs on worker productivity: A meta-analysis. *Personnel Psychology, 38,* 275–291.

Hacker, W. (1985). Activity: A fruitful concept in industrial psychology. In M. Frese & J. Sabini (Eds.), *Goal directed behavior: The concept of action in psychology* (pp. 262–283). Hillsdale, NJ: Erlbaum.

Hackman, J. R., & Oldham, G. R. (1975). Development of the Job Diagnostic Survey. *Journal of Applied Psychology, 60,* 159–170.

Henderson, R. (1984). *Performance appraisal.* Reston, VA: Reston Publishing Company.

Hunter, J. E., Schmidt, F. L., & Jackson, G. B. (1982). *Meta-analysis: Cumulating research findings across studies.* Beverly Hills, CA: Sage Publications.

Ilgen, D. R., Fisher, C. D., & Taylor, M. S. (1979). Consequences of individual feedback on behavior in organizations. *Journal of Applied Psychology, 4,* 349–371.

Ilgen, D. R., & Klein, H. J. (1988). Individual motivation and performance: Cognitive influences on effort and choice. In J. P. Campbell & R. J. Campbell (Eds), *Productivity in organizations* (pp. 143–176). San Francisco: Jossey-Bass.

In 't Veld, J. (1988). *Analyse van organisatieproblemen* [Analysis of organization problems]. Leiden/Antwerpen: Stenfert Kroese.

Jones, S. D. (1985). *Mediating mechanisms of the feedback-performance relationship.* Unpublished doctoral dissertation, University of Houston.

Jones, S. D., Buerkle, M., Hall, A., Rupp, L., & Matt, G. (1993). Work group performance measurement and feedback: An integrated comprehensive system for a manufacturing department. *Group and Organization Management, 18,* 269–291.

Jones, S. D., Powell, R., & Roberts, S. (1990). Comprehensive measurement to improve assembly line work group effectiveness. *National Productivity Review, 10,* 45–55.

Katz, D., & Kahn, R. L. (1966). *The social psychology of organizations* (2nd ed.). New York: John Wiley.

Katzell, M. E. (1975). *Productivity: The measure and the myth.* New York: AMACOM.

Kendrick, J. W. (1984). *Improving company productivity.* Baltimore, MD: Johns Hopkins University Press.

Kirpatrick, D. L. (1960a, January). Techniques for evaluating training programs, Part 3: Behavior. *Training and Development Journal,* pp. 13–18.

Kirpatrick, D. L. (1960b, February). Techniques for evaluating training programs, Part 4: Results. *Training and Development Journal,* pp. 28–32.

Kirpatrick, D. L. (1959a, November). Techniques for evaluating training programs, Part 1: Reaction. *Training and Development Journal,* pp. 3–9.

Kirpatrick, D. L. (1959b, December). Techniques for evaluating training programs, Part 2: Learning. *Training and Development Journal,* pp. 21–26.

Kopelman, R. E. (1990). Objective feedback. In E. A. Locke (Ed.), *Generalizing from laboratory to field settings*. Lexington, MA: Heath.

Kopelman, R. E. (1986). *Managing productivity in organizations: A practical, people-oriented perspective*. New York: McGraw-Hill.

Kulik, J. A., & McKeachie, W. J. (1975). The evaluation of teachers in higher education. In F. N. Kerlinger (Ed.), *Review of research in education*, Vol. 3 (pp. 210–240). Itasca, IL: F. E. Peacock.

Lacho, K. J., Stearns, G. K., & Villere, M. F. (1979). A study of employee appraisal systems of major cities in the United States. *Public Personnel Management, 8*, 111–125.

Latham, G. P., Mitchell, T. K., & Dossett, D. L. (1978). The importance of participative goal setting and anticipated rewards on goal difficulty and job performance. *Journal of Applied Psychology, 63*, 163–171.

Latham, G. P., & Wexley, K. N. (1981). *Increasing productivity through performance appraisal*. Reading, MA: Addison-Wesley.

Locke, E. A., & Latham, G. P. (1990). *A theory of goal setting and task performance*. Englewood Cliffs, NJ: Prentice Hall.

Locke, E. A., Latham, G. P., & Erez, M. (1988). The determinants of goal commitment. *Academy of Management Review, 13*, 23–39.

Marsh, H. W. (1987). Students' evaluations of university teaching: Research findings, methodological issues, and directions for future research. *International Journal of Educational Research, 11*, 253–388.

Marsh, H. W. (1984). Students' evaluations of university teaching: Dimensionality, reliability, validity, potential biases, and utility. *Journal of Educational Psychology, 76*, 707–754.

Marsh, H. W., & Overall, J. U. (1979). *Validity of students' evaluation of teaching: A comparison with instructor self evaluations by teaching assistants, undergraduate faculty and graduate faculty*. Paper presented at the Annual Meeting of the American Education Research Association, San Francisco.

Matsui, T., Kakuyama, T., & Onglatco, M. (1987). Effects of goals and feedback on performance in groups. *Journal of Applied Psychology, 72*, 407–415.

McCullough, J. M. (1984, June). To measure a vacuum. *Training and Development Journal*, pp. 68–70.

Meehl, P. E. (1954). *Clinical vs statistical prediction: A theoretical analysis and a review of the evidence*. Minneapolis: University of Minnesota Press.

Miedema, H., Santbergen, B., Thierry, H. K., & Meyer, J. (1989). *Beloningsonderzoek bij de bankorganisatie* [Research on compensation at a bank] (Internal Report). University of Amsterdam: Work & Organizational Psychology.

Mitchell, T. R., & Silver, W. S. (1990). Individual and group goals when workers are interdependent: Effects on task strategies and performance. *Journal of Applied Psychology, 75*, 185–193.

Muckler, F. A. (1982). Evaluating productivity. In M. D. Dunnette & E. A. Fleishman (Eds.), *Human performance and productivity: Vol. 1, Human capability assessment*. Hillsdale, NJ: Erlbaum.

Nadler, D. A., Mirvis, P., & Cortlandt, C. (1976). The ongoing feedback system. *Organizational Dynamics, 4*, 63–80.

Naylor, J. C., Pritchard, R. D., & Ilgen, D. R. (1980). *A theory of behavior in organizations* (p. 299). New York: Academic Press.

Newstrom, J. W. (1978, November). Catch-22: The problems of incomplete evaluation of training. *Training and Development Journal*, pp. 22–24.

Overall, J. U., & Marsh, H. W. (1980). Students' evaluations of instruction: A longitudinal study of their stability. *Journal of Educational Psychology, 72*, 321–325.

Paquin, A. R., Jones, S. D., & Roth, P. L. (1992, April). *The Hawthorne effect when evaluating productivity gains.* Paper presented at the meeting for the Society for Industrial-Organizational Psychology, Montreal.

Phillips, J. J. (1983). *Handbook of training evaluation and measurement methods.* Houston, TX: Gulf.

Pritchard, R. D. (1992). Organizational productivity. In M. D. Dunnette & L. M. Hough, (Eds.), *Handbook of industrial/organizational psychology* (2d ed.) (vol. 3, pp. 443–471). Palo Alto, CA: Consulting Psychologists Press.

Pritchard, R. D. (1990). *Measuring and improving organizational productivity: A practical guide* (p. 248). New York: Praeger.

Pritchard, R. D., Bigby, D. G., Beiting, M., Coverdale, S., & Morgan, C. (1981). Enhancing productivity through feedback and goal setting. *Air Force Human Resources Laboratory Technical Report* (AFHRL-TR-81-7).

Pritchard, R. D., Jones, S. D., Roth, P. L., Stuebing, K. K., & Ekeberg, S. E. (1989). The evaluation of an integrated approach to measuring organizational productivity. *Personnel Psychology, 42,* 69–115.

Pritchard, R. D., Jones, S. D., Roth, P. L., Stuebing, K. K., & Ekeberg, S. E. (1988). The effects of feedback, goal setting, and incentives on organizational productivity. *Journal of Applied Psychology Monograph Series, 73,* 337–358.

Pritchard, R. D., Kleinbeck, U. E., & Schmidt, K. H. (1993). *Das Management-system PPM: Durch Mitarbeiterbeteiligung zu höherer Produktivität* [The PPM management system: Employee participation for improved productivity] (p. 255). Munich: Verlag C.H. Beck.

Pritchard, R. D., & Montagno, R. V. (1978). The effects of specific vs. non-specific, and absolute vs. comparative feedback on performance and satisfaction. *Air Force Human Resources Laboratory Technical Report* (AFHRL-TR-78-12).

Pritchard, R. D., Montagno, R. V., & Moore, J. R. (1978). Enhancing productivity through feedback and job design. *Air Force Human Resources Laboratory Technical Report* (AFHRL-TR-78-44).

Pritchard, R. D., & Roth, P. J. (1991). Accounting for non-linear utility functions in composite measures of productivity and performance. *Organizational Behavior and Human Decision Processes, 50,* 341–359.

Pritchard, R. D., Weiss, L. G., Hedley, A., & Jensen, L. A. (1990, Summer). Measuring organizational productivity with ProMES. *National Productivity Review, 9,* 257–271.

Ross, J. E. (1981). *Productivity, people and profits.* Reston, VA: Reston Publishing.

Saaty, T. L., & Vargas, L. G. (1981). *The logic of priorities.* Boston, MA: Kluwer-Nijhoff.

Sawyer, J. (1966). Measurement and prediction, clinical and statistical. *Psychological Bulletin, 66,* 178–200.

Sawyer, J. E., Pritchard, R. D., & Hedley-Goode, A. (1992). *Comparison of non-linear ProMES versus linear procedures for obtaining composite measures in performance appraisal.* Unpublished manuscript.

Schmidt, F. L., Hunter, J. E., McKenzie, R. C., & Muldrow, T. W. (1979). Impact of valid selection procedures on work-force productivity. *Journal of Applied Psychology, 64,* 609–626.

Schmidt, K.-H., Kleinbeck, U., Ottmann, W., & Seidel, B. (1985). Ein Verfahren zur Diagnose von Arbeitsinhalten: Der Job Diagnostic Survey (JDS) [An instrument for diagnosing job content]. *Zeitschrift für Arbeits- und Organisationspsychologie, 29,* 162–172.

Shine, L. C. (1973). A multi-way analysis of variance for single-subject designs. *Educational and Psychological Measurement, 33,* 633–636.

Sink, D. S., & Smith, G. L., Jr. (1994). The influence of organizational linkages and measurement practices on productivity and management. In D. H. Harris, P. S. Goodman & D. S. Sink (Eds.), *Organizational linkages: Understanding the productivity paradox*. Washington, DC: National Academy Press.

Staufenbiel, T., & Borg, I. (in press). Computer aided design of productivity measurement and enhancement systems. In F. Faulbaum (Ed.), *Softstat '93*. Stuttgart: Fischer.

Staufenbiel, T., & Borg, I. (1992). HISYS, a program for the scaling and measurement of hierarchical systems. In F. Faulbaum (Ed.), *Softstat '91* (pp. 161–166). Stuttgart: Fischer.

Stone, D. L., Gueutal, H. G., & McIntosh, B. (1984). The effects of feedback sequence and expertise of the rater in perceived feedback accuracy. *Personnel Psychology, 37*, 487–506.

Stone, E. F. (1985). Job scope–job satisfaction and job scope–job performance relationships. In E. A. Locke (Ed.), *Generalizing from laboratory to field settings* (pp. 189–206). Lexington, MA: Lexington Books.

Swanson, R. A. (1989). Everything important in business and industry is evaluated. In R. O. Brinkerhoff (Ed.), *Evaluating training programs in business and industry*. New Directions for Program Evaluation, No. 44. San Francisco: Jossey-Bass.

Tuttle, T. C. (1983). Organizational productivity: A challenge for psychologists. *American Psychologist, 38*, 479–486.

Tuttle, T. C. (1981). *Productivity measurement methods: Classification, critique, and implications for the Air Force* (AFHRL-TR-81-9). Brooks AFB, TX: Manpower and Personnel Division, Air Force Human Resources Laboratory.

Vroom, V. H. (1964). *Work and motivation*. New York: Wiley.

White, R. W. (1959). Motivation reconsidered: The concept of competence. *Psychological Review, 66*, 297–333.

Index

ABOUT THE EDITOR

ROBERT D. PRITCHARD is Professor of Psychology and Director of the Industrial/Organizational Psychology Program at Texas A&M University. He has worked for more than 20 years in organizational performance and productivity and has published many articles and several books on the subject.

ISBN 0-275-93907-3

EAN

HARDCOVER BAR CODE